GERALDINE MCCAUGHREAN was born in North London and has a degree in Education. She has been writing full time for many years and has won the Whitbread Award, the Guardian Children's Fiction Award, the Carnegie Medal and, most recently, the Blue Peter Book Award.

The stories in *100 World Myths and Legends* were originally published in four separate volumes – *The Golden Hoard, The Silver Treasure, The Bronze Cauldron* and *The Crystal Pool.*

ALSO BY GERALDINE McCAUGHREAN

Britannia : 100 Great Stories from British History
Britannia on Stage
God's People
God's Kingdom
Stories from Shakespeare

GERALDINE McCAUGHREAN

100 World Myths and Legends

Illustrated by Bee Willey

FIRST PUBLISHED IN FOUR VOLUMES

*The Golden Hoard, The Silver Treasure,
The Bronze Cauldron* and
The Crystal Pool

ORION

For Jenny Felton

This edition first published in Great Britain in 2001
by Orion Children's Books
a division of the Orion Publishing Group Ltd
Orion House
5 Upper St Martin's Lane
London WC2H 9EA

The stories in this volume were originally published in four
separate full colour editions:
The Golden Hoard, The Silver Treasure,
The Bronze Cauldron and *The Crystal Pool*

Text copyright © Geraldine McCaughrean 1995, 1996, 1997, 1998
Illustrations copyright © Bee Willey 1995, 1996, 1997, 1998

The rights of Geraldine McCaughrean and Bee Willey to be identified
as the author and illustrator respectively of this work have been asserted.

A catalogue record for this book is available from
the British Library

Typeset at The Spartan Press Ltd,
Lymington, Hants

Printed and bound in Great Britain by
Clays Ltd, St Ives plc

ISBN 1 84255 035 7

Contents

CONTENTS

CONTENTS

The Golden Wish

A GREEK MYTH

THERE WAS ONCE a fool. Of course there have been far more fools than one, and fools more often than once. But this particular fool was a king, so his foolishness mattered. He lived in Greece, at the foot of Mount Olympus, and his name was Midas. All he thought about was gold. All day, while the golden sun shone, he shut himself away in dark vaults counting tinny gold. All night long, while the golden firelight glimmered, he shivered over his accounting books reading the words to himself:

> *Twelve bars of gold in my vaults*
> *Twenty plates of gold on my table*
> *Ten rings of gold on my wife*
> *Four hundred gold coins in my tax coffers . . .*

The centaurs, unlike Midas, valued only fun and wine. One day (and on many others, too) a centaur took too many drinks and stumbled into Midas's garden.

'I am lost,' he told the King.

Midas set the centaur on the right road for Olympus.

'Such a friend! Such kindness!' exclaimed the centaur, joyfully kicking up his heels. 'How can I thank you? A wish? I shall grant you one wish.'

Now Midas knew that these centaurs, these horse-men, grazed on

I

the slopes of Olympus and drew magic from the holy mountain. His heart leapt to his mouth. 'A wish? You mean anything? I wish that everything I touch turns to gold!' He said it quickly, before the centaur could withdraw the offer.

'Ah. I should have warned you. People have asked that of the gods before, and . . .'

'Your magic isn't powerful enough! I knew it.'

'Oh, I can grant it,' said the centaur, flicking flies with his long tail. 'But you'll be sorry.'

'*No, I won't!*'

The centaur pronounced no spell. He did not spit or clap or chant. So when he trotted away towards Olympus, Midas felt sure no magic had passed between them. 'Boaster! Braggart!' he yelled after the galloping horse-man, and pounded the garden wall with his fist.

The wall felt smooth under his hand. It gleamed and glittered in the sunlight.

Gold.

Midas ran to his treasury and touched all the brass coins. They instantly shone gold – and not just the coins, but the jars they were in and the door of the treasure-house.

Gold.

Midas ran through the palace stroking and slapping every stool, bench, table and urn. They all turned to gold. His china and statues, his weapons and chariot all shone, more exquisite and precious than anything he had ever dreamed of owning. 'When we charge into battle,' he told his horse, patting its fat rump, 'we shall dazzle our enemies, you and I!'

The horse did not respond. It stood quite silent and quite still between the traces of the chariot: a perfect gold statue of a horse. Midas was a little startled, but after a moment he shrugged his shoulders. It made a fine statue for his new golden palace. And fresh horses can be bought by the dozen if a man has the gold to buy them.

'A feast! A festival! Where's my Chancellor? Where's my cook? Invite everyone! Spare no expense! Let the world know that Midas has gold! Midas has gold enough to buy up every sword, every horse, every acre of land in the world! I shall be unconquerable! I shall be worshipped! I shall be the envy of every man from the poorest beggar to the richest millionaire! I shall *be* the richest millionaire! A millionaire a million times over! Cook, where are you?'

His cook rushed in, carrying the King's lunch. He could not help but stare round him at all the changes to the room – the gold ornaments, the golden furniture. Midas snatched the bread impatiently off the tray and bit it. 'Huh? What are you feeding me these days? Rocks?' When he threw down the bread in disgust, it skidded across the golden floor. A golden loaf.

Food too, then? Midas took a drink to steady his nerves.

At least, he tried to take a drink. But the wine, as it touched his lip, turned to gold, to solid, metallic, unyielding gold. Midas stared. The cook stared. 'Don't just stand there! Fetch me something I can eat!' And he gave the man a push.

Ah well, there are more cooks in the world, for a man with limitless gold.

Midas sat down on the ground beside the golden statue of his cook. His clothes, one by one, in touching his skin, had been turning to gold around him, and he found that he was suddenly very, very weary from wearing them.

He had not meant it to be like this when he asked the centaur to . . . He had not meant food and clothes and people and horses . . .

Midas began to wonder. How long does it take for a man to starve to death?

Just then, his queen came in and, ahead of her, their little daughter. Midas tried to warn her. He tried to stop the girl running to him with outstretched arms. But the child was too young to understand. Her little fingers closed round Midas's hand – and stiffened, and grew cold, and could not be prised open again. Her face and features, too, hardened and set, and the eyes were plain gold orbs in their golden sockets, the golden mouth frozen, for ever half-open to speak.

'Oh Zeus! Oh you gods! No! Not my daughter! Not my little girl!' He ran past the Queen, past the guards, his arms burdened with the monstrous weight of a small clinging golden child. He ran out of his golden palace and its golden gardens: the flowerheads jangled as he brushed by them. He ran across golden grass to a forest and blighted it with a golden canker. He ran through orchards till the sight of the fruit maddened him with hunger. He started up the rocky slopes of Olympus, staggering under the weight of his lifeless daughter.

How long does it take for a man to die of loneliness? Or a broken heart?

'Take back this curse! What did I ever do to you that you punish me like this?' When he kicked off his heavy golden shoes, the golden grass spiked his soles like needles.

'Curse? I thought I granted you a wish,' said a familiar voice. The centaur trotted out of a nearby cave.

'I was a fool! I see that now! I was a fool! But does a man deserve to lose his daughter – to die – just because he's a fool?'

The centaur picked a few stalks of grass and nibbled them thoughtfully. 'I did try to warn you. Perhaps I've done you a favour, after all, if it has taught you something about yourself . . .'

'Wonderful! I shall die wise, then!' said Midas.

The centaur blew through his lips. 'If you take my advice, you'll go to the river and jump in,' he said.

'*Kill* myself, you mean?' gasped Midas.

'No, you fool. *Wash* yourself.'

At the banks of the river Midas did not hesitate. If the water did not turn to gold and crush him, then the weight of the metal child clasping his hand might pull him under and drown him. But he did not care. He flung himself into the river, and its water closed over his head. As he surfaced, his daughter surfaced beside him, spluttering and terrified, not knowing why or how she came to be swimming. 'Father? Where are all your clothes?'

Together they carried buckets of water back to the palace, and flung it over cook and horse, over stool and table and coins. The colour of gold was loathsome to Midas, and he was not content until he had undone all the alchemy of his magic golden touch.

Never again did he dream of gold – except in nightmares. Never again did he yearn to own gilded ornaments and mounds of yellow riches. No, no! For Midas had learned his lesson, hadn't he?

Now he thought about jewels, instead.

Shooting the Sun
A CHINESE MYTH

IMAGINE A TREE with a spread of branches and twigs as intricate as the blood vessels of an eye. Imagine its trunk twelve thousand spans high, roots plunging as far as the earth's hot core. Imagine a rookery of nests in the topmost branches, each the size of a galleon, each the cradle of a boy-child. And imagine the parents of those children, Di Jun, god of the eastern sky, and his wife Xi He.

In the ancient days of China, Di Jun and Xi He had ten sons, strong and handsome, each with a yellow suit, a scarf of orange and a cloak of flame. Each morning their proud mother whistled up the dragon which lay coiled around the great tree where she lived, and harnessed it to her chariot. Then, with one of her boys beside her, she drove to the edge of the eastern sky. There she set him down – Lung or Wu, Yanxi, Ming or Xang – and with a last comb of his hair or damp finger to clean a smut off his nose, she left him there to walk the path across the sky. Each boy, you see, was a sun.

Many footprints tamped flat that blue, celestial path. For many thousands of mornings this same routine took place. But after a thousand years more, the boy-suns grew into boisterous, roistering louts too vain and wilful to do as their parents told them.

They liked to do everything together, and had no patience to wait ten days for their turn to light the world. Thus it came about, in the reign of Emperor Yao, that the Chinese Empire was blighted by a terrible vandalism. The leaves of the trees blackened and curled. The

5

feathers of the cranes singed and moulted. Fishponds boiled and the rhododendrons burned like a million campfires on the hills of China. For there were ten suns burning all at once in the sky.

Corners which were gardens in the morning were deserts by the evening. Even nightfall did not bring a respite from the dreadful heat, the fearful drought, for the ten suns stayed in the sky all the time, playing sports and horsing wildly about. The earth below never knew the healing balm of cool darkness. The people clamoured at the Emperor's gate, begging him to do something. And each one of them had ten shadows at his feet, because of the ten glaring suns in the sky.

Emperor Yao travelled across the ocean to the valley where the great tree grew, and he stood at the bottom and hailed Di Jun with all the respect that one king can offer another. 'O marvellous ruler of the eastern sky, will you not ask your royal children to do as they once did, and walk the sky's path one at a time? The world is burning, the sea is steaming, and soon the only water left will be the tears of my people!'

The great tree shook in every limb. 'O Emperor, no words are harder for a father to speak, but my sons are my shame! They have lost all respect for the word of their parents. Neither their mother nor I can shame them into obedience. Not threats or bribes, not shouts or politeness humble these roaring boys! But tell your people I will not abandon them to fire and scorching. I have sent Yi the great archer of the sky, with his red bow and ten white arrows, to shoot down my delinquent sons!' On an outer branch of the tree, Xi He could be seen sobbing, while her dragon lay panting far below her, half-buried in crisp leaves fallen from the drought-stricken tree.

Emperor Yao bowed low and returned to his people with the good news. Though no one saw Yi in person, nor the red curve of his bow, many claimed to have seen his white arrows streaking skywards.

BANG! One sun exploded in a ball of fire and spun in the sky like a Catherine wheel. As it fell, it changed colour – from white-hot to blood-red, from red to umber, umber to brown. Then each flame turned to a black feather in the body of a black crow, and the dead crow landed, feet up, with an arrow in its breast.

BANG! BANG! The suns fell like oranges from a shaken tree. Four, five, six. 'Blessings on you, Di Jun!' cried the people. 'You have valued our lives and our world above the lives of your ten sons!'

'Ten?' said the Emperor to himself with a start. He shielded his eyes and glanced up at the sky. Four suns were left, blazing down on the earth, roasting the bears in their caves, the turtles in their shells. 'Will he shoot down all ten?' Suddenly it dawned upon Yao that Di Jun meant every last son to die. Yi the archer had ten arrows in his quiver, and when he fired the last one, the world would be plunged into total darkness. Instead of too great a heat, there would be none, and the birds would shiver in the trees and the fish be frozen in ponds of solid ice.

'Quick!' he said to the courtier standing beside him. 'Run to where Yi is shooting, and steal the last white arrow in his quiver!'

Without question, the courtier set off to run – over parched meadow and dry stream, over charred bushes and burned forests. As he ran, the shadows which streamed out behind him decreased in number from four to three, and a black crow fell at his feet. As he ran, the temperature dropped, and another black crow fell.

Just as the courtier glimpsed Yi, his red bow as bent as any dogwood tree, the bowstring twanged and a ninth sun exploded in a whirligig of flame. A ninth crow plummeted to the ground.

Yi reached behind him and felt for the last arrow. He fumbled, looked in his quiver, then looked around. He saw nothing but the dust flying up behind a running man who did not stop when called.

He did not stop, in fact, till he reached the court of Emperor Yao, and presented his emperor with a single white arrow. Meanwhile, the last of Di Jun's suns was running towards the eastern horizon, too afraid to look behind him. He disappeared over the rim of the world, and night fell on the Day of Di Jun's Anger.

That one son was so frightened by what had happened that he might never have shown his face again in heaven. 'The Celestial Bowman will shoot me down, Mama!' he wailed piteously.

But his mother simply bundled him into her dragon chariot next morning, and ordered him out again at the edge of the eastern sky. 'So he will, if you don't behave yourself better in future, my lad!' and she pointed an imperious finger out along the sky-blue pathway.

As soon as his back was turned, she watched him begin his journey with her head on one side and a fond smile on her face. She was so grateful to Emperor Yao for saving the life of her youngest son that she allowed him sometimes to ride in her dragon chariot, and they would tour the boundaries of China together discussing such things as tea and chess.

George and the Dragon

A PERSIAN MYTH

As the sun rose, the town opened its gates, as if it were yawning. As if it were yawning, it shut them again. Left outside were a goose and a nanny goat – the last animals in the whole town. The goose honked balefully, the goat pressed itself against the gate, sensing danger. Then a large shadow swamped them in darkness, a flash of flame burned up the shadow, and goat and goose were gone. When the people of the town peeped over their high palisades, nothing remained but a scattering of charred bones and a sprinkling of white feathers. The dragon had been fed for one more day.

No one any longer left the town to tend their crops or travel to market. They simply waited, prisoners within their own walls, while the besieging dragon circled them, scratching its hide against the wood walls, sharpening its claws on the gates. It had slithered out of the lake – a beast longer than night and hungrier than quicksand. Its scales ran with slimy sweat, and its jaws dripped acid saliva. Wherever it trod, the grass withered and died. The stench wilted the cherry blossom and cankered apples on the bough.

Princess Sabra had seen the beast from the top window of her tall room, high in the royal palace, where she watched for help to come. But no help came, for no one knew of the town's plight, or if they did, they dared not come near. Having seen the dragon once, Sabra hung her cloak over the window so that she might never see it again. But she could not shut out the sound of crying in the streets, of screams and shouting, of fights and quarrelling. All the animals in the city had been fed to the dragon. Now the King had given orders for a lottery.

The name of every man, woman and child was entered in the lottery, and whosoever's name was drawn would be turned out to feed the dragon. The King closed his doors against the angry protesters. 'It is necessary,' was all he would say, shouting through the thickness of the door. 'Do you want the dragon to tear down the city walls looking for its food?'

And the dragon found the taste of human flesh to its liking, and came earlier each morning to be fed.

Then, one day, the knocking at the palace door did not stop. 'Open, Lord King! Princess Sabra's name has been drawn in the lottery!'

'No! No! Her name should never have been entered! My daughter? Never!' But his subjects (though they loved their princess dearly) had no pity left in their hearts. Terror had wrung them dry of it. 'We have lost our loved ones – our husbands, our wives, our sons and daughters. Give up the Princess Sabra, for she must feed the dragon in the morning!'

A flagpost stood outside the gate. To this, each day, the victim was tied with strong rope, blessed with kisses and tears, and left alone to await the dragon's hunger. On the summer morning when Sabra took her place beneath the flag, the sky overhead was full of mare's-tail clouds, and the fields full of poppies. Birds sang in the scorched orchards, and the sun glinted on the poisoned lake. Above her, the blood-red banner flicked its lolling tongue, and the city bell began to toll dully – *chank chank chank*.

Suddenly, a horseman appeared on the skyline: she might not have seen him but for the sunlight gleaming on his metal helmet and the dazzling white of the shield across his back. He stopped to look around him, wondering, no doubt, at the blackness of the country-side, charred, burned, dead. Sabra wondered, in turn, whether to shout a warning. There was still time for him to escape, whereas everyone in her city was surely doomed, one by one, to die in the dragon's jaws.

All at once, the birds stopped singing. Through the soles of her feet, Sabra felt the ground tremble. Through the walls of her soul, she could feel fear crushing her heart. Out of the pool, out of its subterranean lair, the dragon raised its head to see what morsel waited by the city gate. Out it heaved itself, lidless eyes rolling, nostrils dilating. Its tongue unfurled suddenly from behind its teeth, forked and flickering. There was a smell of sulphur and filth.

Sabra opened her mouth to scream, but fear was strangling her. Instead, she heard a voice, loud and calm and demanding of attention. 'So. I have found you at last,' said the knight. 'Evil made flesh.'

The dragon cast a look over its shoulder, and the lobeless earholes sucked in the words. It looked the knight over and then turned back towards Sabra. No meal so delectable had yet been placed before it, and nothing could disrupt its lust to feed.

But as it scuttled towards her, on bowed legs and splayed feet, the knight rode at full tilt and crashed his horse, flank against flank, sidelong into the beast.

It turned in irritation and snapped, but the knight was too quick, and galloped out under its tail. 'Know this, beast, that I am George of Lydda and the shape of your undoing. I am here to make an end of you!'

The baggy jaw gaped in a grimace like a laugh. A ball of fire burst at the horse's feet as the dragon spat its contempt. The mare reared up, her mane singed short by the heat, but George stayed in the saddle, spurring her forwards once more, driving his spear deep into the dragon's haunch.

The beast seemed to feel no more pain than from a bee-sting, and rubbed himself against the town wall, breaking off the shaft of the spear and opening a gap in the long palisade. Its tail brushed Sabra as it turned, and the razor-sharp scales snagged her dress to ribbons. With a single blow of a webbed claw, it knocked over the knight's white mare.

George rolled clear, drawing from the side of his saddle a broadsword, as bright and as long as day. And there, where he had risen, he took his stand, white shield raised over his head. A torrent of fire splashed over the snowy heraldry and turned it to silver ash, but from beneath the burning buckler the knight struck out – a slash to the snout, a lunge to the breast, a charge into the green coils of snaking, dragony neck. Sabra shut her eyes. She could not remember how to breathe, how to make her heart beat. A carpet of fire unrolled at her feet and set her dress alight.

But a hand extinguished the flames, and another brushed her long hair back off her face. 'The beast is down, lady. If I might borrow your sash, you may see foulness conquered by purity.'

Sabra opened her eyes and saw George loop her sash around the dying dragon's throat. Its thrashing tail lay still, its laboured breathing ceased with a quiet sigh, and the fire of wickedness burning in its soul went out like a penny candle. 'I fought you in the name of Christ Jesus, who is goodness made flesh,' George whispered into the beast's ear. 'So you see, you stood no chance.'

Then the gates of the town opened like a great cheer, and out poured the people to stare, the children to clamber over the dragon's carcass. The King embraced George, and thanked him a thousand times. 'Stay! Stay and marry the Princess Sabra and rule the kingdom after I am dead . . . !'

But George thanked him graciously, exchanged smiles with the Princess, then remounted his horse. 'I am on a journey,' he said, 'which does not end here.' Sabra watched her knight ride away, she noticed that his shield was no longer scorched, but white again, and that a red cross embellished it now; a simple blood-red cross.

Skinning Out

AN ETHIOPIAN MYTH

WHY GO TO all the trouble of creating people and then let them wear out? It is like building a cart and not nailing on the wheels: sooner or later they will fall off – and what good is the cart then?

The Maker, who moulded and shaped the Galla people, was neither forgetful nor slipshod. You may see it in the people – as tall and willowy as fishing rods and beautiful as ebony. And his intent never was to let their beauty wane. But of course the blazing sun over Ethiopia dries soft skin and puckers it into wrinkles. Though the babies gleam like stones from the bottom of a stream, the old men and women bend and wrinkle like the tree whose roots can no longer reach water.

'Go to the Galla, Holawaka,' said The Maker to his messenger bird, 'and tell them, when their skins start to wrinkle and to weigh heavy, to slip them off and leave them where they fall. Underneath hides a new beauty, as the butterfly hides within the caterpillar.'

The brightly coloured bird, who sat preening her purple feathers with a beak of scarlet, cocked her head. 'Very well,' she said. 'But how shall I know the Galla from the rhinoceros or the giraffe, from the hyena or the lioness? These creations of yours all look the same to me – no feathers, no beaks, no plumes . . .'

'The Galla are as tall and willowy as fishing rods and beautiful as ebony,' said The Maker. 'How you do *talk*, Holawaka.'

So Holawaka flew down to the earth, still talking, but only to herself. Presently she met Tortoise. 'This is not the Galla,' she said, 'for it is squat and round and its face is far from lovely.' So she flew on by. Soon, however, she saw Snake.

'Now this fellow *is* as tall and willowy as a fishing rod and as beautiful as . . . what was it, again? Ah yes, beautiful as emeralds.' And she asked, 'Would you care to know the secret of staying young and never growing old?'

Snake, not surprisingly, cared a great deal. So Holawaka showed him how to slough his skin and slither out. The skin was left behind, delicate as paper, diamond-patterned and translucent in the sunshine.

'Of course, if I had been The Maker,' said Holawaka, who liked to talk, 'I would have given you people feathers to fly with. Then you could have nested among the treetops and dived for fish in the lakes, and left single feathers like licks of paint on the ground.' On and on Holawaka talked, though Snake had long since gone to tell his children the secret of staying young and never growing old, and she was speaking only to his sloughed skin. When she noticed this, she hopped back into the sky and home to The Maker's orchard where she perched on his fruit trees.

'Did you give the message to the Galla?'

'Yes, yes . . . though I'd have called him *long* rather than *tall*.'

By the time the mistake was realized, the world was set in its ways, and The Maker was busy elsewhere. That is why the men and women of the Galla (and the rest of us for that matter) grow wrinkled and old with passing time, and the passage of many suns. Don't trouble to go looking for Snake to learn his secret. You will never find him – only empty snakeskins, crackling and translucent.

Robin Hood and the Golden Arrow

AN ENGLISH LEGEND

ENGLAND WAS A country in despair. When the wind blew through its forests, the trees groaned and the leaves sighed. It was a country ruled by foreign invaders, and while the Normans fed richly off the fat of the land, the conquered Saxons made do with the crumbs that were left.

Saxon and Norman knights had ridden away in comradeship behind the glorious banners of King Richard, and gone to do battle in the Holy Lands. But the Normans left behind to rule England kept up the old tyranny. Prince John, Richard's brother, proved as barbaric as Richard was chivalric. He appointed men like the Sheriff of Nottingham and Guy of Gisborne: robber barons who sat in the great grey keeps of their granite castles and plotted to grow rich. They taxed and fined and robbed their Saxon subjects until starvation sat by every Saxon hearth. They dispossessed the poor who could not pay, the proud who would not pay, and anyone whose fortune they wanted for themselves.

Robin of Locksley, for instance, was cheated of his father's land by Gisborne. Where was the law to protect his rights, grant him justice? Gone to the Crusades with the King. Law and Justice no longer existed in the England ruled by Prince John.

Unless they lived on in Robin Hood.

That same cheated Robin of Locksley, to preserve his life, slipped away into the green forest and disappeared. Soon afterwards, a mysterious figure was glimpsed by travellers, dressed all in green, with green-feathered arrows in his quiver and green mosses streaking his cheeks. No one knew at first whether the 'Man of Sherwood' truly existed or not. But then strange things began to happen.

Fat Norman merchants were robbed of their gold, and next day thin Saxon children found gold beneath their pillows. Cruel tax collectors were 'relieved' of all their takings. Then money would fly in at the windows of widows, and flour fall like snow on starving villages. The mysterious Robin Hood was robbing the rich to feed the poor, and though the Norman soldiers hunted him like the hind, they could never find him. He had made the greenwood his own stronghold.

One by one, men persecuted or pursued by Norman law headed for the forest to join Robin Hood and to wear the 'suit of green'. They were outlaws to the Normans, but heroes to the Saxons. Their very existence burned like a green gleam in the imagination, a flame of hope.

'A tournament? Will there be archery?' asked Robin casually, waxing his bowstring with a stub of candle.

'That's the main event!' said Friar Tuck, tucking into his meal. 'First prize is a golden arrow, presented by Gisborne himself.' The Friar's words emerged speckled with breadcrumbs and flecks of fat. 'Open to any archer in the land. The Prince himself is going to be there, so they say, the swine.' Tuck was the only man in Robin's band not to wear the suit of green. In his brown habit, he could come and go to town unnoticed, unquestioned, and bring them news, messages from wives and sweethearts, gifts from well-wishers. He was able, too, to deliver Robin's little 'presents' to the poor of Nottingham.

Today his news was of a grand archery contest to be held within the castle walls. The outlaws, sitting around their campfire, greeted the news quietly, remembering other such festive holidays spent with their families.

'We know, without going, who's the best archer in England, don't we?' said Alan-a-Dale loyally, and all the outlaws shouted in one voice. '*Robin Hood!*'

'It would be pleasant to prove it, even so,' murmured Robin.

'You *wouldn't*! You never would!' Much the Miller was horrified. 'Tell him, Little John! Tell him it's too dangerous!'

''S probably a trap,' said Will Scarlett gloomily. 'The Sheriff probably means to lure Robin inside the castle – thinks he won't be able to resist competing for a stupid golden arrow.'

'Let's not disappoint him, then!' declared Robin, jumping to his feet.

There was a streak of recklessness in Robin which scared his Merrie Men. It was hard enough to keep alive in the inhospitable greenwood, without a man wilfully creeping into the stronghold of his worst enemy. And for what? An arrow of shiny gold that would not even fly?

The sun glinted on the golden arrow. The cushion it lay on was of blood-red velvet.

The castle grounds were bright with striped pavilions and painted flag-poles, the sky jagged with pennons. Tourney armour caught the sun and dazzled the eye. Chargers cloaked in cloth-of-gold stamped their hooves and jingled plumed bridles. It was a holiday in Nottingham and, for once, the brown and ragged townspeople were also allowed inside the castle precincts.

Entrants for the archery contest stood in a huddle: the best archers in Prince John's guard, the best archers in the Sheriff's employ, professional marksmen and amateur huntsmen. There were a few Saxons, too – arrowsmiths and bow-makers, for the most part. Impatiently they queued up to shoot at the distant butts.

Suddenly there was a flurry of excitement, as a young man in a green tunic was seized by castle guards and wrestled to the ground. 'We knew you couldn't stay away, Robin Hood! Got you at last!'

But it was not Robin Hood at all, just a boy wearing green. Gisborne ground his teeth. He found archery tedious, and now he was obliged to sit through a whole afternoon of it.

Some arrows went wide, some buried themselves in the grass, ripping off their feather fletches. The butts looked like porcupines by the time all the bowmen had loosed their flights. Last of all, an old man, bent and bearded, shuffled to the firing line, carrying his arrows in a raffia basket. He began, with shaking hands, to fit an arrow to his bowstring.

'Get away, old man. Clear off!' they told him. 'This is a young man's sport. Go home.'

'All comers, it said,' croaked the old man.

'He's holding up the competition! Get rid of him!'

'Oh, let him make a fool of himself. Takes less time than arguing.'

The old man nodded and doddered, peered down the field at the butts as if he could barely see them, then feebly tugged back on his bowstring. The arrow plunged into the golden heart of the target.

'Fluke.'

'Lucky!'

'Not half bad, Grandpa.'

The competition continued, with everyone disqualified who did not hit gold. Round by round it became harder – the butts were moved farther off – and more bowmen were eliminated. But the luck of the old man held. The crowd began to warm to him: he was a ragged Saxon, after all. Every time he fired, they cheered. Every time a Norman missed, they cheered, too.

It came down to just three men: a Norman sergeant-at-arms, hand-picked by Guy of Gisborne, a pretty French knight in chequered velvet . . . and the old man, frail and lame, whose clothes had more holes in them than the canvas target. The butts were moved still farther off – so far now that they were scarcely in sight.

As the French knight took aim, a silly lady in the stands jumped up and waved to him for luck. It spoiled his concentration and the arrow went wide.

But the sergeant-at-arms fired the perfect shot. His arrow hit the gold dead centre. Even the Saxon crowds gasped with admiration and began to turn away. The contest was plainly over.

The old man congratulated the sergeant, who spat in his face and laughed. The nobles in the stand were rising and stretching themselves, stiff after so much sitting. The old man took a green-tipped arrow from his raffia basket and laid it to his bow. 'I'll just see what I can manage,' he quavered.

His arrow flew like a hornet. The thwack, as it hit canvas, sounded like an explosive charge. It pierced the selfsame hole as the sergeant's arrow, and dislodged it, leaving only one arrow thrumming with the force of impact.

'Did you see that?'

'Why? What happened?'

'He did it! Old Grandpa did it!'

The nobility milled about in their enclosure. As the old man approached, twisted and limping, to receive his prize, Prince John pointedly turned his back.

Guy of Gisborne picked up the golden arrow between finger and thumb and dropped it at the vagrant's feet. 'You shoot quite well, old man,' he said grudgingly, but there was no reply. He saw that the archer's face was turned not towards him but towards the Lady Marian. The mouth was hidden by the bird's nest beard, but the eyes were wrinkled with smiling. And the Lady Marian was smiling back!

'Well done, sir! Oh, well done!' she said.

'You are kind, beautiful maiden, past all my deserving,' said the winner.

Now you ought to know that Sir Guy of Gisborne thought of the Lady Marian as his future bride (even though she did not care for the idea). He was furious to see her smiles wasted on a filthy, decrepit Saxon. He took hold of the shaggy beard to yank the rogue's head round to face him. The beard came away in his hand. The archer sank his teeth in Gisborne's clenched fist, then sprang backwards.

It was as if he had left his old age in Gisborne's grasp and been restored to youth. There stood a handsome youngster, straight-backed, bright-eyed and laughing.

'*Robin Hood!*' breathed Gisborne, and for a moment the two men looked at one another with bitterest hatred.

Then a voice in the crowd shouted, 'Here, Robin! Over here!' A riderless horse, slapped on the rump, galloped towards the pavilion; Robin leapt into the saddle. The flying stirrups struck the faces of the guards who tried to stop him.

Gisborne was first to mount up and give chase, while Marian crammed her long plaits against her mouth and gazed after them. 'Oh ride, Robin, ride!' she whispered under her breath. She alone among the spectators had recognized Robin Hood beneath his disguise – but then she was in love with him, and he with her.

The crowds scattered from in front of the galloping horses, as Gisborne pursued Robin towards the castle drawbridge. The golden arrow shone in Robin's hand. A cry rose spontaneously from the beggars and children by the gate: 'Ride, Robin! Ride!'

But Gisborne was close behind, well mounted, and his sword out, whereas Robin's horse was a poor thing. His disguise allowed for no weapon: a longbow cannot be used in the saddle.

'I've a score to settle with you, you filth, you thief!' panted Gisborne, and the blade of his sword sliced the green feathers from Robin's arrows. 'You've robbed my tax gatherers, stirred up the peasants, and thumbed your nose at me out of the greenwood tree! Well, now I'll show that scum of yours that their magic Robin Hood is nothing but common flesh and blood!' This time his blade shaved the hair from Robin's neck. They thundered over the castle drawbridge side by side.

'And I have a score of scores to settle with you, Gisborne!' panted Robin. 'You robbed me of my father's land. You tread down the poor and make widows and orphans weep! You drove me to live like an animal in the greenwood . . .'

Gisborne swung, and Robin's hot blood flew back in his face, in his eyes.

'. . . *when everyone knows that you are the animal!*' Robin turned in the saddle and struck out, using the only weapon he had.

Watching from the castle yard, the crowds saw the two horses part. One went left, towards the forest, the other right, towards the town. It looked as if Gisborne had unaccountably turned aside and let Robin Hood escape.

A short while later, the bully's horse ambled down the streets of Nottingham town, reins dangling, foamy with sweat, hooves skidding on the cobbles. Shopkeepers and housewives, accustomed to the man's cruelty, drew back fearfully against the walls. Then one by one they stepped out again. They had seen the golden arrow shaft shining in the centre of Gisborne's crested surcoat, its point sunk deep in his heart. And they had seen death staring out of Gisborne's open eyes.

Greater tyrants remained, tyrants who made Gisborne seem like a gentleman. Until the true King of England returned, his subjects would continue to groan and suffer at the hands of Prince John and his robber barons. Only the existence of Robin Hood – out there – dressed like Spring among the greenwood trees – kept poor people from despair. The mere mention of Robin's name kept their hearts beating. The telling of his thousand daring exploits warmed them even when there was no fuel on the hearth. In the depths of a cruel winter, Robin was the green promise that Spring always returns.

Brave Quest

A NATIVE AMERICAN MYTH

HE HAD NOTHING: no parents, no possessions, no position in the tribe but to be laughed at and scorned. Once, he had been handsome, but being handsome in deeds as well as face, he had tried to return a fallen eagle-chick to its nest and been gouged and gored by the parent birds. Now his face was hideously scarred, and though his name was Man-of-Little, everyone called him Scarface.

'Why don't you ask Marvellous-Girl to marry you?' they jeered. 'You love her, don't you? What a perfect pair you'd make! The dove and the crow!' Their spite rained down on him sharp as arrows.

Of course he loved Marvellous-Girl: everyone did. Braves of every tribe for a hundred miles around came to ask for her in marriage. They all went away disappointed. How could Scarface even tread in the prints of her moccasins or pain her eyes with the sight of his ghastly face? If they had not goaded him, he never would have done so. But their cruelty stirred in him the dregs of an old pride, and he went to the lodge of Marvellous-Girl, and stood by the closed doorway.

'I love you, Marvellous-Girl. If a strong arm and a faithful heart can do you any service, take me for your husband. I stand at your door and sorrow, for what hope of love has a boy like me? But what love can do for you, I will do, for I am filled with love.'

To his amazement, the woman inside did not shriek with laughter.

The door flap lifted and her face appeared, as lovely as the new moon. 'I can marry no one, Man-of-Little, but if I could, there is no one I would sooner have. For you are gentle and good, and your hair would be pleasing under my hand.'

For a moment, Scarface could barely think. The face slipped out of sight, like the moon passing behind a cloud. 'Why can you not marry?' he called, and the pigeons on the corn flew up in surprise.

'Because I am promised to the Sun.'

'No!' He could hear her moving about inside the dark lodge, preparing a meal: the Sun's betrothed, the girl he loved. He bit back his jealousy. 'You are greatly honoured, then.'

Her rustling movements stopped. After a moment she said, 'I would have felt more honoured, Man-of-Little, to be married to you.'

Astonishment, like a fountain, leapt up within Scarface. 'Then I'll shoot the Sun out of the sky!' he cried, and the vultures, picking over bones among the litter, took off in alarm.

'Shssh!' Her face appeared, lovelier than the moon. 'Don't anger him. But you could go to the Sun's Lodge, if you dared, and beg him to release me. He might take pity on us. If he does, ask him to touch your face and heal that scar of yours. Then everyone will know he has renounced his claim and blesses our marriage.'

'I'll go!' cried Scarface, and an eagle flying overhead heard him and dropped its prey.

Though he took food, the journey was so long that it was soon used up, and he lived on roots, berries and wild honey. Though he knew the paths to the east of the village, his journey was so long that he soon reached woodland paths he had never trodden before. Though he asked every person he met, 'Where is the Sun's Lodge?', no one knew, and the journey was so long that he soon met with no more people. Instead he entered wild places inhabited only by animals.

Though he was young and strong, the journey was so long that at last he thought he could go no farther and sat down on a log. Polecat came trotting by, as black and white as snow on coal. 'I am looking for the Sun's Lodge!' said Scarface to the Polecat.

'In all my life I have never seen it. But Bear is wise. Ask the Bear.'

So Scarface searched out the Bear and found him scratching the bark from a tree, licking the insects from his paws. 'I am looking for

the Sun's Lodge,' he said, quite fearless (for he had so little to lose that were the Bear to eat him, he would be little worse off).

'In all my days, I have never seen it,' said Bear, 'but Beaver goes where I cannot. Ask the Beaver.'

So Scarface asked Beaver, who was building a lodge in the lake.

'In all my travels I have never seen the Sun's Lodge,' said Beaver. 'But Wolverine is cunning. Ask the Wolverine.'

So Scarface searched out Wolverine, but by the time he found him, he was both famished and exhausted.

'The Sun's Lodge? Of course I know where it is,' said the Wolverine. 'But where is your canoe? You can hardly cross the Great Water without a canoe!'

'If that's where it is, I shall swim across!' declared Scarface. But that was before he saw, for the first time, the Great Salt Waters of the ocean, so vast that a man's life might be swum out amid its valleys and mountains. There on the beach, Scarface sat down and wept tears as salt as the sea. He knelt back on his heels and addressed himself to the sky.

'Rightly was I named Man-of-Little at my birth, for I have neither the face nor the strength, nor the magic, nor the luck to make good of my life. Was it for nothing that I was born? I wish those eagles had eaten me, limb and life, rather than leave me here, on the shores of my shortcomings!'

A pair of eagles flying overhead heard him and swooped down. He raised his arms over his head, but he had no shield or weapon to fend them off.

The eagles' talons closed around his arms, and their beaks gripped his hair. Then, with a deafening clatter of wings, they lifted him – up and out over the ocean.

'There you are, young friend,' they said, setting him down on the farthermost shore. 'We regret that our mistake has spoiled your life so far, but we do what we can in recompense. Follow that yellow path. It leads to the Lodge of the Sun.'

With a whoop of joy, Scarface leapt along the path, his strength renewed, his hunger forgotten. Night had fallen, and he had only the moon to light his way. Presumably the Sun was indoors, sleeping in his lodge.

Just before dawn, he began to see, strewn along the path, various pieces of clothing and weaponry: a quiver of arrows with golden shafts, a headdress of white egret feathers, a gold spear, a tunic sewn with gilt thread, and moccasins of the softest kind. He stepped carefully over them, wondering at what kind of warrior owned such splendid things. Suddenly the leaves of a tree exploded overhead, and a youth plunged down on to his shoulders with a blood-curdling war-cry.

They rolled over and over together on the ground. Scarface easily broke free, but the young man did not seem much put out. 'Why didn't you pick them up?' he asked breathlessly, putting on his tunic again and collecting up his possessions.

'All those beautiful things? Because they weren't mine,' said Scarface.

'Pity. I could have challenged you to a fight for taking them – you must be out-of-the-ordinary honest, that's all I can say!' Scarface sat on the ground, winded and a little bewildered. 'Oh! You don't know me, do you? I'm Morning Star, son of the Sun. He'd like you, my father. I make him angry, because I'm always doing what he tells me not to do. But he'd like you, I should think.'

'I'm not so sure,' said Scarface, with a wry smile. But Morning Star had already run off up the path.

'Let's go killing whooping cranes!' he called over his shoulder. 'The Old Man says I mustn't – so it must be fun. Race you to the lake!'

Scarface got to his feet and ran after Morning Star. 'If your father says you shouldn't, maybe you should respect the wisdom of his age!' His words came back at him, echoing off the shale sides of a valley dry but for a small lake glowing in the dawn. Around it, a flock of cranes sipped the water through long spiky beaks.

As Morning Star rushed at them, brandishing the golden spear, they rose up into the air – a clumsiness of bony wings and horny legs. Then they dropped down again, enveloping Morning Star in a blizzard of feathers. He gave one long, loud scream.

Without time to waste on fear, Scarface ran headlong into the storm of birds. Their long beaks were like tent pegs driven home with mallets. The leading edges of their wings were sharp as blades, and the clawed feet which kicked him were hoof-hard.

But with his fists alone, he bruised their scarlet beaks. With his bare hands he tore tail feathers from them in handfuls until they rose, squawking indignantly, and flapped away down the shale valley. Morning Star lay still along the ground, his body bleeding from a dozen wounds. Scarface lifted him gently and carried him back to the yellow path and up to the door of the Sun's Lodge.

'What have you done?' demanded the fearful orange face which answered his knocking. It was blotched and marked in a hundred places by spots of old age. 'Did you do this to him?'

Scarface could feel the hairs of his fringe frizzle, the lashes of his lids scorch. 'He tried to go hunting whooping cranes by the lake in the valley. The birds mistook him for a foolish boy with too little respect for the advice of his father.'

The heat of the Sun's fury cooled instantly, and he hurried Scarface indoors – into the largest and most magnificent lodge ever raised on a forest of poles. Scarface laid Morning Star on a heap of buffalo hides, fearing he must already be dead. But the merest caress of the old man's hand closed the wounds in Morning Star's body, and restored him to perfect health. So he was able to tell his father about meeting Scarface, about his out-of-the-ordinary honesty, about the whooping cranes blotting out his sky . . .

'You have saved my son's life,' said the Sun solemnly. 'How can I repay you?'

Once, twice Scarface opened his mutilated mouth to speak. But though courage had brought him through woodlands, over the ocean and up to the lodge door, he dared not speak. 'You will destroy me where I stand, if I say the words in my heart.'

'Are you not a guest in my lodge, and my son's best friend? . . . And Man-of-Little, do you think I don't recognize you? Do you think I don't glance down, once in a while, as I cross the sky each day? Do you think I don't listen, too? I was overhead in the sky the day you spoke to Marvellous-Girl at her door.'

'Then touch my face and tell me I may marry her!' Scarface blurted.

The Sun reached out an elderly hand spotted as any leopard, and chucked Scarface under the chin like a little child. 'Let me give you clothes and food for the journey,' he said, 'and water to wash yourself.' As to Scarface's request, he said not a word.

It was not until Scarface looked down into the bowl of water which the Sun brought him, that he saw his face, perfect, restored, healed.

When Marvellous-Girl saw it, she reached out a hand too, through the doorway of her lodge, and touched his cheek. She did not even notice the quiver of golden arrows he was carrying, or the tunic sewn with gilt thread, or the headdress of egret feathers. 'Tell the tribe's women to prepare for a wedding,' she said. 'Tomorrow, I think. At noon. When the Sun will be directly overhead.'

They called their firstborn son Eagle, and the sons which followed after, Polecat, Beaver, Wolverine and Bear. But their daughter, of course, they named Woman-who-loves-Sunshine.

Saving Time

A POLYNESIAN MYTH

THE PACE OF life is gentle on the sea-washed islands of Polynesia. Days are long and sunny, and no one hurries to get their work done or rushes a meal when it can be lingered over in the twilight.

It was not always so. Once, the People of the Islands rolled out of their beds at first light and scampered to their boats or to their plantations, dashed to do their work, never stopped to talk or sit – only to snatch a bite of food before the light failed.

'Quick, man, pick those coconuts while you can see which are ripe!'

'Quick, woman, beat that tree bark into cloth while you can see what you are beating!'

'Quick, child, find me bait for my fishing hook while you can still find the worm casts on the sand.'

But many was the time that fishing canoes put out to sea in the morning only to lose sight of land in the failing light and go astray amid the night-dark waves. For the days were very, very short, the Sun speeding across the sky like a thrown ball, the daylight gone in the blinking of an eye.

One day, Maui sat in front of his family hut. The Sun had already set and only firelight illuminated his family's anxious faces as they gathered to eat the evening meal. Some of the food was spilled as the bowls were passed out; there was so little light to see by.

'This food's not cooked,' complained a grandmother.

'I'm sorry. There wasn't time,' said Maui's mother.

'There's nothing for it,' said Maui, jumping up. 'The day must be lengthened or how can we ever hope to get our work done between waking and sleeping?'

'Tell it to the Sun,' grumbled some of the elders. 'He rushes across the sky like a stone from a catapult and is gone in a twinkling.'

'Then I must make him slow down!' said Maui confidently, and strode off along the beach.

First he fell over a turtle and then he fell over a canoe, for the moon was young and the beach was dark and Maui could barely see his hand in front of his face.

'What are you looking for?' called his sister, Hina.

'For a length of rope,' Maui called back, peering around him without success.

'Don't you think you'd best wait till morning,' suggested his sister, 'when there's more light?'

In the morning, Maui found a length of rope made from coconut fibre and tied it in a noose. Then he walked to the eastern horizon (which took him the rest of the day), where a charred and gaping pit marked the spot at which the Sun leaps into the sky.

He circled the pit with the noose and, holding the other end of the rope, sat well back, through the long night, awaiting sunrise.

With a blinding, blazing bound, the Sun leapt out of his pit, hurtling towards his noonday zenith. The noose snapped shut around his shaggy head of flame – but the old Sun was moving so fast that the rope simply snapped like a spider's thread, and the great ball of fire never even noticed that he had been snared.

Maui returned home and, with the help of all the children, gathered up every coconut husk on every beach of every island. He stripped the hair shells and rolled the fibres into strands of coir. Then he plaited the fibres into a rope so strong he might have towed an island with it. He tied a noose in the rope and took it to the eastern horizon where, once again, he laid a snare to catch the rising Sun.

With one flaring, glaring bound, the Sun leapt into the sky and pelted towards his noonday zenith. The noose pulled tight around his shaggy head of flame – but no sooner did it touch the great heat of the incandescent Sun than it frizzled into flames, dropping away in a flurry of ash as the Sun hurried onwards.

The day was so short that by the time Maui reached home, it was already night-time again. He crept into the family hut and felt his way to where his sister Hina lay sleeping on her mat. With his sharp fishing knife, he cut off her long hair, purple-black with magic and as glossy as the night sea outside. Plaiting it into a rope, he made one last purple-black noose. By dawn, it was in place around the pit of sunrise.

With a whirling whoop of white fire the Sun leapt into the sky and flew towards his noonday zenith. But he was brought up short by the jerk of a snare. Hina's plaited hair closed tight around his throat, and he choked and struggled and thrashed about, kicking and scrabbling to break free.

'I will let you go on one condition!' shouted Maui, hanging on grimly to the end of the purple-black rope. 'In future you must pass more slowly across the sky, so that the People of the Islands have a longer day, and can get their work done!'

The Sun rolled and spun, tugged and leapt, like a giant tunnyfish caught on a fishing line. But Maui was a great fisherman and he fought the Sun to a standstill. At last he hung panting in the air, great gouts of molten flame dropping like sweat from his golden face.

'I agree. I agree. From now, I shall creep across the sky as slowly as a turtle across a beach. Now let me loose.' Maui loosened the noose of Hina's magic hair, and the Sun walked sedately towards his distant noonday zenith.

The days, after that, lasted from slow lilac dawn through leisurely golden hours and into a sunset as pink and orange as a reef of coral. At such times, when the People of the Islands linger over their meal and watch the beauty of the Sun's descent, they can still see some strands of Hina's hair caught in the Sun's corona, streaking the evening sky.

Of course, what the Sun does when finally he dives into his pit at the western horizon is entirely his own affair. Freed from his promise to Maui, he may soar and swoop, circle and somersault as fast as any turtle beneath the waves.

The Lake that Flew Away

AN ESTONIAN LEGEND

DO YOU SUPPOSE a lake has no feelings? No sense of pride? No self-esteem? Do you think that it can lie untended without suffering? Its weeds run riot, like unkempt hair; its fishes choke beneath the autumn leaves; its banks crumble under the feet of drinking cattle.

Lake Eim in Estonia is a vast tract of water a hundred fathoms deep. In the beginning, trees which seeded themselves around it drank its water and flourished, dense and leafy. A forest grew. So did the darkness within it. And soon, within the darkness of trees lurked a darkness of men.

Brigands and bandits made their lairs in the black entanglement of lakeside trees. They fished the lake for their suppers, and they spent long hours sprawled in drifting boats, dangling grappling hooks into the deeps. For it was rumoured the lake held great treasures from an earlier civilization. The men did not dredge the shallows, or clear the weed, or cut back the nettles that mustered at the waterside. That would have been hard work, and they had forsworn hard work.

So why did their pockets jingle with gold, and their gambling last all night? Because each time a traveller passed through the wood – a pilgrim or a merchant – they cut his throat and threw his body in the deep, dark waters. The blood stained Lake Eim. The blood shamed Lake Eim. Red blood stained the bankside flowers and dripped from the bending grasses on to the face of the lake. The blood soured and fouled the still waters of the lake, till it shivered with a hundred cat's-paws, even on a windless day.

In horror and disgust, the lake seethed, and bubbles of marsh gas rose from the rotting weed on its bed. 'I will not be stained with the sin of these wicked men. I shall leave this place!'

The Robber Chief, stirring in his sleep, heard the slap-slap of water on the lake shore. He heard a *suck-shuck* as of mud parting company from a boot or a boat. Drops of water fell on the roof, and he thought. 'Rain,' and turned over to sleep again.

Suddenly, hands were pulling at the covers and voices shouting in his ear: 'Come quick! Come quick! The lake is . . . well, it's . . . the lake, it's . . .'

'The lake is what?' demanded the Robber Chief, grabbing a bandit by the throat. 'What is the lake doing, that you wake me in the middle of the night?'

'Flying away, Chief!'

'Flying away.' The Robber Chief pulled the blankets over his head and cursed his cronies, body and soul.

'It's true, Chief!'

'Like a carpet, Chief!'

'Up and away, Chief, all silver and glittering!'

The Robber Chief rolled out of bed and stumbled to the window. Overhead in the sky hung a billion gallons of water, shining like metal plate, thick as cumulus clouds, spreading out to all points of the compass, a translucent ceiling. If it were to fall . . .

The bandits stood stock still, waiting for a billion steely gallons to fall on their heads like the end of the world. Minute after minute they listened to the gentle hiss of moving water cascading through the sky. Then the moon bobbed into view again, like a fishing float, and the danger was past.

'Well? What are you waiting for?' bellowed the Robber Chief. 'Get out there and make the most of it! There'll be fish by the barrel-load, too, there for the picking up! And treasure! Don't forget the treasure! All there for the taking!'

As they pelted down to the lake, dawn was just rising.

'The boats have gone, Chief!'

'Who needs 'em? We can walk!'

They plunged on, up to their knees in mud. The lake bed was certainly alive with wriggling movement. And treasure chests lay about, smashed open at the hinges and steaming in the early sun.

A bandit thrust his arm into one of the chests, then drew it out with a shriek. The chest was full of frogs! Another was full of water snakes, another lizards. Not a fish, not a single bearded barbel or dappled trout lay stranded by the lake's departure. But every lizard, reptile, newt, salamander, frog and slug that had lived in the mud of the lake was crawling now towards the shore.

The brigands shrank back in revulsion – only to see the nasty slimy livestock of the lake crawl past into their dens, into their beds, into their boots and bags and hats.

They burned everything – their lairs and all they had stolen. They razed the forest to its stumps, then trudged away, their wicked lives in ashes, leaving an empty crater encircled by fire.

Meanwhile, Lake Eim carried its careful burden of fish and treasure through the sky. It flew so high that people below looked up and said, 'What cloud is that hiding the sun?' Hunters looked up and said, 'What flock of birds is that blacking out the sun?'

Then the lake came to a land parched and cracked, brown and destitute for want of water. The poor peasants there held out their hands, hoping the cloud might spare them a few drops of meagre rain. Then suddenly, out of the sky it swooped – a sluicing wealth of water, which seemed to glitter with jewels.

'Make me a bed to lie in, and I shall stay with you,' offered Lake Eim, in a voice like a thundering waterfall.

The peasants snatched up their hoes and spades. The children dug with their hands; the women wheeled away the dry earth in barrows. Inside a week they made a bed for the lake, and Eim settled into it, with a sound like a weary groan. Fish danced on their tails on the surface, while each circular ripple washed ashore a trinket of gold or a few silver coins. Several little boats bobbed about, too, on the choppy waves.

First the peasants thanked God, with prayers in the church. Then they thanked the lake, with flowers that they floated on its face. They planted willow trees and dug cattle troughs, made osier beds in the shallows, and built jetties out from the shore. They channelled water to their fields, and the fields flourished. They built a town and fed it on fish, and the town flourished. (All the fish fry they returned, so that the fish stocks thrived.) In short, they cared for the lake, and the lake cared for them.

Which is as it should be.

If you don't want your bed full of newts.

Admirable Hare

A LEGEND FROM SRI LANKA

FOR A FEW brief years, the ruler of the skies lived on earth as Prince Siddhartha, who was later called Buddha when he became wiser than any other man. But just once, they say, he met an animal whose kindness was an example and a marvel, even to the gods.

One night, the Buddha, who lived as a wandering hermit, got lost in a forest in Ceylon. The dense canopy of leaves overhead obscured the guiding stars. The smooth, blank moon poured its light only into the forest clearings, like milk into cups. In one of these clearings, the Buddha met a hare called Sasa.

'Your face is the face of a good man,' said the hare, 'but your expression is that of a man who has lost his way.'

'True, my velvet-eared friend,' admitted the Buddha. 'I am lost.'

'Then permit me to guide you to the edge of the forest.'

'I'm afraid I have no money to repay such kindness,' said the Buddha, thinking that perhaps the hare earned a living in this way.

'Sir,' replied Sasa, bowing gracefully from his slender hips, 'the debt would be all mine, if you would allow me to help you on your way, and share conversation with me as we go.'

So the Buddha was steered through the wood by this most charming hare, and as they walked, they talked. Sasa was hungry for any wisdom the Buddha could spare him. The Buddha was simply hungry, but did not say so.

33

At the edge of the wood, Sasa said, 'I know this meagre forest and how long you have been lost in it. You must be very hungry.'

'You are indeed shrewd in judgement, my velvet-skinned friend,' replied the Buddha. 'I'm famished.'

The hare sat back on his heels. 'That will not do. Indeed, it will not. Please do me the honour of skinning and eating me. I am reasonably plump, as you can see, and too young for my meat to be tough. Here – I'll build you a fire so that you can cook me.'

Leaving the Buddha no chance to protest, Sasa dashed to and fro, gathering firewood into a heap which he lit with the spark from two stones. 'Thank you for teaching me so much of which I was ignorant,' said the hare, bowing once more from his slender hips. 'Enjoy your meal.' And with that, he leapt into the flames.

With the speed of a hawk, the Buddha's hand shot out and caught Sasa by his long velvet ears. Once, twice he swung the creature around, then threw him upwards, upwards. The hare smashed through the spreading canopy of a tree, and leaves and twigs rained down on to the Buddha's upturned face. But Sasa kept on flying, upwards, until he hit the very face of the moon.

'Such a generous creature shall not die – no, never!' the Buddha called after him. 'In future, let the world look up at night and see my friend, Sasa-in-the-Moon, and remember how noble a creature he was, and how kind to a penniless hermit!'

For though he was Buddha-in-the-Wood, with no bite of food to call his own, he was also Buddha, Ruler-of-the-Skies, and had only to reach out a hand to fulfil his every wish.

Sasa lived on in the moon – you can see the happy shape of him dancing. Many a traveller lost at night has looked up and found encouragement in seeing him there.

All Roads Lead to Wales

A WELSH LEGEND

THE COUNTRYSIDE OF Europe is struck through with roads as straight as if they were drawn on the map with a ruler. Though some have been broken by frosts, and weeds have grown through the cracks, and mud has buried them from sight, still they are there, just below the surface, like the main arteries of the land, bearing blood to its heart. This is a story told by men who found the roads and wondered at their marvellous straightness and excellent construction, wondered at the men who had built them and then disappeared without trace from the ruined villas nearby.

Maximus was Emperor of Rome, and no one was more fit to be so. The known world paid him homage and its merchants met in his market places. When he hunted, it was in the company of great men, and when he hunted that day, thirty-two kings rode in his party.

The heat of the day made the landscape quake. The dogs yelped away into the distance. Sleep rose up from the ground mixed with the dust from his mare's hooves, and cloaked Maximus in weariness. He lay down on a grassy river bank, and his centurions made a shelter of their shields to ward off the sun's heat. Beneath his dark shell, Maximus slept, and while he slept he dreamed – a dream so vivid that the events of the morning grew gauzy and unreal.

He flew along a river in his dream, or leaned so far over the prow of a ship that he saw only the water speeding below him. Upstream he

35

sped, towards the source of the river, higher and higher till he came at last to a mountain – surely the highest in the world. Crossing the peak, he found another river issuing from the far side. He followed it down through the foothills, through fields and forests to its estuary and the sea. At the mouth of the river stood a city, its houses clinging to the skirts of a castle with towers of yellow and green and grey. At the foot of the castle wall, the sea rocked a fleet larger than all the navies of Rome. One ship in particular drew his eye, for its planks were alternately gold and silver and its gangway was a bridge of ivory.

Maximus, in his dream, crossed the ivory bridge just as the silk sail of the gilt and silver ship filled and billowed in his face. The ship carried him over sea lanes and obscure oceans to an island more beautiful than any he had ever seen. Still a strange curiosity carried him onwards, across the island from coast to coast, where he found the far side more lovely yet. Though its mountains were clad in mist, and tressed with rain, its valleys were fleecy with sheep and the river he followed was chased with silver spray. Once again, it was at the river's mouth that his dream brought him to a castle; inside the castle to a hall; inside the hall to a table. There it set him down.

Two princes were playing chess, while an old king sat nearby carving more chess pieces: knights and bishops and pawns. He looked up at Maximus, but a girl seated beside him was quicker in getting to her feet. Her hair, circled with gold, lifted and blew as she beckoned for Maximus to sit beside her in a chair of red gold. Thigh against thigh, arm against arm, hand against hand they sat. Then the Princess rested her cheek against his, turned her face towards him, smiled and offered him her mouth to . . .

A baying of hounds, a blare of horns, a thudding of hooves, and the shell of shields over the Emperor's head fractured and let in the sunlight. 'Your Majesty? Are you well? Such a very long sleep in the middle of the day! Perhaps the heat . . .' The sunlight and noise washed away the dream, the joy, the face of his beloved princess. Maximus awoke with a cry like a man stung by wasps, and clutched his hands to his heart. His hounds tumbled round him, and thirty-two kings stared.

On the way back to the palace, Maximus said not a word, and for a whole week afterwards would neither eat nor sleep, speak nor leave his room. It was as though, with the ending of the dream, he had breathed out a breath and could not draw the next. Physicians whispered outside his door. Rumours spread through the city that melancholy had conquered the invincible Maximus, and the thirty-two kings murmured among themselves.

Suddenly Maximus burst from his room: 'Summon my three finest men and saddle the best horses in Rome!'

He sent the three out into the three divisions of the earth, to search for the pieces of his dream: the country, the river, the castle, the two young Princes, the daughter, the King. He described every detail of his dream and said, 'Look, and do not stop looking until three years of looking have found nothing! For this dream went out of me like blood from a wound, and I fear my life depends on finding that place, that woman, that kiss.'

The three messengers departed into the three divisions of the earth, and each found islands, and each found rivers, each found castles and each found kings within them. But of the beautiful country of Maximus's dream – nothing.

They came home forlorn and fearful, and found the Emperor a shrunken man, like a sail emptied of wind. Rebellion was stirring in thirty-two dark corners of the Empire, because Maximus cared too little to put it down. 'I shall never see her again, and I left my heart in her keeping,' was all he said.

Then one of the messengers said, 'Master, won't you go yourself and look for the pieces of your dream? For the dream was sent to you and not to us!' It was so insolent a thing to say that the messenger trembled with fright. Maximus lifted his head and parted the fingers which covered his scowling eyes.

'Wise man!' he cried. 'What you say is true!'

Putting on his hunting clothes once more, he took the selfsame mare from the stables, then rode into the green hills, allowing the horse to ramble and amble, on tracks and off. When she grew thirsty, the mare stopped by the banks of a river, and Maximus dismounted too and bent to drink.

'I have been here before,' he said, all of a sudden, as the water raced by beneath his breast. 'This is the river of my dream!'

This time he commissioned thirteen messengers to follow the river upstream to its source. 'Let each man stitch to his cape a sleeve of gold, so that whatever country he comes to, there he shall be recognized as a messenger of Maximus, Emperor of the Romans! I would go myself, but I have rebellions to quell!' The Emperor seemed quite his old self again.

The thirteen messengers followed the river till they reached its source high in the highest mountain they had ever seen. They followed the river which plunged down from the peak and wandered through a dozen countries to the sea. There they found a city and a castle with turrets of yellow, green and grey, a fleet of ships, and a gangplank of walrus ivory. Crossing over it, they took ship on a galleon clinkered with silver and gold.

'. . . Everything was just as you said, master!' they reported back a hundred days later. Their golden sleeves were caked with sea salt and dust, but their eyes shone brighter than gold. 'In a hall, in a castle held in the arms of a river, we saw an old man carving chess pieces, and two boys playing nearby. And there in the centre of the room was a maiden in a chair of red gold!'

'Did you speak? Did you ask her name?' Maximus scarcely dared to hear them out.

'We did as you commanded us, and fell on our knees before her and said, "Hail Empress of Rome," and told her your story from sleeping to waking.'

Maximus was as pale as death. 'What did she say?'

'"Sirs," she said, "I don't doubt what you tell me. But if the Emperor loves me, let him come here and fetch me himself. My name is Elen."'

After that, Rome stirred like a man waking. The army streamed out of their barracks; the shopkeepers swarmed to the palace with supplies; the ladies waved kerchiefs from their windows, and chariots clashed broadside in the gates. The whole might of Rome galloped northwards, northwards and west – across the Alps, across the fields of France. They reached the sea at the castled coast, and took ship for Britain. And every step of the way, Maximus said, 'It is just as I saw in my dream!'

Without pause, Maximus pressed on westward, through the difficult green confusion of Britain's ancient forests until at last he came to Wales. And there, on the farthest shore, amid mountains clad in mist and streams chased with silver spray, he found the castle of King Eudaf.

The Princes Cynan and Adeon sat playing chess, while their father carved new pieces: knights and bishops and pawns. And there, in the centre of the room, in a chair of red gold, sat the Princess Elen.

Into her arms rushed Maximus, and held her close, as though they were lovers who had been kept apart for too long. They married next day.

So dear was Elen to Maximus (and he to her) that he stayed seven years and could not bring himself to leave. His name was reshaped by the minstrels into Maxen, and his nature reshaped into a man of the valleys, where song and poetry are more important than politics of war.

But after seven years, word came from Rome – from a usurper who had filled Maxen's place and wore his imperial crown. '*Since you have been gone seven years,*' he wrote, '*you forfeit the right to call yourself Emperor of the Romans.*'

Then Maxen stirred himself out of his lover's dream, and rode and sailed and climbed and marched back to Rome, to conquer it in the name of Elen. And there he stayed, pruning back the weeds which had overgrown the Empire during seven years of neglect.

Meanwhile, Elen gave orders for straight and sturdy roads to be built across all Italy and Gaul, across Britain and into Wales, so that a man might come and go along them at the speed of a galloping horse, from the centre of the world to the most beautiful corner of the Empire. Felling forests and quarrying hills, fording rivers and draining bogs, her road builders laid down hardcore and clinker, slabs and kerbs, never going round an obstacle but removing it utterly with pick and spade and brute force, letting nothing stand in their way.

These are the roads which the frosts chipped, the weeds invaded, the mud washed out. But they were built so true, so deep-founded, so straight, that they still cross the landscape like ruled lines.

To and fro rode Maxen of Rome, to and fro between the centre of the world and the most beautiful corner of his empire – even in summer's heat, or winter's muddy flood. And all so that he might sleep in the arms of Elen, a dreamless, blissful sleep.

Rainbow Snake

AN ABORIGINAL MYTH

IN DREAMTIME, OUR ancestors walked the Song Lines of the Earth, and thought about us, though we did not even exist. The Earth they walked was a brown flatness, its only features a few humpy huts built to keep off the sun, the dark, monsters and falling stars. Little tribes of people talked together in their own languages, and sometimes got up and danced their own magic dances. But even magic in those days was brown, drab and unremarkable, for there were no colours to conjure with.

The only colours shone in the sky. Sometimes, after a storm, as rain gave way to sun, a distillation of colours hung in the air, spanning Australia: the Rainbow. And that rainbow, like the people below it, dreamed, thought and had longings in its heart. 'I will go down,' it thought, 'and find a tribe of people who think as I think, and dance as I dance, and we shall enjoy each other's company.'

So the Rainbow drank all its own magic, and writhed into life. Whereas before it had been made only of falling rain and sunlight, each raindrop turned into a scale and each glimmer into a sinew of muscle. In short, it transformed itself into a snake. Twisting and flexing, its body a blaze of colour, it snaked its way down the sky to the edge of the Earth. Its jaws were red, its tail violet, and in between, its overlapping scales passed through every other shade.

But the Rainbow Snake was massively heavy. As it slithered along, it carved a trench through the featureless countryside, and threw

40

aside mounds of mud. Because it was so huge, the trenches were valleys, and the mounds mountains. The next rain which fell was channelled into rivers, and puddling pools, so that already the world was altered by the presence of the Snake.

Rainbow Snake travelled from the Bamaga Point southwards through the bush, and every now and then raised its scarlet head and tasted the air with its flickering tongue. It listened too, with its lobeless ears. Sometimes it heard voices, but did not understand them. Sometimes it heard music, but the music moved it neither to tears nor laughter. 'These are not my kind of people,' it thought, and went on southwards, always south.

Then one day, it found a happy, laughing people whose language it partly understood and whose music made it sway – rear and sway, sway and dance – to the rhythm of the didgeridoo.

The dancing faltered. The dancers froze. The music died away. For towering high above them, jaws agape, the people saw a gigantic snake with scales of every colour in the rainbow. Its eyes closed in rapture, it swayed its sinuous body in time to the music.

When the music fell silent, it opened its gigantic eyes and looked down at them. Mothers drew their children close. Warriors fingered their spears. The Snake opened its mouth . . .

'I am Rainbow Snake, and you are my kin, for you speak the same language I think in, and make the music I have heard in my dreams.'

An elder of the tribe, still balanced on one foot in mid-dance, looked up from under his hand. His bright teeth shone as his face broke into a smile. 'In that case, you're welcome, friend! Lay yourself down and rest, or lift yourself up and dance – but don't let's waste another moment's fun!' The people gave a great shout of welcome, and went back to feasting.

Next day, Rainbow Snake coiled itself round the village, and sheltered it from the wind. Its flanks shaped the land during daylight hours, and in the evening it ate and drank and talked with the villagers. It was a happy time. Even afterwards, it was remembered as a happy time.

After all its travels, the Snake knew more dances than the people did, and from its place in the sky, it had seen more wonders. It taught them all it knew, and in honour of Rainbow Snake, the people decorated their bodies with feathers and patterned their skin, as the snake was patterned (though in plain, stark white).

Then it happened, the terrible mistake.

Dozing one night, mouth wide open, Rainbow Snake felt the pleasant tickle of rain trickling down its back and splashing in its nostrils. The patter of something sweet on its rolled tongue it mistook for rain, and closed its mouth and swallowed. Too late, it realized that the shapes in its mouth were solid.

Two boys, looking for shelter from the rain, had mistaken the Snake's huge mouth for a cave and crept inside. Now they were deep in its coiling stomach, and the Snake could not fetch them back. What to do?

Keep silent and hope the boys were not missed? No. The tribe were certain to notice, and would guess what had become of the lost boys. Admit to eating them, and listen to the mothers weep and reproach it? No. Better to slip away noiselessly, forgoing old friends and seeking out new ones.

Away it went, slithering silently, slowly and sleepily away over the wet ground, colourless in the starlight. It wrapped itself around Bora-bunara Mountain and slept.

Waking to find Rainbow Snake gone and the two boys lost, the tribe did indeed guess what had happened. They did not shrug their shoulders and they did not sit down and weep. Instead, they grabbed their spears and hollered, '*Murder!*' Then they followed the Snake's tracks, plain to see in the wet earth. They sped along the valley carved by its leaving, and had no difficulty in finding its resting place on the peak of Bora-bunara.

The Snake's dreams were pleasant and deep. Its stomach was full, and its contented snores rolled like thunder down every side of the mountain. Boulders tumbled, and shale cascaded, making a climb treacherous. But three brothers clambered nimbly up the rocky escarpments, knives clenched in their teeth. They slit open the side of Rainbow Snake; scales fell in a rain of indigo, green and blue. They opened the wound and shouted inside to the boys . . .

But the great magic of which the Snake was made had part-digested the children. Out past the rescuers fluttered – not boys, but two brightly coloured birds. Their plumage was indigo, green and blue. Soaring high in the sky, they circled the mountain twice, then flew off, singing joyfully in the language of the birds.

The three brothers looked at one another and shrugged. Why

grieve for boys who have been turned into birds? Their story has ended happily, after all. Only when they turned to make their descent did they see their friends and neighbours at the bottom of the mountain, jumping, gesticulating and pointing up at the Snake.

The Snake had opened his eyes.

Feeling a pain in its side like a stitch, the Rainbow Snake experienced a sudden draughty coldness in its stomach. It felt, too, a leaking away of its magic, like blood. And worst of all, it felt *betrayed*.

'I knew my little mistake might end our friendship,' it hissed, 'but I never realized it would stir you up to such *insolence*! Attack the Rainbow Spirit? Cut open your benefactor? Shed the scales of a Sky Creature? I'm hungrier now than I was before. And how do you think I shall satisfy that hunger, eh? I know! *I'LL EAT YOU, EVERY ONE!*'

The tongue which darted from its mouth was forked lightning. Its tail drummed up thunder. It crushed the mountain like bread into breadcrumbs, and thrashed the outback inside out and back to front.

In their terror, some people froze, some ran. Some even escaped. Some wanted so much to get away that they ran on all fours and wore down their legs to the thinness of jumbuck. Some leapt so far and so high that they turned into kangaroos. Some, in hiding under rocks, became tortoises and turtles. Others, who stood stock-still with fright, put down roots and turned into trees; others climbed them and turned into koala with big frightened eyes. Some leapt off Bora-bunara and flew away as birds. And some burrowed deep and became platypuses.

To escape the rampage of venomous Rainbow Snake, they became anything and everything, transforming the landscape almost as much as the angry serpent was doing with its lashing tail.

At last Rainbow Snake exhausted itself and, leaving behind a trail of destruction, hurled itself headlong into the sea. Through the half-circle of the setting sun it slithered, like an eel swallowed down the world's throat.

And next morning, it was back in place again, as though it had never left: the Rainbow, spanning the sky like a breath of peace: a miasma of rain and sunlight, a trick of the light. A reminder of stormy nights.

But when the airy Rainbow Spirit looked down on the Earth

below, the landscape it saw was transformed. So too were the lives of our ancestors, for some were animals and some were plants, and those who were still men and women were wiser men and women by far.

Juno's Roman Geese

A ROMAN LEGEND

VEII WAS AN Etruscan city, a place of rumour and legend, full of treasure. At the very height of the Roman Empire, Rome set its sights on conquering Veii, but for ten years it stood besieged but unconquered. Camillus, commander of the Roman army, wanted to capture it more than anyone, wanted it more than anything. He fell on his face before the altars of the gods and prayed for success. And he wondered how to enter a city which for ten years had kept out all attackers.

'I shall not enter by force, but by subtlety, silently and in secret,' he thought. Then he summoned his engineers and showed them a plan of the city. 'If we were to dig a tunnel under the walls, here, and bring it out here, by the temple of Juno . . .'

Night and day they dug, passing the loose earth back down the passage. Like moles they tunnelled, silent, and black with Etruscan dirt, working in pitch darkness. Then one evening, the soil gave way to something hard. Camillus wormed his way along the narrow tunnel. He stroked the smooth marble overhead with his fingertips. 'We have come up right *under* the temple of Juno,' he whispered.

So after dark, when no footfall came from overhead, Camillus raised a paving stone and peered about. The dark temple was a vast echoing hollow. He felt like a sailor in the stomach of a whale. He felt, too, as if he were being watched. Camillus looked up, looked higher, and drew a gasp of breath. For looking down at him was the

45

monumental figure of the goddess Juno. Seven metres tall, and clad in slightly ragged, rather grubby cotton robes, her eyes looked directly into his. Scraps of litter blew across the temple floor.

'Phew! Only a statue,' he might have said. But he did not. He took off his helmet, stood to attention, and saluted the Queen of the Gods. His lips moved in silent prayer. 'Oh Juno, prosper me this night, and I shall give you a temple finer than this, filled with the scent of burning herbs, and I shall people it with white geese, so that you never stand lonely in the small hours of the night.'

The white marble face looked down impassively, an artefact carved by human hands, nothing more. And yet the clothing blowing round her lent an impression of movement.

'On, men,' whispered Camillus. 'The city of Veii is ours, if the gods are with us tonight!'

One by one, the Romans crawled through the black tunnel and out into Juno's temple. It stood at the centre of the city, so that when they burst out – like adders hatching from a white egg – the city was stung at its very heart, and fell with barely a cry.

Next day, a queue of wagons stood in the market place. The treasures of Veii were being loaded for transportation to Rome. Statues reclined awkwardly in straw-lined carts – even pillars and mosaics were being loaded: everything beautiful, everything deserving of admiration was carefully stowed and driven away.

But inside the temple of Juno, there was a problem. Camillus went to investigate and found his troops standing stock-still round the statue of Juno. 'What's the matter?'

The troops were tongue-tied, embarrassed. 'We were washing her, right, sir? Bathing her, like you told us, sir, and dressing her in new clothes. Suddenly – now, don't be angry, sir . . .'

'Suddenly what?'

'Suddenly she seemed too . . . too *holy* somehow. We're all afraid to touch her, sir.'

Camillus was not angry. He too had felt the aura of holiness which surrounded the great statue of the Queen of Heaven. Instead of shouting at the men to get on with their work, he took off his plumed helmet, bowed to the statue and called, 'Juno! Great Queen of all the gods! Is it your wish to go to Rome?'

The men stared, transfixed. The horses harnessed to the cart at the temple door trembled in their shafts. Then they saw it – everyone saw it: a serene nod of the marble head, the merest closing of the eyes in affirmation. 'I am content,' said the gesture. 'You may take me now.'

Camillus was as good as his word. He did not rest until Juno was ensconced in the finest temple on Capitoline Hill, her shrine decorated with flowers, and the gardens round about busy with Roman geese. Waddling to and fro, toes turned in and hips wagging, the birds made a comical priesthood. But geese are the sacred birds of Juno, and their honking rang out piercingly, reminding the Romans daily to worship the Queen of Heaven.

Rome gobbled up the treasures of Veii and lauded the heroic victor Camillus, carved his statue, and made speeches of thanks to him in the Senate . . . then they put war behind them, preferring peace.

Once, the Romans had looked towards Veii and thought, 'We wish to have its treasure for our own.' But the conquest of Veii and more such cities made Rome herself a treasure-house. Soon others were looking at Rome with hungry eyes and saying, 'We wish to have its treasure for our own.'

One day, a voice was heard in the streets of Rome. At first the people mistook it for the honking of Juno's geese, but it became more plain – deep and mellifluous, but still, perhaps, a woman's voice . . . It woke them from their sleep. It made the night watch shiver. 'Prepare, Rome, beware! The Gauls are coming!'

The Gauls? It was laughable. The Gauls were uncultured barbarians who painted their half-naked bodies and wore animal skins. They had no system of government, no great cities, no drama or literature, no education, no empire. Hardly a civilization to be reckoned with, in comparison with the might of Rome! Camillus might have told them to pay more heed to the voice, but Camillus had been banished to the provinces – a man of war put out to grass.

When the Gauls came, they came like beasts, without strategies or cunning, but with brute force. What they fought, they killed. What they captured, they destroyed. Like fire across stubble they came, and all the fine words in the world could not stop them reaching the gates of Rome.

'Where is Camillus to defend us?'

'Gone to the country! Banished to Ardea!'

'Where are the gods to help us?'

47

'They shouted in the streets, but we wouldn't listen. Too late now! Run! Hide! The Gauls are at the gates!'

Some Romans ran away into the vine-strewn countryside and hid. Those who were fit enough ran with armfuls of belongings for Capitoline Hill. The hill was the city's natural keep – a high, unassailable crag adorned with white temples and glimmering now in the orange light of fires down below. Like surf over a pebble beach, the barbarians, as they pillaged Rome, left no stone where it had lain before. For sheer love of destruction, they pulled the lovely city down round their own ears, for they placed no value on its beauty, found nothing admirable, coveted nothing but blood and terror and death.

Like the sea also, they reached a point beyond which they could not go, for Capitoline Hill could be climbed only by a narrow path, and the besieged Romans could pick off an approaching enemy with ease.

'We have only to wait for you to starve!' bawled the barbarians in their guttural, shapeless language. Then they set about roasting the horses they had slaughtered, and feasting at the foot of the hill. High above them, the Romans watched the fires consume their beloved city, until the heat dried their eyeballs and left them no longer able to cry. Then they wrapped themselves in their cloaks and went to sleep, watched over by the beautiful white statues of their gods.

'Give them time to doze off,' said the barbarian chieftain, gnawing on a hock bone, 'then we'll finish them. Smash their gods and burn their temples.' Beside him, face down on a shattered mosaic floor, a Roman traitor lay amid a pool of bloodstained gold. He had sought to make his fortune by betraying a secret path up Capitoline Hill. The Gauls had taken his information, then cut his throat. Now nothing stood between them and the remnants of Rome.

In the darkest time of night (as when Camillus had burrowed under the walls of Veii), the Gauls crawled and scrambled up the side of Capitoline Hill, daggers in their teeth and rags around their swords to keep metal from clanking against rock. The Romans generally fought their battles by day, after grand speeches, cleansed by prayer, in full sight of the sun. But the Gauls came creeping, sneaking, worming their way up the precipitous path, to slit throats under cover of dark.

At the foot of Juno's statue, the sacred geese fussed and fretted. Their big feet paddled across the chequered floor with a *plash plash plash*.

Hand over hand came the Gauls. Nearly there now. Mouths full of filthy curses, the blood lust rising. An arm over the low wall of a terrace, a knee, a cautious lifting of one eye . . .

'*Haaaaaarkhkh! Haaaaaarkhkh!*'

They were met by orange jabs of pain. Hard white wings beat at their eardrums, and huge black feet, hard as bone, paddled on their upturned faces. Geese!

With pecks and kicks, the geese dislodged the first attackers, then their honking woke the sleeping Romans. '*Haaaarkhkh! Haaaarkhkh!*' It was louder than braying donkeys. One Gaul, in falling, dislodged others: an avalanche of Gauls. Beakfuls of hair sprinkled the marble terraces.

Once awake, the besieged men and women fought with all the valour of true Romans. Morning found the Gauls licking their wounds like kicked dogs, and bemoaning the 'winged monsters' which had beset them in the dark. They would make no more night-time assaults on Capitoline Hill. Besides, the Romans were now on their guard against sneak attacks. And within the week, the cry went up from the roof of Juno's temple. 'Camillus! Camillus is coming!'

Camillus came in behind the Gauls and, scouring them out of the fire-blackened ruins of Rome, drove them into the Tiber. He dealt with them as a man might an infestation of woodlice. And although the destruction left behind was terrible, still forests do grow again after forest fires. In fact, they grow more vigorous and green and beautiful than before.

As for the geese, they were declared heroes and heroines of the battle, crowned with laurel and feted with corn. They fretted and fussed about, like old aunts embarrassed by overmuch attention. But it seemed to Camillus, as he sprinkled corn from a silver pan, that Juno looked on with an expression of pride. Their honking was a note more self-important, too. 'Make way for Juno's geese,' they seemed to say. 'Make way for Juno's *Roman* geese! We saved *her* temple! We saved *her* city!'

John Barleycorn

AN AMERICAN MYTH

No sooner did they lay eyes on him than the men of the farms decided to kill John Barleycorn. Though he had never done them harm, Farmer Mick and Farmer Mack, Farmer Mock and Farmer Muck ganged up on him in broad daylight and tumbled him to the ground. They dug a hole and buried his body in a field, and though the rooks flapped out of the treetops and circled overhead, no one else witnessed the dreadful crime.

Fingers and faces numbed by the raw cold, the four assassins trudged silently to the inn and, beside a log fire, tried to warm their hands round tankards of cold water. April rain spattered the windows, and the rookeries in the treetops faded from sight as the afternoon sky grew dark.

The way home took Farmer Mick past the field where John Barleycorn lay buried, but it was too dark to see the place where the clods of earth were piled on his yellow head.

The days grew longer and the sun warmer. Farmer Mick and Farmer Mack, Farmer Mock and Farmer Muck often drank water together at the local inn. They were kept busy milking and lambing, while their wives made butter and skimmed cream off the bowls in the dairy. None of them saw what the rooks saw from high in the trees – a single sharp green finger poking out between the clods, a long, reaching arm . . .

Then one evening, Farmer Mick stumbled into the inn, breathless, pointing back the way he had come. 'Have you seen? Have you seen? John Barleycorn's up again!'

Their arms slung round each others' necks, the farmers peered out through the low dirty window. 'Ach, he's nought but a green boy. We'd be wasting our time to chase after him!' And they settled to a game of skittles instead.

One particularly sunny day, however, as Farmer Mick walked down to the village, he saw, out of the corner of his eye, John Barleycorn swaying and dancing over his grave, his long yellow beard wagging as he silently sang to the rooks in the trees.

When the others heard the news, Farmer Muck declared, 'Let's get him!' and grabbed up his scythe. Farmer Mock took his sickle, and all four, armed with blades, rampaged out into the field.

Snick-snack, they sliced clean through him at the knees, but John Barleycorn only laughed as he fell.

Whip-snap, they bound him round where he lay, but John Barleycorn only laughed as they tied the knot.

Bump-thump, they manhandled him as far as the barn, and threw him down on the floor, where they beat him with sticks until hairs from his long beard flew amid the sunbeams. So violent and savage were they that sweat poured from their foreheads and dripped in their eyes, and their mouths were circled with a white and dusty thirst. But John Barleycorn only laughed as they pounded him.

They took his blood and bones and hid them in the water butt – and no one knew (except for the rooks in the trees) what they had done.

Then they had a feast, because John Barleycorn was dead. Mrs Mick and Mrs Mack, Mrs Mock and Mrs Muck baked loaves, and the farmers rolled the barrel from the barn all the way to the inn. The innkeeper stabbed a spike through the keg's side, and fitted a tap in the hole. And when the liquor inside glugged out into their tankards, it sounded for all the world like laughter.

'I give you a toast!' cried Farmer Mick. 'John Barleycorn – may he live for ever, God bless him!' and the others took up the toast: '*John Barleycorn!*'

A strange thing to say, you may think, about someone you have just murdered. But not if you think first of a stalk of barley – how it grows from a seed into a green shoot; how it sways in the wind, ripens to gold in the sun and grows a whiskery beard. Reapers reap it, threshers thrash it, brewers nail it into casks. So next time Farmer Mick and Farmer Mack, Farmer Mock and Farmer Muck stagger home from the inn, their arms round each others' necks, and singing fit to frighten the rooks away, raise three hearty cheers for John Barleycorn and the barley wine that's made from him.

Well? Do you think that's water they've just been drinking?

The Singer Above the River
A GERMAN LEGEND

A HEARTBROKEN GIRL once wandered the banks of the River Rhine. Her lover had chosen to marry someone else, and her heart was a rock within her, heavy and hard. She searched the fields for somewhere which did not remind her of her lover. She searched the woods for somewhere she could forget him. She searched the riverbank for somewhere she might sleep without dreaming of him. And when she found nowhere, she sought to end all her sorrows by dying. She threw herself from the huge black rock which juts out over the Rhine like an angry fist. Her name was Lorelei.

But even in death, Lorelei found no peace. Her soul was not permitted to rest. She was doomed, for taking her own life, to live on, in the shape of a nymph, perched on the craggy rock from which she had fallen. Her beauty was greater than it had been in life, her voice ten times more lovely. But in place of grief, she nursed a terrible hatred for young men.

As shadows appear with the sunrise, so with sunset Lorelei appeared: a wraith, a twilight shadow. Any sailor, looking up through the dusk as he sailed by, might see a white arm beckoning from the summit of the cliff. A sweet face, barely distinguishable in the half-light, would call to him, sing to him, sing such a song that he felt himself falling towards it. His hand would tug on the tiller as the voice tugged on his heart. Powerless to resist, he would steer for the crag, heel towards the grey crag and the jagged boulders which lay heaped at its feet.

As his boat split, and water closed over his head, each drowning sailor was still looking upwards, still listening to magic music. Then, as the top rim of the setting sun dipped below the horizon, Lorelei would disappear.

Word spread of the maiden on the rock – the siren who lured men to their deaths. One young man, Ronald, son of the Count Palatine, became obsessed by the thought of her. He boasted that he would lift the curse on the river. He would both remove the hazard to shipping (which was making the Rhine unnavigable) and win himself a bride in the same night. He would climb the rocks, up to the nymph called Lorelei, and snatch her from her dizzy lair. He would close her singing mouth with kisses, and rescue her damned soul by the power of true love.

In short he fell in love with the idea of Lorelei, and believed there was nothing he could not do, because that is what love does to a man.

'Ferryman, ferryman, row me past the Lorelei Rock.'

'No, not for brass money, young sir, I will not.'

'Ferryman, ferryman, I'll pay you silver.'

'Not even silver, young sir, would make me row by the Lorelei.'

'Ferryman, ferryman, then I shall pay you gold.'

The ferryman hesitated. 'How much gold?'

'Enough,' said Ronald.

So, late in the afternoon, the ferryman settled his oars in the rowlocks, and rowed out into the current, with Ronald standing at the bow. The ferryman kept his back always to the rock so that he could not glimpse the nymph and succumb to her magic. But Ronald fixed his eyes on the rock, and his face grew bright in the light of the setting sun.

Suddenly she appeared, the invisible taking shape, like salt settling out of sea water.

'Come,' said her hands, waving. 'Come,' said her arms, beckoning. 'Come,' said her sweet red mouth, 'come and take me home!'

'Row faster, ferryman,' urged Ronald, 'for I must climb the rock before the light fails and she disappears!'

The ferryman did not alter the steady, rhythmic dip of his oars, steering a straight course down the centre of the river.

'Faster, faster, ferryman! Look, she is ready to come with me, if I can just reach her in time!'

The ferryman said nothing, for he had seen it all happen before.

'Faster, faster, you fool!' cried Ronald, as the ferryman eased the boat carefully, carefully down the current. 'You must get closer, or how can I gain a grip on the rock?'

The ferryman shipped his oars. 'This is close enough, young man. You don't want to die so soon. Think what a sweet life lies ahead of you. I'll take you no farther.'

'Cheat! Cheat!' raged Ronald, thinking only of the present. 'I gave you gold to carry me to the rock face!'

'But what good will your gold be to me when I am dead? You have your money back, and I shall row you safe ashore.'

All the while, Lorelei beckoned, whistled, sang like a calling-bird: 'Come to me, love! Come and fetch me down!' In his passion to reach the singing nymph, Ronald snatched one of the oars and began to use it as a paddle. The rowing-boat rocked wildly under him and began to spin. The currents near the cliff face took hold of it and it gathered speed. Ronald gave a whoop of triumph. Too late, he realized that it was speeding towards disaster.

As the boards split between his feet and rocks came through the floor of the boat, Ronald was flung into the cold water. It held him like the arms of a woman. It covered his face with cold, wet kisses, and drew him down to join the company of other sailors wrecked on the Lorelei. The nymph high above smiled, kissed her fingertips and, leaning over the cliff edge, waved down at the drowning men, laughing.

The Count Palatine broke his chain of office between clenched fists when he was told of his son's death. 'Kill that *thing* on the rock! And if it is dead already, pen its soul and torment it, slowly, for a thousand years!'

Every soldier in his service armed himself with axe or mace, pike or broadsword. The troops set sail for the Lorelei in as huge a ship as had dared to pass through the reach for many years. And when they reached the rock, it was morning and they had all day to make the climb. Studded boots scuffing the rock face, mailed gloves clinging to the fissures, they climbed, with ropes and crampons, pitons and picks. They could not hear the cry of the starlings or the redstart round their heads, for they had wax crammed in their ears to shut out the magic song of Lorelei.

Just as the first man's fingers reached over the brink of the beetling rock, the sun's bottom rim touched land. Lorelei appeared, one moment invisible, the next a woman as lovely as the trees swaying in the distant landscape.

'That's right. Come, my dear fellows. I have kisses enough for all of you! Come here, my handsome soldiers. Come home from the hardships of war to the softness of peace. Come. Come!'

But the soldiers were the cruellest and the bitterest men in all Germany – the Count had made certain of that. They had no daughters, no wives, no sweethearts. As they clambered on to the flat top of the black outcrop, Lorelei could see their ears stuffed with wax, their hands holding maces and pikes and swords.

'Despair, demon, for the Count Palatine himself has called for you to die or, if you are dead, for your soul to be penned and poked like a pig.'

'Then I call on the river!' exclaimed Lorelei, jumping to her feet and raising her voice above theirs. 'You Rhine! Save your daughter Lorelei from these . . . these *beasts* disguised as men, who haven't a heart or soul between them!'

Far below, the sound of the river altered, so that the climbing soldiers looked down. They saw a wave heave itself up, as though the river itself were drawing a deep breath. The wave, as it rolled, gathered momentum, sucking water from the shore and piling it, fathom upon fathom, into a tidal wave. The wreckage of thirty ships was stirred up from the riverbed and broken anew, scattering flotsam down the flooding river.

Still the river filled, rising, rising up the sides of the gorge, until it sucked at the boots of the mountaineering soldiers. Just when they thought they had escaped its torrential spray, a second wave broke against the rock, soaking them to the skin. A third plucked men from the rock face and left them swinging on their ropes like spiders on lengths of thread. But those who had reached the top already crawled, relentless as limpets, across the wet black rock, closing in on Lorelei.

With a scream of defiance, she leapt headlong into the mountainous waves . . . and disappeared. She vanished, as surely as salt sprinkled on to water. The setting sun turned the raging river to the colour of blood before the turbulence settled, the waters fell quiet and the Rhine rolled on, black and implacable, into the coming night.

Never again did the nymph beckon from the top of the black rock, luring men to their deaths. But many were the young girls who had their hearts broken by young men, and too many were the young men who went on to become soldiers, steely in body and soul, and deaf to the sweetest singing.

How Music was Fetched
Out of Heaven

AN AZTEC MYTH

ONCE THE WORLD suffered in Silence. Not that it was a quiet place, nor peaceful, for there was always the groan of the wind, the crash of the sea, the grumble of lava in the throats of volcanoes, and the grate of man's ploughshare through the stony ground. Babies could be heard crying at night, and women in the daytime, because of the hardness of life and the great unfriendliness of Silence.

Tezcatlipoca, his body heavy as clay and his heart heavy as lead (for he was the Lord of Matter), spoke to Quetzalcoatl, feathery Lord of Spirit. He spoke from out of the four quarters of the Earth, from the north, south, easterly and westerly depths of the iron-hard ground. 'The world needs music, Quetzalcoatl! In the thorny glades and on the bald seashore, in the square comfortless houses of the poor and in the dreams of the sleeping, there should be music, there ought to be song. Go to Heaven, Quetzalcoatl, and fetch it down!'

'How would I get there? Heaven is higher than wings will carry me.'

'String a bridge out of cables of wind, and nail it with stars: a bridge to the Sun. At the feet of the Sun, sitting on the steps of his throne, you will find four musicians. Fetch them down here. For I am so sad in this Silence, and the People are sad, hearing the sound of Nothingness ringing in their ears.'

'I will do as you say,' said Quetzalcoatl, preening his green feathers

58

in readiness for the journey. 'But will they come, I ask myself. Will the musicians of the Sun want to come?'

He whistled up the winds like hounds. Like hounds they came bounding over the bending treetops, over the red places where dust rose up in twisting columns, and over the sea, whipping the waters into mountainous waves. Baying and howling, they carried Quetzal-coatl higher and higher – higher than all Creation – so high that he could glimpse the Sun ahead of him. Then the four mightiest winds plaited themselves into a cable, and the cable swung out across the void of Heaven: a bridge planked with cloud and nailed with stars.

'Look out, here comes Quetzalcoatl,' said the Sun, glowering, lowering, his red-rimmed eyes livid. Circling him in a cheerful dance, four musicians played and sang. One, dressed in white and shaking bells, was singing lullabies; one, dressed in red, was singing songs of war and passion as he beat on a drum; one, in sky-blue robes fleecy with cloud, sang the ballads of Heaven, the stories of the gods; one, in yellow, played on a golden flute.

This place was too hot for tears, too bright for shadows. In fact the shadows had all fled downwards and clung fast to men. And yet all this sweet music had not served to make the Sun generous. 'If you don't want to have to leave here and go down where it's dark, dank, dreary and dangerous, keep silent, my dears. Keep silent, keep secret, and don't answer when Quetzalcoatl calls,' he warned his musicians.

Across the bridge rang Quetzalcoatl's voice. 'O singers! O mar-vellous makers of music. Come to me. The Lord of the World is calling!' The voice of Quetzalcoatl was masterful and inviting, but the Sun had made the musicians afraid. They kept silent, crouching low, pretending not to hear. Again and again Quetzalcoatl called them, but still they did not stir, and the Sun smiled smugly and thrummed his fingers on the sunny spokes of his chairback. He did not intend to give up his musicians, no matter who needed them.

So Quetzalcoatl withdrew to the rain-fringed horizon and, harnes-sing his four winds to the black thunder, had them drag the clouds closer, circling the Sun's citadel. When he triggered the lightning and loosed the thunderclaps, the noise was monumental. The Sun thought he was under siege.

Thunder clashed against the Sun with the noise of a great brass cymbal, and the musicians, their hands over their ears, ran this way and that looking for help. 'Come out to me, little makers of miracles,' said Quetzalcoatl in a loud but gentle voice. *BANG* went the thunder, and all Heaven shook.

The crooner of lullabies fluttered down like a sheet blown from a bed. The singer of battle-songs spilled himself like blood along the floor of Heaven and covered his head with his arms. The singer of ballads, in his fright, quite forgot his histories of Heaven, and the flautist dropped his golden flute. Quetzalcoatl caught it.

As the musicians leapt from their fiery nest, he opened his arms and welcomed them into his embrace, stroking their heads in his lap. 'Save us, Lord of Creation! The Sun is under siege!'

'Come, dear friends. Come where you are needed most.'

The Sun shook and trembled with rage like a struck gong, but he knew he had been defeated, had lost his musicians to Quetzalcoatl.

At first the musicians were dismayed by the sadness and silence of the Earth. But no sooner did they begin to play than the babies in their cribs stopped squalling. Pregnant women laid a hand on their big stomachs and sighed with contentment. The man labouring in the field cupped a hand to his ear and shook himself, so that his shadow of sadness fell away in the noonday. Children started to hum. Young men and women got up to dance, and in dancing fell in love. Even the mourner at the graveside, hearing sweet flute music, stopped crying.

Quetzalcoatl himself swayed his snaky hips and lifted his hands in dance at the gate of Tezcatlipoca, and Tezcatlipoca came out of doors. Matter and Spirit whirled together in a dance so fast: had you been there, you would have thought you were seeing only one.

And suddenly every bird in the sky opened its beak and sang, and the stream moved by with a musical ripple. The sleeping child dreamed music and woke up singing. From that day onwards, life was all music – rhythms and refrains, falling cadences and fluting calls. No one saw just where the Sun's musicians settled or made their homes, but their footprints were everywhere and their bright colours were found in corners that had previously been grey and cobwebbed with silence. The flowers turned up bright faces of red and yellow and white and blue, as if they could hear singing. Even the winds ceased to howl and roar and groan, and learned love songs.

Whose Footprints?
A MYTH FROM GHANA

D O YOU SUPPOSE God made the world all by himself? Of course not. He had help. He had a servant. Every Fon in Abomey knows that. The servant's name was Legba, and he took the blame for whatever went wrong.

Whenever the people saw a wonderful sunset, or made a huge catch of fish, they gave thanks to God and said, 'Great is our Creator, who has made all things wonderfully well!'

Whenever they fell over a rock, or the canoe sank, they said, 'Legba is making mischief again. That villain Legba!'

Now Legba thought this was mortally unfair. 'Why do I get all the blame?' he complained.

'That's what you're there for,' said God. 'It wouldn't do for people to think of God as anything but perfect. It would set them a bad example.'

'But they hate me!' protested Legba. 'They hang up charms at their doors to keep me out, and they frighten their children with my name: "Be good or Legba will come and steal you out of your bed!" How would you feel?' But God had already sauntered away towards the garden where he grew yams. (This was in the days when God lived on Earth, among all that he had made.)

God tended those yams with loving care and attention. If the truth were told, he was kept so busy by his gardening some days, that things could go wrong in the world without him really noticing. It did not matter. Legba got the blame, naturally.

Legba sat down and thought. Then Legba stood up and spoke. 'Lord, I hear that thieves are planning to steal your yams tonight!'

God was horrified. He sounded a ram's-horn trumpet and summoned together all the people of the world. They came, jostling and bowing, smiling and offering presents. They were rather taken aback to see God so angry.

'If any one of you intends to rob my garden tonight, I'm telling you here and I'm telling you now, and I'm making it plain as day: that thief shall die!'

The people clutched each other and trembled. They nodded feverishly to show they had understood, hurried home to their beds and pulled the covers over their heads until morning. God watched them scatter and brushed together the palms of his great hands. 'That settles that,' he said, and went home to bed himself.

Legba waited. When all sound had ceased but the scuttle of night creatures, the flutter of bats and the drone of snoring humanity; he crept into God's house. God, too, was snoring. Legba wormed his way across the floor, and stole the sandals from beside God's bed.

Putting on the sandals, he crept to the yam garden. Though the shoes were over-large and tripped him more than once, he worked his way from tree to tree, removing every delectable yam. The dew glistened, the ground was wet. The sandals of God left deep prints in the moist soil . . .

'Come quick! Come quick! The thief has struck!'

God tumbled out of bed, fumbled his feet into his sandals and stumbled out of doors into the first light of morning. When he saw the waste that had been laid to his garden, the shout could be heard all the way to Togo.

'Don't worry! Don't worry!' Legba hurried to console him. 'Look how the thief has left his footprints in the ground! You have only to find the shoes that made those footprints, and you will have caught the culprit red-handed . . . -footed, I mean.'

Once more, the ram's-horn sounded, and the people pelted out of their huts and horded into God's presence, trembling.

'*Someone* has stolen my yams!' bellowed God. '*Someone* is about to *DIE*!'

They all had to fetch out their sandals, and every sandal was laid against the footprints in the garden. But not one fitted. Not one.

'Legba! Try Legba! He's always doing wicked things!' shouted the people, and Legba felt that familiar pang of resentment that God did not correct them. It would have been nice if God could have said, 'Oh not *Legba*. He's entirely trustworthy. He helped me create the world. He's my good and faithful servant.' Not a bit of it.

'*Legba! Have you been stealing from me?!*'

Willingly Legba produced his sandals. Willingly he laid them alongside the footprints in the garden. But not by any stretch of the imagination did Legba's sandals fit the prints beneath the yam trees.

'Perhaps you walked in your sleep, O Lord?' suggested Legba, and the people all said, 'AAAH!'

God tried to look disdainful of such a ridiculous suggestion, but the eyes of all Creation were gazing at him, waiting. He laid his great foot alongside one of the great footprints, and the people gasped and laughed and sighed with relief. It was just God, walking in his sleep, ha ha ha! God was to blame after all!

Then they began to wonder – God could see the question form in their faces – if God had sleepwalked once, perhaps he had sleep-walked before. And if God stole in his sleep, what else might he get up to under the cover of darkness, under the influence of his dreams?

God glowered at Legba. He knew Legba had something to do with his embarrassment, but could not quite see what. Instead, he stamped his sandalled foot irritably and said, 'I'm going! I'm not staying here where no one gives me the respect I deserve! I'm going *higher up*!'

So God moved higher up. And he told Legba to report to him every night, in the sky, with news of what people were getting up to.

Of course what Legba chooses to tell God is entirely up to Legba. But the Fon of Abomey have been a lot nicer to Legba since God went higher up. A lot nicer.

The Death of El Cid
A SPANISH LEGEND

DON RODRIGO DÍAZ de Vivar was cursed with pride. It was pride which caused his banishment from the court of King Alfonso of Spain. It was pride which made him swear never to cut his beard until his banishment was repealed. It was pride which made him venture out from Alfonso's tiny corner-kingdom into the part of Spain that had been occupied by Moors from North Africa, where it was certain death for any Christian to go.

Into Moorish Spain he charged, first with a dozen men, then with a hundred, then with a thousand at his back. Before him fell village after fortress, city after port. And from every victory he sent the spoils back to King Alfonso, his King, his lord and master, to whom his obedience never faltered. Still the King did not pardon him, but many more young men left Alfonso's kingdom to join Rodrigo de Vivar and find their fortunes in conquest.

The Moorish occupiers were swept away like rabbits before a heath fire. Families who had lived for generations in Spain, and thought themselves its owners, fled to Africa or had to buy back their lives and freedom from Rodrigo de Vivar. They called him, in their own tongue, El Siddi – the War Lord – and his own men took it up: 'El Cid! Viva El Cid!' He captured Moorish towns like so many pieces in a game of chess.

At last only one black piece was left standing on the board of Spain: Valencia, the treasure-house of the Moors. Not till then did the

African might of Islam stir itself. Valencia must not be allowed to fall, or all Spain would be in the hands of Christians.

Before the fleets of Africa could touch Spanish shores, Valencia had fallen, and El Cid, the victor, had made the exquisite city his own. Sending for his wife and family, he celebrated the marriage of his two daughters, and gloried in the King's forgiveness. His joy was complete. He decided to live out his days in Valencia, for there is nowhere lovelier under God's gaze.

On the night of the double wedding, a little, cowardly, creeping man crawled through the flowery grass on his belly, with a heart full of envy. He pushed a knife through the cloth of a tent, and stabbed El Cid in the back, sinking his blade up to the haft.

Within days, the Moorish legions landed in thousands and tens of thousands, and laid siege to the city – pitched their tents among the orange groves and awaited with impatience the day Valencia's citizens would thirst and starve to death.

'But we have El Cid!' cried the people in the streets. 'With El Cid to lead us, we have nothing to fear!' And they jeered over the walls at the besieging army. 'El Cid will crop you like oranges!'

But El Cid lay bleeding on his bed, his life ebbing away. Nothing but a miracle would put him back astride his horse at the head of an army. When word spread of Don Rodrigo's injury, terror and despair poisoned the streets like acrid smoke.

'El Cid is dying!'

'El Cid is at death's door!'

'El Cid is dead!'

No word came from the window of his house. No news, either good or bad, came from the lips of El Cid's wife, the lovely Jimena. She sat beside her husband's bed, her long hair spread on the coverlet, and her eyes resting on the distant sea. When at last she opened the door, it was to say, 'Fetch El Cid's horse to the door and you, Alvar Fanez, come and help Don Rodrigo to put on his armour.'

Alvar was El Cid's closest friend, his most trusted servant. He ran into the room in a fervour of delight. The saints had restored his master's health! El Cid was fit to lead his army into battle!

Alvar Fanez fell back, his mouth open to speak, his heart half broken by what he saw. The craggy features of Don Rodrigo de Vivar lay whiter than the pillow, his eyes were shut, his hands lay crossed on his breast.

'He's dead,' was all he could think of to say.

'Yes,' said Jimena, simply and calmly, 'but his name will live for ever, and it is his name which must save the city today. Help me arm my husband one last time, and tie him on to his horse. I believe that El Cid can still carry the day, if only he shows himself on the battlefield.'

Alvar Fanez did as he was asked. Together – though it was a terrible ordeal for the two alone – they tied Don Rodrigo to his horse for one last ride. Jimena kissed her husband farewell. Alvar Fanez mounted, and led the general's horse to the city gate.

Ahead went the incredulous whispers, the gasps of happy amazement in the half-light of morning.

'El Cid is alive!'

'He's going to head the attack!'

Silently, so as to surprise the sleeping Moors, the army mustered in the streets behind the gate. Division upon division formed rank. As dawn broke, the knights of El Cid struggled to hold their horses in check between the shadowy houses of Valencia.

At the crash of the crossbar unfastening the gate, El Cid's horse Babeica pawed the ground. It leapt past Alvar Fanez in the open gateway and lunged into the lead, as it had in a hundred battles.

The Moors, waking to the sound of galloping horses, looked out of their tent flaps to see the hosts of El Cid riding down on them. The knights of Islam called for their armour. Their squires ran to and fro with weapons and bridles. 'To arms! To arms!'

'Huh!' sneered King Mu'taman of Morocco, walking with showy disdain to the stirrup of his mount. 'My assassin has cut the heart out of El Cid. My spies have confirmed it. And what is an army without its heart?'

Then he saw a sight which struck such horror into him that his foot missed the stirrup and his shaking legs would not hold him. He fell to his knees, calling on the one true god of Islam for help. 'Can the man not die? Is this why he brought our empires to nothing? Is he immortal? Is it a ghost we have to fight now?' For riding towards him – directly towards him – was the tall, erect, unmistakable figure of El Cid, conqueror of Spain, in full panoply of armour but bareheaded, his long grey hair and beard streaming.

The King's trembling fingers searched for his lance, and he threw it at the chest of El Cid. But though it struck home, the conqueror did not flinch. It was his horse's hooves which trampled the King of

Morocco and which tumbled his tasselled tent to the ground. El Cid rode on, so appalling the superstitious enemy that they flung themselves into the sea sooner than face a ghostly enemy who would not, could not die.

Out of the orange groves and along the beaches of Valencia rode Don Rodrigo de Vivar, on his last foray. From the city walls, Dona Jimena watched till he was no longer in sight. But she shed no tears. She knew it was not the ghost of El Cid out there; it was his flesh, his blood. But neither was it El Cid himself. She knew that the soul of El Cid was at rest, and that his spirit was ranging free, untethered and invisible, high above the heads of his victorious army.

The Man Who Almost Lived for Ever

A MESOPOTAMIAN LEGEND

Long ago, when the history of Humankind could still be carved on a single pillar, there lived two friends. One, Adapa the Priest, was the wisest of men. The other, Ea, was the friendliest of the gods. But you would have thought they were brothers. Ea taught Adapa many things never before known by mortals – how to speak magic, for instance, and carry it in the fingers of his hand.

Adapa was fishing alone one day, in a stretch of water where the river Euphrates widens into a gleaming lake. A storm sprang up and spilled him out of his boat, wetting his venerable beard and his priestly robes and his dignity. Adapa swam to the shore and pulled himself out, dripping wet. Then he pointed a finger at the South Wind and pronounced a curse, as Ea had taught him to do.

> *Come down on you the very worst;*
> *May every power of yours be burst.*
> *You have a mighty wrath incurred,*
> *Therefore be broken, like a bird.*
> *Oh vile South Wind, I call you CURSED!'*

Like a great albatross shot from the sky, the South Wind drooped and faltered. One wing was snapped by Adapa's piercing curse, and the wind limped to its nest with an eerie, lamenting cry, and left the banners of seventy kings drooping. The gods in Heaven were shocked.

'Who taught this small worthless man of the Earth the magic words of Heaven? Ea? Why have you shared our secrets with this puny mortal? Summon him before us, to explain himself!'

Ea told Adapa of the summons. 'Don't worry, friend. You have wisdom enough to speak well, and I will commend you to the gods. Tammuz and Gizidu will meet you at the gates, and conduct you before the throne of Mighty Anu. I have asked them, too, to speak well of you in the Courts of Heaven . . . Just one word of advice.' Adapa, who had already begun to rehearse what he would say to the gods, looked round at the change in Ea's voice. 'Be on your guard, Adapa. The gods are cunning, and you have angered them. They may offer you bread and oil to eat. On no account accept it. It may be poisoned.'

Meanwhile, the gods discussed among themselves what was to be done about Adapa and his great knowledge.

'We could strike him dead,' said one.

'We could just tell him never to use magic again,' said another.

'We could always make him immortal, like us,' said a third.

'Or there again . . .'

Shortly, Tammuz and Gizidu led Adapa in front of Anu's throne.

'Adapa, you are accused of cursing the South Wind and of breaking its white wing with the magic words of the gods. Is this true?'

'I admit it,' said Adapa. 'The South Wind wrecked me and endangered my life.' The gods listened. Some nodded, some glared, some leaned their heads together in debate. Adapa began to feel more confident. 'As for the curse I used, I was taught it by my good friend Ea, who has introduced me to many such marvels.'

'Before I give judgement,' said Anu suddenly, 'you must take some refreshment. You've had a long journey. Tammuz! Bring bread and oil!'

It was a gracious offer, courteously made, but Adapa flinched. Tammuz lifted a tray from a table: a flagon of oil and a broken loaf of hot sweet-smelling bread.

Though Adapa was very hungry, he held up a regal hand.

'With your indulgence, I won't eat. I've had enough already. I rarely take more than one meal a day.'

To Adapa's alarm, the Mighty Anu suddenly fell back in his throne and slapped his knees. 'You see? You see!' he bellowed at the other, lesser gods. 'You see how stupid these little Earthmen are? Adapa, you're a fool, for all your wisdom! I said you weren't worthy! I said you wouldn't know what to do with it! But I never thought you'd turn it down! Ha ha ha! Turned it down! No immortal would have been so stupid! Go back to your temples and your prayers. Go back to your *little* life full of *little* achievements. Go back with your talk of visiting Heaven: no one will believe you. Go home now, Adapa, for we offered you the bread and oil of everlasting life, and you turned it down. So die!'

Adapa ran all the way back down to Earth. For the rest of his short life, he went over and over that day in his head – and how he had come to make his worst of all mistakes. Had the gods tricked him? Or had Ea? It was Ea who had told him not to eat. Had Ea given his advice in good faith?

Ea and Adapa no longer fished together in the lakes of the Euphrates, because Adapa could never be sure. Once such doubts have entered a friendship, the friendship has already begun to crumble. Ea and Adapa fished together no more, and one day, when the South Wind had recovered its strength, it spilled Adapa into deeper water, where he drowned.

He was only mortal, after all.

Stealing Heaven's Thunder

A NORSE MYTH

IN THE HIGH halls of Valhalla, across the Rainbow Bridge in the realm called Asgard, Thor the God of Thunder woke. He lay for a while between the damp softnesses of dark cloud, and contemplated the day ahead.

'Today,' he said, 'I shall reshape the mountains with my hammer, smash the ice cap to the north into glassy splinters, and make the valleys boom like cannon fire. I'll strike lightning from the anvil Earth and shoe Odin's horse with gold from the mines of Middle Earth!' He rolled out of bed, clutched about him a robe of black fur, and reached for his blacksmith's hammer.

It was not in its usual place.

He searched under the bed and in every cavernous cupboard of his chamber. He searched the stairways and corridors of Valhalla, in every trunk and chest, on every landing, in the smithy and the treasury, his temper growing with the increasing daylight.

'*WHERE'S MY HAMMER?*' he bellowed at last, and Valhalla shook.

Other gods joined in the search. Queen Freya herself, wrapped in her flying cloak, soared among the pinnacles of Heaven, thinking to glimpse the hammer from the air. Then Odin, King of the Gods, banged a door or two, and scowled.

'It's plain that Thor's hammer has been stolen. Who would – who could – steal such a prize, but those grunting grubs, the Giants?'

'Take my cloak, Loki,' said the Queen, 'and go quickly to the Realm of Giants. Find out if it is true.'

Loki sped across the Rainbow Bridge, down through the ether, and, tumbling like a pigeon, landed at the gate of the Giants' castle.

'It's true we have Thor's hammer,' bragged the largest of the castle's warriors, Din. 'It's true, too, that you will never find where it's hidden. For I've buried the great hammer called Thunderbolt under clods of clay, one mile underground, and the place is known only to me.' Din scratched his tunic of mangy bear fur, and a cloud of dust enveloped them both. He sneezed, wiped his nose on a mat of greasy hair, and leered at Loki. 'I want a bride, see. And that's my bride-price: Thor's hammer in exchange for a wife!'

Loki was almost relieved. 'I'm certain that somewhere in the world Odin can find you a suitable . . .'

'Oh, I *know* he can,' Din interrupted, cleaning out his ears with a piece of stick, 'and he won't have to look far to find her. I mean to marry Freya. Just for once, what's good enough for the gods might be good enough for me. Now you go and tell Odin: no Freya, no Thunderbolt! And let him send her soon – within three days! I'm weary of being a bachelor.' Loki turned in disgust to go. 'Oh, and say she must bring that flying cloak of hers! And her magic golden necklace!' Din laughed till his nose ran and, blowing his nose between finger and thumb, flapped his hands together with all the grace of an elephant seal.

On the return flight, Loki considered the filthy bargain. Odin would never agree to giving away his wife. He would declare war at the very suggestion. But, in the meantime, what damage would the Giants do to Middle Earth with Thor's hammer? They would flatten its crags, terrorize its occupants. The little humans would blame the gods for their persecution, and the foundations of Valhalla would shake at the consequences. By the time he crossed the Rainbow Bridge of Asgard, Loki had formulated his own solution to the problem.

'Lord Odin, King of Gods and mightiest of us all, I bring word from the thieves who stole Thor's hammer. They have placed a price on its return . . .'

Three days later, bride and escort set out from Valhalla, canopied beneath Queen Freya's cobalt-blue cloak.

Seeing the two figures descend out of the sunshine, Din clapped his hands once more. 'Prepare a feast! Come, brother Giants, and be my guests! Today is my wedding day!' The worm-eaten table in the Castle of Giants groaned under the weight of food. Barrels of wine were stacked as high as the bat-infested vaults of the roof, and a place of honour was cleared among the litter for the bench of bride and groom.

First Loki entered, then the bride, veiled and shining behind him. 'I bring Freya, formerly Queen of Heaven,' announced Loki grandly, 'to be Queen among Giants and wife to Din!'

Din looked on with a fixed grin of sheepish delight, as the bride seated herself and lifted her veil to eat. Two golden plaits as long as bell ropes coiled themselves on the floor to either side of her. She leaned forward and took a rack of lamb, reducing it to a pile of bones in moments. Next she ate a side of beef and three brace of partridge. Then, impatient of the servingman's slowness in filling her glass, she took the jug from him and emptied it in a single swig.

'You certainly do enjoy your food,' giggled Din admiringly. 'A woman after my own heart. But how do you keep your figure?'

Loki, seated on Din's other side, caught him by the sleeve and whispered confidentially, 'She's been so agitated at the thought of meeting you, my lord Din, that she hasn't eaten for three days. She's making up for lost time, that's all.'

Din scratched his neck with a hambone. 'Agitated, eh? Is that good or bad?' he whispered back.

'Oh, my dear fellow!' Loki had his head almost inside the Giant's gigantic ear, so as not to be overheard. 'I think she must have nursed a passion for you this many a year! You've never seen a woman in such a fever to get to her wedding, I do assure you! That Odin – he may be handsome, clever, noble, brave, powerful . . . but he's not every woman's idea of the ideal lover, you know?'

Din turned crimson with delight, and exhaled a sigh with breath like rotting cabbage leaves. 'She loves me?' Turning to his bride, he said, 'Well, don't be shy, then: kiss me, woman!'

Blue eyes looked back at him, as wild as the sea, then changed to the colour of ice, before darkening to scarlet. They blazed in their sockets, those eyes.

Din gulped and shuffled back along the bench, edging Loki on to the floor without noticing. 'Why's she looking at me like that?'

'Passion,' replied Loki succinctly. 'Now, there's just the matter of Thor's hammer . . .'

He had almost reached his feet again when Din clapped him violently on the back and sent him sprawling. 'Of course! I'm a man of my bond! Thor's hammer for a bride, I said, and that's what I meant.' A nod of his great head sent a dozen servants running, spades in hand, to unearth the hammer called Thunderbolt. When they returned with it, Din had just plucked up the courage to tickle the back of Freya's neck with his big fingers.

The servants grunted and staggered under the hammer's great weight, and the table collapsed as they set it down. But nothing could dent Din's pleasure. 'I'd like to see Odin's face when he finds out his beloved Freya's left him for a giant like me!'

For the first time, the bride spoke. 'Then you shall have your wish, Din!'

Pulling off her plaits, the bride snatched up the stolen hammer and whirled it round, before letting it fall on the top of Din's verminous head. Freed of his disguise at last, Odin smashed the tuns of red wine, brought down the vaulted roof. He knocked giants as far as the northern sea and the Baltic Straits. He frightened off their giant cows and stampeded their giant horses, and left their armoury a tangle of twisted metal in the bottom of a fjord.

Only the thin air of Asgard could cool his blazing temper, and he berated Loki continually on the flight back for thinking up such a plan. 'A giant paddling his fingers in my neck, indeed! A giant trying to kiss me!'

Queen Freya saw them rising, like gulls on a warm wind, and greeted her husband's return with pleasure, though she had no idea where he had been.

'Why ever are you wearing that dress, Odin?' she asked. 'It doesn't suit you at all . . . But I'm glad to see you've brought Thor's hammer back. He's been wretched without it.'

Reunited with his Thunderbolt, Thor, God of Thunder, raced around Heaven, striking sparks from the crags of Norway, fires from the peaks of Iceland. He bruised the clouds to a blackness, then split them and loosed a cascade of rain on the fires he had just lit with lightning. Never was there such a storm as the night Thor got back his hammer.

But within the high halls of Valhalla, Freya and Odin slept through the storm undisturbed, while Loki, alone and unthanked, brooded on the idea of making more mischief . . .

Anansi and the Mind of God

A WEST INDIAN MYTH

NANSI WAS AN African. Spider-man Anansi. But he stowed away on a slave ship to the West Indies, so now he turns up in Jamaica and suchlike, as sneaky as a tarantula in a hand of bananas. Spider-man Anansi, Anansi the Trickster. They do say Anansi's the cleverest creature next to God . . . or was it Anansi said that?

Now Spider-man Anansi was a clever man,
But he got to boasting he was God's right hand.
Said God, 'Anansi, if you're really so smart,
You can tell what I'm thinking in my heart of hearts.
There's three things I want, and if you're my peer,
You'll have no trouble in fetching them here.'
Well, Spider-man Anansi, he up and fled,
Swinging down from Heaven on his long black thread.
He ain't one clue what he's s'pose' to fetch back,
But he ain't gonna let God Almighty know that.
He seeks out the birdies, one, two, three;
Says, 'Spare one feather for Mister Anansi!'
Asks every bird for just one feather,
Then Anansi-man, he sews them together.

He sews him a glorious rainbow suit:

76

Feather pyjamas, feather mask and boots,
Then off he flies high up in the sky,
And he dances about till he takes God's eye.
God says, 'Well Lordy, and upon my word!
Who's gonna tell me 'bout this rainbow bird?
I know I didn't make it, so who else did?'
And he asked the mack'rel and he asked the squid.
He asked the turtle and he asked the dog,
And he asked the monkey and he asked the frog,
And he asked the bird, but it just jumped by,
Giving out a perfume like a rainbow pie.

Now God's advisors racked their brains all day,
But they couldn't find but one thing to say:
'Anansi's the man who could solve this case.'
Says God, 'But I sent him on a wild-goose chase!
I sent him to fetch three things to me:
So I fear that's the end of old Anansi.'
'Why? What did you send him for, Lord?' ask they.
'For the night and the moon and the light of day.
Not that I said so. No, I made him guess,
'Cos he got to boasting he was better than best.
But now he's gone, well, I'm sorry, kinda -
That I told Anansi to be a read-minder.'
All the creatures laughed, but God wasn't luffin',
When away flew the bird like a shaggy puffin.

It was no sooner gone than who comes in,
But Spider Anansi in his own black skin.
In came Anansi with a bulging sack.
Says, 'Sorry I kept you, Lord, but now I'm back.
Anansi-man's back and I think you'll find
I've brought you the three things were on your mind.'
So he reaches in the sack and oh! what a fright,
He plunges Heaven into darkest night.
Out comes the moon next with a silv'ry shine
And God says, 'Mercy me, I thought I'd gone blind!
Touché, Anansi-man, you got me licked.
I don't know how, but I know I been tricked.'

Then Anansi pulls out the great big sun -
All its terrible bright illu-min-a-tion,
And it burns God's eyeball in a place or two,
And it gives him pain, and it spoils his view.
So when God looks down now from his throne on high,
There's a patch he misses with his sun-scorched eye.
You can bet that Spider-man knows where it be -
That patch of ground God Almighty can't see.

Is that where you're hiding, Mister Anansi?

How Men and Women Finally Agreed

A KIKUYU MYTH

HAVING CREATED ALL the beauties of Africa, the Creator of course chose the most lovely for his home – the Mountain of Bright Mystery. There he lived invisible, like a patch of sunlight travelling over the mountainside, and from there he could see all over the world.

To his three sons, he offered three gifts: a hoe, a spear, a bow and arrow.

Masai, a fierce boy who loved a fight, chose the spear.

'Then you shall be a cowherd and live on the plains where the grazing is sweet,' said the Creator to Masai.

Kamba, who loved to eat meat, chose the bow and arrow.

'You shall be a hunter in the forests where the wild beasts have their lairs,' said the Creator to Kamba.

Kikuyu, a gentle, industrious boy, chose the hoe – which pleased his father greatly. After the others had left, the Creator kept Kikuyu by him and taught him all the secrets of agriculture – where to sow, when to reap, how to graft and propagate, which insects to encourage and which to drive away. He led Kikuyu to the top of the Bright Mountain and pointed far off.

'You see there – in the centre of the world – where those fig trees stand like a crowd of whisperers? Make your home there, my son, and may your life and the lives of your children be happy.'

The figs were large and juicy, the shade deep and dark. But those were not the best things about the grove of fig trees at the centre of the world. When he got there, Kikuyu found awaiting him a beautiful wife – Moombi – and nine lovely daughters, each as dark and sweet as a fig.

For a long time, Kikuyu lived happily, planting a garden in the shade of the fig trees, as well as fields round about. His daughters helped him, singing while they worked, and the sound of Moombi's laughter rang out from time to time as she pounded maize with her pestle.

But as he watched the bees fumbling the flowers, heard the birds sing in courtship, saw the sheep lambing in the long grass, Kikuyu could not help but wonder how his daughters would ever marry and have children to make them laugh as Moombi laughed. One day, the whole family left the grove of fig trees and trekked back across the plain, past the forests and back to the Bright Mountain, to ask the Creator's advice.

'I would like the sound of men's voices in my fields and, to tell true, my nine daughters would greatly like the sight of men's faces coming home from the fields at night,' Kikuyu confided in his father. 'What should I do to have sons-in-law?'

'Go home, Kikuyu. Go home. And remember – the name of Kikuyu is precious to me, but the name of Moombi is sacred.'

Too gentle to press his request any further, Kikuyu did as he was told, and the family trooped back, past the forest and over the plain, to the fig-tree grove.

There, leaning on their hoes, stood nine fine young men, a little startled to find themselves so suddenly called into being by the Creator. When they saw Kikuyu's nine daughters, their faces broke into the broadest of grins.

'Oh, Papa!' cried the girls, behind him. 'Aren't they *lovely!*'

Kikuyu considered the words of the Creator. 'Is marriage agreeable to you?' he asked the young men.

'Yes, sir!'

'And is marriage agreeable to you, daughters?'

'Oh *yes*, Papa!'

'And is it to your liking, Moombi, that our daughters marry these young men?'

'High time, and none too soon!' declared Moombi, laughing loudly.

'Then I have only this to say,' announced Kikuyu. 'My daughters may marry you, young men . . .'

'Oh, thank you!'

'. . . provided you take the name of Moombi for your family name and obey your wives in all things.'

The young men made no objection, and their marriages were long and happy. When after many years, a couple died, their hut and hoe and inheritance passed to any daughters they might have, not to the sons. The daughters chose whom they wished to marry – taking two or three or ten husbands if they wished, and that is how the family of Kikuyu and Moombi grew into a tribe.

After many generations, the men grew restive. One was jealous of his wife's other husbands. One objected to doing all the washing. One resented bitterly that his wife beat him when the sheep got loose in the garden. One felt sorry for his sons, that they would never inherit a thing. So the men muttered mutinously together, deep in the fig tree groves, and plotted to end their wives' supremacy. But what could they do? The women fought better, ran faster, cursed louder and thought quicker than their menfolk.

So the men waited their chance. They waited until the women were all expecting babies. They waited till their wives were all half as big as hippopotami and waddling like ducks.

'*We* want to be in charge now,' the men announced one day, and all the women could do was press their hands to the smalls of their backs and groan.

After that, the men took as many wives as they wanted: two or ten or twenty, and some beat their wives when the sheep got loose in the garden, and some put their wives to washing and cooking all day. When they held council, only men were invited, and, of course, they passed laws in favour of men.

'Wives!' they said one day. 'We have decided we no longer want our children to carry your female family names. Our families shall have male names from now on. And no longer will the tribe be called the Moombi Kikuyu, after a woman, but rather the . . .'

'*Enough!*' A sun-wrinkled mother, big as a wildebeest and quite as handsome, stood up. She drew her brightly dyed robes around her big baby-filled belly and settled the scarlet cloths on her head. 'In that case we will bear you no more sons,' she said. 'The name of Kikuyu is precious in the ear of God. but the name of Moombi is sacred. If you do this thing, we who are pregnant shall give birth only to daughters; afterwards we shall bear no children at all! If you want sons, from now on, give birth to them *yourselves*!'

The other women began to laugh and nod. The men looked down at their own thin waists and narrow hips and considered the possibility. Have children? No. That was one privilege the women were welcome to.

'What are we called?' asked the wildebeest woman.

'Moombi! Moombi!' answered the women and began to chant the sacred name of the first wife: *'Moombi! Moombi! Moombi!'*

'What are we called?'

'Moombi! Moombi! Moombi!'

The men bowed their heads and shuffled their feet in the dust.

'How are we called?'

'By the name of our mothers! Moombi! Moombi! Moombi!'

'Who was our first mother?'

'Moombi! Moombi! Moombi!'

'What shall we call our daughters?'

'Moombi! Moombi! Moombi!'

'And what shall we call our sons?'

The men drummed their hoes against the ground, joined in the chanting, and consoled themselves that it was a small concession to make. They were still the ones in charge. Really.

'Moombi! Moombi! Moombi!'

First Snow

A NATIVE AMERICAN MYTH

THE WORLD WAS complete.

'And yet it could be better still,' said First Man, gazing up at the night sky. So he and First Woman and Coyote searched about for something to make midnight still more beautiful: a single golden stone to embed in the northern sky, three glowing red pebbles, and a handful of glittering dust which whirled and whorled in a wild, disordered dance.

'I believe we have finished,' said First Man. 'Life is still hard for the People, with famine and thirst in between the rains, but it is better than before, when we lived below, in the kernel of the world.'

'I have one present more to give them,' said Coyote.

Next morning, the People woke to see a brightness brighter than sunshine in the doors of their hogans.

They ran outside, and saw a strange and beautiful white powder falling from the sky. The first snow ever to fall on the world was whitening the bluffs, pillowing the ground, and settling in glittering swags on the trees. Flakes hung on the warp and weft of the weaving looms, like blossom on a spider's web.

The People stood stock-still, their hands outstretched, catching the snow on their palms. It was not cold. First Woman blinked the snowflakes off her eyelashes and shook them from her hair. She took a spoon and lifted a mouthful of snow to her lips.

It was delicious.

The people licked their snowy fingers.

It was delectable.

Soon everyone was scooping up the fallen snow, cramming it into their mouths. It tasted rather like buffalo dripping. They caught the falling snow in baskets, stuffed it into skin bags and stored it up in jars. They filled their pockets and piled it on the papooses. The women carried the white stuff back to their hogans in their skirts, and kneaded it into wafer bread.

'At last we shan't be hungry any more!' they sang. 'Now everything is perfect!' And they feasted greedily on the magic sky food, until they grew too thirsty to eat any more.

Coyote had filled a cooking pot with white handfuls from a drift of snow. He lit a fire and smoke curled up into the sky, fraying it to grey. He began to cook the snow. The People crowded round to see what delicious stew he was making. But as they watched, they began to shiver.

First the snow in the pot turned grey, then to transparent liquid, seething, bubbling, boiling and steaming, cooling only as the fire burned out. As it did so, the snow on the trees wept and dripped and dropped down in icy tears. The white on the ground changed to a grey slush that soaked the children's moccasins, and the women let fall their skirtfuls of snow, crying, 'Oh! Urgh! So cold! So wet! Urgh! Oh!' The old people drew their shawls about their heads and shook their wet mittens, disconsolate.

'Now look what you've done!' cried First Woman, wrapping herself tight in a dozen shawls. 'Our lovely food has rotted away and there's nothing left but the juices. What a wicked waste! You always were a troublemaker, Coyote! In the time before the world, you were always making mischief, stealing, tricking, complaining. But this is the worst! You've made all our beautiful sky flour melt away!'

The People tried to pelt him with snowballs, but the snow only turned to water in their palms.

Coyote simply drank from the pot of melted snow, then shook his head so hard that his yellow ears rattled.

'You don't understand,' he said gently. 'Snow was not meant for food. It was sent down upon the five mountaintops for the springtime sun to melt, drip joining drop, dribble joining trickle, stream joining river, filling the lakes and pools and ponds, before it rolls down to the sea. Now, when you are thirsty, you need not wait for the rain, or catch the raindrops in your hands. You can drink whenever you please.

'The snowmelt rivers will water the woods and swell the berries for you to pick. The streams will turn the desert into grass-green grazing, so that your sheep put on wool like fleecy snow. And out there, on the plains, the bison will wade knee-deep in seas of waving grass, and grow into fat and shining herds.

'The dusty hunter can wash the sweat from his face where the young women's long wet hair streams out like weed. The children can leap and swim beside waterfalls where the poet makes verses.

'And at the end of the day, if you are still, and patient and quiet, the deer may come down to drink, and the swallows sip flies off the surface of the stream. The women weavers can wash their wools, and dye them brighter colours of the autumn woods.

'And when the summer dust settles and the ants swarm around the food baskets, and the flies buzz after the dirt, we shall wash our homes clean and sluice the summer sickness out of doors.

'Quick! There will be fish coming down the rivers – gold and silver and speckled like brown eggs. Make fishing rods and nets! Catch and bake the fish over your fires! They will taste better than any snow.

'And when First Snow falls out there in the canyons and winding places, you huntsmen will be able to find the tracks of the woolly bison with barely a glance. The footprints of the secret hare will be as plain to read on the ground, as the stars arc in the sky.

'These are the uses of snow.'

'So *that* was the present you had to give us, Coyote!' said First Woman, smiling.

'Oh!' yelped Coyote. 'No! The snow almost made me forget!'

He ran to his hogan and fetched out several bags which he opened and spilled on the ground. There was seed inside – maize and beans and squash – and these were his present to the People. They planted gardens, and the snowmelt watered the soil, so that their gardens grew into magic larders of food far more delicious and nutritious than snow.

So next year, when the First Snow fell, the People held a great feast to celebrate its coming, with sweet, pure water to wash down the food from their gardens. Having drunk snowmelt from the very mountain peaks, it seemed as if they themselves were brothers and sisters of the Five Holy Mountains.

Above them hung the glitter of the stars, below the glisten of snowflakes and lapping water. And in the lake floated the reflection of Moon and the yellow Dog Star.

Coyote sat back on his haunches and howled his music at the sky.

Ragged Emperor

A CHINESE LEGEND

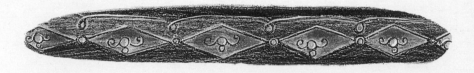

IF ALL CHILDREN took after their parents, Yu Shin would have been a wicked, feckless boy. His father was a flint-cold man who thought with his fists, except when he was plotting some new torment for his son. Yu Shin was often lucky to escape with his life.

But Yu Shin was nothing like his father, nor even like his mother, who lifted not a finger to help her poor boy, and let him work like a slave around the farm. 'Fetch the water! Feed the animals! Clean the stables! Weed the ground!'

Yu Shin did it all, and with good grace, too, as though his parents were the dearest in the world, and the work his favourite pastime. Inwardly, though, he was sometimes crushed with weariness and misery at the thought of being so unloved.

In truth, his favourite pastime was to read and study. Whenever he could, he crept away to the schoolmaster's house and sat at his feet, listening to any and everything the wise man said. 'Always remember, Yu Shin,' said the teacher, 'not all men are like your father. Whenever things look black, have courage and pray. Life will not always be this hard.'

Not always be this hard? No. It got harder. Yu Shin's father dimly perceived that his son was becoming more intelligent than he; that bred in him a kind of fear. And when Yu Shin grew tall, strong and handsome, his father grew even more afraid. Soon he would not dare

87

to beat and kick and bully the boy, just in case Yu Shin should hit him back. No, the boy must be got rid of.

'Yu Shin! It is time for you to make your own way in the world. Out of my great generosity, I'm going to give you the Black Field, to live on and grow fat. There! What do you say?'

Now the Black Field was a patch of ground the old man had won playing mah-jong. It was miles away in the shadow of mountains, and having been to look it over, he had come home disgusted, telling his wife, 'It's nothing but wilderness. I was robbed.'

Yu Shin knew all this, and his heart shrank at the idea of banishment to the Black Field. But he remembered the words of his teacher and bowed dutifully to his father. 'I am grateful for your tender care and for this most generous gift, dear Father.' His father gave him one last kick, for old time's sake, and laughed till he split his coat.

Arriving after the long walk, Yu Shin found the Black Field even worse than he had imagined. Thorny weeds and briars choked acres of stony dirt. Here and there lay a dead tree, there and here a boulder big enough to shatter a plough. Not that Yu Shin had a plough – only his bare hands to work the worthless plot. A ramshackle hut no bigger than a tool shed slumped in one corner of the field, empty of furniture and full of draughts.

Yu Shin took a deep breath. 'Oh gods and fairies, you have watched over me till now, watch over me here, too, that I may not die of starvation or despair.' Then he bent his weary back, and began to pick up stones, throwing them aside, trying to expose some little piece of soil to plant.

As he worked, he happened to look up and see a distant dust cloud moving towards him. As it came closer, he could make out large grey shapes. *'Elephants?'*

Not just elephants, but a flock of magpies too, escorting the herd like black-and-white fish over a school of whales.

Yu Shin felt oddly unafraid. Even his malicious father could not have organized a stampede of elephants to trample him. So he stood his ground, and the elephants lumbered straight up to him, streaming past to either side. Flank to flank, trunks waving, they stationed themselves about the Black Field, wrenching up tree stumps, pushing aside boulders. Under their gigantic feet, the smaller stones crumbled to dust. The magpies swooped and darted in between, uprooting weeds and thistles and slugs, fluttering under the very feet of the elephants, perching to rest on their great swaying backs.

'Oh thank you, beasts! Thank you so much!' cried Yu Shin, scrambling to the top of a heap of stones to survey his land afresh. The soil was black and crumbly now, rich with elephant manure and just waiting for a crop. 'Let me fetch you water! Rest now, please! You're working yourselves too hard!'

But until the elephants had finished their work, they neither ate nor rested. Then they formed a line in front of Yu Shin and dropped on to their front knees, in a respectful bow, just as if he were someone who mattered! The magpies circled three times round his head before flying away – a black-and-white banner streaming over an army of marching elephants.

They were no sooner gone than more visitors came into sight. Narrowing his eyes against the low sun, Yu Shin saw nine young men walking ahead of a rider – a girl with a cloak of shining hair reaching almost to her tiny feet. At the gate of the Black Field, the nine bowed low. 'Your field needs planting, sir, and your crops will need tending. Grant us the honour of working for you.'

'Oh but where could you sleep? How would I pay you? How could I feed you until my crop is grown?' Yu Shin cast a desperate glance behind him at the ramshackle hut no bigger than a tool shed. And lo and behold! It was all mended! Big rain clouds were coiling over the mountaintop, and he begged his visitors to hurry inside before the downpour began. But as he opened the door for them, Yu Shin stopped short.

'What do you see, sir?' asked the young men.

'One would think, by your face, sir, that you saw an elephant in your living-room,' whispered the girl.

'No. No elephants,' whispered Yu Shin.

But there *was* room enough for eleven to sit down and dine, and afterwards to lie down and sleep. The inside of the hut had become as huge as a mansion, and along a trestle table lay a feast for eleven, just waiting to be eaten.

Yu Shin did not sit down at the head of the table: he sat the girl there. He did not serve himself until everyone had filled their bowls. He did not bore his guests with talk of elephants and magpies, but asked politely about their journey and what books they had read lately. And, of course, they talked about farming.

But to the girl he barely spoke. His rank was too humble for him ever to speak of love to such an elegant beauty. Even so, when he looked at her, it was the only topic which sprang to mind. 'I would welcome your help,' he told them, 'but as friends not farmhands. For you can't possibly be of lower rank in the world than I am!' and he laughed, so that all his guests laughed too.

Every day, out in the Black Field, Yu Shin worked as hard as anyone. Within the year, the whole province was talking of the Black Field – not just of its record harvests, but of the oddly happy little community which farmed it.

The rumours reached Yu Shin's home. 'Curse the boy,' said his father, grinding his teeth. 'He's done it all to spite me!'

The rumours reached the Emperor, far away in the Imperial City. 'Send for Yu Shin!' said the Emperor, and that is a summons no man can refuse.

Yu Shin had no idea why he had been summoned. His ten friends offered to keep him company, which was heartening, but when, after twelve days of walking, the white spires of the Imperial City came into sight, Yu Shin trembled from head to foot. 'Oh gods and fairies. my dear teacher told me always to have courage. Lend me some now, for mine is almost used up!'

The girl came and put her hand on his sleeve. 'You have done nothing wrong, Yu Shin, therefore you have nothing to fear from the Emperor. Have courage a little while longer.' And it seemed to Yu Shin that she knew something that he did not.

'YU SHIN!' bellowed the court usher. 'BOW LOW BEFORE THE EMPEROR OF CHINA!' Yu Shin's nose was already pressed to the imperial floor. High on the Dragon Throne, clothed in gold, the Emperor clapped his frail, pale hands. 'Listen, Yu Shin! Hear me, people of the Imperial Court! The eyes and ears of the Emperor are everywhere. For many years now my spies have brought strange news from the borders of my empire: of a boy who was meek and obedient to his parents, uncomplaining and brave, who was born wise, but had the greater wisdom to listen to others. I was curious. So I sent my nine sons and my only daughter, to see if the stories were true, to see if this paragon truly existed. They tell me that this same boy is also just, generous and courteous, that all people are equal in his eyes, and all are his friends. I am old now, and my strength is failing. I mean to step down from the Dragon Throne. That is why, Yu Shin, I have sent for you. To take my place.' Yu Shin lifted his nose off the floor, eyes round with wonder. 'My daughter looks on you with love. Marry her. Then if you rule China as you have farmed the Black Field, China will flourish as never before!'

History does not record what Yu Shin's father said when he heard the news. Oh, history says that Yu Shin's rule was a golden blaze of achievement, but rarely mentions that he was a farmer's son, for who would ever dream a peasant boy could become the Emperor of China?

History does not mention, either, what became of Yu Shin's father. But those elephants must have dumped their trunkfuls of tree stumps somewhere, then settled down. Those magpies must have dropped their beakfuls of weeds and thistles somewhere, then roosted.

The Boy Who Lived for a Million Years

A ROMANY LEGEND

THERE WAS ONCE a boy – the son of the Red King – who had the ambition to live for ever and never to grow old. So he said to his father, 'Give me a horse and my inheritance, and I shall travel the world till I find what I am seeking.'

Now the Red King was rich, and Peter's inheritance came to six sacks of ducats – far too much to carry. So he carved a treasure chest out of rock, and buried it with his treasure inside, under the city wall, marking the place with a cross. 'I shall come back for this when I've found the place where I can live for ever and never grow old.'

Over and under and into and out travelled the Red Prince Peter, for eight years, until he came to a continent called Forest, all covered in trees. In the forest grew an oak tree. And enthroned in the tree sat the Queen of Birds – not an owl or an eagle but a green woodpecker.

'What do you seek in my dappled kingdom, young man?' she asked.

'A place to build my castle where I shall live for ever and never grow old.'

'Then build here,' said the Queen, 'for I and my friends shan't die till I have pecked away the last twig of the last branch of the last tree in this forest.'

'In that case, you will die one day,' said Peter, 'and this is not the place for me.'

He travelled along and throughout, wherever and however the

lanes took him, for eight years more. And he came at last to a palace of copper set amid seven mountains, each one a different colour of the rainbow. Inside the gleaming copper palace lived a Princess more beautiful than any in all the undulating world. On her walls were written, a million times, the name 'Peter', and in her picture frames hung nothing but portraits of him.

'In my mind's eye I have seen you, and I have loved you ever so long, Prince Peterkin,' she said.

Now many men would have ended their search for happiness then and there, but Prince Peter was utterly single-minded. 'I shall stay in no place with no woman unless she and I can live for ever and never grow old.'

'Then you were meant for me!' exclaimed the Princess, flinging her arms round his neck. 'For those who live in the Copper Castle shan't grow old or die till the wind and rain have worn the seven mountains flat.'

Red Peter wriggled free and pushed her roughly away. 'Then that day will surely come. I've seen the rain and I've heard the wind, and this place is not for me.'

On and away, farther than far, the Red Prince travelled for eight years more, until he came to a pair of mountains, Gold and Silver, and nearby, the lair of the Wind. To Peter's surprise, the Wind, for all his fame and strength, appeared to be only about ten years old.

'I have searched the world over for a place where I can live for ever and never grow old,' said Peter to the Wind. 'You roam far and wide; tell me where I can find such a place.'

'You have found it,' said the Wind.

'Until?'

The Wind looked puzzled. 'You spoke of "always" and "never",' he said, 'and so did I. Stay if you will, and go if you care to, but here you will never grow old or die.'

Red Prince Peter crowed with delight, and accepted the Wind's invitation. There was fruit enough in the trees and colour enough in the sunsets to satisfy any man. There was water enough in the streams and time enough for everything.

'Only take one piece of advice,' said the Wind. 'Hunt on Golden Mountain; hunt on Silver Mountain. But don't go hunting in the Valley of Regret or you will be sorry you did.'

The mountains of Silver and Gold had game enough to satisfy any hunter. For a hundred years Prince Peter hunted there, and hankered after nothing, not even the beautiful Princess in her palace of copper. Not one hair of his head turned grey, not one joint in his body grew stiff, and it seemed to him that no more than a week had passed. Even his horse remained young.

Then one day in one of the many centuries, found Peter chasing a deer. The deer leapt over branch and log, over river and ditch, off the Mountain of Gold and into more shadowy groves, damper and darker and *deeper down*. Realizing he must have strayed into the Valley of Regret, Peter immediately turned back. But all the way home he had the strangest feeling of being followed – a feeling he could not shake off.

Into his heart crept a small wish: to see his home again. Later it grew to a longing, later still, a burning ambition. After a while, he missed his home so much that he was sorry he had ever left his father's city.

'I'm leaving now,' he told the Wind, who shrugged.

'Tell me something I didn't already know,' said the Wind.

On his way home, Prince Peter passed the place where the seven mountains had stood. Through the teeming rain, all he could see was the copper palace, green with verdigris, overlooking a flat and dismal plain. As he passed by the window of the Princess, the rain washed away the last stony grain of the last mountain, and the palace buckled and fell with a clashing crash. The Princess reached out a withered hand towards the Red Prince, and cursed him as she fell.

Eight years later, Prince Peter passed across the continent called Forest, but all that remained of the forest was a single twig held in the claw of a green woodpecker. The woodpecker, Queen of the Birds, drilled to sawdust that last twig of the last branch of the last tree, then fluttering into the air, fell dead at Peter's feet.

He did not pause to bury her, but galloped on towards home, the city of the Red King, his father. But when he reached the place . . . there was no city, hardly one brick on another, and not a living soul he knew. 'Where is the city of the Red King?' he demanded of an old man.

The old man laughed. 'That's only a legend, sir. Never really existed. Or if it did, 'twas in a time before history books were wrote.'

'Nonsense. The Red King is my father, you fool!' said the Prince.

'His city stood here – a city of five thousand souls – not thirty years since! Did it burn? Was it sacked?'

The old man closed one eye and sniffed. 'Were you born mad, sir, or did it come upon you sudden?'

Exasperated, Prince Peter dragged the old man to the spot where his treasure lay buried – six sacks of ducats, under the castle wall. 'I'll prove it to you!' he declared.

Breaking open the ground, he dug out the stone chest and, with his sword, prised it open, breaking the blade as he did so. The lid fell back with a dusty crash. 'There! What did I tell you? Six sacks of ducats!'

'Yes, sir, but you did not speak of the other.'

Peter looked again. To either side of the six sacks sat two old crones, one dark, one fair.

'My name is Old Age,' said the dark-haired one, taking Peter's wrist in a bony hand.

'My name is Death,' said the fair, grasping his other wrist.

And that is where Prince Peter, son of the Red King, met his death after a million years of life.

So I'll wish you happiness and long life – but not so long as a million years, for that, in my opinion, would be a kind of a curse, rather than a blessing.

Sea Chase

A FINNISH MYTH

ILMARINEN THE BLACKSMITH knew that only one gift would be good enough to win him the daughter of Lady Louhi of Lapland for his bride. He did not know what it was, but he knew it would be his best work. So he took a swan's feather, a cup of milk, a bowl of barley and a strand of wool, and forged them in his furnace into a single magical gift.

The first time he opened the furnace door he found a golden bowl. But he broke that between his hands and threw the pieces back into the fire, fuelling the furnace even hotter. The next time he opened the door, he found a red copper ship, perfect in every detail. But he crushed that between his hands and threw it back into the flames, fuelling the furnace hotter still. The third time he found a little cow with golden horns; the fourth a plough with silver handles. But none of these things was good enough to win the consent of Lady Louhi. For she ruled the Northland, where the ice growls and night lasts all day and the halls are hung with icicles, like Lady Louhi's heart.

The fifth time Ilmarinen opened the furnace door he found – a something: a sampo. He did not know what it was, but he knew it was the best thing he had ever made. So he sailed with it to the Northland in a boat of copper, and won the daughter of Louhi for his wife. Lady Louhi took the sampo and built for it a hollow copper hill whose door locked with a dozen keys, and inside the hill the sampo worked, its lid whirled and its magic flowed into the icebound ground . . .

Sadly, Ilmarinen's bride was no sooner won than lost again. She died, melted away in his arms like ice in spring. So he went back to the Lady Louhi and asked for her second daughter.

'No!' said Louhi. 'You have squandered one treasure of mine; shall I see you squander another?'

'Then give me back my sampo,' said Ilmarinen. 'I have not had its worth in wives.'

'Give me back my daughter and I shall give you back your sampo,' said Lady Louhi bitterly. 'Not before.'

Ilmarinen could see why she would not part with the sampo. Since his last visit, Lapland had changed past all recognition. Where there had been snowfields, now barley waved golden and ripe. Where once only reindeer and husky dogs had left their tracks in the snow, fat cows and sleek horses grazed in flowery meadows. And where icicles had hung from the eaves of Louhi's cabin, golden ornaments tinkled in a balmy breeze. Only now did Ilmarinen begin to understand just what a wonder he had made.

Boldly, Ilmarinen seized Louhi's second daughter, flung her over his shoulder and ran for the shore. But though he got clean away, he had sailed only five leagues when the girl, before his very eyes, turned into a seagull and flapped back to land.

By the time Ilmarinen reached his Finnish home, he had abandoned all idea of marrying. All he could think of was getting back the sampo. 'I made it, after all,' he complained to wise old Väinämöinen.

'Then we should share in its magic,' the old man agreed.

Three heroes set sail that summer: and three more different men Finland never forged. There was good old Väinämöinen, sensible and sage; Ilmarinen, dogged and strong; and Lemminkäinen, rash and passionate as a fool in love. With three at the oars, the little boat fairly leapt through the waves.

. . . Too fast for the health of the Giant Pike who lay in wait. Bandit of the sealanes, it plundered the high waves for whale and sturgeon, seizing them in its jaws and eating them, bone and caviar. But when it gaped to swallow the boat of Väinämöinen, the ship's bow rammed it, the proud prow pierced it . . . and the heroes ate pike for five days. Out of the jawbone, Väinämöinen made himself a kantele – a kind of harp with bones for strings; he used the teeth to pluck a tune. And so it was to the sound of music that they came to Pohjola. In place of a beach, huge copper rollers lay at the water's edge for rolling ships in and out of the freezing sea. Beyond the rollers, between the pine trees where day-long dark had once clung, the sun now dazzled on Louhi's cabin and on the copper hill. A gull swooped down and pecked Ilmarinen on the head.

'What brings you here?' asked Lady Louhi, bare armed in the balmy warmth of her cabin's porch.

'The joy of your company and the sampo which has made your frosty land a paradise,' said Väinämöinen. 'Since Finland made it, shan't Finland enjoy its magic too? Let us share!'

But the sun had done nothing to melt the ice in Lady Louhi's heart. 'Can one squirrel live in two trees?' she said. 'Lapland has the sampo now and no one shall take it from us!'

If Väinämöinen was annoyed, he did not show it. He simply took out the kantele – the pike-jaw harp – and began to play. The music was sweeter than mead, the notes softer than snowflakes on the lids of those listening. Louhi made to rise from her chair, but fell back, as all around her the lords and ladies, the soldiers and slaves of the Northland slumped down asleep.

The three heroes tiptoed past them, up to the copper hill. Ilmarinen pushed butter in the keyholes of the dozen locks, while Väinämöinen sang strange and low wordless songs. The door swung open, and the sampo was theirs!

One side was grinding out fair harvests, one peace, one wealth, while the bright lid spun amid a galaxy of sparks.

Past the cabin, over the copper rollers, out into the surf went the three brave raiders, dipping their oars as softly as wings, stealing away from the Northland. But Lemminkäinen was bursting with pride and pleasure. 'We should celebrate!' he declared. 'We should sing!'

'No. We should not,' said Väinämöinen in a whisper. But Lemminkäinen would not be told.

'We came and we stormed the copper hill!
And now we'll sing till the sun stands still
How Finland's heroes stole the Mill
Of Happiness, and took their fill!'

A crane roosting on a sea rock rose lazily in the air and flapped inland. It flew to the cabin of Lady Louhi; it woke the Lapps from their magic sleep. 'The Finns have opened the copper hill! The Finns have stolen the sampo! Arise and give chase!'

Over the copper rollers thundered the Lapp ship – huge as a castle, with a hundred men at the oars and a thousand standing. And Louhi at the stern cursed as she held the tiller:

> *Come from the seabed, Gaffa's child!*
> *'Come, you Mist-moisty Maiden!*
> *Come from the seabed, Gaffa's child!*
> *Stormclouds with thunder laden,*
> *Come and turn the calm sea wild!'*

A hundred miles away, Väinämöinen's boat was suddenly wrapped in mist as thick as sheep's wool. Lemminkäinen's song, first muffled then stifled, fell silent. The three heroes could not see as far as each other's faces; they might as well have been alone on the wide ocean. Without sight of the stars, how could they steer a course for home? Without sight of the sea, how could they avoid the reefs and shoals of shallow water?

Väinämöinen picked up the kantele and began to play. If the mist were magic, so was his music. For the fog began to glow and gleam, to run and steam. It turned to a golden liquor which poured into the sea, a cataract of honey. Lemminkäinen opened his mouth and swallowed the sweetness greedily. Ilmarinen wiped his sticky hands and pulled on his oar. The sea ahead was clear, the water round them a puddle of honey, astonishing the fish.

But Louhi and her men had gained ground.

A mile farther, and the sea around Väinämöinen's boat began to seethe. Out of a geyser of bubbles burst the murderous great head of a sea monster. With scales of slate and teeth of razorshell, the oldest child of Gaffa the Kraken broke surface and gaped its jaws to bite the boat in two.

Väinämöinen threw his cloak, and as the monster chewed it to rags, leaned out over the water and took hold. His fingers pinching both the green frilled ears, he hoisted Gaffa's child high out of the water and hooked it to the mast by its earlobes. The boat sat low in the water and filled up with a terrible smell, but as the monster dried in the sun, its roars subsided to whimpering.

'Tell us, O Gaffa's child, why you have come,' said Väinämöinen (though while he spoke, Louhi was gaining ground).

'The Lady Louhi conjured me to kill you,' sobbed the monster, 'but if you let me down, you may go on your way for all I care.'

What a splash the creature made as it hit the water; for some time it lay rubbing its ragged ears. They were watching it still when the storm came up behind them, and the clouds began to hurl lightning and thunderbolts. The sea rose, the sea rolled, the sea writhed into waves like spires of spume. One after another the pitchy waves beat against the little boat, washing over the low rails, filling the bilges with saltwater and chips of ice. A few more waves, and the boat would founder. Lemminkäinen had no breath left to sing: he was too busy baling.

One wave, bigger than all the rest, crashed down on their heads and washed the pike-jaw harp out of Väinämöinen's hands, washing it over the side, sinking it in six thousand fathoms.

Väinämöinen's lips, wet and cold and trembling with sadness at the loss of his harp, would not pucker at first. But he wiped them dry and whistled long and low – a noise so loudly magic that it brought all the way from the cliffs of Finland the great Sea Eagle whose wings span Bear Island and whose beak made the fjords. From its tail Lemminkäinen pulled two feathers the size of castle walls and battened them to the boat's sides; so high that the sea could not break over them, so glossy that the boat slipped all the faster through the vertiginous seas.

But meanwhile, Louhi and her men had gained more ground.

The heroes looked back and thought they saw a cloud. They looked back and thought they saw a flock of birds. They looked back and knew they were seeing a ship as huge as a castle, crammed with warriors. Suddenly Louhi was on them: a hundred men pulling on a hundred oars and a thousand more standing.

Väinämöinen fumbled in his pocket. He pulled out his tinderbox and from it took a sliver of flint. Over his left shoulder he threw it, as you or I throw spilled salt, and as he did so, he sang:

> 'Grow reef, and crack their prow;
> Rocks arise to rack them – now!'

The tiny shard grew to a pebble, the pebble to a stone, the stone to a boulder, the boulder multiplied a millionfold. A reef grew in that instant, so sheer and sharp that it slashed the sea to foam.

Too late Louhi saw it lying across her path. The hull shook and the hundred rowers fell from their benches while the thousand warriors sprawled in the bilges. Seams parted, planks splintered and the sea surged in. As her ship fell apart round her, Louhi clapped the clinker sides under her arms, the rudder under her coat-tails, and telling her men. 'Cling tight to me!', the Lady Louhi took flight.

She became an eagle of wood and bone, with talons forged from swords and a beak from axeheads. With a shriek of hatred, she swooped on Väinämöinen's boat out of the north-western sky, one wingtip sweeping the sea, the other brushing the clouds.

'Oh for a cloak of fire now, to keep off this fearful bird!' muttered the old hero, and he called out, 'One last time I say, let us share the sampo! Let's share its magic!'

'No! I won't share it! I shan't share it!' shrieked the woman-eagle plumed with soldiers, and her metal talons snatched the sampo out of Ilmarinen's lap.

So Väinämöinen pulled his oar out of its rowlock and, whirling it three times round his head, struck out at the swooping eagle of wood and bone. Plank and men and weapons showered down. The wood wings buckled, the tail feathers dropped their burden of men into the sea. But the sampo – oh the sampo! – it fell from her claws into the green, seething sea!

The three heroes leapt to their feet in horror. The Lady Louhi soared into the cloudbanks with a terrible cry. Only the lid of the marvellous sampo dangled from her finger. 'I'll knock down the moon!' she ranted. 'I'll wedge the sun in a cleft of cliff! I'll freeze the marrow in your bones for this, thieving Finns!'

Väinämöinen tossed his long grey hair defiantly. 'You may do much, Louhi! God knows, you have done enough! But the sun and moon are God's, and beyond your reach and mine. Here our battle ends, and here our ways part!'

The enemies turned in opposite directions: Väinämöinen to the south, Louhi to the north. The Lapland she found on her return was very different from the one she had left. Silent, sunless and clogged with snow, groaning under the weight of hard-packed ice, it was once again home to wolves and bears. Only the magic of the sampo's lid brought back the herds of reindeer out of the gloomy forests, brought singing to the lips of the drovers, and pride to the Lapp nation who live at the top of the world.

The three heroes rowed home. No singing now from Lemminkäi-nen, for the sampo was lost and so was the magical harp. 'The best and the last I shall ever make,' said Väinämöinen mournfully.

But whether by accident of tide, or whether by order of the sea king Ahto (in thanks for the new harp he cradled on his lap), something wonderful greeted them, bright amid the seaweed and shells of the beach. Pieces of the marvellous sampo had washed up on the Finnish shore, and with them better fortune than the Finns had ever known. From then on, the harvests grew taller in the fields, the beasts fatter, the treasury fuller, the people happier than they had ever been before. Poets, most of all, found the air aswarm with words, and dreamed their greatest verses – sagas of sampos, heroes and the sea.

Dragons to Dine

A HITTITE MYTH

Taru took his lightning in one hand and his thunderbolt in the other and went out to fight the dragon Illuyankas. From Aleppo to Kayseri it lay, a mountain range of a monster, armoured with scales as large as oven doors, and green as the mould that grows on graves.

Behind it lay the ruins of cities, fallen forests, plains cracked like dinner plates, lakes drunk dry. One yellow eye surveyed the devastation done, the other looked ahead to lands as yet untouched. That eye came to rest on Taru, god of wind and weather, armed for battle and calling its name.

'Illuyankas! Illuyankas! Stand and fight! You have cracked open this world like an egg and chewed to pieces everything Mankind has made. But you shall not take one step more! All the weather of the world is in my quiver, and the gods have sent me to stop you where you stand!'

Illuyankas yawned gigantically, and licked the moon with a rasping tongue. When Taru mustered the clouds and blew them over the dragon's back, drenching it in rain, the rainwater evaporated in clouds of steam. When blizzards enfolded the beast in driving snow and sleet, the icy droplets simply cascaded off it in torrents of meltwater. Taru tore shreds off the north wind and, shaping them in his hands, pelted the dragon's head. But Illuyankas, though it rocked back on its heels, only snapped its jaws shut around the missiles and cracked them between its bronze teeth.

For a time, Taru drew back his wild weather and let the sun scorch the dragon's back. But Illuyankas's hide, like a roof of glass, reflected the sunlight, and it rebounded on Taru, dazzling him and wilting the lightning in his hand.

Tara pounded on the dragon with thunder. He whipped it with whirlwinds. But after a day, Illuyankas merely flicked its tremendous tail and flung Taru seven miles into the sky before continuing to graze on the people and villages of the Earth. Lifting its snout and flaring its nostrils, it let out a beacon of fire and a roaring whistle – a summons – and from below the earth, out through the craters of volcanoes everywhere, came smaller, squirming dragons, the children of Illuyankas.

They feared nothing from the paltry people scurrying like ants between their claws. For not even the people's gods could stand in the way of Illuyankas and its kin. Leaping and careering in a boisterous, playful trail of destruction, the great green family came to the palace of the goddess Inaras. That was where, for the first time, they saw a smiling face. It startled them to a standstill.

'Welcome! Welcome, glorious creatures!' cried Inaras, spreading her arms in a gesture of hospitality and gladness. 'Won't you rest and eat? See! I've prepared a meal for you. If you are going to rule the world from now on, you must be honoured as kings are honoured and feasted like emperors.'

Laid out on the ground in front of the palace were white cloths a mile long, strewn with dishes of gold. In the dishes was food of every kind – fish baked and fried, vegetables raw and cooked, meat roasted and rare. There were barrels of wine and casks of beer, sherbets and curds and cheeses. There were cakes and loaves, baskets of nuts and tureens of caramel sugar. Honey-soaked halva was heaped as high as haystacks.

The dragons browsed at first, taking a lick here, a taste there. But soon they were gorging frenziedly, so delicious were the offerings Inaras laid before them. All day and all night and for three more days and nights the dragons dined, and Inaras never slept, so intent was she on bringing them more food, more drink, more deliciousness.

The dragons began to feel sleepy, and stumbling a little against the pink palace walls, they turned for home. Their bellies were so bloated, their eyes so heavy that it was all they could do to find the individual entrances to their underground lairs. Belching and hiccuping, the baby dragons rolled into their volcanic craters and thrust their heads into the tunnels from which they had emerged. *Oof.* Neck and shoulders passed inside. *Oooff.* Their stomachs did not.

So fat were Illuyankas and the lesser dragons that they could not manage to climb back through their doors. They could not reach their warm nests, their lava troughs, the vats of molten rock at which they drank to recharge their dragonish fire. And when they tried, they could not back out again, either. It was Inaras's turn to light beacons and to whistle. Out from the ruins of their villages, out from the rubble of cities and farms and the fallen forests came all the little people of the Earth, carrying enough new rope to bind the moon to the sun.

They ran to where the dragons stood, heads underground, stomachs and hind-quarters in the sun, writhing and tugging to free themselves. The people bound the dragons and hog-tied them, roped them, knee and ankle, and peeled off their scales, leaving the dragons pink and vulnerable, naked and sunburned.

'Thank you, Taru, for your fierceness and bravery!' they sang. 'But thank you, Inaras, even more, for your cunning and your cooking!'

Inaras inclined her head graciously and invited the people to finish up the crumbs of the dragons' feast. And Taru (when he came back down from the sky) held off bad weather until the people had had time to mend their roofs.

Guitar Solo
A MYTH FROM MALI

IN A PLACE where six rivers join like the strings of a guitar, lived Zin the Nasty, Zin the mean, Zin-Kibaru the water spirit. Even above the noise of rushing water rose the sound of his magic guitar, and whenever he played it, the creatures of the river fell under his power. He summoned them to dance for him and to fetch him food and drink. In the daytime, the countryside rocked to the sound of Zin's partying.

But come night-time, there was worse in store for Zin's neighbour, Faran. At night, Zin played his guitar in Faran's field, hidden by darkness and the tall plants. Faran was not rich. In all the world he only had a field, a fishing-rod, a canoe and his mother. So when Zin began to play, Faran clapped his hands to his head and groaned, 'Oh no! Not again!'

Out of the rivers came a million mesmerized fish, slithering up the bank, walking on their tails, glimmering silver. They trampled his green shoots, gobbled his tall leaves, picked his ripe crop to carry home to Zin-Kibaru. Like a flock of crows they stripped his field, and no amount of shoo-ing would drive them away. Not while Zin played his spiteful, magic guitar.

'We shall starve!' complained Faran to his mother.

'Well, boy,' she said, 'there's a saying I seem to recall: when the fish eat your food, it's time to eat the fish.'

So Faran took his rod and his canoe and went fishing. All day he

106

fished, but Zin's magic simply kept the fish away, and Faran caught nothing. All night he fished, too, and never a bite: the fish were too busy eating the maize in his field.

'Nothing, nothing, nothing,' said Faran in disgust, as he arrived home with his rod over his shoulder.

'Nothing?' said his mother seeing the bulging fishing-basket.

'Well, nothing but two hippopotami,' said Faran, 'and we can't eat them, so I'd better let them go.'

The hippopotami got out of Faran's basket and trotted away. And Faran went to Riversmeet and grabbed Zin-Kibaru by the shirt. 'I'll fight you for that guitar of yours!'

Now Zin was an ugly brute, and got most of his fun from tormenting Faran and the animals. But he also loved to wrestle. 'I'll fight you boy,' he said, 'and if you win, you get my guitar. But if *I* win, I get your canoe. Agreed?'

'If I don't stop your magic, I shan't need no canoe,' said Faran. ''cos I'll be starved right down to a skeleton, me and Mama both.'

So, that was one night the magic guitar did not play in Faran's field – because Faran and Zin were wrestling.

All the animals watched. At first they cheered Zin: he had told them to. But soon they fell silent, a circle of glittering eyes.

All night Faran fought, because so much depended on it. 'Can't lose my canoe!' he thought, each time he grew tired. 'Must stop that music!' he thought, each time he hit the ground. 'Must win, for Mama's sake!' he thought, each time Zin bit or kicked or scratched him.

And by morning it really seemed as if Faran might win.

'Come on, Faran!' whispered a monkey and a duck.

'*COME ON, FARAN!*' roared his mother.

Then Zin cheated.

He used a magic word.

'*Zongballyboshbuckericket!*' he said, and Faran fell to the ground like spilled water. He could not move. Zin danced round him, hands clasped above his head – 'I win! I win! I win!'- then laughed and laughed till he had to sit down.

'Oh Mama!' sobbed Faran. 'I'm sorry! I did my best, but I don't know no magic words to knock this bully down!'

'Oh yes you do!' called his mama. 'Don't you recall? You found them in your fishing basket one day!'

Then Faran remembered. The perfect magic words. And he used them. *'Hippopotami! HELP!'*

Just like magic, the first hippopotamus Faran had caught came and sat down – just where Zin was sitting. I mean *right on the spot* where Zin was sitting. And then his hippopotamus mate came and sat on his lap. And that, it was generally agreed, was when Faran won the fight.

So nowadays Faran floats half-asleep in his canoe, fishing or playing a small guitar. He has changed the strings, of course, so as to have no magic power over the creatures of the six rivers. But he does have plenty of friends to help him tend his maize and mend his roof and dance with his mother. And what more can a boy ask than that?

Sadko and the Tsar of the Sea

A RUSSIAN LEGEND

THERE WAS A time when Russia was peopled with heroes, and every day brought adventure. All the deeds were great and worth the doing, and all the cargoes were king's ransoms. Even so, these heroes – the *bogatyri* – were not the greatest powers on Earth, and they were still bound by laws and etiquette and taxes. So when Sadko the Merchant set sail with a cargo of gems, he *ought* to have paid tribute to the Tsar of the Sea.

Suddenly, with a jolt which spilled sackloads of rubies along the deck, the ship stopped moving. The wind tugged at the sail, waves spilled over the stern, but the ship stood as still as if it were rooted to the seabed. The crew looked over the side, but there was no sandbar, no reef. A terrible realization dawned on Sadko.

'The Tsar of the Sea wants his toll!' he exclaimed. 'Fetch it! Pay it! Fetch twice the amount! How could I have been so forgetful, so lacking in respect?' Scooping up a handful of pearls, another of emeralds and two of diamonds, he spread them on a plank of wood and, leaning over the side, set the gems afloat.

'More sail and on!' cried the captain, but the ship stayed stuck fast, like an axehead sunk in a log.

Sadko smote his forehead, tore his coat and leapt on to the ship's rail. 'It's no good! The Tsar is affronted! My offence was too great! He requires a life, and a life he shall have!' So saying, he fell face-first on to the plank, scattering pearls and soaking the fur collar of his coat. 'Take me!' he cried (for this *was* the Age of Heroes).

Nothing happened except that the plank floated away from the ship, the ship from the plank. The captain sailed on without a backward glance, and Sadko lay face-down on the sea, wondering about sharks. The ocean rocked him, the sun shone on his back. Sadko fell asleep.

So he never did know how he came to wake in the palace of the Tsar of the Sea. Its ceiling was silvered with mother-of-pearl, its vaulting the ribs of a hundred whales. Conch-shell fanfares blew from towers of scarlet coral, and where banners might have flown, shoals of brightly coloured fish unfurled in iridescent thousands. Seated on a giant clam shell, among the gilded figureheads of shipwrecks, sat the Tsar of the Sea, half-man, half-fish, a great green tail coiled around the base of his throne.

'Your tribute, my lord . . .' began Sadko, flinging himself on his face and sliding along the smooth-scaled floor.

'Think nothing of it,' said the Tsar graciously. 'I had heard of you. I wanted to meet you. This to-ing and fro-ing over the ocean was your idea, I hear.'

'It shall stop and never be thought of again!' offered Sadko.

'Not a bit. I like it. Good idea,' responded the Tsar, his walrus moustaches flowing luxuriantly about his ears. 'It shall be a thing of the future, believe me. D'you play that?' He pointed a fluke of his tail at the balalaika which had fallen from inside Sadko's coat and was floating slowly upwards and out of reach.

Sadko made a porpoise-like leap to retrieve the musical instrument and began casually to pluck its strings. He claimed modestly to have no skill, no musical talent, nothing worthy of the Tsar's hearing. But he played, all the same, and the Tsar's green face lit up with pleasure. He began to thresh his great tail and then to dance, undulating gently at first like a ray, then tossing aside his turtleshell crown and somersaulting about the palace. The goblets were swept off the tables by the backwash. The hangings billowed, rattling their curtain rings.

Naturally, the courtiers followed suit, plunging and gliding, the narwhal beating time with its twisted horn. But none danced as energetically as the Tsar, hair awash, barbules streaming, as he tumbled over and over, spinning and whistling.

High above, on the surface of the sea, waves as high and white as sail-sheets travelled over the water and fell on ships, shrouding them in spray. Lighthouses tumbled like sandcastles, cliffs were gouged hollow by breaking surf. A storm the like of which the seas had never seen raged from the Tropic of Capricorn to the Tropic of Cancer, because the Tsar of the Sea was dancing to Sadko's balalaika. Sadko's ship and twenty more besides came sailing down, drowned sailors caught in their rigging, spilling cargoes on the tide.

Seeing his mistake, Sadko tried to stop, but the Tsar only roared delightedly, 'More! More music! I'm happy! I feel like dancing!' So Sadko played on and on, in bright, major keys suited to the Tsar's cheerful mood. At last, with a tug that cut his fingers to the bone, Sadko pretended accidentally to break all the strings of his balalaika, and the music twanged to a halt. 'I regret . . . my instrument . . . not another note . . .' he apologized.

'No matter. I was getting tired anyway,' panted the Tsar, throwing himself down on a coral couch. 'My chariot will take you home.' Sadko was conveyed in a shell chariot drawn by salmon, out of the palace caves, in from the ocean and up a saltwater river to its freshwater source.

The experience had so shaken him that, for a long while, he did not set foot on a ship, but made all his journeys overland. Near where the Tsar's chariot had set him down, he built a warehouse where other merchants could store their goods. It was a novel idea no one had ever had before. But the spot was far from his native city of Novgorod, and he did wish to see his home again before (as was the fate of *bogatyri*) he turned to stone, a boulder in the landscape of history.

Apprehensively, he went to the banks of the River Volga with a plate of salted bread and fed it to the river. 'Oh River, will you carry me home to the city of my birth, now that we have dined together?'

The fish ate the bread, but it was the river which thanked him. 'You, Sadko, are a man who knows the worth of water.'

'Of course! No man can live in it, no man can live without it,' said Sadko, and the Volga gurgled with pleasure.

'I must tell my brother that one! "No man can live in it, no man can . . . " Very good! On second thoughts, why don't you tell him yourself? Share some of your excellent bread with my brother, Lake Ilmen, and see how he rewards your generosity.'

So Sadko threw salted bread on to the waters of Lake Ilmen, and though the fish ate the bread, it was the lake which thanked him.

'You, Sadko, are a man of the future,' said Lake Ilmen in his whispering, reedy voice. 'May I suggest you cast three fishing nets over me, for I have a present for you from my great grandfather, the Tsar of the Sea.'

Sadko cast the three nets, and to his astonishment and the amazement of everyone who helped him that afternoon, the nets filled with all manner of *salt sea* fish – cod and bass, sturgeon and wrasse – and silver salmon, too, though it was not the season, not the season at all! There were so many fish and it was so late in the day that the catch needed to be stored overnight. Sadko's warehouse was the very place.

But in the course of the night, a subtle change overtook the fish in Sadko's warehouse. By morning, when the doors were opened, there was no smell, no smell at all. And all the fish – stacked high as the rafters of Sadko's warehouse – had turned to ingots of solid silver.

In a way, the end began that day. For afterwards, the *bogatyri* of Russia stopped adventuring and doing great deeds. They took to trade: buying and selling, transport and distribution, marketing and striking deals. They made millions of roubles, and their warehouses reached almost to the sky.

But their wealth fired the envy of foreigners, and Russia was invaded by brutish, bad-mannered barbarians. The *bogatyri* fled – or withdrew, perhaps, to discuss economic sanctions. While they debated, they turned, one by one, to stone – boulders in the landscape of history. Were it not for the rivers babbling about them, the lakes whispering their stories, the sea roaring out their names, we would hardly know they had ever existed.

The Armchair Traveller

AN INDIAN LEGEND

HE WAS NO beauty, it's true. In fact compared with his brother Karttikeya, his looks were downright bizarre. There was his colour, to begin with: blue is not to everyone's taste. Nor are four arms and a pot-belly. Nor are trunks and tusks. But then Ganesa's head *was* second-hand, his own having been cut off by Shiva in a moment of temper and replaced with the nearest one to hand, in the hope no one would notice. Even so, elephants are wise animals, and what Ganesa lacked in obvious good looks he made up for in wisdom. His library was huge. He read even more greedily than he ate, and he ate all day long.

Ganesa and his brother wanted to marry. Their sights were set on Siddhi and Buddhi. Although the obvious solution might seem that they should marry one each, fiery and quarrelsome Karttikeya saw things differently. 'I'll race you round the world, Ganesa,' he said. 'Whoever gets back first shall have them both!'

Ganesa munched on a pile of mangoes before answering. 'That seems acceptable,' he said, spitting pips out of the window. Never once did he lift his eyes from the book he was reading.

With no more luggage than his bow and arrows, Karttikeya leapt astride his trusty peacock (laughing aloud at the absurd idea of his fat, squat brother struggling round the globe behind him) and sped into the distance, a streamer of iridescent green and purple feathers and a flash of silver. He would be married and his first child born before Ganesa even got home!

'Well?' squeaked the mouse which lived somewhere between Ganesa's ears. It raced up and down his bony head. It shouted into his flappy ear. 'Hurry! He's faster than you! Get moving!'

'All in good time,' said Ganesa, and went on reading.

'Don't you *want* to marry Siddhi and Buddhi? They're lovely!'

'Intelligent, too,' said Ganesa. 'At least Buddhi is. Siddhi, I would estimate, is more of an achiever.' He chewed slowly on a heap of melons while sucking strawberries up his trunk for later. 'This really is an excellent book.'

'No time for reading!' urged the mouse. 'Aren't you even going to try? Don't you think you can do it? Karttikeya may be fast but you and I can push through jungles better than he. We could make up time in South America and Indonesia! Get on your feet! You won't win just sitting here!'

'Well, that's as maybe,' said Ganesa through a mouthful of onions. 'Let us not pre-judge these matters.' His trunk reached out and took down another gigantic tome from his bookshelves. Then he settled back in his chair and shot peanuts into his open mouth with uncanny accuracy.

Round the fat world raced Karttikeya. He swam rivers, hacked his way through forests, and traipsed over fly-blown deserts. He saw the most wonderful cities in the world, some armour-plated with ice, some half-submerged in flowers and ivy. He met kings and climbed mountains. He watched harvests of wheat and seaweed and olives; he fought wild beasts with fur, with feathers, with scales. There was no time for wondering why the towers of Sumeria lay in ruins, or why the night sky sometimes filled with trickling colours at the top of the world. He was too intent on winning, on beating his elephantine brother, on the stories that would be written of this epic race.

'Summon the musicians! Prepare the wedding feast! I am back! Karttikeya has returned!' His peacock looked bedraggled and tattered. Karttikeya was covered in dust, leaves and barnacles, and his clothes were full of sand. 'Buddhi? Siddhi? . . . *You!*'

There sat Ganesa in his armchair, munching thoughtfully on cumquats and reading a copy of the *Puranas*. 'Where have you been?'

he asked his dishevelled brother. 'We couldn't start the wedding without the bridegroom's brother.'

Now Karttikeya, though he did not have the head of an elephant, was not altogether stupid. He suspected that Ganesa had not been *right round* the world, as he had. Indeed, he did not stop short of thinking Ganesa had never even levered his big rump out of that armchair. So he decided to shame him in front of Buddhi and Siddhi, and to show him up for a cheat.

'Tell us, brother. What did you think of China?'

'Which part?' replied Ganesa. 'There's so much. The green pinnacles of the Yangtse, or the man-made marvels of Pekin?'

'Huh! . . . Was Siberia cold enough for you?' Karttikeya persisted.

'I preferred Greenland, myself – all that volcanic activity, those hot geysers – such astonishing shapes they make as the droplets freeze. And the fjords of Scandinavia – ah! – more indentations than the blade of a saw!'

'Since you were ahead of me,' said Karttikeya sarcastically, 'I'm surprised I didn't see the path you beat through the rainforests.'

'Mmm, well, the forests regenerate so quickly,' explained Ganesa. 'That's why they've all but reclaimed those ziggurats. I notice a similarity – don't you? – between the ziggurats and the pyramids of Egypt. Do you suppose there is any truth in that story about Naramo-Sin sailing west with his mathematics?'

On and on Ganesa talked, pausing only to accept a grape from Buddhi, a pomegranate from Siddhi. The women sat at his feet spellbound by the pictures he painted of distant lands, their people, their philosophies, their legends. 'I particularly like the Native American myth – so poetical in form. For instance . . .'

'All right! All right! You win!' said Karttikeya, slumping down, exhausted. 'You win. You may have your brides.'

Siddhi and Buddhi laughed and hugged each other with delight.

'Thank you, brother! How very gratifying!'

'But admit it, brother, just to me, just for the sake of history, *did* you really travel round the world?'

Ganesa tapped his bony skull with one of his four hands. 'In my mind, dear brother. In my mind. You don't always have to visit a place to find out about it. That's why I treasure my books.'

Buddhi and Siddhi gazed round them at the high shelves full of books and scrolls, and smiled as though they had just been given the world for a wedding present. Then they fetched Ganesa another hand of bananas and sat down to hear more stories.

Uphill Struggle

A GREEK LEGEND

YOU CAN DEFY the gods just so often: they will always have the last word. The Immortals, you see, have time on their side. They only have to wait, and the disrespectful will be brought to their knees by old age and the fear of dying.

Sisyphus, though, feared nothing. He did not give a fig for their trailing clouds of glory, for their thunderbolts or lightning. In fact, as he said more than once, he thought they were a bunch of rogues and that living at the top of a mountain must have affected their brains, for they were all as mad as bats.

When Zeus, King of gods, mightiest of the mighty, stole the wife of River Alopus, Sisyphus went and told Alopus straight out – just like that. 'It was Zeus, the philandering old devil. He's got your wife. I saw him take her.'

That was too much for Zeus, King of gods, mightiest of the mighty. '*Death! Go and tell Sisyphus his time has come!*' he spluttered, as the jealous husband swirled round his ankles, set urns and couches afloat, and rendered heaven awash with mud.

Sisyphus took to his heels and ran. Death lunged at him with a sickle, but Sisyphus ducked. Death tried to fell him with a club, but Sisyphus jumped just in time. Death loosed avalanches and wild animals, but Sisyphus bolted for home and slammed the door, jamming it shut with furniture.

'I can't hold him off for long,' he told his wife. 'So listen. When I'm dead, I want you to throw my body in the rubbish pit and have a party.'

'Oh but dearest . . . !'

The door burst open and, with a gust of wind and a crash of furniture, Sisyphus fell dead, his soul snatched away to the Under-world to an eternity of dark: silenced by the gods..

'He has *what?!*'

'A complaint. He wishes to complain, your lordship.'

Hades leaned forward out of his throne, eyes bulging, and his herald cowered in terror. '*Just who does he think he is?!*'

'A poor benighted soul, shamefully and shoddily treated,' said Sisyphus, entering without permission and stretching himself out face-down before the Ruler of the Dead. 'I complain not of dying, Lord Hades. Far from it! It's a privilege to share the dwelling place of yourself and so many eminent ghosts! But my wife! My wretched wife! Do you know what she has done?'

Hades was intrigued. 'What has she done?'

'*Nothing!*' cried Sisyphus leaping up and clenching his gauzy fists in protest. 'No funeral rites! No pennies on my eyelids. Not a tear shed! She simply dumped my body in the rubbish pit! She's a disgrace to the very word "widow"!'

Hades nodded his infernal head slowly, so that his piles of pitchy hair stirred within his chair. 'The rubbish pit. That's bad. She shall be punished when she too dies.'

'No need, my lord! Don't trouble yourself! Only send me back there, and I shall make an example of her that will teach the Living a lesson in caring for the Dead!'

'SEND YOU BACK?' Hades was stunned by the boldness of the suggestion. 'Would you come straight back afterwards?'

'The moment she's been taught a lesson, I promise,' said Sisyphus. Hades hesitated. 'Do you know, lord? She never even laid a tribute on *your* altar in remembrance of me!'

'*Then go back and teach her the meaning of respect!*' cried Hades, leaping up in his excitement. '*Appalling woman!*'

'Excelling woman,' said Sisyphus kissing his wife tenderly.

'I did right?'

'You did perfectly. Here I am to prove it – first man ever to escape the Underworld!' He shook vegetable peelings out of his hair, having only just recovered his body from the rubbish pit. He had promised to return to Dis, Land of the Dead, by midnight. But by midnight he would be fishing on the seashore, by morning dozing among the lemon groves, the sun on his back. Sisyphus felt so full of life that he could have palmed Mount Olympus and thrown it out to sea like a discus! 'They haven't the wit they were born with!' he told his wife. 'And I, Sisyphus, have the wit to outwit them from now till the revolution! One day soon, humankind will rise up and rout the gods as they routed the Titans before them. I'm *never* going back!'

When Sisyphus did not return to Dis as promised, Hades loosed his hounds on the scent. Black as tar, they came panting out of the earth, tongues lolling over bared teeth. From their Olympian palaces the gods watched, smirking, as the dogs closed on their prey, submerged him in their pitchy pelts and dragged him down to Dis.

'Such nerve! Such daring!' said Hades towering over his prize. 'I am so impressed, I mean to do a deal with you, my audacious friend. You see that hill, and that boulder? Simply push that boulder to the top of the hill, and you shall go free, leave here, live for ever, *go home*.'

And so Sisyphus pushes his boulder up the hill. He has been doing it now for four thousand years. His hands bleed, his back is twisted and bent. Every time he gets to within one push of the top, the gods on Olympus swell their cheeks and – *pouf* – the boulder rolls thundering down to the bottom. He must begin again.

Nearby, Tantalus, condemned for his crimes to a pool of fire, never able to taste the sweet cool water placed just out of reach, looks up and takes his only scrap of comfort in an eternity of torment. 'At least I am not Sisyphus,' he tells himself, 'rolling his rock for ever and a day.'

But Sisyphus, as he slides down the rocky slope on his bare feet, and sets his shoulder to the stone for the millionth time, says, 'One day soon Man will rise up against the gods, and then . . . and then!'

Bobbi Bobbi!

AN ABORIGINAL MYTH

IN THE DREAMTIME, when the world was still in the making, the Ancient Sleepers rose from their beds and walked across sea and land, shaping the rocks, the plants, the creatures, arranging the stars to please the eye.

I remember. Or if not I, an ancestor of mine, or if not he, a sister of his ancestor. Our memories are blurred now, but we do remember: how the Ancient Sleeping spirits walked the Earth during Dreamtime, and made things ready for us.

The snake spirit, Bobbi Bobbi, on his walk, heard crying and came upon a group of human beings newly brought to life.

'Does the world not please you for a place to live?' he asked.

'It would please us,' sobbed the people, 'if we were not so *hungry!*'

So Bobbi Bobbi searched his dreams for a kind of food, then gave it shape from a handful of soil. He made one flying bat and then another. Big they were, and meaty, each one a meal to feed a family. By the time Bobbi Bobbi walked on his way, over the brand-new world, the sky behind him was black with bats.

Binbinga lit a fire. Banbangi his sister crept up on a bat where it hung by its toes from a tree.

Crackle-rattle! The bat heard her, for its hearing was sharp and, just as she reached into the tree, it spread its leathery wings and flapped away.

Banbangi tended the fire. Binbinga took a stone and went to where the bats hung in a row by their toes from a cliff. He leaned back to throw.

Crackle-rattle! The bats heard him, for their hearing was keen, and just as he threw his stone, the bats spread their leathery wings and and flapped away.

Bobbi Bobbi, walking home through the red light of evening, heard crying. Once again, he came across the little new-made people – now looking more gaunt and desperate than before – and asked them what was wrong. But all they could do was point up at the sky at the flittering swarms of bats.

'We can't reach them. We can't catch them. All day we hunt them, but they won't be caught!'

Now Bobbi Bobbi was angry, because when he made a thing, he made it for a good purpose and not to find it fooling about in the red light of sunset. In his anger he beat his chest, till the ringing of his ribs gave him an idea.

With the sharp blade of the sickle moon, he cut a slit in the side of his chest, reached in his hand, and pulled out a rib, a single rib. Taking a squinnying aim on the circling bats, he flung the rib – it flew with a singing whistle – and tumbled a fine fat bat out of the blood-red sky!

The little people jumped and cheered, but not so high nor as loud as they jumped and cheered at what happened next. Bobbi Bobbi's rib-stick came whirling back out of the scarlet sky – right to his hand, right to the very palm of his hand!

Bobbi Bobbi gave his marvellous rib to the hungry newcomers and – wonder of wonders! – even when they threw it, it knocked the bats from the sky then swooped home again to their hands. 'Boomerang', they called it, a treasure entrusted to them by the gods. A very piece of the gods.

No wonder they grew proud.

They knocked down more bats than they could eat, just to prove they could do it. The best throwers even boasted that they could knock down the birds . . .

'. . . the clouds . . . !'

'. . . the moon . . . !'

And as they strove to outdo one another, Binbinga threw the boomerang so hard and so high that he knocked a hole in the sky!

Down fell rubble and blue dust, on to the ground below. Winds escaped through the gap, stars showed at midday, and the handiwork of the Ancient Sleepers was spoiled.

Now Bobbi Bobbi was really angry, because when he made a thing, he made it to good purpose, not to see it played with by fools.

Before the boomerang could arc back through the tear in the sky, Bobbi Bobbi reared up, caught it in his mouth and shook it with rage.

'Quick! Before he swallows it!' cried Binbinga.

'He mustn't take it from us!' cried Banbangi. And they ran at the great snake spirit, scrambled up his scaly body, clambered up his trunk towards the broad, toothless rim of his mouth. They each took hold of one end of the precious boomerang. In their ignorance, they actually tried to pull it out of Bobbi Bobbi's mouth!

But the snake spirit only dislocated his jaw (as snakes can) to widen the gape of his cavernous jaw, and swallowed Binbinga and Banbangi, swallowed them whole.

A great silence fell over the newly made world, broken only by the *rattle-crack* of the last remaining bats.

For a long while, the flying bats cruised the sky above the new-made people. Daily they increased in number, just as the hunger increased in the bellies of those below. When, at last, Bobbi Bobbi relented and gave back the rib-stick, it was only in exchange for their promises to use it as it was meant to be used – for catching food.

The Gingerbread Baby

A MYTH FROM PALESTINE

LEILA PUT IN the bread and closed the oven door. She drew a deep breath and sighed; there was sea-salt in the air. 'While the bread bakes, I just have time to stroll down to the harbour,' she thought. 'I must see the sea today.'

Down at the waterfront, a ship was loading. Leila had no sooner stepped aboard than it set sail, and carried her over three oceans and five high seas till she came to a land rather like her own. Down by the docks, the houses were shabby and the people poor. A home was one room and a meal was one raisin and the reason was poverty.

A young widow stood by her door, big-bellied with yet another baby, and weeping fit to break your heart. 'Another mouth to feed,' she said, 'and where's the food to come from? Even our poor dog is starving to death.'

Leila wished she had brought the loaf of bread with her, for truly this whole family was as thin as a bunch of twigs. The dog, too. As it was, Leila felt in the pockets of her gown and there was not so much as a coin for her to give the widow.

Higher up, the houses were large and beautiful, each room as big as a lesser man's house, each meal a marvel, and the reason was wealth. Even so, a woman stood on her golden balcony and wept fit to break your heart.

'What's the matter?' asked Leila.

'Nothing your kindness can cure, old lady,' sobbed the woman.

'My husband the sultan hates me, because I have given him no children!'

'*He* has given *you* no children, you mean!' said Leila. 'These men! How they complain about the least thing! You dry your tears and let an old lady advise you.' She whispered in the sultana's ear, and the young woman, though she shook her head – 'It will never work!' – did just as she was told.

When the sultan came home, she told him, to his great joy, that she was expecting a baby. Then, every day, Leila padded the sultana's dress a little more, so that she really did look as though she had told him the truth. Meanwhile, each day, Leila also cooked a morsel of gingerbread, and took it down to the garden gate and fed it to a bony little dog who poked his nose through the bars.

After eight months, Leila went to the kitchen and made more dough than usual. She pinched the gingerbread into the size and shape of a baby, and baked it in the palace oven, wondering as she did so, if her own bread at home was baked yet.

Every day, the sultan came asking, 'Is the child born yet?' At last he heard the words he longed for. Leila peeped round the bedroom door and told him, 'Your dear wife has given you a beautiful child, your eminence. As soon as she is strong enough, she will bring the boy to you in the garden.'

There, amid the tinkling fountains and orange trees, the sultan sat singing for sheer joy. Watching from her balcony, the sultana cradled her gingerbread baby . . . and sobbed fit to break your heart. 'Did you really think he would be fooled, Leila?' she wept. 'Do you think my husband is blind and stupid? It is a lovely baby you baked for me, but anyone with two eyes and a nose can tell it's made of gingerbread!'

'Yes, indeed,' said Leila happily. 'Anyone with two eyes a nose and a tail.' She told the sultana to go down to her husband, carrying the child. 'But not too tight, you hear?'

Leila ran downstairs ahead of her, ran to the garden gate where every day she had fed the bony dog. Sure enough, the dog was there again today and, at the smell of gingerbread wafting over the gardens, began to drool. Leila unlatched the gate . . .

'I come, O husband, to show you our lovely child,' said the sultana, her voice full of fright.

The sultan sniffed. 'Well, he *smells* better than most babies,' he said.

Just then, with a flash of fur, one bark and a rattle of skinny bones, a dog bounded over the fountain and seized the 'baby' in its mouth.

'Call the guard! Shut the gates! Stop that dog!' yelled the sultan desperately. But no one was quick enough to catch the mongrel with its meal of gingerbread wrapped in priceless lace. The dog ran straight home – down to the docks – and shared its good fortune with the widow and her hungry, fatherless children.

The crumbs were still falling when Leila hurried in, breathless from the long trot. She went straight to the box in the corner (which was all the widow had for a cradle) and lifted out the tiny, half-starved baby boy crying there with hunger. 'Listen,' said Leila. 'How would you like your baby to live in a palace, with all the food he can eat, growing up loved and safe, to be a sultan one day?'

'Better than words can say,' said the widow. 'But how?'

'Trust me,' said Leila. Picking up the beautiful white shawl from the floor, she wrapped the real baby in it and carried him out to where the palace guards were searching the streets.

'All is well!' she said. 'This family rescued the baby before the dog could hurt him.'

When the sultan heard that, he gave command that the widow should receive a reward – a reward so huge that the family need never go hungry again. And hugging the baby boy to his chest, he carried it home to his wife.

Imagine the sultana's surprise, having lost a gingerbread baby, when she got back a real live son. She was too happy to quibble.

Leila sniffed the air and smelled baking bread. 'Time I was going,' she said, and climbed aboard a ship making ready to sail. Over three oceans and five high seas it carried her, to the harbour below her own little house. As she opened the door, the wonderful smell of baking bread greeted her like a friend. 'Just in time,' she said, and taking her loaf out of the oven, cut herself a slice to eat with a glass of hot, sweet tea.

The Price of Fire

A MYTH FROM GABON

FROM THE LEAFY canopy of the forest hang the long, looping lianas, leafy ropes of creeper like tangled hair. Within the loop of the longest liana, God used to sleep away the hottest part of the day, swinging in his viny hammock. His mother said the climb was too tiring now, so she dozed on a tree stump down below, remembering.

The dark damp of the forest floor is a chilly place, especially for an old lady. So God invented fire to keep Grandma God warm: a morsel of sun, a kindling of twigs, and there it was one day, crackling merrily and casting an orange glow.

Manwun came shivering down the forest paths, looking for berries. He saw the fire, saw God's mother asleep in its glow, and thought, 'I could use that stuff to keep *me* warm.' So he stole the fire, and ran for home as fast as he could manage with an armful of burning twigs.

Grandma God stirred, shivering, and bleated up into the trees, 'Son! Son! Someone has stolen my fire!'

God leapt from his hammock at once and, using the ropes of creeper, swung from tree to tree with a piercing yell. He quickly caught up with the thief, swooping low over his head and snatching back the stolen fire.

But Manwun went home and told his village about fire. Soon Mantoo came creeping by and, waiting till Grandma God fell asleep, stole the fire from in front of her. She dreamed of ice, and the chattering of her teeth woke her. 'Son! Son! Someone has stolen my fire!'

Swinging hand-over-hand, from tree to tree, God went after the thief, and though Mantoo had almost reached the edge of the forest, he too felt the red-and-yellow treasure snatched from his grasp as God went swooping by with a whoop of triumph.

'We could just *ask* him for some fire,' suggested Woman, but no one listened to her.

Manthree made careful plans before he left for the forest. He knew that God would be on the look-out for sneak-thieves creeping through the undergrowth. So he sewed together a coat of feathers – one from every kind of bird – and practised hour after hour. First he jumped from logs, then from branches, then from hilltops, until he could fly with all the skill and speed of a bird.

Dozing on his liana swing, all God saw was a flash of colour as Manthree went by. He never suspected a bird-man had swooped on Grandma God's fire and snatched it up, kindling and all.

'Son! Son! Someone has stolen my lovely fire!' she bleated, and God gave a weary sigh, for he had done enough chasing for one day.

Swinging hand-over-hand, whooping from tree to tree, God went after Manthree: he could just make out the glimmer of orange and red among the treetop fruits. Quick as a swallow, Manthree darted between the dense trees. He reached the edge of the forest and burst out into the bright sunlight of the plain, soaring and looping over rivers and valleys. Out in the open, God had to make chase on foot, wading and jumping, running and climbing, till at last, he sprawled exhausted on a sunny hillside to catch his breath. 'All right! All right! You may have fire! The day is too hot and the world too big for me to chase you any more. Have it and be done!'

Manthree (whose feathers were starting to char from carrying the fire) gave a great cheer, and took his prize home. God, on the other hand, dragged his feet all the weary way back to the forest.

'I've given them the fire, Mother!' he called as he approached the tangle of lianas and the dark, damp tree stumps beneath. 'I decided they could have some too. It will set the world twinkling at night, and their cooking will taste better. Was I right, do you think? I'll make you some more, of course. Mother? Mother?'

Grandma God lay curled up beside the circle of ash where her fire had once burned. She was cold as death, and no fire would ever warm her again.

First God wept, then he swore to make Manwun, Mantoo, Manthree and the rest pay for stealing fire from his poor, frail old mother. 'When I made them, I meant them to live for ever. But now, for doing this, let them taste the cold of Death! Let every man, woman and child grow old and cold and die!'

So that is why old folk complain of the cold, and shiver on the warmest days, and why, at last, the flame of life gutters and goes out in their eyes, no matter how close they make their beds to the campfire.

The Hunting of Death

A MYTH FROM RWANDA

AT THE START, God thought the world of his people: their smiles, their dancing, their songs. He did not wish them any harm in the world. So when he looked down and saw something scaly and scuttling darting from nook to cranny, he gave a great shout.

'People of Earth, look out! There goes Death! He will steal your heartbeat if you let him! Drive him out into the open, where my angels can kill him!' And fifty thousand angels flew down, with spears, clubs, drums and nets, to hunt down Death.

All through the world they beat their skin drums, driving Death ahead of them like the last rat in a cornfield. Death tried to hide in a bird's nest at the top of a tree; he tried to burrow in the ground. But the birds said, 'Away! God warned us of you!' And the animals said, 'Shoo! Be off with you!'

Closer and closer came the army of angel hunters. Their beating drums drove Death out of the brambles and tangles, out of the trees and the shadows of the trees, on to the sunny plain. There he came, panicked and panting, to a village.

He scratched at doors, tapped at windows, trying to get out of the glare of the sun, trying to get in and hide. But the people drove him away with brooms. 'Go away, you nasty thing! God warned us about you!'

The angel huntsmen were close to his heels when Death came to a field, where an old lady was digging.

'Oh glorious, lovely creature!' panted Death. 'I have run many miles across this hard world, but never have I seen such a beauty as you! Surely my eyes were made for looking at you. Let me sit here on the ground and gaze at you!'

The old lady giggled. 'Ooooh! What a flatterer you are, little crinkly one!'

'Not at all! I'd talk to your father at once and ask to marry you, but a pack of hunters is hard on my heels!'

'I know, I heard God say,' said the old woman. 'You must be that Death he talked of.'

'But *you* wouldn't like me to be killed, would you – a woman of your sweet nature and gentle heart? A maiden as lovely as you would never wish harm on a poor defenceless creature!' The drum beats came closer and closer.

The old woman simpered. 'Oh well. Best come on in under here,' she said and lifted her skirt, showing a pair of knobbly knee-caps. In out of the sunlight scuttled Death, and twined himself, thin and sinuous, round her legs.

The angel huntsmen came combing the land, the line of them stretching from one horizon to the other. 'Have you seen Death pass this way?'

'Not I,' answered the old lady, and they passed on, searching the corn ricks, burning the long grass, peering down the wells. Of course, they found no trace of Death.

Out he came from under her skirts, and away he ran without a backward glance. The old woman threw a rock after him, and howled, 'Come back! Stop that rascal, God! Don't let him get away! He said he'd marry me!'

But God was angry. 'You sheltered Death from me when I hunted him. Now I shan't shelter you from him when he comes hunting for your heartbeat!' And with that he recalled his angel huntsmen to Heaven.

And since then no angel has ever lifted her skirts to hide one of us, not one, until Death has passed by, hunting heartbeats.

Young Buddha

AN INDIAN LEGEND

SWEET AND PURE as dewfall on a spring morning, Queen Maya was loved by her husband and people as much as any goddess. One night, she dreamed that an elephant, white as milk, raised its trunk in salute over her. In her dream, its phantom whiteness came closer and closer, trumpeting, moving right through her own transparent body. When she woke, she was expecting a child. With such a beginning, no ordinary boy. His very name meant 'bringer of good'.

From the first moment, Prince Gautama was remarkable. He was no sooner born than he took seven steps, looked around him at the astonished waiting-women and midwives, and said, 'This is the last time I shall come.'

He understood, you see, without anyone teaching him, how life goes round and round, each soul quitting one body only to be born afresh in another: each life a new chance to strive for perfection, to escape the endless treadmill of rebirth. But despite his childish wisdom Gautama was as ignorant as any other newborn baby of the world outside his nursery.

'One day he will give up his kingdom!' cried a woman of such age and wisdom that her milky old eyes could see into the future. 'He will be a mighty teacher, greatest of all the teachers, bringing peace to countless millions!'

'Oh no, he won't!' cried the King, for Gautama was his son and his

131

intended heir. He wanted for Gautama what every father wants – a life of ease, a life of pleasure, a life of plenty. 'My son shall be happy!' said the King.

So, when Prince Gautama went out for a chariot ride, crowds of people lined the streets: healthy, well-fed, handsome people with smiling faces. Anyone ugly, anyone crippled or pocked by disease, anyone starving or threadbare or weeping was swept off the street, along with the dung and the litter, by squads of royal guardsmen.

The King found his son a beautiful girl to be his wife, and filled the palace with music, fountains and works of art. For all the young Prince knew, the whole world was a paradise of joy and unfailing loveliness. The gods above shook their heads and frowned.

One day, despite the efforts of the royal guards, despite the King's commands . . . and because the gods care only for the truth, Gautama went riding in his chariot. And he saw an old man, wrinkled and bent and weary from a lifetime of work.

'Who is he? *What* is he?' Gautama asked his chariot driver. 'I have never seen the like.'

Then the chariot driver could not help but explain: how everything – people and animals and plants – grow old and feeble and lose their first, youthful bloom. It is the truth; what else could the poor man say? When Gautama got home that day, he did a great deal of thinking.

Next day, despite the efforts of the soldiers, despite the King's commands, and because the gods care only for the truth, Gautama went riding again. And he saw a woman with leprosy lying beside the road, hideous and racked with pain.

'Who is she? *What* is she?' Gautama asked his chariot driver. 'I have never seen the like.'

Then the chariot driver could not help but explain: how sometimes people and animals and plants get sick and suffer pain or are born disabled or meet with terrible injuries which scar and mar their bodies. It is the truth; what else could the poor man say? Before he fell asleep that night, Gautama did a great deal of thinking.

Next day, despite the royal guards, despite the King, and because the gods care only for the truth, Gautama saw a dead body lying unburied at the roadside. 'What is that?' Gautama asked his chariot driver, seized with clammy horror. Then the chariot driver could not help but explain: how everything, everyone dies. It is the truth; what else could he say? Before the moon set that night, Gautama was a changed man.

He no longer took any pleasure in the dancing girls who tapped their tambourines and shook the golden bells at their ankles. He had no appetite for the delicious meals, no patience with the games he had once played. Taking a horse from the stable, he rode like a madman, searching for some solace in the great empty countryside beyond the city wall.

But as he rode, it seemed to him that the very fields were screaming under the sharp ploughshares of the farmers; that the woodsmen were breaking the spines of the trees with their merciless axes; that the insects in the air and worms in the soil were crying, crying, dying . . .

In a lonely glade, under the shade of a rose-apple tree, Gautama found a measure of peace. Like a man balancing a million plates, he reached a perfect stillness and balance. He saw the whole, how the world was, with all its evil, and he perceived that somewhere beyond its noisy hurtling waterfall of misery – if he could just reach through the crashing torrent – there was a place of peace and stillness.

Giving away all his jewels, all his possessions, he left his father, left his wife, left even his young son. It was no easier for him to leave them than it was for them to lose him but as he told them, 'It is the fear and pain of such partings that make life unbearable. That's why I have to go and discover a different kind of life untouched by any such sorrow.'

In his search for understanding, Gautama tried to go without food and drink, to ignore his body so that his mind could fly beyond and away from it. But starving himself only left him sleepy and weak and his thoughts cloudy and muddled. And so he bathed his poor, bony body in the river and the riverside trees reached down their branches in sheer love, to help him from the water. Gautama took food.

Later, as he walked through the forest, a giant snake, king of its breed, reared up before him, its head as high as the tallest tree. 'Today! Today, O wisest of men, you shall have what you desire! Today you will become a Buddha!'

So sitting himself down, cross-legged, under a holy tree, Gautama vowed that he would not move once more until he had grasped the reason for life itself. He practised meditation, freeing his mind like a bird from a cage, to soar through past, present and future, through place and time and all the elements.

At the sound of his whispered chanting, Mara, god of passion, fretted and raged and fumed and quaked. He summoned his sons and daughters, his troops and his weapons. '*Destroy him!*' he commanded. 'If he finds a way to rid the world of Wanting and Longing and Anger and Ambition and Greed and Fright I shall have no empire left, no more power than a blade of dead grass trodden underfoot!' At Mara's command. Thirst and Hunger, Anger and Joy and Pride and Discontent all hurled themselves at the fragile, silent, solitary man seated under the tree.

But they might as well have hurled themselves against rocks, for Gautama was beyond their reach, out of their range, his soul united with the gods, his thoughts as large as the Universe. Gautama had become a Buddha. And now, when the very word 'Buddha' is spoken, *his* is the face which fills a million minds, with its knowing, tender, smiling peace.

The Woman Who Left No Footprints

AN INUIT LEGEND

THEY HAD NO children, but they had each other. And so great was the love between Umiat and Alatna that they had happiness to spare for their neighbours. An old lady lived nearby with her granddaughter, and if it had not been for the kindness of Alatna and Umiat, who knows what would have become of them during the harsh winter months? As it was, Umiat caught them meat to eat and Alatna sewed them warm clothes. That little girl spent so much time playing at their house, she might as well have been their own daughter.

Then one day, Alatna disappeared. She did not get lost, for then she would have left footprints. She did not meet with a bear, for then there would have been blood. No. Her footprints went ten paces out of the door and into the snow . . . then disappeared, as if Alatna had melted away.

Umiat was desolate. He beat on the door of every house, asking, 'Have you seen her? Did you see who took her?' But no one had seen a thing, and though the people tried to comfort him, Umiat only roared his despair at them and stamped back home. From that day on, he did not eat, could not sleep, and if anyone spoke to him, he did not answer. Someone had taken his wife away, and he no longer trusted a soul.

Then one evening the little girl came and took him by the hand. Silently she led him to her grandmother's house and the old lady said,

'You and your wife were good to us. Now it is time for us to help you.'

She gave him a magic pole, an enchanted staff of wood. 'Drive this into the snow tonight. Then tomorrow, go where it points. It will take you where your heart desires to be.'

For the first time a flicker of hope returned to the man's sallow face, and he took the stick, stroked the little girl's hair, and went home to sleep. The stick he drove into the snowdrift by his door, and sure enough in the morning it had fallen over towards the north. Umiat's one desire was to be with his wife, so he picked up the stick, put on his snowshoes and tramped north. The old woman and the little girl stood at the village edge to wish him well. 'Remember!' the old woman called. 'The name of the stick is October!'

Each time Umiat rested, he stuck the stick in a snowdrift and, each time, the stick keeled over (as sticks will that are driven into snow). But Umiat trusted the old woman's advice. And after three days' journey through the wildest terrain, the stick sensed the closeness of Alatna. It pulled free of Umiat's hand and set off at a run: it was all Umiat could do to keep up with it! End over end it poled through the snowy landscape, and Umiat sweated in his fur-lined coat with running after it.

The stick led him to a valley well hidden by fir trees and hanging cornices of snow. And in the valley stood the biggest snowhouse he had ever seen, smoke coiling from the smokehole. Outside the door hung something like a huge feathery cloak.

As Umiat watched, a man came out of the hut and lifted down the garment. As he put it on and spread his arms, Umiat could see: it was a gigantic pair of wings.

So *that* was why his wife had left no footprints! This bird-man had swooped down out of the sky and snatched her away. At the thought of it, Umiat's fists closed vengefully round the magic stick. But the bird-man had already soared into the sky and away, the sun glinting on his fishing spear.

Alatna recognized her husband's footfall and ran to the door even before he knocked. 'I knew you'd come! I knew you'd find me! Quick! We don't have long. Eagling will be back as soon as he has caught a walrus for supper. And he has such eyesight, from the air he could spot us for sure!'

'Then we'll wait for him,' said Umiat calmly, 'and buy more time.'

Instead of starting back for the village at once, Umiat hid inside the snowhouse.

When, with a walrus dangling from each claw, the villain landed outside the door, Alatna went out to greet him 'Is that all you've brought me? Is that all you care for me? I said I was hungry! A couple of miserable walruses won't make me love you, you know! Now fetch me two whales and we shall see!'

So Eagling put on his wings again, despite his weariness, and flew out of the valley towards the sea. And while he was gone on this marathon journey, Umiat put Alatna on his back and they left the valley. Leaning on the magic stick now for support, Umiat strode out as fast as he could go.

But by the most disastrous stroke of luck, Eagling's return flight brought him swooping directly over their heads! A vast sperm whale dangled from each claw, and at the sight of his prisoner escaping, Eagling gave a great cry of rage and let his catch fall.

The impact half-buried Umiat and Alatna in snow, but they were not crushed. They scrambled over the huge flukes of the whales tails and made for a river gorge where there were caves to hide in. Crawling into one, they lay there holding their breath, hoping Eagling would think them crushed beneath the whales.

Eagling was not so easily fooled. He saw where they had gone, knew where they were hiding, though the narrowness of the gorge prevented him swooping on them. 'You shan't escape me so easily!' he cried in his shrill, squawking voice. And plunging his huge clawed feet into the river, he spread his wings so as to dam the flow completely.

Little by little, water piled up against his broad chest and his massive wingspan, deeper and deeper, flooding the river till it burst its banks, till the gorge began to fill up like a trough.

'Oh my dear Umiat, I'm sorry!' cried Alatna. 'You should never have tried to rescue me! Now look! I've brought death and disaster on both of us!' They held each other tight and tried to remember the happiness of their time together in the village. They thought of the little girl next door and so of the old lady who had lent Umiat the running stick . . .

'*And its name is October!*' cried Umiat, remembering all of a sudden the old woman's last words to him.

Just as the floodwater lapped in at the mouth of the cave, into its menacing, swirling depths, Umiat threw the magic stick with a cry of, 'October!'

In the second that it hit the river, the stick brought to it the month of October – that very day, that very moment in October when the rivers slow and gel throughout the arctic wilderness; when they slow and gel and fleck with silver, thicken and curdle and freeze.

Eagling, submerged up to his chin in the rising river, wings outstretched, was trapped in the freezing water as surely as a fly in amber. Umiat and Alatna stepped out on to the ice and crossed gingerly to the other side, pausing only to pull one feather defiantly from the bird-man's head.

Within the day, they came in sight of the village. And there the old lady and the little girl stood, waiting and waving.

'I'm sorry! I have lost your magic stick, Grandma!' Umiat called as soon as they were close enough to be heard.

'But you have found your heart's desire, I see,' she replied. Then, watching Alatna and the little girl hug and kiss and laugh for joy, she said, 'I think we've all found our heart's desire today!'

Sun's Son

A MYTH FROM TONGA

'Who's your father? Can't you say?
Where's your father? Gone away?'

OVER AND OVER the other children chanted it, until Tau burst into tears and ran home to his mother. 'Who is my father? I must have a father! Tell me who he is!'

His mother dried his tears. 'Take no notice. Your father loves us both dearly, even though he can't live with us, here.'

'Why? Why can't he? Is he dead?' His mother only laughed at that. 'Who *is* he? You must tell me! I have a right to know!' On and on Tau nagged until at last his mother gave in and whispered in his ear, 'You are the son of the Sun, my boy. He saw me on the beach one day, loved me, shone on me, and you were born.'

She should never have told him. Tau's eyes lit up with an inner sunlight, and he bared his teeth in a savage grin. 'I always knew I was better than those other boys. I never liked them, common little worms. Well, now I've done with them. Now I'll go and find my father and see what *he* has in mind for me!'

His mother wept and pleaded with him, but Tau considered himself too splendid now to listen. Pushing a canoe into the sea, he paddled towards the horizon and the Sun's rising place. 'Tell your father I still love him!' his mother called.

As the Sun came up, Tau shouted into his face, *'Father!'*

'Who calls me that?'

'I! Tau! Your son! I've come to find you and be with you!'

'You can't live with me, child! My travelling has no end. I have always to light the islands and the oceans!'

'Then at least stay and talk to me now!' called Tau.

And the Sun was so moved to see his human son, that he actually drew the clouds round him and paused for a brief time over the drifting canoe. 'I suppose you will become a great chief on Tongatabu when you grow up,' said the Sun proudly.

'Stay on Tongatabu?' sneered Tau. 'Among all those common people? Not me! I want to ride the sky with you each day!'

'I regret, you cannot,' said the Sun. 'But you are lucky. There's nowhere lovelier than Tongatabu and no one sweeter than your mother . . . I must go now. The world expects it of me.'

'Is that all you can say?' retorted Tau resentfully. 'Is that all it's worth, to be the son of the Sun?'

The Sun was rising from the ocean now, shedding his disguise of cloud, shining brighter, and brighter, hurrying to make up time. 'Tonight my sister the Moon will rise in the sky. She will offer you the choice of two presents. One is brotherhood, the other glory. Choose brotherhood, my son! For my sake and for your dear mother: choose brotherhood! It will make you happy!' His booming voice receded to the bronze clashing of a gong, as the Sun reached his zenith in the noon sky.

'Brotherhood, pah! He wants me to be like all those others,' said Tau aloud to himself. 'He wants me to forget who I really am and be mediocre, like the rest. He doesn't want me. He doesn't care one coconut about me.' Full of self-pity, Tau curled up and went to sleep in the bottom of the canoe.

He was woken by a piercing white whistle which made him sit bolt upright. There in the sky, like a mother's face looming over a cradle, the Moon his aunt looked down on him. 'Have you come to give me my present?' he asked rudely.

She scowled at him. 'Who do you take after? It isn't your mother and it certainly isn't your father. But yes, I have a present for you. Tell me, which do you want?'

Hanging down from her horns, like the pans of a pair of scales, hung two identical packages. Neither was big and neither was recognizable for what it was. 'This is glory, and this is brotherhood,' said the Moon.

'Give me glory!' barked Tau.

'Think, nephew. One of these gifts will do you good, one will bring you harm. Please choose carefully!'

'I told you already!' said Tau. 'I know what my father wants: he wants to forget all about me. He wants me to go back home and forget who I really am – prince of the sky! He's afraid that if I take glory I'll be greater than him – burn him out of the sky. That's what. Give me glory! Give it now!'

She reached out the other package – brotherhood – but he paddled his canoe directly into her round silver reflection on the sea's surface, and scratched it, so that in pain she let drop her other hand. Snatching the parcel called 'glory', Tau hugged it to his chest.

He ripped off the wrappings and there, as beautiful as anything he had ever seen, was a seashell round and red and luminous as a setting sun. 'Now I shall be a god,' said Tau. 'Now I shall be worshipped instead of doing the worshipping. Now everyone on Tongabatu will bow down and worship *me!*'

But first the fish came to worship Tau.

Startled by a sudden rushing noise, he looked up and saw the surface of the ocean bubbling and churning, as every fish for miles around came shoaling towards the magic of the red shell. Dolphins and flying fish leapt clean over the canoe. Sharks and tunny herded close, rubbing their sharp scales against the boat in ecstasies of adoration. The spike of a marlin holed the boat. The fluke of a whale struck the sea and showered Tau in spray. Shoals of tiny, glimmering fish sped the frail vessel along on a carpet of colour, while ray flapped darkly out of the water to trail their wings over the canoe's nose.

'No! Get away! You'll drag it under! Get off the canoe!'

But the fish were in a frenzy of worship, entranced by the glory Tau held clenched in one hand. The canoe was swamped in seconds and plummeted down from under him. And although Tau was carried along for a time, on the writhing ecstasy of the fish, as soon as the red shell slipped from his hand, they let him go, let him sink. Thanks to the shark, his body was never found: he who would have been elected Chief of Tongabatu, if only he had valued his fellow men. If only he had chosen brotherhood.

Biggest

A JAPANESE LEGEND

WHEN THE PEOPLE of Kamakura decided to cast a statue of the Buddha, their love for him was so enormous that the finished masterpiece was the biggest in the world. Cast in gleaming bronze, it caught the sun's light like the burnished waves of the evening sea – until, that is, a temple was built to house it, a temple rising almost to the sky. The statue towered over the people who had made it, and they were full of wonder, for they were sure they had never cast the look of calm and kindness on the huge bronze face. News spread through the whole world that the Buddha of Kamakura was the biggest, the loveliest, the most wonderful thing under the heavens.

When word reached the Whale, the Whale said, 'Nonsense!' It shook so hard with scornful laughter that waves slopped against fifteen shores. But on every one of those shores, fishermen mending their nets were busy talking to each other about the wonder at Kamakura: '. . . It's the biggest, the loveliest, the most wonderful thing under the heavens, you know . . .'

'But *I* am the biggest, the loveliest, the most wonderful creature under the heavens,' said the vain creature. 'That's how I know these stories cannot be true!'

Still, the rumours played on his mind, until he could bear it no longer. With a whistle, he summoned his friend the Shark and asked him, 'Can there be any truth in these stories?'

'I'll find out,' said the Shark, and swam to the shore of the ocean at Kamakura. From the water's edge she could see the new temple rising almost to the sky. 'That must house the Buddha,' she thought. 'Big! But how big! And how can I find out? I can't swim up the beach or swing from tree to tree.'

Just as she was about to give up, a small rat came scuttling by with a fishhead in its jaws. 'Sir! Would you do me the very great favour of going up to that temple over there and measuring the statue inside it?'

'The Buddha?' said the rat. 'Certainly! It's always a pleasure to go there. It is the biggest, loveliest, most marvellous thing under the heavens, you know.' Away trotted the rat, up the hill, in under the temple door, and round the base of the statue.

Five thousand paces! The Shark shook and shivered at the sheer sound of the words. Five thousand paces? What would the Whale say?

'*Five thousand paces?* From where to where? From nose to tail? From stem to stern? Whose paces, and how long is their stride? Believe the word of a rat? Never!' That was what the Whale said.

But though he tried to ignore the news, he could not put it out of his mind.

'There's nothing for it,' he said at last. 'I'll just have to go and see this pipsqueak for myself.'

And so he took down from the Continental Shelf his magical boots, and put them on.

The tides rose high that night. Rivers flowed upstream, waves broke with such a surge that seaweed was left hanging in the trees. Moonlit meadows were flooded with saltwater, when the Whale waded ashore that night, in his magic boots. Dripping and glistening, he rolled his blubbery way up the hill and slapped with one fin on the great carved temple doors.

The priests were all sleeping, so no one heard him knock. No one, that is, but the Buddha, dully luminous in the candlelit dark. The candle flames trembled, as a voice like distant thunder said, '*Come in!*'

'I can't come in,' said the Whale. 'I am too vast, too huge, too magnificent to cram myself into this little kennel!'

'Very well, then, I shall come out,' said the Buddha mildly, and by bending very low, he was just able to squeeze through the temple doors. As he straightened up again, the Whale blinked his tiny eyes with shock. The Buddha, too, stared with wonder at the sight of a Whale in magic boots.

The noise of the temple gongs vibrating woke a priest. Glancing towards the Buddha's bronze pedestal he saw, to his horror, that the statue, the precious wonderful, adored statue, was gone! Had thieves come in the night! Had the Buddha sickened of so many curious visitors? The priest ran shouting out of the temple. 'Help! Quick! The Buddha is . . . is . . .'

There, eclipsing the moon, stood two gigantic figures, deep in conversation amid a strong fishy smell.

'The very person we need!' said the Buddha, spotting the priest. 'Perhaps you would be so kind, sir, as to settle a small query for this excellent cetacean? Could you please measure us both?'

The priest fumbled about him for something, anything he could use for measuring. Untying his belt, he used that. One . . . two . . . three . . . scribbling his measurements in the soft ground with a stick.

When he had finished, the priest fretted and fluttered, he stuttered and stammered: 'I sincerely regret . . . I'm dreadfully sorry . . . I can't lie, you see, I have to tell the truth, your divinity . . . but the Whale is two inches bigger than you.'

'Knew it!' The Whale whirled round in his magic boots, shaking the ground, setting all the temple bells jangling in the breeze he made as he blew out triumphantly through his blow-hole. 'I knew it! I knew I was the biggest, grandest, most marvellous creature beneath the heavens! Never doubted it for a moment!' And away he strode, leaving a smell of fish in the air and large, deep bootprints in the ground.

'Oh master, are you very distressed?' the priest asked of the statue. 'We could fetch more bronze and make your feet thicker, your forehead higher!'

The Buddha smiled a peaceable smile, utterly unconcerned by the night's events. 'It means nothing to me and much to him that he should be the biggest. Think nothing of it. I am very content to be as I am. Please don't lose another moment's sleep over it.'

The priest mopped his brow and crept back inside the temple. A handful of peaceful words followed him, fragrant with the scent of the blossoms outside.

'Besides . . . the Whale has still to take off his boots.'

'I Love You, Prime Minister!'

A FRENCH LEGEND

THE EMPEROR CHARLEMAGNE conquered the world . . . then was conquered himself by a woman. He fell in love with Princess Frastrada from the easternmost regions of his vast Empire, and such was his passion for her, his adoration, that Prime Minister Turpin always suspected some magic at the bottom of it.

Frastrada was beautiful, gentle and good, but was she so far above every other woman, that Charlemagne the Mighty gazed at her all day long, could not bear to be apart from her, took her on every campaign, and invited her to every conference of state? Turpin had his doubts.

When Frastrada died, he was certain. Somehow she had cast a spell over Charlemagne, and the magic did not even end with her death. Now the Emperor sat by her body, rocking and groaning, cradling Frastrada in his arms and wetting her cold face with his tears. All government was forgotten, all affairs of state let go. He would not eat or drink, nor leave the room where her body lay; would not permit the Princess to be buried.

The Prime Minister could not let this unhealthy state of affairs go on. So when at last the distracted Emperor fell asleep across the bed, exhausted with crying, Turpin tiptoed in and began to search. He did not know what he was looking for – what charm, what amulet, what magic hieroglyph – but he searched all the same, until just before dawn, he glimpsed something in the dead Princess's mouth.

Poor Frastrada. Her love for Charlemagne had been so desperate, that she had begged her eastern men of magic for a charm: something which would ensure her all-powerful husband never tired of her. They forged her a magic ring. Growing ill, realizing she was about to die, Frastrada looked at the ring on her hand and wondered what would become of it. Would another woman wear it and be loved by Charlemagne as much as Frastrada had been loved? No! The thought was unbearable. So, in the hope of remaining the one true love of Charlemagne's life, she slipped the ring into her mouth just as Death stole her last breath.

'Who's there? Frastrada? What—' Charlemagne was stirring.

Turpin, sooner than be found robbing the dead Empress, slipped the ring on to his own finger just as his master sat up, fuddled with sleep. Charlemagne opened his eyes and saw his . . .

'Dearest Prime Minister!'

'Good morning, my lord.'

'How wonderful to see you! I'd forgotten how very handsome you are. What, hasn't this woman been buried yet? How remiss. Oh, Prime Minister! Oh dear, *dear* Prime Minister, may I just say what a comfort it is, at a time like this, to have a man like you by me I can rely on.' And flinging both arms round Turpin, Charlemagne dragged him away to breakfast.

Inwardly Turpin crowed with delight. He had saved the Emperor from dying of grief, and therefore saved the Empire from crumbling into chaos. Besides, all Turpin's advice would now sound as sweet as poetry in Charlemagne's ears. He got permission for his favourite road building schemes, he got laws passed, he got posts at the palace for all his friends and relations . . . not to mention the presents – horses, chariots, a few small countries . . . All because he was wearing the magic ring.

Even so, after a time Turpin began to wish that perhaps the ring were not *quite* so powerful. Just when he wanted some peace and quiet, the Emperor always wanted to talk, to hold hands, to listen to music with his dear Prime Minister. On campaign, Turpin had to sleep in the Emperor's tent. And the generals in the army, the princes, the kings of minor provinces gave him very odd looks as Charlemagne stroked his hair and bounced Turpin on his knee. Turpin's wife was put out, as well.

In fact, Turpin began to be extremely sorry he had ever put on the ring. But how could he be rid of it? Give it to someone else? No! That someone would be ruling the Empire before long, whispering new policies in the Emperor's ear and being given all the privileges of a . . . well . . . a prime minister.

Could he bury it? What if Charlemagne became rooted to the spot where the ring was buried, fell passionately in love with a garden bed or half a metre of desert sand? What if Turpin were to drop it in the sea? Would Charlemagne hurl himself into a watery grave?

Turpin examined the ring with utmost care. Around the inside was engraved an inscription: 'From the moon came my magic; in the moon my magic ends.' Had the ring fallen from the moon, then? Oh no! How could a mere prime minister return it there? Night after night, Turpin walked sleepless around palace or camp, turning the problem over in his mind.

One moony night, when the imperial army was camped in a forest, Turpin crept from the Emperor's tent, desperate for a little solitude. He wandered among the trees, a broken man. He simply could not stomach one more poem composed to the beauty of his nose, one more statue of him raised in a public place, one more candlelit supper where Charlemagne gazed at him – 'How I love you, Prime Minister!' – all through the meal. Enough was enough. Turpin resolved to run away.

But just then, he found himself beside a lake. It was large and smooth, with a reflection of the moon floating at its heart. Impetuously Turpin pulled off the ring. A little smudge of gold flew over the water. A small splash at the centre of the moon's reflection set ripples spreading. The ring was gone for ever.

Dawn came up while Turpin walked back to the Emperor's tent. As he lifted the flap, the sunlight fell across Charlemagne's face and roused him.

'Yes, Turpin?' said the great man, raising himself on one elbow. '*Must* you bring me problems of state quite so early in the morning? What is it?'

Turpin bowed low respectfully and backed out, letting the tent flap fall. 'Nothing, my lord. Nothing that cannot wait.'

Outside, Turpin gave a little skip and a hop. The spell was broken. He was a free man, a happy man – apart from the explaining he had to do to his wife.

The army struck camp, the Emperor mounted up, and a thousand banners fluttered on their way through the forest. Within the hour, they came to the lake. 'Stop!' cried Charlemagne. Turpin chewed anxiously on his glove. The Emperor gazed about him, one hand over his heart, smiling open-mouthed with wonder. 'I've never seen anywhere like it! What do you say, Turpin? Isn't this the loveliest spot you ever saw?'

'Magical, my lord.'

His knights and courtiers looked about him, puzzled. Pretty, yes, but a tree is a tree and a lake is a lake. But Charlemagne, not realizing that the drowned ring was still working its magic, found the forest clearing too ravishingly beautiful for words. He could not tear himself away. All day long he strolled its shores, picked flowers from its banks.

'I shall build a palace here, my greatest palace, my home. One day, when the world is all mine, I'll live here, I'll be happy here. If only Frastrada could have seen this place . . .'

True to his word, Charlemagne did build a palace in the forest, beside the lake, and whenever war and politics permitted, he lived there. A little town grew up around the palace – Aix-la-Chapelle it was called – and wherever Charlemagne travelled, however far afield, he never could quite put Aix from his mind. No more than he could ever quite forget his dear dead wife, Frastrada.

And the Rains Came Tumbling Down

A MYTH FROM PAPUA NEW GUINEA

'WHAT WE NEED are houses,' said Kikori.

'What's one of those?' said Fly (since houses had not yet been invented).

'Somewhere to shelter from wind and sun and rain – other than this cave, I mean, with its spiders.'

Fly pretended to be unimpressed, but liked the idea. Kikori suggested they build a house together, but Fly had ideas of his own about building the very first house and he was sure they were the best.

Kikori built a wood frame, then wove the leaves of the rei plant into five glossy waterproof mats: one for a roof and four for the walls. It was laborious, painful work. The sharp leaves cut his hands and irritated his skin, but the finished house was so fine that his family broke into spontaneous clapping.

Not Fly. He had long since finished his house and returned to watch, with much shaking of his head and carping. 'How long you took! Look at your hands. Makes me itch just to think. And it's *green*. Do you seriously think people want to live in green houses?'

'How did you make yours, then?' said Kikori patiently.

Kikori examined Fly's house, his head on one side then on the other. Fly's framework of branches had been daubed all over with mud. The mud had dried into clay, and now the hut crouched on the ground like a collapsed beast, boney with protruding sticks.

'What happens when it rains?' said Kikori.

At that moment, a clap of thunder sent them both darting back to their huts, mustering their wives and children. The monsoon broke as if the green sky had split, and the rains came, as they come every year to Papua New Guinea. Every view was lost from sight behind a curtain of rain. Every sound was silenced by the deafening hiss of the downpour.

Inside Kikori's house, he and his family sat listening to the thunderous rattle of water on rei. But the interwoven leaves threw off the rain as surely as a tortoise's shell, and they stayed warm and dry. They sang songs and planned which crops to plant in the sodden earth.

Fly, too, sat with his family inside his new house. The rain ran down its brown sides, and gradually the clay walls turned back to mud around them. The mud oozed and trickled. It slopped down like cow pats on to Fly and his wife and children, smothering them from head to foot in brown slurry.

But not for long. Soon so much icy rain was pouring through the roof that they were washed quite clean again. The children's teeth chattered, his wife moaned gently to herself, ground her teeth and wrung out her hair. When the rain slackened briefly, she went out with a panga and cut a great pile of rei leaves, dropping them down at the door.

'When you've made a house like Kikori's,' she said, 'I and the little ones will come and share it with you. In the meantime, we're going back to the cave.'

Fly, as he sat ankle-deep in mud, contemplated the unfairness of life and whether he ought to invent dry rain.

Four Worlds and
a Broken Stone

A NATIVE AMERICAN MYTH

THE PEOPLE OF Peace will tell you that three worlds existed before this one, and before that a Nothingness flowing from never to ever.

Taiowa, though invisible himself and without form, pictured a solid universe. So he created a creator – Sotuknang – to be its architect. Sotuknang shaped the First World, called Endless Space, and into it, down a thread as fine as one of his own hairs, dropped Spider Woman, fat with the eggs of magic. Those eggs hatched into the very first people.

If you met them, of course, you would hardly recognize them as kin. There is not much of a family resemblance. For they, those most ancient of our ancestors, never grew old, never spoke, and never hunted the animals with whom they shared Endless Space. Also, they had no tops to their heads. Taiowa was able to drop wisdom into their minds like golden honey off a spoon. No learning by their mistakes, no puzzling or studying, no struggling with the meaning of things. Understanding came to them as sweetly as honey, and in among it were the seeds of language.

After a while, the People of Endless Space were muttering to one another, passing comment on the world around them. The animals, alarmed by this new secret, tried to speak themselves. But beaks and muzzles and snouts are not made for more than calling a mate, warning of danger. Noticing the difference between them, the animals drew away, hid among the trees and down burrows, thinking, 'They are ganging up against us.'

Far from it. The People of Endless Space no sooner had language than they began to quarrel – to lie, to boast, to curse and shout insults. Some drew away from the rest, hoarding their treasure of words like money they begrudged spending.

Sotuknang was disgusted. Like a blacksmith who throws bad work back on to the forge, he lit a fire under that world called Endless Space, and burned it to the ground.

The people saw the flicker of fire, and there was sweet wisdom enough in their heads for them to observe the animals, and learn from them. When they saw the ants run underground, the people followed, sheltering deep under the earth from the inferno. When they emerged, a Second World had been built: a world called Dark Midnight. It was gloomy and a little scary. At either end – at North Pole and South – sat giant brothers, steadying the globular world.

Living underground had forced shut the people's open-topped heads somewhat, so now they found it harder to understand what the gods wanted them to do. Still, one or two things they did invent which Sotuknang had never even thought of. For example, instead of sharing everything, they *sold* what they had for money, or exchanged it for goods. 'What do you mean, you can't afford it?' they would say. 'Nothing comes for free in this life!' They began to haggle, to cheat one another, to steal what they could not afford. Soon the streets of the world were full of people crying their wares.

They sold food to the animals and sold the animals to each other. They sold the land they stood on and the water in the rivers. In the world called Dark Midnight, they sold candles to one another, and complained that times had been better once, in the world of Endless Space.

'Enough!' said Sotuknang. 'Twin of the North! Twin of the South! Leave your places! The mind of God requires *Change!*'

Twice the earth rolled over, as the Twins let go of its axletree. The round world was as shaken as a pebble in the surf. Oceans slopped over the dry land. Cargo ships far out to sea were picked up and dashed down on market-places miles inland. The deserts drowned, and with them the scaly salamanders and crackling locusts. Fresh-water rivers were lost in a saltwater surge, and with them the herons and the turtles.

But the people – some of them at least – had the wit to follow the ants below ground again. And the sea had no sooner withdrawn than out they crawled to inspect the Third World left by the tidal waves: Kuskuara.

Ideal building land. They shaped adobe, they made mud bricks, they cut stone blocks and cut down timber. They built cities in wood and stone and brick and clay, with houses and temples, meeting halls and silos. Before long, someone said:

'Our city is better than your city.'

'Our land stretches to the horizon!'

Banners declared: 'Trespassers will be stoned. Keep out.'

Generals proclaimed: 'We must fight for what we believe in!'

The people answered: 'WAR!'

From the bones of trees and the feathers of birds, they built flying machines, and swooped over rival cities showering them with rocks and pitch. Their enemies built newer flying machines to do combat in mid-air with the bomber flying machines, and when flying machines crashed on to the crowded cities, ran with buckets to put out the fires.

At last there were so many fires that only Sotuknang could put them out. His tears swelled the oceans until the oceans joined hands and bled one into another. Whole cities, whole city-realms drowned – even the ants beneath them. Whole continents softened into mud and slid away, and with them the shape and existence of Kuskuara.

But the people – some of them at least – had had the wit to climb into hollow reeds and float away on the rising water. Bobbing about over acres of ocean, the survivors of Kuskuara kept a lookout for land. But there was no land left. Seagulls perched on the reeds and, riding out the flood alongside them, flew in search of dry land. But they came winging back, beaks outstretched, sagging wearily into the wave troughs, exhausted for want of solid ground to rest on.

'Peace, peace,' said Spider Woman. 'I who saw Endless Space and Dark Midnight, who saw Kuskuara come and Kuskuara go, shall live to see more worlds yet. For if the mind of Taiowa wishes a world to exist, then he won't rest till he has succeeded.'

She was right, of course. One morning they looked out across the oceans and saw land. The Fourth World had come into being: World Complete.

Standing on the shore was a gigantic man – huge, terrifying, his eyes alight with visions he was seeing in his head, and in his hands a hammer and chisel such as sculptors use to carve rock.

'Come ashore!' he told them. 'I am Masaw, Guardian of the World Complete. Come ashore! I have things to tell you.'

Masaw had dreamed dreams. Though the top of his head was closed, the gods had found surer ways of imparting wisdom to this wise giant. He took them inland to a place called Four Corners – a desert landscape planted with towers of dark rock. On one such mesa, Masaw had carved the story of his dreams. The people threw down their bundles of belongings and began to scrape together the dirt for building homesteads.

'No!' said Masaw. 'Not yet! You are not yet fit to settle in the Complete World! You have truths to learn, wonders to see, problems to solve.' Picking up a large flat stone, he broke it, as easily as a biscuit, into four equal parts. Then he parted the people into four groups according to the colour of their skins – red, yellow, white and black – and gave each group one fragment of the stone. To North, South, East and West he sent them, far and wide over the face of the Complete World. 'Come back when you have done journeying and meanwhile remember just one thing.'

'What must we remember?' asked everyone, eager to obey.

'Never to forget,' replied Masaw.

First to come home were the red tribe. Long before the continental plates bumped and groaned into their present positions, the red tribe were back, building their villages around the Black Mesa, calling themselves the Hopi, which means 'Peace'. They read Masaw's carvings now and trembled: his dream carvings spoke of unspeakable terrors to come. But what, and why?

When the white tribe came back, they had forgotten everything – their piece of stone, the words of Masaw, their narrow escape from fire and flood. They did not recognize the red tribe as their brothers – nor the yellow, nor the black. In fact, they came home armed with guns and swords and firebrands, ready to fight or kill or capture anyone who stood in their way. They peered at the Black Mesa with eyes as blind as drunkards, seeing only a jumble of words and pictures, understanding nothing.

'See here?' said the Hopi gently, 'this bowl of ashes falling out of the sky? One day it will scorch the dry land and set the oceans boiling! The future is written here on this rockface.'

But the white tribe could only see scribbles and scrawls.

Now, luckily, it is your turn. Look closer. See that blue star drawn on the Black Mesa? One night, when the Fourth World has burned down, wick and wax, and left only a puff of smoke behind, the time will have come for a Fifth World, a final world, just as Taiowa intended, just as Sokutnang wished, just as Masaw dreamed, just as the People of Peace long for. See that blue star? Watch for it. Everything else has happened just as Masaw said it would. So watch out for the blue star rising.

The Needlework Teacher and the Secret Baby

A EUROPEAN LEGEND

WHEN ANZIUS WAS Emperor of Constantinople, a certain Prince Hugh, of the royal house of Ameling, came to manhood. His father was dead; it was time for Hugh to take up his rightful position as king. But he had no sooner grown *up* than he began to grow his hair *down*. He sent for a seamstress and had dresses made. He also took up embroidery. What his family and friends thought, who knows?

Now when Hugh set his mind to a thing, he never gave up. So soon there was no finer 'needlewoman' in all Europe than Prince Hugh of the long-flowing hair and longer frocks.

He had his reasons, of course. Hugh had heard tell of a princess – Princess Hilde – most beautiful, most intelligent, and most wronged of women. For her father had sworn she should never marry, and had shut her away in a tower, out of reach of ambitious men like Hugh. Nothing but rumours about her escaped that tower-palace, like bees escaping a hive.

It was not done out of cruelty. Her father Walgund loved his daughter. Perhaps he loved her too much to share her. Perhaps he thought his brick-built tower and brass locks could keep out Death. For in those days, Death roamed as free and common as the wolves in the great green forests.

Hugh set his heart on having the mysterious princess for his wife. So he travelled to Walgund's realm of Thessaly and, putting on his

156

prettiest dress, presented himself at Walgund's castle with gifts of gold and embroidered linen. He said he was a refugee – a noble-woman orphaned by war, without a friend in the world.

Walgund was a chivalrous man; he could hardly turn the noble-woman away (even if she did make him uneasy, standing three spans taller than he). Besides, his wife had seen the lady's embroidery. 'Oh, such artistry! You simply must teach our daughter Hilde how to sew like this!' she said.

Hugh did.

Princess Hilde took a liking to her needlework teacher which startled even her. Perhaps it was that deep, rich voice, or the strength of those big hands guiding Hilde's fingers over the canvas. Or was it the unusual *smell* of that long coarse yellow hair? Within days, they were the best of friends.

So Hugh taught Hilde his best secret of all. 'I have to admit, I'm not quite what I seem . . .' he whispered, grasping her hand and laying it against the roughness of his unshaven cheek.

The weeks which followed were blissfully happy. Hilde secretly married her needlework teacher, and they spent all day together inside the grim High Tower. Then one day Hugh said, 'I must go home now and tell my ministers that I've found the perfect wife to be my queen. Then I must find some way to persuade your father to bless our marriage. Trust me: I'll be back before you even miss me!' And he cut his long hair and left a hank of it in her trembling fingers. He exchanged his dress for a shirt and trousers he had sewn himself, and slipped away from Thessaly and the High Tower.

But Hugh did not come back in days or even weeks. Though Hilde sighed sighs and wept tears and yearned with all her heart, he did not come. Even nine months later, as she secretly gave birth to a baby in the loneliness of her stone prison, there was no sign of Prince Hugh, though she never lost faith in his promise and her love never wavered.

Naturally she could not keep such a secret all by herself. She told Joan, her most loyal and trusted waiting woman, who came and went with rattles and shawls and washing, and a broad smile on her lips. When the Queen made her daily visit to the High Tower to see her daughter, Joan would smuggle the baby away and hide him, so there was no risk of the Queen hearing him cry. Together Joan and Hilde kept secret the very existence of the baby boy. 'What shall you call him, lady?' asked Joan.

'His father can name him when he returns,' said the Princess, for she never gave up hope that Hugh would come back and claim her for his queen.

So where was Hugh? What business of state could possibly keep him so long from the beautiful Hilde? Nothing but war – a dire and deadly war, which spread like plague sores over the whole body of Europe. Soon even King Walgund was riding out to do battle with the enemy, and in the course of the war, found himself fighting side by side with Prince Hugh.

The war ended. Weary and scarred, but triumphant, a dozen armies turned for home. Peace settled like summer dust over the hills and shores of Thessaly. Hugh travelled home with Walgund. A thousand times he had it in his mind to say, 'I love your daughter. Take me for your son-in-law.' But the time never seemed quite right.

Hilde woke with a start to hear running footsteps on the stairs. 'Joan! Joan, quick! Someone's coming! Take the baby and hide him!'

They passed in the doorway, Joan and the Queen. The Queen never suspected that the bundle of washing in Joan's arms was really her grandchild.

'Hilde! Hilde! get up. Get dressed. Wonderful news! Your father has sent word: he's coming home today! He has friends with him. There'll be banqueting tonight; help me prepare. Think of it, child! The war's over!'

Down the stairs hurried the old nurse, and out at the postern gate. She waded downhill into the deep grass beside the castle moat, and there she laid down the sleeping baby. 'Sleep a while longer, little darling. I'll come back for you in two chimes of the church bell.'

But on the stairs, she met the Queen coming down, and the Queen had things for Joan to do. 'Wash the royal bedlinen and sharpen the King's razor. Mull him some ale, and strew fresh herbs on the floor of the Great Hall. Then go and tell the poultryman to kill some geese for dinner – oh, and gather may branches to decorate the castle.' In fact, she kept the old nurse busy till long after midday.

The very first moment she could, Joan slipped out of the postern gate and down towards the moat. She was worried sick about the baby – big enough to crawl, to cram poisonous berries into his mouth, to grab at wasps. She parted the grass. She parted it again. She stood and listened to the flies hatching on the surface of the moat. But there was neither sight nor sound of the baby, no trail nor trace. It was as if he had never been born. In the distance, the great dark forest seemed to raise its branches in anguish and rend its green hair.

As Walgund rode through the forest, he breathed deep the familiar smells of home. He could just glimpse the tip of the tower he had built to house his beloved Hilde.

'If you ever have a daughter, Prince Hugh, take my advice and lock her in above five storeys of stone and behind seventeen doors of oak. Have her taught needlework and music and solitaire. Then she can't break your heart or her own.'

'She might die of boredom,' said Hugh under his breath, but King Walgund did not hear: he had just glimpsed the fleeting grey streak of a running wolf, and his sword was already half out of its sheath. Walgund dug in his spurs and his horse leapt forwards.

But the horse's hooves all but trampled the she-wolf's den. Five, six, seven wolfcubs, with teeth like needles and eyes as bright as mercury, rolled and wrestled and yelped in a furry heap, and there in the midst of them, a little boy baby sat snatching at their tails and rubbing his face against their fur, laughing with delight.

'By the saints! What a boy!' whispered Walgund, breathless with amazement. 'What I'd give to have a grandson like that!'

Hugh's heart leapt into his throat. 'How?' he wanted to shout out. *How will you ever have any grandchild at all, unless you let Hilde marry?'*

But just as the words formed on his lips, back came the she-wolf, terrible, murderous, and Hugh did the only thing he could. He leapt out of the saddle and snatched the baby from between the wolf's very jaws.

'Look what we found in the forest, my dear!' called Walgund to his queen as he rode in under the portcullis. 'A wolf child!'

Not only his wife but his daughter came out to see, and yet it was a daughter Walgund scarcely recognized. Her hair was wild and loose, her face white, her eyes swollen from crying.

'She must have missed me a great deal,' thought Walgund.

'She must have thought I was never coming back,' thought Hugh.

Hilde ran towards the men, arms outstretched and shrieking.

'She must have thought I was dead,' thought Walgund.

'She's going to give away our secret!' thought Prince Hugh.

But Hilde ignored both men. She saw only her little boy – the one she had searched for all afternoon, the one she had thought drowned in the moat or eaten by wild beasts. Pulling him out of Hugh's arms, she covered him with kisses, laughing and crying both at once. The Queen stared. Walgund stared. Hugh stared. But Joan just smiled.

When everything was explained to Walgund, he brooded a long time before he spoke. 'A man may look to his children for obedience,' he said at last, 'but he'll be disappointed. A man may look to his children for surprises: they're guaranteed. A man can ask his daughter to live without love . . . But then how can she give him a splendid grandson like this? Let his name be Wolf! . . . that's if you agree, Prince Hugh.'

'His name shall be Wolf,' said Prince Hugh, 'if mine can be "son-in-law".'

'Then I've gained a son and a grandson, all in one day!' exclaimed Walgund. 'And there aren't two boys in all Christendom I would be more proud to come by!'

Culloch and the Big Pig
A CELTIC LEGEND

ULLOCH WAS CURSED with the curse of Love. His wicked stepmother doomed him, out of magic spite, to love Olwen, daughter of Ysbaddaden. And the curse was no sooner spoken than Culloch fell madly in love – even though he knew neither the colour of Olwen's eyes nor the features of her face. For all he knew, she might take after her giant father and stand head-high to the hills.

'Giant' is not a big enough word to describe Ysbaddaden, for he never sat in one room of his castle but he filled three – one with his head, one with his body and one with his legs. His hair, all unkempt and uncombed, filled a fourth.

As Culloch rode up to the castle, he was greeted by Olwen herself – a comely girl, scarcely two-storeys tall. Cramming her plaits into her mouth in anxiety, she pleaded, 'Turn back! Turn back! No one has ever asked for my hand and lived! For on the day that I marry, it is prophesied my father shall die!'

Pausing only a moment to gaze into Olwen's eyes, Culloch went straight inside. He thought, when he first entered, that Ysbaddaden was asleep. But servants came running with two enormous forked sticks with which they propped open the giant's eyelids.

'What do you want and why are you here?' Ysbaddaden asked in a slurred voice, as if his tongue were similarly heavy.

'Your blessing and the hand of your daughter, sir!'

'Didn't you know?' said Ysbaddaden. 'She weds. I'm dead. It's written in the stars.'

'I'm truly sorry to hear that,' said Culloch. 'But your life seems wearisome to you, anyway, or why do you lie on your face in the straw?'

'I only lie on my face because my hair hangs so heavy. Come back tomorrow, and you shall have my answer.'

Culloch felt he could spare one day, and turned to go. But Ysbaddaden snatched up a sharpened wooden spear, and threw it at Culloch's unprotected back. Cunning Culloch spun round, snatched the spear out of the air and threw it back the way it had come. It struck Ysbaddaden on the knee – 'Ouch!' – but Culloch said nothing, simply walked out into the yard.

When he returned next day, Ysbaddaden had thought up a string of excuses. 'I'm busy. I'm not well. I never see visitors on any day with a T in it. Come back tomorrow.' As Culloch turned to go, the giant threw another spear. This time its point was smeared thick with poison that spattered and scorched the floor as it flew. Culloch caught the spear, spun it round one finger and flung it back the way it had come. It stuck Ysbaddaden in the hand – 'Argh!' – and his groans followed Culloch out of the castle.

Next day, Ysbaddaden, swathed in bandages, began to make more excuses. 'The stars are not favourable. I never liked Wednesdays . . .' but Culloch interrupted him.

'I think we should discuss terms, before you get hurt any more. What must I do to win your daughter? Name it!'

'Very well,' said Ysbaddaden. 'Fetch me the means to cut my hair.'

'That's simple! I'll borrow my cousin Arthur's sword, Excalibur!' said Culloch at once.

But Ysbaddaden shook his fearful head, and set his hair tumbling through all the chambers and anterooms of his castle, lively with lice. 'My hair can only be cut with the magic comb and shears of the Great Pig Troit. Fetch them, and Olwen is yours!' And he smiled at the thought of a task so plainly impossible.

'Now *that* is a quest befitting the Knights of the Round Table!' declared King Arthur, as his young cousin knelt before him in the throne room of Camelot. 'We shall help you, Culloch, and you shall have your bride!'

Arthur and his knights rode with Culloch to the far coast of Wales.

When the Great Pig Troit saw the brightness of their armour, saw the boar-spears in their hands, he sharpened his tusks and pawed the ground. 'You may have found me,' said the Boar, 'but now you have to catch me!'

Twrch Troit was no ordinary boar, nor had he always been one. Once he had been a king. But his nature was so evil and his sins so many that they had pushed their way out through his skin – at first like black stubble at his chin, then as thick black bristles all over his body. His dog-teeth had grown into tusks, and his crimes had weighed him down, till he could only move on all fours: a man transmogrified into a boar. It was not hard to find him, for he left a trail behind him of crumpled trees, of houses stove in, of gored hillsides and trampled flour mills.

Now Troit ran down the coastline of Dyfed, past Blaenplwyf and Cei-bach beach, across Ynys-Lochtyn point towards Strumble Head, then inland among the Preseli Hills. Up the watercourses of Taf and Cynin and down the valleys of Tywi, into the Black Mountain crags he ran. Past Castle Cennen they chased that Big Pig, and over the Brecon hills where Troit paused for breath.

'Hold, Troit! We mean to have those shears and comb from between your ears, but you may keep your golden crown and that ugliness you call your face!' bellowed King Arthur.

'The shears and comb are my treasure!' replied Troit in a snarl strung with saliva. 'Before I part with them, I shall carve you into such shapes your own womenfolk will not recognize you!' And he charged, scattering the knights and leaving the prints of his iron hoofs cut in the Beacons for ever. Then he was off again, darting and dodging through the Vale of Ebbw, across Arthur's own estates of Caerleon.

Beating their spears on their shields and loosing bloodcurdling yells, the Knights of the Round Table barely paused for breath. Though their caparisons were muddy and their cloaks spiked with thorns, though their faces were masked with dust, and their horses mantled with bracken and ivy, they drove the giant boar over flat watermeadows. Ahead lay the River Severn as big as the sea.

Through the shallows, from sandbar to mudbank, the boar staggered until, on the shoals called Middle Ground, he stood at bay, slashing the water to white rags. Grey waves broke against the bristly flank, and the salt-water washed it white. Arthur's knights threw off their heavy armour for fear of drowning. They whirled their long blades, wiped their spray-wet faces with their hair and sinking up to their knees in the wet sand, circled the Boar Troit as if he were the Round Table itself.

Afterwards, no one man took the credit for snatching the golden comb. A great wave spilled Troit off his feet, and the comb tumbled through the water until Arthur's hand snatched it up.

By then, the Great Pig had gone, swimming and snorting, floating and floundering to the far side of the Severn Estuary, on and into Cornwall. Over river and hills and down steep-hedged lanes, the knights of Arthur hunted the Big Pig Troit. The golden shears clanged against his golden crown. The soft Cornish rocks turned to tin under his hooves as he clattered over them.

The knights on foot climbed up behind those on horseback. Arthur's horse was weary and slowing, but his dog Cabel was as fresh as ever, and ran snapping at the Boar's heels, vexing and harrying him with nips of its sharp teeth. In a frenzy, Troit turned and turned until his tusks were a blur of whirling white.

Spurring on his horse to one last effort, and with a sweep of Excalibur, Arthur sheared through the Boar's topknot of matted bristly hair. The golden crown went spinning one way, the shears another, and Troit bolted baldly over the long peninsula and out into the breaking sea.

He swam on. He may be swimming yet, or rootling and ravening about the seabed, creating havoc among the fishes. But once Arthur had in his hand the comb and shears of the Great Pig Troit, he was content to let him go, out of the Realm of Albion.

Wrapping the strange gifts in white cloth, Culloch bore them back to the castle of Ysbaddaden. Culloch held his breath. Olwen shut her eyes and bit her lip. The servants came running with their forked sticks, and propped open the giant's heavy lids.

'Why have you returned with your quest unfulfilled?' Ysbaddaden demanded, peering at Culloch with bloodshot eyes.

'Our quest is complete. I bring the magic comb and shears from between the ears of the Big Pig Troit. Shall I now cut your hair, Ysbaddaden?'

Locks of the tangled, matted, grimy hair fell, with a noise like autumn. Ysbaddaden lifted his chin off the floor – it was easy now – and sadly smiled. With the merest velvety stubble around his temples and jaw, he looked quite boyish. 'You are to be thanked, Culloch. Your stepmother is to be thanked for bringing you here. For what is life if it must be spent face-down in the dirt? What is a wheel if it does not turn? What is life if it does not end and give way to newness of life?'

Ysbaddaden got up, and the crowd of curious knights gathered by his moat watched him, fingers to his eyelids, leave his castle to tour his lands and estates.

'Culloch. You may consider yourself betrothed to my daughter,' he said as he passed. Then he walked away, head-high with the hills, though his back was bent with age.

'Oh, Olwen!' cried Culloch.

'Oh, Culloch!' cried Olwen, and they kissed there and then on the drawbridge.

The great giant, outlined against the sky, brandished his massive club, in sheer jubilation at the beauty of the spring countryside. Then, leaning his back against a hillside, he melted way, leaving only his white outline in the chalky stone, his shape outlined in sweet green grass.

The Call of the Sea

A LEGEND FROM THE CHANNEL ISLANDS

WHEN THE TIDE goes out in Bonuit Bay, it leaves rockpools studded with limpets and starry with sea urchins. Joseph Rolande, after a day's fishing, would often stroll along the beach smoking his pipe and watching sunset tinge the sea red. One evening he found more on the beach than peace and tranquillity. A woman lay up to her waist in one of the rockpools – as though taking a bath, but crying bitterly into hanks of her long salt-spangled hair. At the sight of her, Joseph blushed and turned away, for she was wearing not a stitch of clothing. But she called out in panic: 'Please! Don't go! Help me! I stayed too long! The tide went out and left me stranded here. Carry me down to the sea or I shall die!' As she reached out towards him, he glimpsed the ripple of scales and a huge tail fin.

'Oh, no! Oh, no!' said Joseph, backing away. 'You're a mermaid, and I've heard what mermaids do! I've heard how you'll lure a man down into your own world and drown him there!'

The mermaid covered her face with her hair. The water was trickling out of the pool and little by little her shining tail was being laid bare. 'I'll die if I dry!' she sobbed.

Joseph was a good man. Besides, she was far too beautiful a creature for the world to lose. So lifting her in his arms – she smelled of salt and sea-pinks – he carried her past the third wave where she spilled out of his arms like a codling.

'Thank you!' she cried, swimming around his thighs, her hair brushing his hands. 'Come with me and let my father reward you! He's king of the sea people, and his treasures fill the sea caves.'

'Oh, no! Oh, no!' said Joseph stumbling out of the water. 'I've heard how your kind lure a man to his destruction. Be off, you and your salt-sea magic!'

Something sharp pricked his palm. She had slid the amber comb from her hair and was pressing it into his hand – a gift, a thank-you present. 'If you ever need my help, pass this three times through the water and I will come.' With a thrash of her gleaming tail, she was gone.

Those words were like seeds in his brain which sprouted and grew, taking over his every thought. He walked the beach every evening, looking in the rockpools for stranded mermaids. Instead of forgetting her, the features of her face grew clearer in his mind. Those eyes. That mouth. That beauty. Time and again he found himself, without knowing how, down at the water's edge, searching the waves for a glimpse of mermaid. And when he slept, he dreamed mermaid. The amber comb was always in his head when he woke.

'So that's your magic, is it, woman?' thought Joseph. 'That's how you mean to lure me to my death. Well, I'll not give you the satisfaction!' And he left the fishing, left his seashore cottage, and moved inland to farm a field of kale. He put a mountain between him and the sea.

And yet when the sun shone, it drew up seawater to form the rainclouds which gathered over Joseph's field of kale. It was the sea that rained on his roof.

One night, the rain beat on Joseph's roof like a thousand galloping hooves. A storm worse than anyone could remember rived the sea to a frenzy of leaping waves. It drove a ship on to the Bonuit rocks, and the Bonuit maroons sounded.

Every soul who lived in the bay ran to the shore and peered through the downpour. Rain beat so hard on their faces they could barely lift their lids. Waves heaved themselves up to the height of church steeples, and fell in crashing ruins against the shore. All but one of the little boats lying along the shore was overturned and smashed. The screams of the sailors clinging to the wreckage were all but washed away. 'It's hopeless. No one can get to them,' said the Jerseymen.

'Help me to launch my boat!' shouted a voice behind them. Joseph

Rolande came running down the beach. There was grass on his boots from his run over the hill, but he was dressed once more in his fisherman's clothes.

He and his boat disappeared beyond the mountainous waves into the hellish maelstrom of Bonuit Bay where rocks chew each wave to shreds and wicked currents knot and plait beneath the surface. Only when the lightning flashed could those on shore glimpse the little rowing boat and the pounded wreck with its sad clutch of crew.

The lightning burst and faded; it scorched eyes, it coloured the sea. But surely they could not *all* have been mistaken? There was someone else besides Joseph out there . . . A gigantic fish? A drowning woman?

'You called me with my comb and I came, Joseph. At last you called me!'

'Help me save these men!' he shouted back to the mermaid, his mouth full of rain.

And she did. With all the tenderness of a human woman, she caught up each sailor washed off the wreck, and swam with them to Joseph's boat. Half dead with drowning, half mad with fear, they hardly remembered afterwards how they had escaped death. But many of the seventeen sailors saved that night spoke of a woman holding them in her arms, of a man pulling them aboard laughing as he did so and crying, 'All this time! All this time! What a fool I was!'

As the last sailor slumped like a wet fish into the bottom of Joseph's boat, and he pulled for shore, the mermaid swam alongside, her hair flowery with sea foam. 'All this while I thought you had forgotten me!' she called.

'All this while I thought your kind was wicked – that I mustn't give in to your beauty! Thank you for coming. Thank you for helping!' Joseph shouted above the storm's clamour.

He beached the boat, and the locals crowded round, praising his bravery. But as they helped the rescued sailors up the beach to shelter, they looked back, only to see Joseph pushing his boat once more into the dreadful surf. Had he seen another soul to rescue?

'No! You've done enough! Don't go, Joseph!' they called, but their voices were snatched away by the wind.

Joseph put out to sea and never returned. He did not need to.

Someone was waiting for him beyond the third wave – 'And all this time you were a true friend!' – someone with an amber comb in her hair and in her hand the keys to the Kingdom of Undersea.

The Crystal Pool

A MELANESIAN MYTH

THE SEA WAS not always so big, glazing the globe blue, roaring in the ears of dry land. Believe it or not, the sea was once no more than a single secret saltwater spring where an old woman went to draw water for cooking: it made her vegetables taste good.

Often and often, her two sons, Spy and Pry, saw her go out and come back with a brimming pan. They saw the pan when it was empty, too: rimy with white dust.

'Where do you go to, Mama mine, and where do you fill your cooking pan?' asked Pry, but she would not tell him.

'Let us go with you, Mama mine, and help you carry the pan,' said Spy, but she would not take him: said she knew them both for mischief.

So one day, without asking, they followed her – saw her draw back a cloth, fill her pan and put back the cloth lid.

When she had gone, they crept out. They too pulled back the cloth. There underneath was a small sparkling crystal pool. One stride would have straddled it. Spy cupped his hand, took a taste and pulled a face. Pry tried too: 'Pah!' Nothing but a brackish puddle.

Reflecting the sky, the pool blinked a blue eye. It began to bubble and gurgle, gush and rush. It fountained up between their guilty fingers.

'Oh, Spy, now what have you done?'

'Nothing! It was your idea!'

Water splashed over their feet and went on rising. It swirled round their ankles. Taking fright, they ran in different directions – each still holding a corner of the cloth, so that it tore clean through. They ran, but the water ran faster, curling and coiling into waves, heaping and humping into great glossy swells which swamped the stones, drowned the desert, hid the hills, besieged the mountains. Whole villages were swept away like bird nests. Whole herds and hoards of beasts and birds were rolled off their feet and washed free of their wings and fur.

When the old woman saw the sea coming to submerge the land under sky-high fathoms of salt water, she snapped twigs from a magic tree, hitched her skirt past her knees, and went down to meet it. In a straight line at her feet, she planted the twigs, watering them with magic words.

On came the rolling, smashing, tumbling breakers, crashing into a spray which enveloped the old woman and hid her from sight. But as their foam fringe touched the magic fence, they drew back, sucking the sand, stirring the stones, sinking with a soughing sigh, back, back and back.

The ocean ceased to grow. Though sea now outstretched the land, it never rose beyond those magic twigs. Even now, when the full moon tugs and rucks the seven seas to and fro, to and fro, the twigs do not wash away.

But those two torn strips of sopping cloth dangling from the hands of Spy and Pry can no more cover the ocean now than a butterfly's wings can cover a continent. Nor ever will.

Race to the Top

A MAORI MYTH

IN THE VERY Highest Heaven, Papa Io prepared three presents for the Human Race. He took three baskets and into one put Peace and Love. Into the second he put Songs and Spells. Into the third he put Help and Understanding. The people of Earth would need all these if they were to get along with one another successfully. And Papa Io knew all about the importance of getting along. He had two sons, Tane and Whiro, who could no more agree than fire and water. He had put Tane in charge of light, Whiro in charge of darkness; the jobs suited their temperaments perfectly, he thought. For Tane was all brightness, kindness and goodness, while Whiro (although Io wept to admit it) was gloomy, evil and dangerous.

Naturally, when the three baskets were ready, it was easy to choose which son should deliver them. Io stuck his head out over Heaven's parapet and called through his speaking trumpet, 'Tane! Come up here! I need you to take these gifts to Humankind!'

Now Whiro knew full well that whoever delivered such fine presents to the people of Earth would win them, heart and mind. They would never stop thanking or praising the messenger. The thought of praise appealed to Whiro. So, while Tane climbed the Great Tower of Overworlds, storey by storey, up the ladders which led from one floor to the next, Whiro set off to climb the *outside* of the Tower. Like ivy, like a fat black spider creeping silently up a wall, he raced his brother skywards, determined to reach the top first. In his

172

pockets were all the tools of his trade, all the tricks which would give him the advantage . . .

It was slow going. But by the time he reached the second storey, Whiro found Tane was already on the third. So, out of his pocket he pulled handfuls of mosquitoes, sandflies and bats. 'Kiss my brother for me, my dearios,' he said, and flung them in the air.

Unsteadily balanced on the ladder between worlds, Tane was suddenly engulfed in a cloud of flying black particles. They flew in his eyes, his ears, his mouth and up his nose. He bent his head down against the swarm, clinging to the ladder with one hand while, with the other, he fumbled in his pocket. At last he tugged out a twist of north wind as big as a towel, and waved it round his head. The insects and bats were swept by a frosty gusting gale miles out to sea.

So, when Whiro, climbing the outside of the Tower, reached the third storey, Tane was already well on his way to the fourth. Whiro put his hand in his other pocket and drew out, like a fisherman's maggots, a handful of ants, centipedes, hornets, spiders and scorpions. 'Say hello to my brother from me, sweetlings,' he said, and threw them in the air.

Half-way up the next tall ladder, Tane heard a crackling, and was suddenly, vilely beset by creepy-crawlies. They swarmed through his hair, infested his clothing; they stung his bare arms and cheeks and calves. Feeling in his pocket, he found no rags of wind, nothing at all to swat them away. There was nothing he could do but shut tight his eyes and mouth and go on climbing – higher and higher – from the eighth to the ninth to the tenth storey.

Gradually, the air became thinner, purer. The holiness emanating from the magic realms above filled the upper storeys with a glorious perfume. The disgusting crawling creatures began to fall away, overcome, like mountaineers succumbing to altitude sickness.

Outside, on the wall of the Tower of Overworlds, even Whiro began to flag. His arms and legs ached. His fingers could barely grip. When he looked down, his head swam at the vertiginous drop. He would never make it as far as the eleventh storey before Tane.

Spotting a small window in the side of the Tower, Whiro slipped through it, feet first, and found himself on the ninth floor. Very well. If he could not catch Tane on the way up, he would ambush him on the way down. Hiding himself in the shadows behind the ladder, he settled down to wait . . .

In the uppermost Overworld, welcoming hands helped Tane from the ladder and led him before Papa Io. And there, while pink evening clouds drifted between the white pillars of Highest Heaven, Io entrusted his three precious presents into Tane's keeping. 'Give them to Humankind with my love and blessing,' said Io. 'And tell them to watch out for that infernal brother of yours. He's a tricky one, that Whiro, though I weep to say it about my own son.'

Carefully, carefully, Tane started back down, the baskets balanced neatly on top of one another. The perfumes of Highest Heaven were heady, and he was feeling a little light-headed as he stepped on to the ladder from tenth to ninth Overworld. He had only one hand free to grasp the rungs now, and he could not properly see where to place his feet.

Suddenly a hand grabbed his ankle and wrenched him off the ladder. He fell, the baskets tumbling on top of him, on top of Whiro who was just then sinking his teeth deep into Tane's thigh.

There in the darkness they fought, good and evil, sparks and foulness spilling from the folds of their clothing. Their panting breaths sped the clouds across the evening sky. Against a blood-red sunset, the Tower of Overworlds trembled and rocked, while the birds screamed around its shaken frame: 'Help! Murder! Ambush!'

Whiro was rested. He liked a fight, liked to inflict pain, whereas his brother was naturally a gentle soul. But Tane knew, as his brother's hands closed round his throat to throttle him, that if Whiro once got hold of the baskets, he would either spill them or use them to take control of the Earth and its people. He slapped feebly at his brother's chest, but there was no pushing him away. He reached out a hand across the creaking floor; his fingers brushed a fallen basket; the lid came off and rolled away into the darkness. A wordless song and a single magic spell spilled into Tane's open palm.

Suddenly a sacred, magic warmth crept up his wrist and arm, into his aching muscles, inspiring him to one last effort. Pushing Whiro backwards, Tane toppled him over the edge of the hatchway and – *thud* – down into Overworld Eight; *crash* – down into Overworld Seven; *bang* – down into Six . . . and Five and Four and so, by painful stages, all the way down to the stony Earth.

He was not killed: immortals don't die. And the whole episode did not serve to sweeten his nasty temper. Picking himself up, Whirro snarled, 'Not deliver the baskets? Well then, I shall make Humankind some presents of my own! Sickness for one! Crime for another! DEATH for a third!' And he slouched away to find baskets big enough for all the miseries he had in store.

Small matter. Tane delivered the three baskets safely to the people of Earth. So after that, they were armed against anything Whiro could hurl at them. The only lasting damage was to the Tower. Shaken and rocked by the titanic struggle on the ninth floor, its rickety structure teeters now, condemned, on the world's edge. It would not carry the weight of the smallest child, let alone the great bulk of Papa Io climbing down from the sky. So Humankind are on their own now. They will have to make do as best they can with what the gods gave them.

Lamia

AN INDIAN LEGEND

HE THOUGHT THAT he came on the place by chance, but that was not quite true. A deer led him to it. Ali Mardan Khan followed the creature deep into the forest, to the shores of a lake, before it eluded him among green shadows. Not two moments later, he heard weeping.

A woman sat with her back to a tree, her hair plaited with wires of gold and silver, her dress bright with mirror sequins, so that she glistened like a fallen star. At the sight of him, she stretched herself at his feet, hands clasped in supplication.

'Don't be afraid,' said Ali Mardan, raising her up. 'You're on my land here, and no harm will come to you. But who are you?'

She said she was a princess from over the mountains – from war-torn China. 'My father was defeated in battle. Of all my family only I escaped. I have wandered for weeks through the mountains.' Not one jet-black hair was out of place, not a fold of her dress creased, but he believed her instantly. For surely the gods had reached out to preserve this unearthly beauty. The flower boats that plied his Kashmiri lakes were no lovelier than Princess Amali, her voice so soft, sibilant and sweet.

'You are welcome to make my home your own,' said Ali Mardan.

'If you were to offer me marriage, I would not refuse,' said the Princess, looking shyly through her lashes. His fate was sealed.

There on the banks of the lake, Ali Mardan built his bride a palace in keeping with her loveliness. She wanted peace and solitude, she said, and to be alone with him; he was only too glad to agree. Only one thing marred those beautiful early days of marriage: Ali Mardan began to suffer fearful stomach pains.

'Let me nurse you,' said Amali. 'I'm gentler than those brutal physicians of yours with their leeches and scalpels.' And so tenderly did she care for him, night and day, that Ali Mardan every dawn reproached himself for feeling no better.

One day, as his manservant helped him walk about in the garden, breathing the scents of the forest, they came across a wandering holy man, small and bony as a pigeon, asleep under a tree.

'Shall I throw him out of your garden, sir?' asked the servant.

'Certainly not. Holy men are a blessing from heaven. Fetch a bed out here, and have food prepared for him when he wakes. I must lie down now. The pain, it's too . . .'

When the holy man woke, he was delighted to find himself on a soft couch surrounded by trays of food. He sought out his host to thank him. 'I am sorry to find you unwell, sir. Perhaps I can repay your kindness with my own humble knowledge of medicine.'

He examined Ali Mardan, asked questions, and strummed his lower lip, rapt in thought. 'Are you by any chance newly married, sir?'

'Why, yes! I am!'

The man smiled. 'Then the remedy is plain, and I shall supply it! Let me cook dinner tonight.'

He picked all the herbs, ground all the spices. But although he cooked exactly the same meal for Ali Mardan as for the Princess, he sprinkled a handful of salt over Amali's plate. If she noticed, she said nothing and the meal passed without incident.

By midnight Amali had a raging thirst. She got out of bed, and went to the water jug. But the jug was empty. She went to the door. But it was locked. She went to the window. But its grille of wrought iron was designed to keep out thieves: no way out.

With a glance at her sleeping husband, Amali stretched herself, reaching up as though she would touch the ceiling. Her body grew thinner; her bones seemed to melt away. Her skin glistened green in the moonlight, and her hair congealed to her back and legs. A serpent ten feet long reared up from the patch of moonlight where Amali had stood a moment before, its jaws agape for water, forked tongue flickering. Out between the filigree ironwork of the window she slithered, and down to the lake, drinking her fill, dislocating her serpent jaws to scoop up the water. Then she slithered back to the palace.

In the shadow of the wall stood the holy man, a little silver hatchet in his hand. The moment her head was through the bars, he struck. But the snake was too quick for him, the scales too tough.

Next morning Ali Mardan summoned the holy man to his room.

'I'm sorry, sir. I wounded her, but I could not kill her.'

'Wounded whom? Is there an assassin loose in my palace?'

'No, sir. A lamia.'

If for two hundred years a snake lives unseen by human eyes, it becomes a dragon. A hundred years more, and it becomes a lamia – a creature of infinite wickedness, able to change into any shape – a bird, a tiger. Worse, it can become a woman and feed on the lifeblood of a man.

'Your wife, sir,' said the holy man, 'is poisoning you with the venom of her kisses. Your only cure is to kill her.'

'Never! No! You're wrong! Aha, I can prove you're wrong! You may have wounded some snake in my garden last night, but not Amali. I left her asleep in bed. Unhurt! See for yourself: here she comes!'

But as Princess Amali entered the garden, her silken cloak blew back: they saw that one of her arms was in a sling. 'I dropped my mirror. I cut myself,' she said when she saw them staring.

When she had gone, Ali Mardan drew a trembling breath. One hand clutched the pain in his side, one gripped the arm of his chair. 'Tell me what I must do,' he said at last, 'to kill a lamia.'

They built a summer-house of shiny lacquered tree bark, down by the lake. It had just a table, a chair, a bed and a big oven.

'Come with me, Amali,' said Ali Mardan. 'The holy man thinks one of my courtiers may be poisoning me. So I shall eat nothing but what is cooked by your own hand, and have no one near me but you.'

The Princess looked doubtful. 'Cook, my love? But I hardly know how . . . being a princess, you know. Besides, I hate ovens.'

'Only a loaf of bread,' he said. 'You can hardly refuse me that.'

The walls of the summer-house were so thin and fine that the shadows of husband and wife could be seen as they kneaded dough together at the table. The smaller shadow turned to place the bread in the oven. The taller moved painfully across behind – and gave her a push.

Into the oven went the lamia! And Ali Mardan staggered from the hut, his arm across his face. Servants came running with blazing torches, and set light to the summer-house: it burned like a chrysanthemum bursting into crimson bloom.

Next day. Ali Mardan woke feeling stronger. He dimly hoped the pictures in his head were left over from some bad dream. But when he climbed out of bed and found his body free from pain, he realized that the death of the lamia – his bride – had truly taken place.

Outside the door stood the holy man, travelling-staff in hand. 'I can safely leave you now, sir, and return to my monastery. But come with me to the lake, if you will.'

'Must I?'

The summer-house was nothing but a pile of ash around the cast-iron oven. Opening the oven door the holy man swept out a handful of ash and a pretty green pebble. 'Choose: the pebble or the ash?'

'The pebble,' said Ali Mardan without thinking.

'Then I shall keep the ash,' said the holy man.

Ali Mardan sat the pebble down on the oven while he stared out across the lake. The lilies were just coming into bloom. Birds were eating seed from the rushes, dragonflies hovering over their reflections. When he turned back, the oven was solid gold.

He pocketed the stone with a smile. 'And what can the ash do?' he asked. But no one answered. The holy man had disappeared among the trees, and Ali Mardan would never know what the ash of a lamia could do. He was glad it had gone. He used the alchemy of the pebble only rarely, when he most had need. It reminded him of his dead wife and the gleam of gold wire in her plaited hair.

Isis and Osiris

AN EGYPTIAN MYTH

IN THE SHIP-OF-A-MILLION-YEARS, Shu rolled the dice.
'Again!' groaned Troth. 'You win again!' And so the God of
Mischief won from the God of Time a whole stash of minutes –
enough, in fact, to make a day. And on that new day, Nut, wife of the
Sun God himself, gave birth. Her peevish husband had cursed her with
childlessness all year round. But on the 366th day of the year, using
borrowed time, Nut was at last able to give birth to four babies. She hid
them on Earth, as kings and queens: Set and Nephthys, Isis and Osiris.

Set could find no one on Earth fit to be his wife – no one, that is, but
his sister Nephthys. So he married her, and they became King and
Queen of Nubia. Their love was so great for one another that they
had none left for the people of Nubia.

Osiris could find no one on Earth fit to be his wife – no one, that is,
but his sister Isis. So he married her, and they became King and
Queen of Egypt. Their love for one another was so great that it spilled
over on to their Egyptian subjects.

In those days, mortals knew nothing about clothing themselves,
growing food, taking shelter from the burning sun. Up until then,
they had simply grubbed about like brute beasts. But Osiris taught
them how to brew beer and to dance, and Isis taught them how to
weave linen, farm crops, make bricks out of the Nile mud. King and
Queen were greatly loved for their teaching; greatly repaid for the
love they lavished on the people of Egypt.

'What a beautiful statue!' cried Isis, as she took her place at the banqueting table. Set had invited all his neighbouring kings and queens to a marvellous feast and, naturally, Isis and Osiris were guests of honour.

'Aha, no statue, this!' laughed Set agreeably, and showed off his latest work of art. It looked like the figure of a man, but there were hinges on one side and latches on the other, and it opened like a trunk. The space inside was just the size and shape of a man. 'If anyone here fits the space exactly, he shall have the chest as a present!' Set announced – astonishing generosity, given that the chest was inlaid with turquoise faience, gold, silver and lapis lazuli.

Up they trooped, those well-fed kings, to try the chest for size. But either they were too fat to squeeze in, or too short to fit. Only Osiris, willowy and tall, fitted to perfection. (But then, of course, it had been tailor-made for him.)

BANG! Set slammed shut the lid and sprang the latches.

'No, no!' cried Isis. 'He won't be able to breathe!'

'All well and good, then!' sniggered Set. 'All my life I have had to watch you and him wallowing in the worship of your loving subjects. Now all that love will come to me – Set – ruler of Nubia and of Egypt!' His troops picked up the chest and ran with it, and though Isis tried to follow, Set held her fast until the coffin-bearers were out of sight.

Alone and bereft, Isis walked north from Nubia back into Egypt along the muddy gulch which called itself the Nile. As she walked, she wept – large brilliant tears which, in falling, startled tufts of dust from the ground. Rivulets of tears became pools, pools became streams, streams swelled the trickling Nile to a river, a torrent. It overspilled its banks, swamping the countryside from the fifth cataract to the delta plain.

'Stop crying! Don't cry!' said a little voice. Other voices joined it. 'Please, Queen Isis! Don't cry any more!'

She blinked down and saw seven scorpions gazing up at her with bulging eyes, imploring her to stop. 'If you cry any more, the flood will wipe out Egypt!' they said. 'We'll help you look for Osiris. Everyone will help you!'

It was true. Isis and Osiris were so loved that all Egypt was ready to join in the search for Osiris, shut up in his airless coffin, stifling to death with every passing second.

*

Looking over their shoulders, the troops of Set saw the Nile floods rolling down on top of them and ran for their lives. They flung aside the jewelled sarcophagus, and the floodwaters of Isis' tears caught it and swept it from swamp to reedbed, reedbed to river, from river's reach to cataract, on down the Nile.

With the help of the scorpions, Isis herself found it. Transformed by magic into a sparrowhawk, she was searching, with hawkish eyes, from high in the sunny Egyptian sky. Suddenly she glimpsed the chest floating in mid-river! But her borrowed wings were weary, her bird body on the brink of exhaustion. All she could do was fly down and perch her hawk's weight on the floating coffin, pecking feebly at the lid.

Her feet felt the beat of a heart through the inlaid lid. Not dead yet, then! Half mad with hope, she pecked furiously. Her beak made a hole. The soul of Osiris struggled like a flame through that hole, and singed the feathers of the sparrowhawk!

But, powerless to free him, Isis fell exhausted from the casket and was washed up on the river bank, while the sarcophagus floated on its way into the maze of delta rivulets, and on out to sea. There, waves washed over it, splashed in at the hole her beak had made, filled the trunk with sea brine.

When Isis awoke, bedraggled on the Nile mud, she found she was expecting a baby – Osiris' son. She was forced to call off her futile search until after the baby was born.

Not for a year, not for a handful of sorry years did Isis finish her search for the treacherous casket. It had embedded itself in the trunk of a young tamarisk tree, and the tree had grown up around it, imprisoning the sarcophagus in yet another layer of wood. Only love guided her to it, only absurd, indestructible hope made her hack her way into its sea-filled compartment.

But Osiris was long since dead.

'Dead and never to be buried!' cried a cruel voice behind her. It was Set, as dogged in his hatred as she had been in her love. He too had searched the Red Land and the Black for the lost casket. Bodies could be buried. Graves could become shrines. People could worship at shrines, adoring the memory of the dead; and Set was determined no one but he should be worshipped throughout the length and breadth of Egypt.

So he took an axe and, in front of his sister's horrified eyes, hacked the body of Osiris into fourteen pieces, flinging them into the Nile. '*Now* love him – what you can find of him!' jeered the murderous Set, as the speeding river carried away the parts and pieces of Osiris.

This time Isis did not cry. She tore her hair and rent her fine linen robes, and she screamed like a gull out at sea. '*A boat!*' she shrieked at the people nearby. 'I must gather up the pieces of my husband and give him decent burial! Make me a boat, for the love of pity!'

'But there are no trees to build a boat!' said the people. 'No trees between here and Memphis!'

'Then cut rushes and make a boat from them!' howled Isis, filling her fists with papyrus reeds and shaking them at the sky.

'The crocodiles will tear it apart!' said the people. But they built the boat. And Isis sailed it, too, careless of whether the green Nile crocodiles, large as boats and monstrous with teeth, tore her or her craft in pieces. Blind to their green raft of bodies closing in, she sailed up and down, reaching into the water, reaching into the bloodstained reeds.

'Why do you not fear us?' demanded the largest of the crocodiles. 'Why do you trespass on our river? Why do you brave our hunger?'

'What do I care about drowning or being eaten?' answered Isis. 'Haven't I pain enough already to fill three worlds? Haven't I lost my darling, body, brain and heart?' And she told the crocodiles (there were several hundred jamming the river now, like logs) the whole story of her husband's murder.

By the time she finished, the log-jam of crocodiles were sobbing and tossing their green jaws from side to side in grief. Some laid water lilies in the bow of the boat, to comfort her. 'Oh, beautiful lady!' wailed the largest, 'we shall cruise the Nile from source to sea and find you every part and piece of Osiris!'

In their baggy green jaws they brought the pieces, as gently as they carried their own eggs. They found every piece but one (which was not important), and Isis took all her husband's remains and carried them ashore.

Far inland she walked, to a place called the Valley of Stones, all boulders and hot rocks cracking in the sun. Only then, in that desolate place, did she really feel her loss. For what good are the parts of a dead man, except for burial in the parched ground? She raised such a clamour of grief that the sky above her quaked. The Ship-of-a-Million-Years, barge of the gods, bucketed about.

'What's that row?' asked Ra, Sun and father of the gods.

'Just a mortal weeping over the body of her mate,' he was told.

'Then for Heaven's sake, someone make her stop!' grumbled the ancient Maker-of-the-World. 'Or how can I sleep?'

Leaning over her parcel of woe, Isis saw the black shadow of a jackal loom over her. 'No! You shan't eat him!' she cried, throwing herself across the body.

'Please,' said Anubis, jackal-headed god, keeper of secrets. 'Don't upset yourself. I have come to help.'

The arts he showed her that day had never been seen before on Earth: how to bandage and anoint a body, how to clothe it in prayers. 'Now,' Anubis said, stepping back from his work, 'now it is only a question of how much you love Osiris.'

She called his name. She shouted out her love. She called so loudly that even in the World-under-the-World, the great serpent of Chaos heard it and flinched.

Anubis grinned a doggy grin. He reboarded the Ship-of-a-Million-Years, and it sailed on across the heavens towards the Gate of Sunset, leaving Isis and her husband in the Valley of Stones . . . hand-in-hand and talking.

He could not stay long, of course. The Living and the Raised-to-Life cannot live in the same world. Osiris left to become King of the Westerners, guardian of the spirits of the Dead. After that, when Egyptians came to die and make the long journey west out of the living world, they no longer feared the darkness of dissolution. They knew that a familiar face would be waiting to greet them in the Land of the West: Osiris, who would raise them to life with love, just as love had resurrected him.

Nor was Isis left lonely for long on the Earth. Shortly she won herself a place in the Barque of Heaven, alongside Thoth and Shu and Ra, Anubis, Nut and the rest. So now each night, as the ship sails under the Earth, she is able to glimpse the glimmering towers of the Westerners and a lean, willowy figure waving, waving his greeting and his love.

The Flying Dutchman
A SAILORS' LEGEND

HIS HOLD HEAVY with precious metals and his decks piled high with spices, Captain Vanderdecken cast off, fore and aft, and gave the order to hoist the mainsail. But the crew at the capstans did not sing as they worked. Even the surf did not whisper under the ship's prow. For the clouds which lay along the horizon were red as fire, and the wind ratched at the sea like a rasp. There was dirty weather ahead; this was no time to be setting sail.

The Dutchman was known for a hard man, but not for a fool. Though he worked his men like dogs, cursing them and keeping their rations short, he was a profiteer, and surely a businessman values his cargo if he cares nothing for his fellow men. Surely the captain prizes his ship, even if he couldn't give a damn for his crew. So, when the storm came, slewing round the bottom of the world, fit to send every ship scurrying for shelter, everyone expected Vanderdecken to turn back and make for shelter.

'We'll all be killed!' the First Mate warned. 'The men are scared silly and there's no priest on board to pray for our souls! Turn back, Captain, turn back, I beg you!'

The Dutchman was sitting in his easy chair on the afterdeck, smoking a pipe, while his cabin boy polished his boots. The chart lay in front of him, a single line marking a route around the Cape of Good Hope. He barely even stirred himself to answer, and then the words crawled from between snarling lips. 'I'll go where I choose,

185

and I'll kill any man who thwarts me,' he said. At his feet, the cabin boy tittered in admiration of his brutal master.

The Mate withdrew, but the frightened crew went on muttering among themselves, scared of their captain, more scared of the sea which rolled down on them like a purple mountain range falling on their heads. The waves were flecked with ice, the wavetops torn ragged by the howling wind.

'If we reason with him, he'll have to see sense,' said one, and led the rest – the entire crew – back down the ship to the afterdeck. 'For the love of God, turn back, sir!' shouted the matelot above the racketing wind. 'It's flying in the face of God to round the Cape in this weather!'

But the only answer he got was the sight of the Dutchman's drawn pistol and the sound of its hammer falling. The seaman fell back over the rail into the boiling sea – fell without a cry. But the wind screamed in the rigging, and the ship groaned from stem to stern. 'I'll go round the Cape whether God wills it or no,' said Vanderdecken, grinning like a fiend, his eyes gleaming. 'Which of you is going to try to stop me now? None? No! Not God nor all His angels shall say me nay!'

The crew stared open-mouthed, each man seeing his own death scrawled in the filthy sky. Then their pallid faces grew whiter still, as that ghostly phosphorescence called St Elmo's fire settled on the ship's mast like a column of cold fire.

A piece broke free and fluttered down to the deck, taking shape, as it fell. Some said wings, some a gown, some a head of snowy hair, some a face of ineffable, unbearable beauty. But only the Dutchman really dared to look into the face of that blazing figure.

'Did you never hear tell, Dutchman, that it's a sin to take the Lord's name in vain?'

The Dutchman only swore vilely. 'Get off my ship. I've business in hand.'

'Turn back, Dutchman. Three times now you have been warned.'

But the Dutchman only cursed foully and lifted his pistol a second time, saying, 'Devil take you.'

BANG. The thunder was louder than the shot. And the bullet passed clean through the phantom of flame, melting into a single waterdrop before falling into the vast running seas.

'You have spoken your mind,' said the figure. 'Now I will speak mine. Every trading man looks to profit from his trade. So, from this bitter night's work, you shall earn ten thousand such bitter weeks. In return for your curse, I'll pay you in millions of curses. Sail on, would you? Then sail on for ever, for your blasphemy, never touching port. No sleep, no food, no drink shall comfort you. These men shan't disobey you again, for I shall leave you no men. Hail no ships for company or aid or news; none will ever draw alongside without rack and disaster overtaking it. The world will soon learn to fear the Fleeing Dutchman, to shun him and curse him, as you have shunned and cursed me tonight!'

No tears of remorse sprang to Vanderdecken's eyes. He bit his thumb at the phantom. 'Me, I thrive on terror! It's all I ever looked for in another man's face!'

'Good,' replied the fiery shape. 'For search the world over and you shall never find Love – no, not in one single face. Sail on, Dutchman. You have all Eternity for your voyaging!'

A wall of water as high as a cathedral burst over the ship. The Dutchman was flung against the wheel, and clung there, eyes and mouth tight shut against the swamping salt-water. When he opened his eyes again, the deck of his ship was washed bare – bare of spices, bare of sailors, bare of anchor or chains, ropes and waterbutts. Bare of phantasms, too. But clinging to the Captain's ankle, the little cabin boy spluttered and gasped and gibbered with cold.

'Ah! Not entirely alone, then!' crowed the Dutchman, reaching down to grasp the boy's hand. But the face which turned up towards him was no longer human. It wore the snarl of a dog, and the hand he took hold of was scaly and rasp-rough, like the pelt of a dogfish. Eyes which had once fawned on Vanderdecken now looked at him with unconcealed loathing.

'My waterbutts gone? Then I shall drink beer!' shouted the Dutchmen defiantly into the rainy sky. 'Fetch me beer, boy, and I shall drink myself blind drunk!'

But when the cabin boy brought the beer, it boiled in the tankard, making the metal too hot to hold; the foam scalded as it blew into his face. And the meat on his plate turned to molten lead. The darkness beneath his eyelids was suddenly full of horrors so terrible that Vanderdecken never again dared to close his eyes.

Without his orders, all the flags at the masthead had changed. Now, all that flew there was a ghastly yellow rag with a central black spot: the signal of a ship contaminated by plague. And though he ran that flag down a thousand times, it was always flying there again next time he looked up. So no port would grant him entry. No ship would come near.

Rumours soon spread, in cosy harbour taverns, among old sailing comrades, as they sat drinking together, sharing a supper of cheese and cold collations. The Fleeing Dutchman, the 'Flying' Dutchman was a devil, his ship cursed by God. It was a ship to steer clear of, a ship damned.

Of course pirates and thieves listened in to the gossip, but heard only the words 'treasure' and 'gold' and 'precious cargo'. Far from steering clear, they went looking for the Flying Dutchman. But those that laid grappling hooks on board, and set foot on the bare, silent decks, never disembarked again. For their own ships sank like stones, just from touching rib against rib with the ship of doom. So Vanderdecken's ship did *not* go uncrewed. Indeed, he gathered around him dozens of the scurviest villains ever to escape hanging. But they hated the Captain, because they were powerless to leave him, and they cursed the day they had set eyes on that yellow plague flag, for their souls were everlastingly in thrall to the Flying Dutchman.

Restless, unresting, the ship sails on around and around the watery globe. Though the boards have been chafed through by the salt-sharp sea, and her ribs laid bare, still she does not sink. Though the sails have been blown to the ragged thinness of rotten silk, still she speeds before the remorseless trade winds. The chart on the Captain's desk is blacker now than a spider's web with the courses he has plotted on his never-ending voyage.

Endless hail and wind and sun have beaten down on the Dutchman's head, so that his brown face is scored with creases, his misery etched for anyone to see. Whole centuries have passed since Vanderdecken learned repentance, learned to crave a kind face, a smile, a hand extended in friendship. But he sees only resentment, loathing, hate, contempt, terror.

Now, the sailors in the portside taverns whisper that God's anger is softening – that once every seven years or so, Vanderdecken is seen ashore, walking the streets of some foreign port, lifting his cap to the ladies, in the hope that one will stop and speak to him, listen to his story, pity him – love him.

But looking into those half-crazed eyes, seeing all that horror, hearing his crimes, what woman could ever love the Flying Dutch-man? So perhaps God's anger is not lessening. Perhaps God has merely found a new way to torment His damned Dutchman from everlasting to everlasting.

Proud Man

A NATIVE AMERICAN MYTH

WISDOM IS POWER so they say, and that makes Gluskap all-powerful. For Gluskap knew everything, and magic besides. He made the world, he rid it of monsters, he fought the stone giants and sometimes, just sometimes, he granted wishes.

One day, four men came in turn to visit him. Each wanted something, some more than others.

'Please, oh please, mighty Gluskap!' said the first unlucky soul. 'All my crops have died and my well's run dry! Now my wife and children are starving and I haven't a morsel to give them! When I ask my friends for help, they call me a fool and a scrounger. Grant me a bite of bread and a jug of milk, if only for my children's mouths!'

'With friends like that, you really do need help,' said Gluskap, and gave the man a cow and whole basket of seed-corn to replant his field.

'Oh, master of the world, I humbly beg you,' said the second man, bowing low. 'See how sickness has scarred my face and weakened my body? Pity my ugliness. All I long for is to be as I was born, an ordinary man, whole and healthy.'

'Whole and healthy is how I made you,' said Gluskap, 'and so you shall be again!' And he healed the man then and there, and sent him off skipping and dancing.

'Oh, Lord Gluskap, in your great mercy!' shouted a loud and scowling man. 'I am cursed with a wicked temper. I scold my wife and hit my neighbours and make my children cry. Before I do something unforgivable, I beg you, take this demon temper out of me!'

Gluskap smiled. 'I always preferred the farmer to the warrior. Take off your shirt and with it your temper. I grant you your wish.' So the man took off both shirt and temper, and left them in the palm of Gluskap's giant hand. The Great Spirit was still holding them when a fourth man arrived.

'Listen here,' said the man. 'You did a pretty poor job when you made me. But I'm a fair man. I'm going to give you a chance to make up for that. Make me taller, for a start, and more handsome. I want to be admired. I want to be the most admired man in my village! Oh, and make me live longer, too.'

Gluskap smiled, but not in quite the same way as before. His fingers closed around the shirt in his hand, and his skin tasted the temper left in its weave. 'Your wish is granted,' he said between gritted teeth.

But the man did not thank him. In fact he didn't say a word. His feet had burrowed deep into the ground, and his spine had stretched, tall and erect. His hair had lengthened, too, so that now it was spiky and . . . green. There he stood: a fine, tall fir tree, as beautiful as any in the forest.

It is true, he did tower over mere men as they rode by; and those passing travellers did admire him immensely. And though they must have grown old and died since then, the fir tree is still there, thriving, to this day. But whether this height and elegance and admiration and long life were quite what the man had in mind, no one will ever know, because the only noise to come from him is the creak of timber and the singing of birds.

Such were Gluskap's powers. Such was his wisdom.

Perhaps you know someone like him; someone who is always right? Someone perfect who never makes a mistake? Yes. Quite. Such people can be . . . wearing, to say the least.

A day dawned when Gluskap's wife had had too much of her husband's marvellous wisdom and (it has to be said) his almighty conceit.

'Of course, there is *someone* who can resist your great powers,' she said, slipping the comment in between the porridge and bread of breakfast.

'I suppose you mean yourself?' said Gluskap, all set to turn her into a sheep or a bush.

'Heavens, no! I mean him,' and she pointed to the baby wriggling on the mat beside the fire.

'Oh, nonsense!' said Gluskap with a tolerant, condescending chuckle. He whistled to catch the baby's attention, and the boy looked up and smiled. 'You see?'

'Hmmm,' said his wife, unimpressed.

So Gluskap called the child to come. But the little baby just smiled and stayed put.

Gluskap put on his most important and solemn face, and summoned the child in ancient words of antique magic.

. . . But the baby just crawled off and played with a feather.

'COME HERE THIS INSTANT!' bawled Gluskap, and although the child's face crumpled, he only crawled to his mother and hid among her skirts. She did not say, 'I told you so.' She did not even smile behind her hand. No, she was wise enough simply to take the baby in her arms and sing him to sleep.

By that time, Gluskap had swallowed his pride, and come to see that there was indeed someone in the world who knew more than he – at least about babies. He took the lesson to heart.

'Wife,' he said. 'It's a wise man who knows his limitations.'

The Silver-Miners

A LEGEND FROM BOLIVIA

WHEN THE SPANISH came to South America, they looked round them at the people, but saw only the gold bands on their arms, the silver rings in their ears. They looked at the great stepped temples, like stairways to Heaven, and saw no gods but only the golden chalices and silver plates the priests held. When they looked at Bolivia, beautiful with holy green mountains, they saw only huge heaps of earth threaded with silver ore. They saw no beauty but in digging, gouging, tearing. They sank silver mines.

Worse. They did not even do the digging themselves, but forced the local people into a slavery of breaking and carrying rocks. The mountain Parichata, husband mountain of Tata-Turqui, guardian of Potosí Town, was torn and pounded with picks and shovels, and his silver ripped out to feed Spanish greed.

'O Parichata, forgive us!' groaned the labourers, swinging their long picks as the midday sun scorched down on them. 'O Parichata, grieve with us!' they sobbed as they staggered beneath huge baskets of rock. 'O Parichata, husband of Tata-Turqui, guardian of Potosí Town, have pity on us! Would that you were made all of mud and had not a grain of silver in you, that you might stand at peace in the landscape, and we beside you!'

But the air was so full of the sound of whips that their prayers seemed to be cracked and broken by the lash in mid-air, and to fall to

193

the ground without ever reaching the ears of the gods. Only the crawling beetles on the ground waved their long antennae and scuttled away.

Each evening, at the end of the day's work, Maro the mule-boy would lead his father's skinny mules up the mountain path to the mines. It was his job to ensure the animals were ready and waiting for the first loads of the following day. The Spaniards paid Maro's father nothing, and the animals were already half-dead with overwork. 'But better they should drop in their tracks,' his father said, 'than that mothers and children should die carrying rocks for these slave-drivers.'

Suddenly, Maro heard ahead of him on the path the clatter of hooves. More donkeys? How very strange. He had thought his was the only team for miles around. And when the mules appeared, they quite took his breath away, for not only were they glossy, sleek and fat, but coal-black in coat and mane. Huge panniers were strapped to both sides of their saddles.

The muleteer driving them wore a straw hat which cast his face into shadow despite a bright moon. 'Out of the way, boy!' he shouted at Maro. 'Clear the path! Go back or die!'

'I shall die if I don't do as the Spaniards tell me,' said Maro, but the muleteer uttered such a fearsome roar that both Maro and his donkeys scampered off the path in terror, and the black mules clattered on downwards, unhindered. Maro ran after all his animals, gathered up their lead-ropes and led them back down to the edge of town.

But his curiosity got the better of him. He could not bear not to know what was happening to his beloved mountain, and going back alone, on silent, bare feet, he hid himself beside the path and watched all night.

He saw, under the moonlight, how the chalky path was alive with insect-life. Whole swarms of gleaming longicorn beetles, bugs and mud-rollers were crawling upwards. Every beetle on Parichata seemed to be closing in on the silver mines.

Rank by rank, the beetles reached the mine workings – where the trees were all felled, the boulders smashed, the flowers uprooted and the mountain's flesh cut to its very bones of silver. There, the Indian in the straw hat was waiting. He touched each beetle with his muleteer's goad, and rolled it on to its glossy back.

But when they rolled back again on to their feet, the feet they stood on were hooves, the legs they straightened were hairy, and their bodies and heads were those of fully grown handsome mules. In place of their antennae were long pink-lined ears, and over their backs the muleteer hung panniers of woven wicker-work.

Out of the mountain flowed molten silver. It spouted and spurted in fountains and springs, directly into the panniers, and there solidified into shining ingots. With both panniers full, each mule turned down the mountain path and came clumping past Maro's hiding place before disappearing into the black distance, leaving only the echo of hooves clip-clopping among the rocks.

The Spaniards arrived next morning, eager and anxious for a new day's loot. Their weary slaves rolled miserably out of bed and crawled up the pocked and scarred mountainside. They found (to their amazement) that there was no silver to mine.

The Spaniards looked – oh, how they looked! – sinking new drill holes, scrambling down every crevice, peeling back the grass as though they would flay the mountain. But they could find no trace of silver, not the merest grain, not the tiniest glitter. It was as if Parichata had been filleted of all his silver bones.

'You won't find any.' Maro spoke up from between the muzzles of his father's mules. His neighbours looked round at him in astonishment. The Spaniards scowled. 'Parichata took pity on us last night. He gave away his silver for the sake of the people.' And Maro went on to tell them how every beetle had been turned into a mule and had carried away the precious ore. The Spanish only snorted with disbelief, but the people of Potosí Town looked down at the ground, and saw no beetles, no, not so much as a leather beetle creeping to and fro.

No one ever discovered where the beetle-mules took their treasure of silver. Perhaps they gave it into the safe keeping of Tata-Turqui, wife-mountain of Parichata, or perhaps they carried it into the valleys, to some secret treasure-house. But though the Spaniards raged and threatened, they had, in the end, to quit Potosí and seek their riches elsewhere.

The scars on the face of Parichata soon healed. Spring brought its yearly treasure of seeds, berries, flowers and sapling trees. And after morning had dropped its dew on every spider's web and leaf and bending blade of grass, Parichata was not entirely without a gleam of silver in the early dawn.

The Men in the Moon
A MYTH FROM KENYA

'**M**URILAY, COME HERE! Murilay, don't do that! Murilay, I've told you before! Murilay, just wait till your father comes home!'

Murilay hunched his shoulders and slunk out of doors. He could hear his mother's shrill voice still scolding inside the hut, her words hunting after him like stinging red ants.

A wooden stool stood beside the door – the carved seat where Murilay's father liked to sit in the evenings and watch the huge sun shimmer and ripple, and the clean sharp-edged rising Moon cut its way like a sickle through the last stems of cloud, the stars raining. 'We may have nothing,' Murilay's father liked to say, pointing at the sky with his knurled and gnarled old walking stick, 'but we are as rich in stars as the next man.'

Murilay liked to watch the sunset, too, but his mother never let him sit down for long enough. 'Eat your supper, Murilay! Wash your face, Murilay! Go to bed, Murilay, and get up a better boy. The boys in the Moon never cheek their mother. The boys in the Moon always do as they're told. The boys in the Moon aren't lazy, idle, good-for-nothing boys like you!'

Murilay seized his chance to sit, for once, upon his father's stool. 'The boys in the Moon are lucky,' he said out loud. 'I wish I could be up there in the peace and quiet.'

The stool rocked, the stool swayed, the stool reared up like a horse, and it was all Murilay could do not to tumble off. The stool took a practice leap into the branches of a nearby tree, and balanced there, quivering with pent-up magic.

Murilay was excited. 'Up, stool, up!' he said. 'Up to the Moon!'

The stool rose further up, resting at intervals on a cloudbank, a ledge of rainbow. Finally, the blue sky gave way to the blackness of space, and Murilay flew on his stool as far as the Moon, where he landed in a pleasant landscape yellow with Moon-bleached grass.

A group of men came by driving cows ahead of them. They cast a wary eye over the boy sitting on a stool in the middle of nowhere.

'Please, gentlemen,' Murilay asked politely, 'can you direct me to the Chief of the Moon People?'

They knew at once he was a stranger, and grinned in a way not entirely friendly. 'You want directions? You earn them. You work for us for a month.'

So Murilay worked for the men, grooming their cows and fetching water from the deep wells of the Moon. His mother's nagging had accustomed Murilay to worse than anything these men could inflict, and he was not unhappy. Time only hung heavy because the food was so *bad*. At the end of each day the cowherds gave him stone-cold porridge, uncooked and indigestible. He might have understood, if they had eaten differently – but they ate the same themselves!

'I have worked one month for you. Now tell me, gentlemen, where I may find the Chief of the Moon People.' The cowherds gave a variety of grunts and pointed out a path. Murilay ran down it before they could change their minds.

The path did indeed bring him to the village of the Moon Chief. It was a dark, dismal place, and very cold. The people huddled under blankets in the doorways of their huts, crunching nuts between broken teeth, or sipping cold porridge. The Chief himself sat on a carved wooden chair watching the Earth rise, like a green-and-blue duck egg, alongside a sprinkling of stars. The first remark he made to Murilay was, 'We may not have much to call our own, stranger, but we are as rich in stars as the next village.' He waved in one fist a giant turkey wing still stubbly from plucking and completely raw.

When he offered Murilay something to eat, a servant brought the meat of a Moon rabbit; that, too, dripped blood.

'Eat, eat, young man! Don't stand on ceremony! You must be very hungry if you've travelled all the way from Earth and done a month's work as well!'

'The gods forbid that I should offend your highness,' said Murilay, 'and I realize that the fault is all mine, but I am accustomed to eating my food . . . how can I say this? . . . cooked.'

'Cooked? How "cooked"? What does it mean?' said the Chief, scowling over his turkey wing.

'With fire,' said Murilay.

'Fire? And what's that?'

The Chief's wives were glaring at Murilay from under the blankets, dark eyes enveloped in wool and temper. Murilay began to see the Moon in quite a new light. He searched about for two flints, pulled a tuft of hair from his head for kindling and – to the great astonishment of the whole tribe – struck a spark.

He fanned it to a flame, fed it with wood and, looking about for food to cook, took the turkey drumstick from the Chief's hand. Warrior bodyguards lifted their spears menacingly. But Murilay persevered in cooking the turkey on the fire, while the People of the Moon were busy discovering the delights of warmth. They crept from under their blankets. They gazed round-eyed at the leaping fire, and burnt themselves trying to pick it up.

'To think that my mother thought these folk were far above us!' thought Murilay, but kept the thought to himself.

When the Chief of the Moon tasted his roast turkey, he at once offered Murilay all his daughters as wives.

Murilay had not been planning to marry so young, but the prospect of marrying seven princesses in one day quite changed his outlook. Gifts of cattle and sheep followed the marriage, and by nightfall, Murilay was proclaimed the greatest magician in the Realm of Stars.

While Murilay grew to manhood, the People of the Moon prospered as they had never done before. By the time he had a hut and a family of children, his wealth was second only to the Chief's.

But sometimes, when he sat on his father's wooden stool and watched the Earth rising, he longed to see, from Earth, the Moon cut cleanly through the last stems of evening cloud. He wanted to see his father again and hear the crows in the treetops at dusk, as shrill as his darling mother.

He decided to go back, but going was not as simple as coming. He might fly back on his magic stool, as easily as the birds hopped between Earth and Moon, but he had his wives and cows and children and sheep to think of. All on one stool, they would find the journey hugely over-crowded. There was a place where the Moon dipped down and the Earth sloped up, and a causeway joined the two. But it would be a difficult, dangerous journey to make. So he sent word ahead, by way of the Mockingbird, telling his family to meet him halfway and help with the cattle.

'Muri-i-i-lay! Muri-i-i-lay! Home soon, home soon!' squawked the Mockingbird, and gave a burst of brash, brittle laughter. 'Meet him halfway to the Moon!'

Murilay's father picked up a stone and threw it. 'Wicked bird! Do you want to break my heart with your lies? My Murilay is dead these seven years!'

'Muri-i-i-lay be home soon!' cackled the bird. But Murilay's mother came after it with a broom, and cursed it with a dozen curses for lying about her poor dead son. The Mockingbird flew back to the Moon and explained the problem to Murilay.

'You lazy, idle, good-for-nothing, laze-in-the-sun-all-day, lying bird!' exclaimed Murilay. 'You never even went there! My parents would never give me up for dead, just because I disappeared for a few years!'

The poor Mockingbird flew back down to Earth and swooped low over the house of Murilay's parents. It snatched the knurled and gnarled walking stick out of the old man's hand. The old man stood up, but the bird flew out of reach of his old, weak hands. He watched until the bird flew out of sight of his old, weak eyes.

Then Murilay had to accept that he must make the journey all by himself, and set off for Earth with his wives and children and cattle and sheep, skidding down the slopes of Moon-white scree.

The cattle slid on their hocks, Murilay skidded on his heels, the white Moon-dust filling his hair and clogging his throat. A trail of milk, white as Moonlight, dripped from the udders of the cows. Murilay's wives and children soon grew tired and rode on the backs of the cows.

Then Murilay grew weary, too, and feared he could go no further. When he reached the causeway joining the Moon to the Earth, he sat down with his head between his knees and wept. For the causeway passed over a bottomless chasm so terrifying that Murilay dared not go one step across it. He was already dizzy with weariness, and his courage was fading fast.

'I will carry you across.'

'Who said that?'

'I did,' said the Bull. 'I'll carry you over, if you promise my reward won't be the butcher's knife. I've seen what your fire does to meat, and I daresay beef is dear to you People of Earth.'

'I promise I shall never eat red meat, if you will carry me over the Ravine of Nothingness,' vowed Murilay.

So the Bull took Murilay on its back and, as sure-footed as any mountain goat, tripped across the knife-edge narrow isthmus to the great meadows of Africa.

That evening, Murilay's father and mother sat on the ground outside their hut. (The stool was gone which had once stood there.) They watched the sun set – saw its big mottled face dip beneath the fumes of dusk and waver like the thinnest wafer of gold leaf. Then the Moon rose, clean and sharp-edged as a scythe, and cut its way through the last stems of evening cloud. The stars rained.

'I would give every star in the sky to see my son again,' said the old man to his wife, and his wife said, 'So would I.'

Out of the darkness came the lowing of a hundred cattle, and off the plain came a herd of Moon-white cows led by a coppery bull. Riding on the Bull was Murilay, their long-lost son, as rich as the richest, as fit as the fittest, as happy as the happiest, pointing at the stars with a knurled and gnarled stick and singing a song he had learned on the Moon.

Dream Journey

A MAORI MYTH

THERE WAS ONCE a great chieftain, whose mind was as wide as the plain, and whose dreams were as bright as sunshine. One night, a dream shone on his sleep that was almost too dazzling to comprehend, but it filled him with feelings of great hope and excitement. 'Go north,' said the voice in his dream. 'Go north, and I will show you the shape of happiness.'

> *Go alone, without a sound,*
> *Like the shadow of a bird*
> *Passing over broken ground,*
> *Or flies' flicker. Be not heard*
> *More than time passing.'*

Kahakura was so thrilled by his dream that he got up at once and ran down to the beach to tell his people. The young men of his tribe stood about, balanced precariously on the seaside rocks, aiming spears at the fish in the water. They would throw, jump in, retrieve their spears and begin again. Their catch lay on the shore – a couple of bass and a flatfish.

'I must go away! I've dreamed a dream,' announced Kahakura. 'I've seen a vision. I've been made a promise by the gods! Stay here and wait: I'm going north to fetch the gift the gods have promised us!'

The young men stood on one leg and stared at him open-mouthed.

Go away? Leave them without a chief and go north into hostile country? Not if they could help it.

'We'll come with you!' they said, jumping down into the surf. 'We'll all go!' They wanted neither to miss out on the adventure nor to see their chief disappear over the horizon without knowing when or if he would return. So although Kahakura insisted he must go alone, they dogged his footsteps round the settlement and stuck as fast to him as his own shadow. Kahakura began to think he might not be able to do as his dream instructed: his own people would stop him making whatever marvellous discovery awaited him in the north.

One evening, when the whole village was dancing, the music loud and the singing cacophonous, Kahakura backed away into the surrounding darkness. He cast a last fond look at his people dancing in a pool of firelight, then turned and began to run – northwards.

For many days, he trekked through the provinces of tribes whose warriors would have speared him as eagerly as fishermen spearing a fish. But Kahakura wove his way through the grey tassels at either end of day, when the ground is carpeted neither with light nor dark.

At long last, he came to a country called Rangiaowhia, fluffy with white flax and fringed with yellow sand. He first glimpsed the sea in the early morning. It seemed to Kahakura that the moon, in leaving the sky, must have fallen and smashed. For the sea was silver with sparkling lozenges of metallic light. Then the water began to rattle and leap, to explode with fish, such crowds of them that they shouldered each other out of the water to somersault in the surf. A feast of fish! Kahakura's first instinct was to race into the surf and gather them up in armfuls – but instead, he hid himself. He was not first on the scene. Someone was already busy catching the fish.

The fishermen were the frail, slender, tiny Sea People – a tribe who live among the ocean waves and come ashore only as often as the Land people put out to sea. Kahakura had heard tell of them, and now here they were – in front of his very eyes – fishing. And not with spears!

Looking once more at the multitude of fish in the bay, Kahakura saw that they were being hauled in and harvested in a giant bag – a spider's web of woven thread, delicate as hair, yet strong as sinew. When the mouth of the bag was closed, inside it were trapped not one fish or two, but one or two *thousand*!

Kahakura stared. '*This* is what I was sent here to see,' he thought.

'A way of catching fish which will feed my tribe for all time! As long as the sea runs and fish run in the sea, we'll never be hungry again! I must take that bag home with me, to copy how it is made.'

From his hiding place, Kahakura watched the Sea People struggle. Though they were pretty with their yellow hair and pale, smooth skins, they were a puny race, narrow-chested, thin-shanked, with pinched moonish faces. It took twenty men to land the catch, whereas Kahakura could have done it with a couple of friends.

The work done, the young men lay about exhausted among their canoes, while their blond-haired women gutted and cleaned the fish. A flock of gulls gathered to eat the offal, and frightened the Sea People's tiny children.

Apart from the other women sat a girl quite different from the rest. She had the task of mending the net. Children sat about her feet, laughing at the stories and jokes she told them, but the other women sat with their backs turned, and threw her not so much as a civil word. Perhaps it was her beauty which made them resent her. Perhaps it was her formidable size which made the men equally unkind. Taller than the tallest fishermen, she had hips like the curving bole of a tree, and arms strong enough to carry a family of children. Her clever hands wove and knotted flaxen thread into the holes where the net had torn. Kahakura was so entranced by the sight of her and her quick, darting fingers that he almost forgot why the gods had sent him to Rangiaowhia.

The net!

He jumped up from his hiding place, thinking to tell the Sea People . . . what? As his head rose above the bushes, he realized he had not even thought what to say, or how to come by the precious net which now lay stretched at the girl's feet. He had nothing to trade for it, no weapon to fight for it, and the language of the Sea People was strange to him. So when they caught sight of him, he spoke with a great loud voice – as people do to make foreigners understand them.

'I am Kahakura of the Maori People! I dreamed a dream and I saw a vision . . . Wait, don't go!'

The Sea People took one look at his towering frame, huge shoulders, broad chest. Then mothers snatched up their children and threw them into the canoes, jumping in after them. The men plunged into the surf and dragged the canoes out to sea.

The big yellow-haired girl took two steps from her seat and fell, her feet tangled in the net she had been mending. Her basket of threads and tools was squandered on the ground. For a moment, Kahakura thought to bundle her up in the net like a giant tuna, and sling her over his back. He had to have her for his wife, stroke that golden hair, and watch her bounce his children on her knee.

But the thought came to him – as clearly as the dream had come to him in sleeping – that a man does not take a wife in the same way as a fisherman takes a tuna. So he stood just where he was, and allowed her to untangle her feet and get up.

She ran a few steps towards the sea – saw her tribe and family paddling away from her, abandoning her, but did not cry out. She looked back to where Kahakura stood wearing a crooked, uncertain smile. He gathered up the spilled tools and thread and handed the basket back to her. 'It is as the gods wish, or my eyes would not have seen you,' he said. And she seemed to understand.

So Kahakura took home to his tribe the amazing secret of fishing nets – how they are used and how they are made. And he took home, too, a wife with golden hair, and curved hips like the bole of a flourishing tree, and strong arms destined to hold a family of children. As long as the sea runs, and the fish run in the sea, the Maori People will never go hungry for fish, nor empty of love. It is as the gods wish.

Roland and the Horn Olivant
A LEGEND FROM FRANCE

THE KNIGHTS OF Charlemagne were like the spring flowers which brighten fields as far as the eye can see. Resplendent with flapping pennons and banners of purple silk, the army prinked its way on high-prancing horses over the faces of the fallen enemy; its minstrels outsang the evening birds. Saddlecloths swept the ground like the skirts of the women waiting at home for the knights of Charlemagne, the finest men in all the world. And finest of them all was Roland.

Even in retreat they were magnificent. They carried their wounds like the red rosettes of victory, and they died with a joke and a prayer. The army of Charlemagne was like the spring which covers the fields in flowers . . . but the Saracens were like the locusts which strip fields bare. Though the Emperor Charlemagne had conquered most of the world, the Saracens denied him the realms of Spain. Their troops massed to turn him back, as tightly packed as bricks in a wall. In the end, there was no more purpose to be served in throwing good men against such a wall to see them break, and Charlemagne withdrew. His knights were the finest in all the world, and the finest of them all was Roland.

'Sir Roland, my friend and pride of my knights,' said Charlemagne, 'command the rearguard, I beg you, and shelter the wounded and the weary from attack as we retreat.'

'I shall, my lord – if we really must leave Spain unconquered.'

'Better to withdraw and come back another day, eh, than grant the enemy our blood to walk in and our shields to decorate their halls . . . ? Do you have Olivant with you?'

Sir Roland nodded and pointed to his horse. Hung by a scarlet cord from his saddle was a huge horn – the tusk of an elephant, carved by Roland's own hand, reamed and bored with fire and hot steel. No one but Roland could blow it, and there was no sound like the shriek of Horn Olivant. 'If you need reinforcements,' said the Emperor, 'sound Olivant, and I shall turn back to help you.'

Roland, in his pride, bridled a little, and his cheeks flushed. 'I shall summon you, my lord, if I prove unequal to my task.'

The army began to move. Like a frozen river thawed by spring, it moved between the craggy mountain passes. First came Charlemagne with his princes, dukes and earls, then his knights, squires and foot-soldiers; next the wagons and the wagonboys, the armourers, farriers and fletchers; the machinery and engines of war. After, came the dead, fetched out of battle by their friends for decent burial in a Christian land; and behind them, moving with painful slowness, came the wounded and the sick, wearing bloodstained banners for blankets, and marching in silence, without breath enough for song.

Behind them came the troops of Roland, half-turned in their saddles to watch for pursuers.

'Charlemagne leaving Spain? By the God I serve, he shall not!' declared the great Sultan in his marble courts. 'Pursue him with sword and arrow and let not one man live who has offended me by setting foot in Spain! No, when your work is done let not two letters of that filthy name hang together: *Charlemagne*!'

At Roncesvalles it happened. The Saracens came down like wolves upon a flock of sheep. When Roland saw the dust raised by their horses' hooves, he wheeled his knights about and deployed them as a blockade across the path, to shield the column of retreating Franks. Roland made a wall of men to stop the Saracen rout.

'We shall be the reef on which they founder!' he shouted to his men, and the sight of his great war horse, prancing from end to end of the human wall, put heart into his battalion and fired them with resolve. 'Ours is the honour of saving Charlemagne's army, that he may go on to win new victories! Ours is the honour of doing our duty! Let us leave the Saracens with one last taste of our mettle! Let's write one last page of history!'

And it seemed as though that page would be written in gold. For five tides of Saracens broke against the reef of Frankish Knights, but it held fast, and they could not break through. Like summer flies the Saracens fell, while the Frankish shields held firm, edge to edge – a palisade painted with heraldic beasts. At long last, the Saracens withdrew and the weary knights drew breath and congratulated one another on their daring and skill.

Then five more battalions of Saracens appeared over the rocky horizon.

So the page of history was to be written in blood, after all. As the five tides broke against the Frankish reef, soldiers too weary any longer to lift a sword were trampled down. Knights wounded in the first onslaught found their limbs too cold to raise lance or axe, and fell beneath Saracen swords. When, at last, the tenth battalion was driven off, the splendour of Charlemagne's rearguard was as tattered as a windfrayed banner. Still, the wall had held. The column of wounded and sick crept away around distant bends in the mountain track.

'The day is ours and all the honour!' cried Roland exultantly. 'I did not sound the Horn Olivant, for we alone did what was asked of us!' He rose proudly in his stirrups.

. . . That was when he glimpsed the dust of five battalions more.

'Sound the horn now, my lord!' exclaimed his sergeant. 'Signal the Emperor that we are outnumbered!'

'And lose the honour of the day? Plead for help, No! Olivant shall not speak today! Not while I have power to lift my sword and men around me who are Franks!'

So the Saracen battalions broke over the reef of Frankish knights and swept many away. Horses clad in Frankish colours lay dead on top of their dead riders, and fallen shields bossed the ground.

Each man spent his life dearly, and took ten Saracen souls with him to the gates of death. Even so, when the third onslaught fell back, nothing more was left of Roland's defensive wall than a knot of fifty exhausted men.

'We have turned them! We have finished them!' exclaimed Roland, crimson from head to foot in the blood of his enemies.

As one man, the fifty lay down with a crash of buckled armour.

They were too weary to raise a cheer. They had seen too many friends die to glory in their survival. A dozen vultures hopped and crouched within arm's reach, but no one had strength to shoo them away. Over the distant mountain ridges, the last of the column of retreating Frankish wounded moved out of sight. Roland watched them disappear with satisfaction.

Turning back, he saw, by the light of the low sun, another five battalions of Saracens closing in fast. Their numbers were as vast as the waves in the sea. They would wash over Roland's rearguard like the ocean over a handful of pebbles.

Fifty men looked at him with despair in their eyes. Fifty swords stabbed the ground, as the knights of Roland dragged themselves painfully to their feet once more.

Only then did Roland reach for his ivory horn. He placed it to his lips, and prayed for breath enough to blow it. He summoned the breath from the four winds, and he blew till his eyes and ears bled.

Olivant gave a blast which froze the Saracen horses in their tracks. Overhead in the sky, birds stricken by the note fell dead on to the helms of the advancing Moors. Elephants bellowed on the dusty plains of Africa, as if stirred by a memory. Boulders rolled and shattered, and the clodded mud shivered into sandy grains.

Roland's horse died beneath him, its great heart shrunk by the terrible noise. And the Horn Olivant – sounded a thousand times in victory – cracked and split in sounding defeat.

Twenty miles away, Charlemagne put his hands to his ears at the sound. He knew the Horn Olivant as well as the cry of his own baby son, as well as the echo of his own voice.

'Roland needs us!' he told his princes and dukes, his earls and knights.

They rode back through the brightly clothed squires, past the muddy foot soldiers, through the feathered ranks of archers, past the wagons and wagonboys. Their frenzied gallop startled the armourers and farriers, shook the machines and engines of war. The dead men slung across their saddles all but woke. The wounded and the sick shuffled aside to make room, for they too had heard the cry of Horn Olivant and knew that Roland was in need of help.

Too late did Charlemagne return to Roncesvalles. Too late did he counter the last Saracen attack. One hundred thousand of the enemy had finally overwhelmed the troops of Roland, and the finest of the Frankish chivalry lay like a field of flowers killed by frost.

Roland himself lay face up to the sky, beside him the Horn Olivant, like a crescent moon cradling the sun. Across his legs lay a Saracen banner, token of respect from one race of knights to another. At the sight of it, Charlemagne wept. 'Oh proud, proud Roland! Why did you wait so long to sound your horn?' asked the Emperor of his finest knight. But Roland said nothing in reply. The lips which had sounded Horn Olivant were silent now, and pale as ivory.

A Question of Life and Death

A GREEK MYTH

THE PEOPLE OF Thebes grew lazy and selfish, and begrudged the things they had once given to the gods. They visited the temple of the sun god Apollo less and less often, left smaller and smaller offerings on the altar. One day, when he found nothing but a half-eaten apple and a sardine, where once there had been whole carcasses of beef, whole sheaves of flowers, he considered the time had come to remind Thebes of its duties to the gods. He sent a monster, a creature of hideous grace, of grotesque magnificence, to devour anyone who set foot outside the town.

The Sphinx – part woman, part lion, part eagle – made her lair above the main highway out of Thebes, couched on a ledge of rock. Whenever a traveller passed by, down she would leap, waving her lion's tail. The traveller, stricken with wonder as much as fear, would gaze up at the tumbling mane of black and gold fur, the soulful features, the gigantic wings raising the Sphinx rampant off the ground. Her shadow cast the whole valley into gloom.

'Answer me this riddle,' she demanded, in a voice as big as doom. 'Which animal has four legs in the morning, two in the afternoon, three in the evening, and is weakest when it has most?'

It was the kind of teaser that might go round at a party, or to pass the time on a journey. And yet no one who trod that road out of Thebes thought the riddle a small or trivial joke. It was a question of life or death. For when they guessed wrongly, the Sphinx tore them cloth from clothes, hair from head, limb from trunk, body from soul, and ate each piece.

Soon no one dared come to Thebes and no one dared leave. The Council sat to discuss the answer to the riddle. The townspeople huddled on street corners, their only conversation the Riddle of the Sphinx. Rewards were offered – the throne of Thebes and the hand of the newly widowed queen in marriage – and people reckless, or penniless, or cocksure enough, risked answering the Sphinx's riddle.

'Which animal has four legs in the morning, two in the afternoon and three in the evening and is weakest when it has most?'

'A giraffe!'

'A circus horse!'

'One of the constellations!'

No one returned to claim their reward.

'A centipede!'

'One of the gods!'

'A cockatrice!'

No one returned.

Then along came Oedipus. He approached Thebes one green morning – and was met by the Sphinx.

'Which animal has four legs in the morning, two in the afternoon and three in the evening, and is weakest when it has most?'

Oedipus shielded his eyes and looked up at the Sphinx, a woman of sumptuous beauty imprisoned in the body of a lion and given only wings to solace her. 'You are only a lion, and though the lion is called King of the Beasts, truly it is not: Man is that. You are only an eagle, and though you may fly high over the earth, you do not rule it: Man does that. You are only a woman, and though you may have had men love, hate or fear you, you are powerless: Man will always oppress you.'

'Answer my riddle!' demanded the Sphinx in a voice as terrible as fate.

'I already have. A man crawls on all fours when he's a baby, on two when he's grown, and leans on a stick in his old age, when he's frail and toothless, "Man" is the answer to your riddle, and Oedipus is the man who answered it.'

At that, the Sphinx gave a scream, like an eagle falling, like a lion caught in a trap, like a woman vexed to the point of desperation. She pounced at Oedipus – over Oedipus – clearing his head with her lion's leap. Over the brink of a gaping ravine she leapt. Her wings opened no more than a book riffling its torn pages, for she had chosen to die on the rocks below.

Thebes whooped with joy, opened its gates once more, and made Oedipus King. Once again they made sacrifices to Apollo and the gods who lived on Mount Olympus. People hardly bothered to remember the answer to the riddle, though they never forgot the Sphinx. Perhaps the true Riddle of the Sphinx is not what she asked, but why she asked it, and why the right answer drove her to such despair.

The Harp of Dagda

AN IRISH MYTH

THEY CAME FROM the four great cities in the sky – from Falias and Gorias, Finias and Murias. They had studied every kind of knowledge at the feet of the cities' Four Wise Kings, but their destiny was to live on earth a while, a tribe like any other. So they came riding down on the wind, hidden by magic clouds, and the home they chose – for were they not the wisest of the wise? – was Ireland. Their chieftain was Dagda, and they were like giant gods to the wild men of the bogs and peat lakes. They were the Good Men, the Dananns.

With them they brought the greatest treasure from each of the four celestial cities: a stone from Falias, a sword from Gorias, a spear from Finias and, from Murias, the bottomless cauldron.

Even in times of famine, the Dagda's Magic Cauldron was always full – of meaty soup, or porridge threaded with golden honey – and no matter how many hungry people dipped in their spoons, it was never emptied, never scraped clean to the iron studs of its bulging belly. No wonder they clamoured to make Dagda King of Ireland, too.

The Magic Stone was placed beneath the throne; and when Dagda seated himself, it roared like a lion, as if to say, 'You have chosen aright. This is the true King.' No king was chosen afterwards unless the stone shouted for him.

In battle the Magic Spear felled twenty men each time it was thrown, and the Magic Sword melted whole ranks of men where they stood.

But greater still than all these treasures was the Dagda's Harp and the Harpist who played it to him at the glimmering fireside. For men can fight their battles with bare hands if need be, and tighten their belts when they are hungry. But no civilized man can live without music and song.

Even the barbarian, spitting into the straw of his squalid hut, wants music to soothe him at the end of a long day's cruelty. That is why the King of the Fomorians set his heart on having the Harp of Dagda.

Nine winged Fomorian warriors flew down on the castle of the Dananns, like skuas mobbing the snowy gulls on the cliffs of Tyree. Shrieking and swooping, they seized the Harpist by his curly hair and lifted both him and his harp high into a stormy sky. The Dananns, rushing to the doorway, shaking their swords at the diminishing shapes in the wild sky, felt rain fall in their faces like the notes of a lament.

'This time the Fomorians have flown one league too far into the realms of wickedness,' said Dagda, his head brushing the roofbeams, his cloak extinguishing the fire. 'Come, Men of the Good, and we shall get back the Harp and the Harpist of Dagda!'

'Shall we strike them dead with the Magic Spear of Finias?'

'Shall we cut them in pieces with the Magic Sword?'

Dagda considered, and upon consideration dropped his voice to a murmur. 'No, children, no. For the Harp has soul enough to yearn for its home, and the Fomorians have too little soul to know the value of what they have. There will be no need to spill blood.'

Three men only, Dagda, Lugh and Ogma the Warrior, travelled to the Fomorian settlement. It took them some time, for they did not fly, but patiently picked their way over bog and heath, sheep track and stony stream till they saw a crooked pall of smoke rising from a crooked roof. The banqueting hall of the Fomorians was crammed with noise, but none was harp music. For the Harp refused to sound and the Harpist refused to play it, and no Fomorian had the art of making music. The King, after an outburst of spleen, had hung the Harp, along with his other hunting trophies, high on the wall.

When he saw the gigantic Dagda filling the doorway of the

banqueting hall, he rubbed his smoke-reddened eyes and grinned. 'Come in! Come in!' he said, thinking to humiliate the Dananns still more with condescending shows of hospitality. 'Cooks! Prepare a bite for the great Dagda. You know what an appetite the man has!'

Three men with shovels set about digging a pit in the floor, a trough big enough to hold a horse. Then the cooks brought cauldrons full of porridge and vats full of milk, and slopped them into the pit until a steaming pond lay at Dagda's feet, looking more like a bath than a meal.

'Most kind,' said Dagda, graciously inclining his head. He pulled from his belt a spoon, or rather a ladle, its bowl so big that a man and woman could have cheerfully gone to bed in it and not fallen out till morning. In a matter of half a dozen spoonfuls, the porridge was gone, though Dagda stayed to scrape round the hole, supplementing his meal with a spoonful or two of gravel and earth.

While the Fomorians sat spellbound by this massive feat of eating, Dagda's eyes searched the smoky hall till they lit on the Harp. Under his breath he began to say,

'O come, my orchard of notes,
Strung with the four seasons of sound.
Come, you breath of spring,
You heat of summer,
You colours of autumn,
You stillness of winter.
Come, you bed of sweet sleep!
Come, you square for dancing!
Come, you weft of woven stories!
Come, you web of captured dreams!
Come, you magic, mouthless, marvellous, musical man of mine!'

The Harp sprang from the wall and plunged like a fish eagle. It cracked against the skulls of the nine Fomorians who had raided the Castle of Dagda, and their black wings sagged around them, moulting in the moment of death. Then it settled in the arms of Dagda, as gentle as Noah's dove returning to the ark.

As the room erupted in chaos, the Fomorian men diving for their swords, the women shrieking with terror, Dagda touched the strings of his harp and began to play – a hearty, happy tune. He smiled as he did so, and the Harpist, who had crept to his feet, smiled too. But the Fomorians did more than smile. They began to laugh! They could not help it. Their shoulders jigged and their big bellies quaked while they laughed just as though they had heard the funniest of jokes.

They held their sides and dabbed their eyes, and those who had half risen to kill the Dananns where they stood, rolled across the table in paroxysms of helpless laughter.

Dagda passed the harp to his son Ogma, who played in a different key – a sad, lilting lament like the grief of a dying swan. The laughing Fomorians, like children at bedtime who have over-excited themselves, burst into sudden hysterical tears. Their eyes streamed and their mouths gaped open, wailing and weeping till the dirty floor was slippery with tears.

Then Ogma handed the Harp to its harpist, who cradled it like a new-born baby and bent his head, low and loving, over the web of strings. The weeping Fomorians, despite their uncontrollable grief, had turned over the table and were starting to throw aside the stools to lay hands on the three Dananns. Some had drawn swords, others spears which they raised overhead, preparing to impale the Good Men against the door.

But when the Harpist began to play, the foremost spear-wielder halted on one foot and leaned backwards. His wailing mouth stretched wider still into a monumental yawn. Then he keeled over backwards like a felled tree. Drunken with sudden sleepiness, the rest of the Fomorians reeled about, cannoning into one another and tumbling to the floor. Some slept propped in the corners, and one hung over the back of a chair.

The King simply rolled out of his throne and into the dogs' basket, where the hounds licked him curiously.

'Until we meet on the battlefield!' said Dagda to the sleeping Fomorians. 'For such is our fate.' Then he and his warriors closed the great doors softly behind them. The sound of snoring followed them all the way back to their castle.

The death of days and the tides of time wrought a change in the men called Good. When the world grew old and sour and villainous, like the Fomorians, the tribe of Good diminished – oh, not in wisdom or skill, but in actual physical stature. They shrank, just as the goodness of the world shrank, and changed their dwelling place once again, from earth to the places beneath the earth. They lived in the green mounds of the lonely places and changed – as the grub changes to a butterfly – into the faeries of Ireland.

And they took with them their treasures: the sword, the cauldron, the spear – all but the Magic Stone. Most certainly, they took Dagda's Harp. That is why, sometimes, you may see a man, all alone and quite without cause, suddenly laugh out loud, or weep into his sleeve, or sit down beneath a tree on a grassy mound and fall asleep with the ease of a child. He has heard the music, you see, coming from underground.

A Nest and a Web

A LEGEND FROM THE MIDDLE EAST

A T FIRST, WHEN Muhammad preached, they said he was mad. But that is not uncommon in the experience of prophets. When his words began to be believed, then he was in far greater danger.

For Muhammad the prophet lived in Mecca, city of the idol-makers, who had charge of the house of the gods and made their money selling idols. In those days, the house of the gods in Mecca held three hundred and sixty idols depicting the gods of a multitude of different religions. People came from all over the pagan world to worship this god, or that goddess, and there was a great deal of money to be made from selling them goods and mementos of their pilgrimage.

But Muhammad spoke of only one God. 'Smash the pagan idols, empty God's house of them. Allah is the one, the only God.'

Now Muhammad was a man of good reputation, with great influence in the city. When he spoke, he fired the hearts of his listeners. He was called the One Who Can Be Trusted, for his fair dealing in business, and he dreamed dreams of the kind lesser men do not.

So the idol-makers trod carefully. 'We'll make you King of Mecca if only you will stop your preaching, Muhammad!' they said. 'Don't you see how this new religion of yours will damage the trade in idols and cut the revenue of the house of the gods?'

But Muhammad did not care about their greedy profits, and he would not stop preaching what God had told him to preach. 'Allah is the one, the only God.'

When bribes did not work, the idol-makers used threats. 'We'll shun all your tribe and buy nothing from them in the marketplace. Perhaps they can put a stop to this foolishness of yours!'

But Muhammad would not stop his preaching. 'Allah is the one, the only God.'

Next, the idol-makers pretended to be tolerant. But Muhammad's following was growing; more and more people began to believe what he was saying. Muhammad knew that the idol-makers would resort to violence soon, to put a stop to him.

Some pilgrims from Medina, four hundred kilometres away, heard Muhammad preach – 'Allah is the one, the only God!' – and they delighted in his message. 'Come and preach in Medina!' they said. 'We want our friends, our families, our neighbours to hear you for themselves. Honour us with your presence! Leave behind Mecca and all those who hate you!'

So Muhammad left Mecca with his wife – left the city where he had grown up, left the house of the gods and the company of his tribe. And he walked out along a new road, into a new Chapter of his life's story.

Only in the nick of time did he leave. For assassins were on the streets that same night, with drawn knives, and murder in their hearts. 'Gone? Left to spread his lies further afield? He must be stopped!' The idol-makers were filled with bitter malice, and went after Muhammad, armed and on horseback, pursuing a pair of helpless travellers.

The ground shook to the gallop of hooves. When Muhammad looked round, the sun shone on naked swords and spear points. There was only one road, and the idol-makers intended to ride it till they rode down Muhammad and trampled his 'message' into the dust.

In a gorge, where the hot sun ricocheted from rock to rock, and the air melted and ran, Muhammad sought a hiding place. He found a cave a little way from the track, clambering over rocks and thorns to reach its dark mouth. He and his wife crept inside – it was cool, like a blessing – and crouched down, silent and still, in the rear of the cave.

But the galloping came closer with every second, and now the noise of voices, too – shouted commands, and swords slashing at the brambles. There was not the smallest chance that the cave would escape attention if the pursuers searched the gorge.

The horses came to a halt directly below. Men dismounted, and footsteps could be heard on the grassless ground. There was a rattle of stones as two soldiers clambered towards the mouth of the cave. Their silhouettes moved across the daylit entrance, and Muhammad's wife huddled closer, pressing her hands over her mouth in terror.

'Look here,' said one of the searchers, 'a pigeon's nest with a full brood of eggs in it.'

The second came to see, but chose not to count the little blue eggs for it would mean brushing his face against a massive spider's web. The web's geometric threads, strung with dewdrops, shimmered in the sunlight, the tapestried work of weeks by some industrious spider. It clad the cliff face and curtained the cave from portal to portal.

'Well, it's plain no one's been this way for a while,' said the soldiers, and turned back down the mountainside.

Muhammad's wife turned to her husband in amazement.

A web? A nest full of unbroken birds' eggs? How had she entered the cave without seeing them? How had they both entered the cave without breaking them? It was impossible, as the soldiers had rightly thought.

Muhammad was deep in prayer, facing towards the holy city he had left behind. His face was at peace, his praying hands steady, not shaking. 'Of course,' thought his wife. Where was her faith that she had feared for their safety? Was not Allah great enough, resourceful enough to protect his own prophet from danger? Was it so incredible that Allah, who made the universe, should have spared the gift of a bird's nest and a spider's web to keep Muhammad and his message alive?

When the idol-makers had gone, Muhammad and his wife continued on their way towards Medina and a new life, breaking free of the past as pigeon chicks break free from their eggs. And eloquent Muhammad went on to weave a web of words which captured the hearts and souls of millions.

Ash

A NATIVE AMERICAN MYTH

A MAN HAD four sons, and three of them were his pride and joy. The fourth was his despair. Squat and ugly, he spent all day lolling by the fire, gazing into the flames, never stirring to do a useful day's work. 'What are you *doing* exactly?' his father would ask, losing patience.

'Just thinking.' His face was streaked with soot, his clothes grubby with sitting in the warm ashes: his brothers called him Ash. They called him a great many other, less flattering names, as well, and threw things at him – fish bones, apple cores, insults. But Ash hardly noticed. The flames' reflection danced in his bloodshot eyes, and he just went on thinking.

To the whole village, Ash was an idle layabout. They could not pass by without kicking him, could not talk about him without a sneer in their voices and a spit in his direction.

The young women went by giggling and chanting:

> '*Ash, Ash, go and hunt!*
> *Or is your hunting knife too blunt?*
> *Ash, Ash, make a wish!*
> *Wish you'd ever caught a fish?*
> *Ash, Ash, by the fire*
> *What made you so awful tired?*
> *Wasn't chasing girls, I bet'ya:*
> *Wouldn't know one if you met her!*'

Then one day the neighbouring tribe issued a challenge: 'Our champion will wrestle yours!'

Ash's brothers, like all the other young men, were thrilled, glad of the excitement, eager to be chosen champion of the tribe . . . until they saw their opponent. Whale Man was as big as a hut and as heavy with blubber as a bull seal. He came through the woods breaking down saplings and knocking bears out of the trees. He picked up a newly carved canoe and threw it like a paper dart, so that it wedged in a mudbank. Then, bellowing like a moose, he kicked a hole in the side of the village long house rather than go in through the door.

'Who's it going to be? Whose head shall I rip off today?'

There was a long wait for volunteers.

The village squirmed with shame. The chieftain pondered how many sealskins he must give his neighbours, to make them go away and take their champion with them.

'I'll fight you,' said Ash, standing up. 'You've put out the fire anyway, with your big feet. So I may as well fight you, to keep warm.'

The giant wrestler began to laugh. The women began to laugh with him, to be polite, and then the men joined in, hoping the giant had a sense of humour. Ash? Wrestle?

'You? You couldn't wrestle your way out of a hammock!' hissed his brothers. 'Keep quiet; you'll make things worse!'

But Ash simply ducked out through the hole in the wall, waited for Whale Man to follow, and then took hold of him by both feet. Ash shook Whale Man like a blanket, till the fleas flew out of his hair, then beat him like a drum, till the stains flew off his loincloth. Ash whirled him about by his ears, and flung him into the next valley where he landed with a noise like rotten fruit. When the chief looked around, the challengers were nowhere to be seen.

'Wow!' he exclaimed.

'Fluke,' said one brother.

'Lucky accident,' said another.

'Trick of the light,' said the third.

But Ash had gone back indoors, anyway, and stretched himself out beside the newly built fire. No one mentioned the matter of the giant again, and he never reminded them.

There was magic in Ash. He must have read it in the embers, or dreamed it in a dream. But somehow there was magic in Ash, and his fellow men chose to ignore it. Magic does not like to be ignored.

Early one morning, a woman emerged from the long house, on her way to fetch water. She looked at the skyline and gave a shriek. For lumbering towards her, larger than any giant, were all the trees of the distant forests – on the warpath.

From every side came trees, roots clawing up the soil, knotting their branches into fists, their heads tossing with indignation. 'We're surrounded! We're done for!' cried the villagers, clinging to one another. 'They'll trample us into the ground!'

Not until the trees were shoulder to shoulder, their branches interlocking, their trunks as close as the bars of a cage, did Ash stir from beside the fire. He stepped to the door of the hut, peered blearily against the bright light, and shouted: 'Stop it! Go back! There's no harm done! My word on it!'

The trees faltered and came to a halt. Their dark green tops bent over Ash, like parents bending anxiously over an injured child. Fir cones fell by the hundred on the long house roof. Then the trees spun round on their roots and trudged away. With the wind soughing through their green needles, they sounded like grumpy whisperers.

'That was a narrow escape,' said Ash's father.

'Near thing,' said his brother.

'Did you hear Ash?' said a second. 'Who did he think he was shouting at? Does he really think he made the trees go?'

'Must be even madder than we thought,' said the third.

The ground rumbled and the sky shook. The villagers, dawdling back to their work, looked up and saw – no, it could not be – the smallest of changes in the familiar view. The horizon did not seem quite the same shape, the mountains not quite as they had been before.

But the ground rumbled and the sky continued to shake. By noon, they realized the dreadful truth – that the far-off mountains were no longer far away. They had picked up their skirts of grass, flexed their bones of rock and were moving, purple-headed with anger, across the coastal plain. Where their shoulders rubbed together, sparks flew, and from their clenched fists, boulders tumbled in avalanches of rage.

You see, there was magic in Ash, and magic does not like to be ignored.

Larger and larger loomed the mountains, closing in on every side, while the villagers ran this way and that, but found no escape.

'Ash! Ash! Come out and speak to them! Tell them to stop! Ask them not to crush us! Help us, do!' they begged, but Ash only lazed beside the fire, watching the magic of the flames as usual. At last he got to his feet, went outside, and held up both hands. 'Peace. Stand still. That's far enough.'

Obedient as dogs, the mountains lay down where they were, jostling, settling, lounging along the ground, the evening sun on their watching faces. This time, when Ash lay back down in his favourite place, the girls brought him food, his brothers brought him drink, and his father threw more wood on the fire.

Now they saw the magic in Ash, his family and tribe stopped calling him a layabout and a fool. Suddenly they were as proud to have him in their midst as any champion wrestler or holy man, and spoke of him boastfully: 'We have a man full of magic! The trees and mountains do as he tells them! We have a man who can think all day, without tiring! If only we had his wisdom. If only we had his magic in us!'

One day, visitors came calling. Six men got out of a fine carved canoe and walked up to the village.

'Greetings. Have you come to buy sealskins?' said the villagers, but the strangers answered not a word.

'Have you come in peace? Or to challenge us to wrestle?' said the villagers, but the strangers answered not a word.

'Have you come looking for bribes? Or warriors? Or craftsmen? Or fishermen?'

But the strangers simply walked straight ahead into the long hut and up to the fire where Ash lay thinking.

'I have been expecting you,' said Ash, looking up at once. Instead of flames dancing in his eyes, they had become strangely blue, the colour of water. 'Is your master ill?'

'He is, young man, and if we do not hurry, he may die before we get back to him. Please come.'

Ash got up and strode down to the canoe with them. He climbed aboard and took up an oar, and his powerful arms helped speed the boat out to sea.

Not far from the horizon, where the setting sun gouged a blood-red whirlpool in the sea, the canoe spun round three times, and sank out of sight.

Standing tiptoe on the shore, the young women wept and Ash's father wrung his hands. 'Death had sent an escort for him! Death has taken away our magical young man!'

But the six messengers were not from Death. They came from the sea caves beneath the setting sun, sent by the strongest man of all. When the canoe touched bottom, all seven got out and began to walk. Rays swam by like blankets on a high wind. Dogfish cruised the canyons of weed-hung rock. The sunlight filtered, in a frail dapple, through the choppy surface of the sea, lighting a silver storm of salmon. Across the sea floor, the six messengers led Ash to a deep sea trench. And there, on a bed of sea grass, lay a man so old that his body was more spirit than flesh. It seemed that some monstrous torturer had skewered him to the bed of the sea, for a huge pole stood on his chest, soaring high, high out of view.

'Ah! You have come at last! At last I may rest. At last!' sighed the frail old man, lifting his head a little. 'For a thousand years I have held up the sky with this pole. For a thousand years, my strength has been equal to the task. But now I am old and dying, and there is no one but you with magic enough in your soul and strength enough in your breast to balance this pole in my place.'

Ash at once lay down beside the old man, and took the end of the pole, resting it on his own chest. The soot that had always stained his face had washed clean away. The smuts that had always dirtied his clothes floated away on the tide.

'I am asking much of you, Spotless One,' said the weary old man. 'What will you do, as the years wash the rocks into sand? What will you do to pass the time away?'

'Oh, that will be no hardship to me,' Spotless One replied. 'I do not know the meaning of boredom. I shall simply lie here and watch the magic of sunlight dancing on the wave tops. And that will help me think.'

The Tower of Babel

A HEBREW MYTH

EARLY IN THE morning of the world, before the human race had grown very large at all, it moved all together, one great tribe of wandering nomads pitching their tents where dusk overtook them.

Then one day, in one year, they decided to exchange tents for houses of stone, and they built a city in the centre of a great plain, and stopped their wandering. When the city was built, they were very proud of it – overly proud of it, for its gateways and market squares, its staircases and turrets convinced them, 'There's nothing we can't do! Let's build a tower as high as Heaven itself, so that people half a world away will see it and wonder!' So they baked bricks and they mixed mortar and they built up . . . and up and up.

When God saw their tower growing, and their pride growing along with the tower, he did not like the idea of the people of Babel reaching so far upwards. So he stamped once, and the ground trembled. He breathed once, and the mortar dried to dust and bled from between the bricks. He took one brick from the base of the Tower of Babel, and it fell. Like Satan falling on his belly in the dust, the Tower of Babel tumbled, and with it the pride and ambition of its builders. Clutching each other, clutching at limbs of wood and lintels of stone, they plummeted to the ground, rolling and bowling in every direction across the great plain.

And when they opened their mouths to bemoan the disaster,

strange words came from between their lips, strange accents and dialects. Tugging at one another's coats, gesticulating with frantic hands, they yelled in each other's faces. But one man could not make sense of what his neighbour said to him; one woman could not make the woman beside her understand.

The great city was never finished. The Tower of Babel was never rebuilt. For with human beings split and divided by differences of language, they found it very hard to work, or even to think, in harmony.

They have never learned the trick of it, not in all these years.

Saint Christopher

A EUROPEAN LEGEND

CHRISTOPHER WAS BORN neither good nor bad, but he knew his worth. 'I'm strong, I'm tall, I can turn my hand to most things. I shall work for only the best. I shall take for my master the most powerful ruler in the world.' So he went down to Hell, to serve the Devil, because he had heard that more people feared the Devil than any other emperor or tyrant. Certainly the Devil's banners were to be seen flying everywhere on Earth.

At the door of Hell, there was a long queue of people wanting to sign in the Devil's service. At last Christopher and one other man were admitted into the presence of the Lord of Darkness, who sat on a throne of fire, eating sparks.

'Swear to obey me in all things,' said the Devil (which was the way of masters and servants in those days).

'What should I swear by?' asked the other applicant. 'By my mother? On my life? By Jesus Christ?' At the mention of Christ's name, the Devil gave a shudder, and his red eyes rolled. Christopher had sudden misgivings. Quickly, he made the sign of the Cross – he had often seen Christians do it – touching his forehead, chest, then each shoulder. Sure enough, the Devil leapt out of his chair and ran. 'Don't do that! Don't! If you're going to work for me, don't ever do that, d'you hear?'

'Work for him?' thought Christopher, as the Devil slammed the chamber door. 'I set out to work for the most powerful master in the world. Plainly this Jesus Christ is more powerful.'

So he made it his business to find out all about Jesus. And he liked what he heard.

'What must I do to serve this Jesus Christ?' he asked a priest.

'Serve your fellow men. Either by prayer, as a monk, or by making yourself useful to those in need.'

'You mean I don't get to meet him? Not meet my own master?'

'Not in this life, Christopher. In this life you will only see Christ's face in the faces of the poor and needy.'

Now Christopher was not of a nature suited to a monk's life, so he decided to make himself useful in some practical way. He built himself a hut beside a river, and whenever travellers needed to cross over, he carried them across the river on his strong shoulders. Whole families of eight and nine children he could carry, though the current was strong and the river cold and wide. As he carried them, he would listen to their sad stories, and make the children laugh and the adults brighten, while he sang a song or told a fable.

One day, a little boy came to the river. 'I want to cross over,' he said.

Christopher swung him on to his shoulders as a swimmer might hang a towel round his neck, and broke into a cheerful song.

But a short way out from the shore, he had to stop singing. The boy was much heavier than he looked. 'I must be getting old,' he told his passenger. 'I've carried ten of your size before now, without thinking twice!'

Halfway across the river, the child began to feel even heavier. Christopher could hardly lift his head or straighten his back. 'What age did you say you were, boy?' But the boy did not reply.

With every step, the boy grew heavier, so that soon Christopher could barely keep his footing. The river shoved at him, and the weight on his back bore down like a bale of wool, a full barrel, a hod of bricks. He staggered and gasped for breath. His mouth was being pushed under, his nose too. He had either to let go of the boy or drown. He turned his face towards the sky and took a last gulp of air. 'I fear, son, that I cannot . . .'

And yet he must. How could he let a child drown whom he had offered to carry? He must get the boy to the shore, even if it cost him his last ounce of strength. The river swamped him. The boy's hand, clutched in his hair, seemed to be plucking out his brain, and yet he plunged on, his face submerged now, his lungs bursting. In his heart, he prayed: not to live, but that the boy should not drown.

At last, his feet felt shallower ground and he crawled up the bank on all fours and dropped on his face beneath the boy.

'Thank you,' said the child, 'but I have no money to pay you.'

Christopher did not want to frighten him by saying how close they had both come to drowning, so he simply rolled on to his back, smiled through his sodden beard, and said what he always said. 'No charge, son. I did it for Christ.'

'You speak truer than you know,' said the boy in a deep, musical voice, then ran away, fast as a deer, across the wooded landscape.

Christopher lay on his back looking up at the sky. And when he had breath enough to speak what he had realized, he shouted up at the birds: 'No wonder he weighed so much! I wasn't carrying a child – I was carrying the greatest man in the world! I met Jesus today, and carried him on my back!'

And that is why travellers pray to Saint Christopher for a safe journey, because everyone needs kindness from those they meet on a journey, a helping hand, a glimpse of Christ's smile on the face of a stranger.

God Moves Away

A MYTH FROM TOGO

'I TELL YOU God lives above the sky. Way up high. Out of earshot almost. We know about these things in Togo.'

'Are you saying God never lived on Earth, among men?'

'Not at all. Of course he did! The sky hung about here, not much higher than a man's head, and God used it for a hammock. But he moved away. Don't you know that? Don't you know why?'

'I know you're going to tell me.'

People were disrespectful, yes. Little children used to wipe their greasy paws on the sky at the end of a meal, and cooks used to tear pieces off, for the cooking pot. I hear it was delicious – gave you wind, but it was delicious.

You know how the women pound corn into meal in this part of the world? With a big wooden bowl to hold the grain, and a huge wooden pestle for pounding it? Bang, bang, bang. Well, naturally the pestle needs to thump down on the corn as hard as possible. So this old lady used to throw the pestle high in the air. It was made from a tree trunk and was as tall as she was, but she could thump that pestle up and down for hours on end, like an elephant stomping on peanuts. And of course every time she threw the pestle upwards, it used to catch God a fourpenny whack somewhere painful. One day it hit him in the eye.

That made him so mad that he packed up and left. He did!

Rolled up the sky and flew right up high, rubbing his eye and muttering.

Of course it was a help to the old woman's work, but a great sadness to everyone else. No more sky in the cooking pot. Nowhere to wipe their greasy hands. And – worst of all – it made a conversation with God so difficult. So hard to make him hear our prayers. So hard to take an argument before him for his judgement.

The old woman did what she could to make amends. She told her children and her grandchildren and every other greasy-handed child in the village to gather up all the pounding bowls.

Some still had corn in. Some had rainwater slopping about in the bottom. Some were old and bruised with fifty years of pounding. But the old lady piled them up, one on top of the next, and climbed up, to ask God if he wouldn't come back down where he belonged.

She nearly made it, too. When she reached the top of the pile and was balanced in the topmost bowl, like an egg in an eggcup, she could almost reach the hem of God's robe. She stood on tiptoe. She hopped as high as she dared, but it made the tower wobble alarmingly.

'One more bowl and I'm there!' she called down to her children. But there were no bowls to be had. 'I know!' she called. 'Take the bottom one out and pass it up to me. Then I'll be able to reach!'

And that is what they did, for it is a foolish child who argues with his grandmother. They took away the bottom pounding bowl – *wobble, clatter, eeek!* – and though the old lady made a snatch for the hem of God's robe, she missed. And that was that.

Wilhelm Tell

A SWISS LEGEND

'To life, Liberty and a free Switzerland!' That was the toast they drank and the oath they swore in secret. But in public, few dared to defy the tyranny of the Austrian Empire. So they paid the heavy taxes, they obeyed the unfair laws, and in secret they dreamed of independence and swore grand oaths, to keep from despairing.

Wilhelm Tell was different. A farmer from a remote mountain farm, he spoke little and thought deeply. So when he swore such an oath, the words dropped like hot sealing wax on to a deed of law, and made those who heard him tremble at the strength of his feelings.

In every respect, Tell was the best of men: best archer, best mountaineer, best helmsman at a boat's tiller out on Lake Lucerne; best friend to have when a friend was needed; best father in all the world, as far as his son Carl was concerned. Many suspected that, since the Austrians had come to power, a temper burned like volcanic lava in Tell's breast, but his friends and family had never seen it flare. It was that family of his which kept Wilhelm at one remove from the politics of rebellion. Only a bachelor can afford reckless exploits in the name of Liberty; a married man has other lives than his own to consider.

One cruelty gave the Austrian overlords a taste for another and another. Men like Baron Gessler delighted in inventing new humiliations to inflict on the Swiss. An edict forbade any farmer the use of a horse or ox to pull his plough. The farmer could haul his own plough, couldn't he, and give the horse and ox to his Austrian betters.

Baron Gessler stalked the streets and lanes, surrounded by body-guards, to glory in the misery he caused. In fact, power was making Gessler a little peculiar, a little wild at the eye, a little unpredictable in his extravagant malice. He placed various of his hats on poles and sent them into the market square of every village, demanding that everyone who passed by must bow to the hat, as though to its owner. Soldiers were posted at the foot of each pole, to ensure everyone complied with the decree.

Old men with arthritic joints were obliged to bend their aching knees to Gessler's hat. Young women carrying babies, farmers laden with bales of hay were called on to pay their respects to the silly hat on high. Milkmaids could not sell their milk in the marketplace until they had curtseyed to Gessler's hat. From the window of an inn in Altdorf, Gessler himself watched, grinning, and thought of the same scene being acted out all over the canton.

It so happened that Wilhelm Tell chose that day to come to town for supplies. Nothing was farther from his mind than to make trouble: he had brought his dear son Carl with him. But no one had told him about the business of Gessler's hat, and as he crossed the square, one of the soldiers suddenly barked like a rabid dog, 'Bow to the hat, why don't you?'

'Why would I bow to a hat?' enquired Tell in his low, shy voice.

'Because it's the hat of Baron Gessler, and it represents him.'

Wilhelm squinted up at the hat. 'It might bear a passing resem-blance to him, I suppose, if he ate less . . . But the day I bow to a hat is the day I grow ears and bray like a donkey. Bow to it yourself.'

With the bang of a door and the breaking of a beer mug, Baron Gessler came bellying out of the inn. A gobbet of chewed apple flew from his mouth as he blared. 'So! You refuse to obey my decree, do you? I've heard of you! You're Wilhelm Tell! I know all about you! You're famous hereabouts, aren't you? People never stop talking about you – what a good archer! what a great mountaineer! And you're a dissident, are you? A subversive? A rebel?'

Suddenly guards were clinging to Tell like squirrels to a tree.

'That's a lot to accuse me of, simply because I insulted your hat,' said Tell calmly.

'So will you bow to it?'

'No.'

Gessler burst into hysterical laughter which puffed out his cheeks and made his forehead red. 'Then your farm's forfeit! I'll lock you up! I'll have you sent to Castle Kussnacht and . . .' Tell's grey eyes looked back at him, cold and unmoved. Gessler racked his brains for something more original in the way of cruelty. The longer Tell retained his dignity here in this public square, Gessler was the one being made to look small. He peered beyond Tell and saw something which inspired his malicious imagination . . . 'Unless . . . '

Tell flexed his arm muscles, which were growing uncomfortable. A guard slithered to the ground. 'Unless?' he asked, peaceably.

'I hear you've a fair art with a crossbow. What a waste it would be to bury such talent in a dungeon!' Gessler looked down at the remains of the apple he had been eating. 'If you can shoot through this apple at a distance of one hundred paces, you can go free.'

'Agreed!' said Tell, taken aback by such uncharacteristically good sportsmanship.

Gessler hiccuped with laughter. 'Guards. Balance this apple on the head of Tell's son, and stand him in front of that tree yonder. That should help make Herr Wilhelm shoot straight!'

Up until that moment, Tell had been so intent on keeping his temper that he had forgotten entirely about Carl, about his little boy standing so still and wide-eyed in his father's long shadow. For the first time Gessler saw the flicker of fear he so loved to inflict. Tell was afraid to make the shot. He would crumble now, in front of all his admiring neighbours, and beg for mercy.

Nobody moved for a long time. Nobody moved until Carl reached out, took the half-eaten apple out of Gessler's hand and set off towards the tree. Along the shore of the lake he walked. One hundred paces? It was more like one hundred and fifty. Carl rested his back against the trunk and looked back at his father, so small now in the distance. 'You can do it, Father!' he called. His high sweet voice rang out as clear as a bell.

The soldiers tied Carl to the tree with ropes. They made as if to blindfold him, too. 'I won't flinch, if that's what you think,' he told them. 'I know my father can hit the apple.'

So he saw the huge crowd that had gathered seemingly from nowhere. He saw his father's face above the level crossbow – pale as snow on the mountaintops. He saw the sun flaring on the water of the lake a blinding brightness. He saw the metal bolt glint in the sun, the flash of a second one held between his father's fingers. Carl held his breath. A cloud covered the sun.

The bolt flew so fast that the twang of the bowstring and thud of the impact were like a single sound. A woman in the crowd screamed, *'You murderer, Gessler!'*, for she had seen, through her fingers, an explosion of white and red as the bolt struck.

But it was only the apple splattering to pulpy pieces. Fragments stuck to the boy's hair, juice trickled into his eyes, as he smiled back at his father. Then a cheer went up from the Swiss crowd that was repeated at every window, shouted down every alleyway in Altdorf: *'He did it! Tell hit the apple!'* Gessler, blustering and foolish, groped for something disparaging to say. 'Not so cocky, really, were you, Tell? Thought it might take two shots?' He pointed out the second bolt between Tell's fingers.

The archer shrugged. 'Oh yes, I thought my first bolt might kill my son. That's why I had a second ready for you, Gessler.'

'Arrest him! Seize him! Traitor! Villain! Assassin!' Gessler ducked behind a member of his bodyguard, his heart leaping with a mixture of terror and triumph, a cold sweat running down his fat neck. 'Your own words condemn you! Take him to Castle Kussnacht and let him wait in a dungeon for the headman's axe!'

A murmur like a hive of bees stirred among the crowd. Then an egg hit the back of Gessler's coat, a hail of pebbles began to fly. If Gessler had wanted to upset the people of Altdorf, he had surely succeeded, for they began to herd forward, like cattle roused by lightning.

'Run, Carl! Run!' cried Tell, and Carl picked up his heels and ran into the shelter of the crowd, which swallowed him up, hid him as surely as if he were invisible.

Arrest Tell? When he had won his freedom like that? Some injustices can be borne, some wickednesses tolerated. But this time Gessler had touched a nerve already rubbed raw by his tyranny. Someone smashed a market stall and began handing out sticks of wood for weapons. Some drew the money from their pockets – worthless Austrian coppers good for nothing but pelting worthless Austrians.

'It's no good, sir. We'll never reach the horses!' shouted the captain of the guard. 'Best get offshore. That's our only hope.' And so they beat an undignified retreat, jogging along a jetty, bundling Tell aboard a small fishing boat. The crowd also broke into a run, shaking their sticks and shouting, 'Get Gessler! Let's put a stop to him once and for all!'

'Steer, won't you?' Gessler pushed a sergeant in the chest.

'B-but I don't know how to —'

'Just do it, fool, before this rabble tears us limb from limb!'

As the space widened between boat and shore, Gessler crowed like a cock. 'Just wait till my *real* troops arrive!' he sneered at the people ranged along the jetty. '*You'll wish you'd never been born!*'

A sudden yaw in the boat made him stagger, and he cursed the helmsman. Then he saw the cause: a storm like a genie summoned from a bottle. Lake Lucerne, too, was rising up against tyranny and injustice.

There were blades of cold and arrows of ice in the wind. They sheered through the rigging and brought down the topsails on to the men below. The unwilling helmsman cowered in the bottom of the boat pleading for the help of a real sailor. 'Free Tell! He knows boats. He can sail anything! Free Tell or *we'll all drown*!'

'So even you admire the lout!' fumed Gessler. His opulent, fur-lined coat was so heavy with rain and spray that his knees were bowing. 'All right. All right! Cut the dog loose.'

The moment his hands were untied, Tell took the tiller of the boat and turned her into the wind. She stopped rolling and pitching and taking in water, and beyond that no one cared where she was heading. Minutes later, they saw the shore dead ahead, spines of jagged rock clawing the waves into an open wound of breaking water, a foaming maelstrom. They stared open-mouthed, letting the driving rain trickle down their throats. Did Tell mean to wreck the boat and take his enemies with him to the bottom of the lake?

At the last second, Tell swung on the tiller, and every man aboard was sent sprawling. The prow reared up like a horse's head, the keel grazed bottom. The boat swung round within its own length, so that it was stern-on to the rock. And from the stern transom leapt Wilhelm Tell – out across a gulf of rioting water, black, deep and deadly. It was a phenomenal leap – a mountain goat's leap from one crag to the next. Only a mountaineer could have made it and held his balance on landing. Only the bravest could have made it in the teeth of a gale, while the wavetops gnashed and the foam flew like blinding snow. Only Wilhelm Tell could have done it with an iron crossbow slung across his back, snatched from the slippery deck the moment before he jumped.

The Austrian guards clung desperately to the boat rail, unwilling to let go despite Gessler's ranting: '*Shoot him! Shoot the villain! Kill him! Don't let him get away, Devil curse you!*'

The boat had the wind behind it now, and was driven out towards the centre of the lake, ropes snaking, sail ripping, and the tiller unmanned. On the shore, clambering agilely over the razor-sharp rocks a figure lithe as an otter reached the safety of dry land.

'I'll see you in Hell for this!' bawled Gessler. 'You so-called soldiers! You and your wives and sweethearts! I'll finish Tell! I'll burn down his farm with his wife and brat inside! I'll burn down every farm on the mountain! I'll burn down Altdorf!' The wind dropped suddenly, as if outbrayed by Gessler's cursing. The rain teemed blackly, but the drifting boat ceased her pitching as the storm stood still in horror.

The figure on the shore laid a single bolt to his crossbow and took aim. A furlong of darkness crammed with rain; half a moon, and all his breath used up. Tell fired. And the insane ranting stopped even more suddenly than the wind's howl had done.

Next morning found the boat adrift in the heart of Lake Lucerne. The soldiers aboard, when asked what had become of the Baron, only pointed over the side at the still, secretive waters. Lake Lucerne is deep. It takes time to give up its captives. But the fishermen of the lake said that a great many fish died that night, as if poisoned by some pollution of the water.

The Swiss will only stand for just so much. They may bend to circumstance. They may bear with misfortune. But ultimately, they are slaves to no one. Within half a handful of years, Switzerland was free of Austria. It has never given up its independence since.

A Heart of Stone

A GREEK MYTH

'Love,' said the King, 'has never troubled me, I'm glad to say.' In fact, King Pygmalion of Cyprus had done rather better than simply not falling in love. He had managed to loathe women, with a deep and deadly loathing, ever since he had been able to tell them apart from men. 'Can't see the purpose of them,' he would say, in a superior way. 'Don't hunt elephants. Don't quarry rocks . . .'

If these seem strange virtues to set any great store by, it should be explained that Pygmalion was a sculptor as well as a king. His notion of true joy was a tusk of ivory or a block of marble, uncut, awaiting the touch of his chisel. He carved animals, heroes, children, pillars . . . and superbly, too. People could almost forgive him his hatred of women when they saw the genius of his carvings.

Venus did not forgive so easily. The Goddess of Love took great exception to his rude and ignorant remarks. Every day, from the slopes of Mount Olympus where the gods of Greece made their home, she could hear the supercilious voice of Pygmalion complaining: how women *talked*, how women *lied*, how women *spent money*, how women were a useless and troublesome invention he could well do without. Not surprisingly, he had never offered up a single sacrifice in the Temple of Venus. One day Venus stamped her foot, and her green eyes flashed with resolve. 'It is time, Pygmalion, to teach you a lesson!'

A stranger knocked at the door of Pygmalion's studio next day – a tall hooded stranger with piercing green eyes.

'Greetings, your majesty. I am a traveller returned from foreign parts where I learned of a contest which might interest you. The King of Crete is offering a laurel wreath for the finest sculpture submitted. I thought of you at once, O King, knowing you to be the finest sculptor in the world.'

'Thank you! I shall carve a bull!' exclaimed Pygmalion, already selecting the ideal block from among the marble stacked in the yard . . . 'The Cretans like nothing better than a charging . . .'

'No, no!' interrupted the stranger. 'The statue must be of a woman. The one considered the most beautiful will be the winner.'

'Oh, but I never . . .'

But when Pygmalion turned round, there was no one to be seen.

Bravely overcoming his disgust, Pygmalion decided to compete nevertheless, and to carve a female figure. He chose the finest marble, sharpened his best tools and asked himself what could possibly make a *woman* seem beautiful. 'A wide, generous mouth,' he thought, 'but not always talking. A pair of large, tender eyes looking only at me. Hair flowing like the weed in a river, fit to drown a man . . .'

The figure which emerged from under his skilful fingers was tall and willowy, bending a little forward. She seemed to be listening with intent interest to everything Pygmalion had to say. 'I think you will do very nicely,' he found himself saying aloud to the sweetly inclined head, as he set down his tools. 'For a woman, you are really quite . . . quite . . . exquisite, if I do say so myself.' But the statue only looked back at him, with white marble eyes and a sweet but brittle smile.

When the King went to bed that night, he could not get the statue out of his mind. It was his best achievement yet, no doubt about it. It was perfect. He had to get up and go back to the studio just to look at it, at her. For the rest of the night he sat there, gazing at her, enthralled by a beauty of his own making.

Next morning he found himself unwilling to crate up his statue and despatch her to Crete. No sooner were the nails banged home than he prised them out again and recovered his masterpiece from the crate, setting her on a plinth where the sunlight flattered her lovely figure, her delicate features, her long curling hair. 'I shall call you Galatea,' he said, but her carved mouth did not respond, either to agree or disagree. She seemed more beautiful every time he looked at her, but cold and still. She seemed on the very point of moving – and yet she would never move. She was only a statue, after all.

For a week, Pygmalion did not leave his studio. His servants brought meat and drink to the door, but he sent them away. His ministers could get no answer to their knocking. They gathered round the door, anxious, worried. Then, when he did finally emerge, he rushed past them, white-faced, and ran all the way to the Temple of Venus on the hill, falling on his knees in front of the altar.

'O Goddess of Love, take pity on me! I'm a fool, I know it! I'm half-mad, I see that! But I can't help myself! I love her! I've fallen in love with my own statue! I deserve to be laughed at in the street – "There goes that fool who lost his heart to a piece of marble!" – but I never knew what it was like before. I never even guessed love could be like this! Pity me, goddess! Take this pain from my heart, this madness out of my brain! I'll carve your statue at every crossroads – if only you'll end this *pain*!'

His voice rang around the cavernous temple. The only faces looking down at him were images of the goddess Venus – tall, enthroned in a sea shell, clothed in locks of hair, carved in pallid stone.

He walked back to the studio, scuffing the heels of his sandals. He might have gone to his palace, but the statue drew him, as a magnet draws iron. He must see it again, even though seeing it only increased his suffering, because it could never be anything but cold, insensible marble.

The look on his face was so terrible that his ministers and servants stepped back and did not try to speak to him. Pygmalion closed the door behind him and leaned against it, his eyes tight shut in self-loathing. 'Oh, what I'd give to be one of those lucky men I used to make fun of – in love with some dancer or priestess or orange-seller!'

'Are you speaking to me?'

He opened his eyes and saw at once that his statue was missing, his beloved statue. '*Where is she? What have you done with my statue?*' The stranger sitting in the seat by the window was so blotted out by the sunlight behind her that he saw only a dark shadow. But when she stood up – 'I'm sorry, what statue?' – he could see her more clearly: a beauty in green drapery and gold sandals, her hair falling in ringlets to front and back of her shoulders.

'I believe I may be a little unwell,' she said, in a sweet apologetic voice, 'for I cannot entirely remember how I came to be here. My name is . . .'

'Galatea,' said Pygmalion at once.

'That's right. How did you know? Or are we acquainted? You do seem rather familiar . . . if only I could remember. But I mustn't keep you from your work. I see you are a very fine sculptor, and I know how artists need peace and quiet.'

Thus Venus gave Pygmalion his perfect woman, satisfied that he had learned his lesson. Besides, she was extremely eager to see those statues he had promised to carve of her standing at every crossroads.

If the gods have one weakness, it is probably their vanity.

Babushka

A RUSSIAN LEGEND

THE STAR SHONE – but then everything in Babushka's house shone, bright and glistening. So that when she glimpsed the new star shining in at the corner of the window, she saw nothing unusual in that. Everyone else in the village was out of doors, pointing and prattling. But Babushka would never waste her time so frivolously. She had a house to keep clean, washing and washing-up to do, weeding and kneading. She was too busy for wonders.

'A new star! See?'

'Never there before!'

'Last night it was over yonder.'

'It's moving!'

'Shifting!'

'Shining!'

'Amazing!'

'Wonderful!'

But Babushka was too busy for wonders.

She heard the new commotion in the street, too, the children ooh-ing and aah-ing, the herrumph of camels and the jingling of bridle bells.

'See their turbans!'

'See their cloaks!'

'See the scrolls and scriptures in their saddlebags!'

But nothing could make Babushka break off from her work until that knock at the door.

'May we rest here tonight, Babushka?' Three travellers stood in her neat little garden; their camels were tethered by the gate. Their clothes were dirty with the dust of many miles, but not so dusty that she could not see the quality and richness of their foreign weave.

'You'd best come in, sirs,' said Babushka in a shy whisper, 'though if you'd wipe your feet on the mat I'd be grateful.'

She bustled about fetching them cheese and milk, dates and nuts, bread and little cakes.

'Sit down and talk to us, Babushka,' said her visitors, but Babushka never sat down. There was far too much to do – especially with visitors in the house. There were blankets to be fetched for their beds, fires to be lit, apples to be polished for their dessert.

After dinner, the three foreign gentlemen, Caspar, Melchior and Balthazar, opened out maps on the table and discussed where their journey was taking them. 'We are following the new star,' they explained, when she brought them extra candles. 'It's leading us to the realm of a new king.'

'A new king. Fancy!' said Babushka, but she was too busy washing up the supper things to say more.

'The Christ of the Scriptures!' said Caspar. 'The Saviour of the World! The star marks his coming – is writing it in the sky!'

'The Saviour of the World? Well, God bless us!' said Babushka.

'We're taking him presents,' said Melchior. 'Gold and spices and rich ointments.'

'Fortunate man,' said Babushka.

'No, no! Only a baby as yet,' Balthazar corrected her. 'A newborn king!'

'Then may he live long, for his mother's sake,' said Babushka and the three turned quickly and looked at her, simply because at last she had stopped stock-still. She stood by the door, her shawl clutched close at her throat. 'I had a child once,' she said, 'but he died.' Then seeing the pity in their faces, she put on a bright smile and set off once more, straightening the ornaments, plumping the cushions, sweeping crumbs from under the table. 'No great matter. I keep busy, Children! They make a house untidy anyway.'

'Come with us, Babushka,' said Caspar.

'Come where, sir?'

'Yes, come with us tomorrow,' said Melchior. 'What's to stop you?'

'Come and the see the Saviour?' said Babushka. 'You shouldn't tease an old woman.'

'Why not come?' said Balthazar. 'You've nothing to keep you here.'

Babushka put her hands on her hips and laughed, though she had not laughed for many years. 'Lord bless you, there's a man talking! Nothing to keep me? Why, there's the washing and the wiping, the sweeping and the shopping, the dusting and the dishes. A person can't just get up and go on the spur of the moment – not someone like me, I mean! It's one thing for you sages and scholars, you thinkers and philosophers!' But she would have liked to go! Indeed she would! Her grey eyes shone as they had not done for many years. 'Besides, I have no present to give the Saviour.'

In the morning, the three sages said to her again, 'Come with us, Babushka! Come and see the Christ child.'

'Maybe,' she said, giving them parcels of food for the journey. 'Soon, perhaps. Maybe I'll follow on tomorrow and catch you up.'

'Don't leave it too late,' warned Melchior, as he mounted his kneeling camel.

So the three sages went on their way, and the bells on the camels' bridles jingled more and more softly as they swayed away into the distance.

Babushka cleaned her house from top to bottom. 'I will go!' she resolved. She washed her clothes for the journey. She mended and polished her boots. 'I do have a present, after all!'

She unlocked the cupboard in the corner of the room and took out the toys which had belonged to her dead child. Then she cleaned and painted and shone and mended them all: wooden dolls and little cups, a ball, a bat, a bear. She worked all day and never noticed how the time sped by, for she liked to be busy. For a time she wept at the memory of her dead child. Then she smiled at the thought of the child newly born. How good it would be to welcome such a child into the world! How fine that the three sages thought that she – Babushka! – was a fit person to meet the Saviour of the World.

At last she packed all the toys into a basket, shut the door of her immaculate little cottage and set off after Caspar, Melchior and Balthazar. The new star in the sky had set, but it was not difficult to follow the trail of excitement and astonishment left behind by the exotic camel train.

She followed them down valleys and over hills, through villages and cities. She followed them to Jerusalem, where they had visited the palace of the Roman Governor. She followed them to Bethlehem, and rested there at an inn.

'Three wise men from foreign parts?' said the innkeeper. 'Yes, they came here, but they've gone now. So have the man and woman – and the baby, too.'

'*The baby was born here?*' asked Babushka in amazement.

'Yes, yes. In the stable. No room in here. What a night we had! Visitors, lights, singing . . . Gone now, though. You're too late.'

Into Egypt, Babushka followed the rumours of Mary and Joseph and their little baby Jesus. North, west, east and south she went on searching for the Christ child. Though her search led her nowhere, and lasted many years, she never gave up. On and on she carried her basket of toys, forgetting that the baby king must have long since grown to manhood.

Thirty years later, passing again one day by the walls of Jerusalem, she saw a terrible sight. Three men had been executed by the Romans, nailed by their hands and feet to wooden crosses on a bare hilltop, to suffer in the sun and to die. The one in the centre wore a crude twist of thorns round his head, like an imitation crown. A crowd of women stood nearby, weeping. One was the mother of the young man in the crown of thorns.

Babushka set down her heavy basket, and put her arms around the woman. 'I lost a son, too,' she said. 'My heart goes out to you.' Then she stooped to pick up her basket again.

It seemed strangely light – as if all the toys had been taken from inside. But no, when she opened the lid, they were still there, as shining and pretty as the day she packed them.

Babushka continued on her way, searching, always searching. But now she decided not to save all the toys in her basket to present to the Christ child. She would give some of them away – 'After all, every child is a child of God!' She felt sure the Christ child would understand, when at last she found him. So whenever she passed the home of a child, she left a little something by the hearth – a trumpet, a puppet, a drum.

Strange to say, her basket – though it was now as light as a feather – never emptied. Whenever she reached her hand under the lid there was still always a variety of toys at her fingertips.

She never did find whom she was looking for – or never realized that she had found him already. She is travelling still, still giving away her toys. She leaves her presents in every Christian country, in every Christian town, on every day of the year. But only on the birthday of the Christ child are her shining gifts visible to the girls and boys who wake in the half-light of morning and remember, 'It's Christmas Day!'

The Pig Goes Courting

A HAWAIIAN MYTH

E WAS NOT a pretty lad. Even his mother and father
blenched at their first sight of him: it was the way his snout
snuffled and his ears drooped and his tusks curled right
back over his ears. His manners left something to be desired, too: the
way he held his bowl to his face and grunted down his food, then
rootled about the floor for what he had spilled. But when it came to
friendship, Kamapua'a was the man to have by you, and when it
came to valour, he made the finest ally in the world. The fact that
Kamapua'a had the head and body of a pig was of no importance to
those who knew him. And he was a god, after all.

He lived on the island of Hawaii, where he spent most of his time
frightening away invaders. There was not a foe born who did not
panic and run at the sight of Kamapua'a in full charge – head down,
shoulders up, tusks gleaming, and venting the most terrifying squeals.
He wielded a palm tree for a club, and while he rooted about for
coconuts to pitch at retreating enemies, would scoop up huge
earthworks and sand dunes, the better to defend the islanders.

Sometimes, however, when Kamapua'a's mind turned from war to
the finer things of life, he would trot off on his human feet, into the
hills and plantations, and whistle at the pretty women swaying by.
The women would laugh and cast a flirting glance, then patter home
to their mothers, giggling. One day, Kamapua'a ventured further
inland – to the mountainous regions – and saw a quite different breed

of woman. She took away too much of his breath for him to whistle. 'Her I shall marry,' declared the pig god, gazing up at the summit where Pele stood, red hair streaming.

Pele was the fire goddess. She lived among her cantankerous relations, the volcanoes, whose grumbling could be heard all over the island. Like them, Pele had a fiery disposition (as you might expect of a fire goddess). She greeted Kamapua'a's proposal of marriage with a cackle of crackling laughter, and kicked pebbles down on his head. Then, standing on the skyline, her hands on her hips, she began to heap such invective on the pig god that his little legs bowed.

'Marry you? *You?* The nut-snuffling, trough-grubbing, bristle-backed hog of a bacon-flitch? You sugar-cane-crashing bore? You yard of lard? Who do you think you're speaking to?'

'I'm a boar, not a bore,' said Kamapua'a, grinning with delight, 'and who else in the world do you think is going to take you, you lump of hot coal, you furnace-mouth, you spark-burned hearthrug?'

Pele thumbed her nose. 'Filthy mud-rolling, rubbish eating, snout-nosed heap of brawn!'

'You collision of glow-worms! Bad-dream-on-a-hot-night! Indigestible bunch of red chillies!'

Pele spat fire, but Kamapua'a simply raised up a mound of earth to deflect it. 'Come down and take the only bridegroom who'll ever have you! Together we'll be pork and crackling!'

So they went on, hurling insults as big as coconuts, until the relations began to join in. The volcanoes trembled, and their vents poured out foul-smelling jets of yellow sulphur. Lightning jumped about excitedly, jabbing a stabbing finger at Kamapua'a and his family and using such words as burned holes in the heavens. Kamapua'a's friends rallied to him in defence of his good name.

It began to look less like a wooing than a war, as the two sides bombarded each other with aspersions and expletives. Words gave way to weapons. At first, Pele only hurled thunderbolts and fireballs, while Kamapua'a threw back cakes of mud and litter off the beach: seaweed and empty turtle shells. But the squabbling escalated.

'Go home, you ugly brute, or my aunts and uncles will erupt and drown you all in molten lava!'

'Look out, Kamapua'a,' muttered his friends uneasily. 'They could do for us if they put their minds to it.'

'Not if we call up reinforcements,' said Kamapua'a, scratching himself luxuriously against a palm tree. He turned his snout towards the sky and bellowed: '*Come clouds! Come sparkling springs, come damp dewfall and splashy sea! Come wet rain and fuming fog! Come moist mists and running rivers! Rise up and teach these volcanoes a lesson that will silence their grumbling for ever! I'll have you pleading to marry me, Pele, you see if I don't!*'

So all the moist things of the islands ganged together. Springwater leapt up and, together with streams and rills and rivers, ringed the mountains round with water. But when the cascades of orange lava spilled from the throats of Pele's ghastly relations, they dissolved the water in clouds of steam. Mountains of ash blotted out the sky, and rained down, hot and choking, on the pig god, till he stood hock-deep in cinders. But he simply blared at the clouds to do their worst, and the clouds burst over the volcanoes and drenched them in torrents of rain.

Magma seethed and bubbled. Brimstone and pumice rattled down on Kamapua'a, white-hot or dripping orange lava. But though he squealed ear-splitting yelps of rage, he also summoned up the fogs and mists that live in the morning forests. Like gigantic ghosts, they advanced on the erupting uplands, grappling and interweaving with the yellow clouds of sulphurous smoke, the plumes of steam. There was a hissing like a million angry snakes, a coughing and choking, a spluttering and sputtering. Then, one by one, like snuffed candles, the volcanic fires went out, and Pele's aunts and uncles were reduced to rumbling grumblers, chuntering and mumbling: '. . . these disrespectful youngsters . . .'

Pele, her red hair hanging in sodden hanks, came stumbling blindly through the dense fog, feeling her way and shivering. Kamapua'a plunged forward and, before her eyes even opened, took Pele's two hands in his. 'Give in to me, Lady of Fire! The world is more water than fire: my longing for you will always be greater than your loathing. Give in. Fire and earth and air and water should work together – make something out of nothing – not reduce the world to dust and ashes! Let's join forces, you and I. I may look more pig than man, but you'll find I'm more god than either.'

She never made a quiet bedfellow. Pele's temper was forever flaring up. But her passion for Kamapua'a, once lit, was as hot as her temper. And soon, when her uncles and aunts grumbled and rumbled at the heart of the island, complaining that the world was changing. Pele would laugh as loud as Kamapua'a, and they would run down to the beach together and drink coconut milk till both their snouts were quite white.

Can Krishna Die?

AN INDIAN LEGEND

MANY GODS HAVE visited the earth. Wherever their feet trod, myths have grown up, and wherever they lived legends are left, like fossils, in the rocks. But none of the gods has stayed long. For gods can only visit by becoming flesh and blood, and flesh and blood are vulnerable like butter in the hot sun.

When the great Lord Krishna was born to live among the cowherds and milkmaids of Yadava, however, it seemed he must live forever. He was so strong that no man or beast or monster could overpower him. He was such a warrior that no enemy could stand in his way. He was so handsome that women cherished him as a child and adored him as a grown man. He had children, and his children had children, and it seemed that Krishna must live to bless and protect his family through endless generations. Old age ran off him like rain off a raven's wing.

Then, one day, a joke went badly wrong. A band of wise men came wandering through the meadows, frail, gaunt, aged, and without one smile between them. The young cowherds of Yadava had no respect for their age and wisdom.

'Let's see if they're really so wise,' said one.

'Let's see if they even know a cow from a bull!' said another.

They called Samba, grandson of Krishna, and dressed him in women's clothes. His long hair was curly and his cheek was smooth, so that once dressed in a sari, he looked as pretty as any milkmaid. In his right hand he held a pestle for pounding rice, under his dress a cushion, and on his face a silly simper.

'O wise men! O sage scholars of a thousand learned words! Cast your clever eyes over this girl and tell us what manner of child she will have when it is born.'

Samba found it all so funny that he let slip the cushion, which fell to the ground with a thud.

The cowherds laughed till their legs gave way: they laughed till the cows took fright. But the sage old men did not laugh. Their sad rheumy eyes looked down at the cushion and at Samba's large, masculine feet.

'So you think it is funny, do you, to make fun of your elders and betters? So you have no respect for the magic of our wisdom? Then with our wisdom of magic *we curse you*!' Their yellow eyes flashed and their gnarled fingers pointed at Samba. 'May that woman's pestle of yours strike dead every young man in the tribe of Yadava!'

Laughter tailed away. The air was cold with the chill of the curse. The leaves on the trees shook.

Before the sage old men had limped out of sight, Samba had smashed the wooden pestle in two. The two halves he burned in the fire till they turned to ash, then he ground the ash into finest dust. Finally he sprinkled the dust into the sea, where it sank.

'There!' said Samba, brushing his hands together. 'How shall the pestle kill us when there is no pestle?' And every man there breathed a sigh of relief. For though they did not fear to die, their insulting joke had put in danger the life of the Lord Krishna.

Down in the dark of the deep-fathomed sea, the powdered ash settled on the sand. Like seed it took root. Like seed it sprang up. Salt sea grasses grew, as straight and brittle as reeds of glass, and in among the stems swam the bright fish of the ocean.

Amid its own bubbling cloud of silver breath, a little fish nibbled the sea grasses, the crawling snail, the wriggling worm . . . and the silver hook inside that worm. With scarcely a struggle, the fish was pulled from the water by a fisherman, who carried it home in delight and ate it for supper with his family. No cowherd this fellow, for he loved the challenge of hunting – boar in the forest, lions in the hills, fish in the sea, and birds on the wing.

The cowherds of Yadava preferred to roast an ox, eat cheese from the creamery, and drink wine from the fruit in the orchards. Sitting on the beach at low tide, they celebrated their narrow escape, and laughed (as loud as they dared) at the thought of foiling that dreadful curse.

Everyone was there – Krishna, his brother Balarama, Samba and all the Yadava cattlemen. The sea ebbed, but the wine flowed – heavy, heady wine. The brittle reeds on the shoreline tinkled like glass chimes in the breeze. They drank in celebration – and the drink make them want to dance. The dancing made them thirsty, and so they drank some more. The drink made them thirstier – as thirsty as if they had drunk the salt sea – so they drank still more.

The ocean rolled, the drinkers reeled. The tide turned, and the mood of the drinkers turned too, from cheerfulness to surliness, from surliness to a fighting madness.

For no good reason, one pushed another. He rolled back in among the reeds and one snapped off in his hand. He threw it like a spear, and it stabbed the young man in the throat. All at once a nonsensical quarrel turned into a frenzied battle. The lads took sides, the sides took arms – they broke off the sharp reeds and hurled them, with drunken lunges, blindly at one another. Balarama was pierced in the back and the cold of the sages' curse chilled him to the marrow. 'Go. Krishna! get away!' he called. Then he dragged himself into the shade of a tree and sat patiently watching Death approach like a ship across the wide sea.

That poisonous curse cankered each graze, turned every cut into a deadly wound. By sunset, not a cowherd was left to call the cows to milking. Every one lay dead on the beach. The milkmaids watching for returning herds waited till night settled over them, and with it a sense of dread.

Krishna alone walked from the beach, his face full of anguish, his heart full of regret. He went deep into the forest, where the light was slight and green. Only the wind through the branches sounded the same as the sea. He thought back over his life – the women he had loved, the children he had cradled, the battles he had won. He thought about the vastness between the stars, the heat within the suns, the length of history and the shortness of life. Not another soul moved through the green shade of the forest.

None, that is, but the huntsman. Today he had left his fishing rod at home and come in search of deer, with bow and arrow. His newest arrow hung at his side – the one tipped with sharpened fish bone cut from the remains of his fish dinner.

A movement, a shadow shape. A deer?

The huntsman drew back his bow and fired, and Krishna, darling of the world, buckled his leg in pain. The arrow tip had pierced the sole of his foot, and the cold curse was already coursing through his veins.

So he laid his earthly life aside. Like a snake who sloughs off the papery glory of its skin to grow the greater, Krishna sloughed off his human form and returned to Heaven – a creature of spirit, a divine being once more, a radiance like the brightness left in your eye after looking at the sun.

The Lighthouse on the Lake
A JAPANESE LEGEND

THERE WAS ONCE a lighthouse-keeper, tall and slender like his lighthouse and as dazzling to women as the light he tended. His name was Jimmu, and he sat in his high tower, feeling like the sun generously bestowing its beams on Lake Biwa.

A beautiful girl, Yuki, who lived on the shores of the lake, saw him out fishing one summer's day, and fell in love, as only a young girl can. Her soul, her life, her heart, her all, she placed in her father's boat, and rowed out to Jimmu. 'I love you,' she said.

Jimmu wound in his hook and attached another worm, looking at the girl. 'Pretty little thing,' he thought, and said, 'I'm honoured. But your parents will never allow us to meet. You're so young.'

'I could row over the lake to your lighthouse after dark. My parents would never even know.'

Jimmu was taken aback. It was such a very daring suggestion! The vast lake is a pretty place on a sunny day, but at night it is an eerie crevasse of gleaming dark between the looming Hira mountains. Yuki was certainly a remarkable girl if she was ready to cross the night lake. And how shameless! To suggest such a lover's tryst with a stranger, without a word about marriage. Jimmu was almost shocked . . . but pleasantly excited too.

'Until tonight, then,' he said, and her face filled with such joy that he congratulated himself on making her so happy.

That night, Yuki slipped from her bed and crept to the waterside.

She launched her father's rowing boat and unshipped the oars. Then, fixing her course by the lighthouse's shining beacon, she rowed towards her handsome lighthouse-keeper.

In her mind, she pictured happy days ahead: marriage, children, a little house like her parents' by the lake shore, a garden in the shadow of the lighthouse . . . When the prow of the boat bumped the steps at the foot of the tall building, a smiling figure stood waiting with outstretched hand to help her ashore. She saw in Jimmu's smile everything she wanted to see: true love, a kind heart, a longing to share his whole life with her. She would help him trim the wick of his lamp, help him polish the mirrors in the lamp-room. She would cook the fish he caught in the lake each day, and bear him sons to work the lighthouse in Jimmu's old age.

Night after night, Yuki visited her lover at the Hira lighthouse. No one ever knew. She rowed through sharp frost, her breath like smoke. She rowed through driving rain, her hair stuck to her like otter's fur. She rowed through summer lightning, when jagged forks jabbed at a meat-raw sky and tore it to shreds.

Jimmu marvelled at her bravery, then he revelled in her love. He even mentioned marriage, in a vague sort of way – and almost meant it. After she was gone – rowing home before dawn could betray her secret – Jimmu would lie awake, looking at the haze of light around his lighthouse window, and wonder at his good fortune.

'She's better than any girl I ever met,' he thought one August night, as he watched her little boat approach along the golden path of light. 'Who else would do this for me? I shall marry her.' The night was windy: the waves were higher than usual, and Yuki's progress was slow.

'Although, really, she ought to show more modesty.'

The little boat pitched and Yuki's oars flailed like the legs of some water-borne insect.

'Perhaps she behaves like this with all the men – a flirt – a man-chaser!' thought Jimmu, '. . . although when would she have time to visit anyone else?'

Yuki stopped rowing to peel the wet hair away from her eyes.

'Perhaps she's mad with love for me because I'm so desirable,' thought Jimmu. 'No one else has ever rowed across the lake to cook me dinner.' His wondering began to change to anxiety.

'Perhaps she's just mad,' thought Jimmu. 'I'd be mad myself if I married a madwoman.' Then came the worst possibility of all.

'Perhaps she's not a woman at all! Perhaps she's a demon sent to tempt me! Maybe she's an enchantress weaving an evil spell, even now, to trap me like a fly in a web! Yes! That's it! She's an evil spirit! A spirit of the lake!'

The heart which had felt so little real affection for Yuki experienced an unfamiliar pang of fright, a quiver of pure self-love. He must show the Powers of Evil that he was not a wicked man at all – no, not at all! He could resist temptation! He had no need of ghostly temptresses! The thought of Yuki's arms round his neck made him shiver with horror, now that his foolish imagination had convinced him she was a dream.

Leaping up the stairs to the lamp-room, he shielded his eyes against the brightness of the burning tallow wick and its mirrored reflections. His own shadow danced hugely against the wall. Jimmu snuffed out the flame with a leather bag, and coughed himself breathless in the acrid smoke.

Out on the lake, Yuki was plunged into total darkness. The golden path of light along which she had been rowing drowned in an instant, and left her blind. Gradually her eyes made out her own pale hands on the oars, the wet oars themselves, but beyond her oar's end, nothing – blackness.

She was instantly disorientated. 'Jimmu! Dearest! The light! The light has gone out! Jimmu! Trim the wick! I can't see the lighthouse! I can't see the shore!'

The darkness fell on her like slurry, stopping up her eyes and ears and nose and mouth. 'Jimmu!' she tried to call, but the wind tore the words from her lips and repaid them with spray. One oar pulled free of its rowlock and drifted away from the boat. 'Jimmu, help me! Shine a light! Call out to me! It's your own little Yuki! Why don't you hear me? Help me. Jimmu! I'm lost!'

In the lamp-room of the lighthouse, Jimmu sat with his hands over his ears, telling himself, 'A demon would say anything to trick a man out of his soul!' He refused to hear. He shut his eyes and ears, and put out the flame of love in his heart as assuredly as he had snuffed out the wick.

Yuki went on calling. Though her little boat was filling with rain, though she had spun and drifted far out into the centre of the lake, still she went on calling: 'In the name of everything we mean to each other, light the light, Jimmu!'

When the second oar broke loose, she tried to retrieve it, leaning out too far. The boat capsized, and Yuki was plunged face-first into the icy black waves. As the cold soaked through her clothes, so the realization crept into her soul.

Jimmu had betrayed her. She saw, with terrible clarity, all that she had been too dazzled to see by lamplight: that Jimmu did not love her at all, had never loved her, cared nothing for her fate. She pulled herself carefully across the upturned boat, straddling the slimy keel.

'I curse you, Jimmu. Do you hear me now? I curse your lighthouse, and I curse you! I curse this lake which carried me to you, and I curse the mountains which looked on and did nothing to stop me! Disaster fall on you as it fell on me the day I saw Jimmu the lighthouse-keeper!' Then she let go her grip on the keel, and allowed herself to slide into the heaving lake, dropping like the lead on a fish-line directly to the bottom.

A jag of wind caught the empty boat and rolled it across the lake, smashing it against the base of the lighthouse. Another roused the waves to riot, foam crests seething into sudden life, ripping the crayfish pots from their tethers. The wind redoubled, pulling slates off the roof of Yuki's little house, and branches off the shoreside trees. Out from behind the mountains came a twist of wind more ferocious than bears or mounted swordsmen. It raced across the lake, wrenching into the sky a million gallons of angry water.

The hurricane struck the lighthouse with wind and water, rubble and fish, wreckage and tree trunks and birds. It crazed the lamp-room like an eggshell, and tore the mortar from between the bricks. Trapped inside, Jimmu glimpsed the night sky through a hundred opening cracks. A moment later, the floor collapsed, and dropped him the height of the lighthouse as if down a deep, dark well.

Next day, nothing remained of the lighthouse on the shores of Lake Biwa. And now, each August, hurricanes spring from behind the mountains and lash the lake into a maelstrom, destroying, uprooting, demolishing the calm remains of summer. They come as regularly as a lover keeping a tryst with her sweetheart, but their twisting embrace is deadly and, at heart, a whirling emptiness.

King Arthur Gives Back his Sword

A CELTIC LEGEND

L EGEND SPEAKS OF a king who ruled when the world had need of heroes, and taught men the nature of chivalry. His name was Arthur Pendragon and his kingdom was in the west. There was druid magic in his hands – a pure, white magic that gave him the strength to strike and the authority to govern. He carried the great sword Excalibur and, by his side, its magic scabbard which protects the wearer from wounds.

He gathered around him a family of knights – good men (or well-intentioned, at least) – and made them swear to seek adventure and fight evil wherever they found it. To teach them humility, he seated them at a round table, giving no one pride of place, not even himself.

But knights are by nature competitive. They are trained from boyhood to win in the joust, to win in battle, to prove themselves the best. Equality and accord are not in the nature of knights. So inevitably rivalries, jealousies, petty differences broke out, which grew into feuds. The company of the Round Table began to split and splinter like a wheel embedded in a rut.

Open rebellion arose at last, led by Mordred, who drew to his side an army big and cruel enough to trample down a legion of angels. Arthur and his faithful knights prepared to fight the last great battle. They were hugely outnumbered, but by a rabble so grubbing, greedy and unremarkable that they amounted to mere brass pennies – dozens needed to equal one silver knight.

Between tents fringed with blood, from daisy-eyed morning to sunflower noon, the two armies fought – cavalry charges like crashing surf, axes hammering out on shields the great drumbeat of war. The dark rabble of Mordred's infantry fell away, but the shining company of Arthur shrank, too. At last, only the black knight-champions of Mordred remained, and fought in single combat with the knights of the Round Table. Man by man they died, not one falling without his opponent paying the same price.

Finally, Arthur and Mordred met in the shadow of a castle wall and a cry went up that silenced the rooks in the treetops. 'All day I have pursued you, Mordred, and you have kept shifting ground. Are you afraid of dying or of damning your soul with treason by fighting your lawful king?'

'I am afraid of nothing,' said Mordred, and the word 'nothing' was in his mouth when Arthur's lance struck him a blow which shattered his armour like the ice on a lake. Looking down at the gaping wound in his chest, Mordred drew back his lips in a snarl. He pushed forward along the lance – as a boar will sometimes thrust on to the hunter's spear – and wielding his broadsword one last time, struck Arthur a blow that cracked his breastplate. 'Die, Arthur Pendragon! Die and be forgotten!'

Impaled on the royal lance, Mordred died on his knees. Arthur fell backwards into the arms of Sir Bedivere. 'Where are my other knights?'

'I am all that is left, sire.'

'What, only one? It is enough,' whispered Arthur. 'It takes only one man to tell the world: this is how it was, this is how it ended . . . Lift me up.'

'I'll fetch a stretcher – the women of the castle will help me carry you indoors. You can rest there. Get better . . .' said Bedivere.

'No. My time has come. Lift me on your back and carry me into that wood over there.' The magic in Arthur's eyes could still command Bedivere's obedience. As Bedivere carried him, Arthur spoke despite his pain. 'I have been here once before. When I was newly crowned, Merlin the Magician brought me here – to the shore of a lake in the middle of the forest. It was here that I was given Excalibur. It is entrusted to earthly kings only once in a thousand years, you know. It made me what I am.'

'Your goodness and God's help made you that, my liege,' said Bedivere, feeling tears cold on his cheeks.

'A witch stole the scabbard, or Mordred could not have wounded me today. But every man must die, Bedivere. Every man deserves to rest.'

It grew dark, but still Bedivere plodded on through the wood, along a baffling maze of paths, carrying Arthur across his shoulders. Suddenly, a lake lay in front of him – an eye of light, mirroring the moon. Bedivere lay Arthur Pendragon down between the roots of an oak tree.

'I haven't the strength, Bedivere. Please – as a last act of friendship – return Excalibur to the lake for me . . .'

'Throw it in, you mean?' Sir Bedivere took the grand sword from Arthur's hip. He was exhausted himself and could barely carry it. It seemed a terrible waste of a sword, an ignoble and obscure end for the mighty Excalibur. So before he got to the lake, he hid the sword under some bracken and turned back towards his master.

'What did you see?' asked the King, pulling himself upright.

'See? Well, I . . . er . . . I saw the ripple stir the reeds, and moorhens hurrying away . . .'

'Liar!' said Arthur in a voice that turned Bedivere's blood to water. 'Go back and do as I said!'

Bedivere turned and ran back to the sword. He *did* mean to throw it, he did almost throw it: twice he whirled it round his head. But then he thought of his task: to preserve the legend of Arthur and his knights, and keep the wonder and faith alive in the hearts of the people. How much easier it would be if he kept Excalibur for the world to see!

So he laid the sword down again on a cushion of moss, and went back to Arthur.

'What did you see?' asked the King.

'I saw a skein of geese and a shoal of fishes rise in a cloud of bubbles . . .'

'Traitor! Villain!' cried Arthur in a voice which turned Bedivere's blood to gall. Clutching the tree, trying to get up, he demanded. 'Must I do it myself, after all?'

'No! No! I'll do it! I will!' Back through the trees Bedivere ran, in a frenzy of regret, thinking that the last words his king spoke to him would be in reproach. He snatched up the great sword, swung it three times round his head, staggering deep into the lake under the huge weight. Then he let it go, and it whirled about and about, a fragment of lightning, a sliver of moon.

In the centre of the lake, just where the moon's reflection floated like a pallid face, an arm clad in white silk reached out of the water – a woman's arm, a woman's hand, but with strength enough to catch Excalibur by its hilt, brandish it three times and draw it down into the lake.

Bedivere went back and told the King what he had seen. It seemed to pacify Arthur, to free him of his anxiety. A smile came to his lips, but he could barely speak any longer.

Suddenly, Bedivere heard behind him the splash of oars and ran to the waterside, thinking perhaps to glimpse the Lady of the Lake bearing Excalibur. But what he saw was a long, slender barge being rowed towards him by three veiled women in tissue-fine robes of grey. They beached the boat and moved ashore past Bedivere, lifting the King to his feet and leading him the short way to their craft. It seemed an easy journey for him, like a man walking to his own bed after a day's hard labour.

Just when Bedivere thought he was dreaming, the women spoke to him. 'We are taking your lord to Avalon.'

'Where he may rest and sleep and recover from the wounds of life.'

'Do not mourn for him.'

'How can I help but mourn?' said Bedivere. 'The world will be lost without him.'

'If there is ever a danger of the world being lost, young man,' said the tallest of the women, 'Arthur will come again, armed with the sword Excalibur. But for now, the world is not lost. Indeed, you saw it saved today from the forces of Evil. Don't forget that when you tell the history of Arthur, when you recount the legend of the Round Table.'

The barge floated out from the shore, two women at the oars, the third cradling the King's head in her lap. He seemed to be asleep now, at rest, and the barge moved silently out across the lake, to be swallowed up by scarves of mist, curtains of diaphanous moonlight, hangings of velvet night.

A Bloodthirsty Tale

A MYTH FROM ANCIENT EGYPT

IT IS A story told all over the world. The Creator makes Humankind. Humankind disappoint their Creator. The Creator destroys what he has made. So it was with Re, in the days when he ruled both the world of people on Earth as well as the family of gods in Heaven.

'People are hatching plots against me! They are rebellious and disobedient. I don't know why I ever created them or any of their kind!' complained Re. 'And yet . . .'

And yet Re was fond of his creation, and did not want to wipe people altogether off the face of the Earth. A small punishment would serve, perhaps, to put the humans in their proper place, to teach them a lesson in humility.

So Re took the third eye from his forehead – the one which shone so brightly, as he sailed the Ship-of-a-Million-Days across Heaven – his eye, the Sun.

When Re wished (as now he wished), his eye took on the shape of a goddess, Hathor. Generally, Hathor was gentle and kind, but since the eye had bulged with fury as Re took it from his head, this time Hathor too was filled with furious rage. Snatching up a sword, she rushed out into the deserts, herding and chasing crowds of people ahead of her like flocks of frightened sheep. She laid about them with teeth and blade, killing and rending, till the human race cried aloud for the gods to pity them.

Only sunset put an end to the slaughter, when Hathor reported to Re in the Ship-of-a-Million-Days and was congratulated for her good work. Re reached out a hand to turn her back into his eye. 'Return to me. O Powerful One. This day shall be remembered for ever in the history of the world!'

But Hathor stepped out of reach. 'Tomorrow I shall kill the rest!' she declared, laughing wildly. 'The sands of the desert will turn red with their blood!' Her hands dripped blood, and she smeared it across her cheeks and hair like warpaint. 'When I have finished my work the history of people on Earth will be at an end! I have tasted their blood and I mean to drink every last drop!'

Re shuddered. 'I've never seen her like this. She means to kill them all!' he realized with a pang of sorrow. He had not meant things to go so far. The people of Earth were, after all, the flowers he had planted for a garden: he did not want them scythed down to the last bright petal.

'Quick!' he told his messengers. 'Go to the Island of Elephantine, in the centre of the Nile, and fetch me its bright red soil!' Crocodiles plunged into the river; cranes flew upstream. There, in the river, as scarlet as the back of the swimming hippopotamus god, lay the island of Elephantine, rich in red ochre. It was smaller by half, after the messengers of Re had scoured away its soil.

'Quick! Quick!' Re told the High Priest of the temple at Memphis. 'Pound this red earth to dust!'

'Quick! Quick! Quick!' he told the servant girls who worked in the fields. 'Brew beer and ferment it with honey!'

All night, the priests pounded and the girls brewed. Then, just before dawn, Re took the dusty dye and seven thousand pints of foaming beer, and mixed the two together till they thickened and congealed into a gleaming red liquor.

One jug at a time, Re poured out the thick red beer on to the ground. Seven thousand jugs of oozing redness he poured out, until he and the priests and the serving girls stood ankle deep in it.

Then he sailed away in the Ship-of-a-Million-Days, as though the fate of the human race were of no concern to him.

Hathor, the eye of Re, woke from her slumbers and remembered her task for the day. She lifted her bloody sword and strode out into the world of people.

Splash, splash, splash, her feet waded into a lake of red. She looked around her and saw, as far as the eye could see, a quaggy mire of gore. 'Indeed, I am the glory of Re that I spilled so much blood in a single day!' And in her bloodlust, she knelt down and drank what she mistook for the blood of Humankind.

She had not remembered it tasting so good! 'If this is how the blood of my enemy tastes, then I shall kill and drink and drink and kill till the last mewling baby has paid for angering my master! Where are they hiding themselves? Let me root them out, these wretches! I, Hathor, am their doom!'

But after drinking a thousand jugs of the blood-red liquor, Hathor found she could not readily get to her feet to go after the remainder of Humankind. She could only manage to sit, with her feet dangling in the red lake, and drink a thousand jugs more.

Soon after, an unaccountable desire to sleep came over Hathor. She squinted up at the Ship-of-a-Million-Days, bearing the gods on high, but it seemed to be spinning about like an angry bluebottle. She watched it for as long as her eyes would stay open, then fell backwards with a splash into the deepest, darkest drunken stupor the world has ever seen.

'Oooh, my head! Oh, my bursting head! Almighty Re, take pity on your servant! I'm not well!' When Hathor woke from her beery dreams, she could remember nothing about the day before. 'How did I get here? What am I doing here? Where is the comfortable forehead of my master. Re? . . . And why do I feel so *ill?*'

Re helped her to her feet, cupped her affectionately in his hands and changed her back into his third eye, settling her in his forehead. Though she was very bloodshot for a while, and glowed less brightly, she was once again a solemn and sober eye who looked down kindly on the people of Earth.

So too did Re, for having seen them come so close to destruction, he had learned to value them as among his best works of creation.

Rip Van Winkle

AN AMERICAN LEGEND

'**W**ELL? YOU GONNA feed the chickens, or what? D'you think that cow's gonna milk herself? S'pose you think sweeping the yard's beneath you! Mother told me it would be this way: me slaving my fingers to the bone and you laying up in bed, thinking you're the King of England!'

Rip Van Winkle rolled out of bed, but still his wife came after him, her bony hand pecking him through his nightshirt. It was five in the morning and today was turning out just like yesterday.

'And chop some wood if you're not too high and mighty! And mend that busted step before I fall down and kill myself. You'd like that, wouldn't you? Then you could drink alcohol and play skittles with those cheap friends of yours . . . And talking of that – I've told you till I'm blue – keep that flea-bitten dog of yours out the house, will yuh? Mother told me it would be this way: marriage.'

Rip wished *his* mother had told him. He wished she had led him aside on his wedding day and said, 'You don't want to do this, son. Here's a gun: go shoot yourself instead.'

He got dressed, swept the yard, chopped wood, fed the chickens and milked the cows. He cooked breakfast for his wife, picked the dog hairs off the rug, and made the beds. It was still only six o'clock and the day lay ahead of him like a pile of rocks.

As he mended the fence, his work took him farther and farther away from the house. The shouting grew fainter and fainter. '. . . *and you let those slugs get to the cabbages again!'* Rip suddenly thought that if he walked way up the hill, he would not be able to hear it at all. His dog Bark looked at him, harassed and hangdog. 'Let's go,' said Rip. And they did.

He knew there would be heck to pay when he got home, but as he climbed between the red pine and maple trees, and breathed the scent of the ferns, Rip hardly cared. He walked and walked up the gorge, deep into the canyon, where the sound of falling water scrawls out every other sound. 'Hear that, Bark? Peace. Perfect peace,' he said.

Up past Sentry Bridge, Minnehaha Falls and Frowning Cliff he climbed, where the sunlight barely trickled through the oaks but the stream plummeted down like silver mercury. And when he reached Rainbow Falls he sat down among the plaited colours of spray. He had never been so far up the glen before. Even his dog sat so still that white-tailed deer and stripy raccoons strolled by, unconcerned, and a chipmunk rolled among the moccasin flowers. At least, Rip thought it was a chipmunk at first.

Then he looked again and saw the hat, the clothes and little boots. And the barrel.

'Dang, blam and fliminy bosh!' cursed the dwarf, as the barrel he had been pushing rolled away from him towards the brink of the falls. He pulled his hat right down, so as not to see it go.

Rip Van Winkle took two big strides and stopped the barrel with his foot. 'Can I carry this some place for you?'

The dwarf pulled his hat off again and peered upwards. 'That's mighty neighbourly, sir, coming from a giant. My back's plumb busted trying to get it up the hill.'

He led the way up a staircase of slippery black stones which led right behind the Rainbow Falls. Half expecting to be washed away, Rip followed with the barrel, and Bark kept close to his heels. Behind the thunder of the waterfall, they found a little door, and behind the door, a great tavern – a cavern of a tavern, noisy with fifty or sixty dwarfs. By getting down on his hands and knees, Rip could just squeeze in through the door. Once inside, there was room for him to stand. At the sight of Rip, the dwarfs stopped stock-still and stared.

'He helped me with the keg!' explained the first dwarf.

'Swell, but who is he?'

'What's he doing hereabouts?'

'Maybe he's dwarf-hunting.' Their voices echoed round the cave and, when Bark trotted in, they cowered against the far wall.

'I'm Rip Van Winkle, and I'm . . . well, I'm hiding from my wife.' (To his relief, there were no women dwarfs in sight.)

The dwarfs let out a single groan. 'Oh, give the man a chair! Pour him a drink! Make room for the unfortunate fellow! Don't we know how it goes! *Chop the wood! Hunt a rabbit! Fetch up the stores.* Set that barrel down Rip, and make yourself at home!'

Rip grinned shyly. 'I'd better be getting back. She'll skin me alive if I don't do some chores.'

But they all rushed at him, and slapped him on the bottom (because they could not reach his back) and hugged his legs, and tugged at his fingers. 'Come and play skittles! You can be on our team!'

'That's not fair! We want him on our team!'

'You can have his dog on your team!'

'And you can have this mug of beer over your head!'

They squabbled and wrestled and giggled throughout the game. And though they lost three balls and broke a flower vase, nobody minded. Time and again, the little men helped themselves to ale from the barrel Rip had carried. 'Have a cannikin yourself!' they kept saying, but Rip only ducked his head and said shyly, 'Better not. The wife doesn't like me to touch strong drink.'

At last, cheered on by his team, Rip scattered the skittles to the four corners of the cavern and five toppled out of the door and over the waterfall.

'We win! We win! Our team wins! Bring the hero a drink!'

It was true, the game had given him a powerful thirst. The tankards were tiny; it couldn't hurt to sip just a thimbleful of ale . . . The dwarfs set down a saucerful for Bark the dog, as well.

At the first swallow, the cavern began to spin. At the second, everyone seemed to be standing on their heads. At the third, Bark seemed to be yawning and turning pink. Then darkness closed in on Rip Van Winkle from all sides.

'Of course. Human. We should have known.'

'. . . not used to fairy beer . . .'

'. . . too strong for him,' said voices out of the darkness.

Then Rip fell asleep, and slept deeper than he had done ever since the day he first shared his big feather bed.

When he woke, there was no sign of the dwarfs. Bark's coat was remarkably dusty, but he woke when Rip patted him. Together they ducked out of the cave. The waterfall was tumbling just as before, the spray still spanning the gorge with rainbows, the white-tailed deer still grazing.

'Now we're for it,' said Rip to his dog, as they tripped up the porch. 'Better mend that step this afternoon, I guess.'

'Who are you?' said the woman at the door.

Rip was almost too startled to speak. 'You're not my wife.'

'George! There's some old-fashioned hobo at the door, says I'm not his wife. George!'

'But I . . . I . . . I live here!'

'George! Says he lives here! You wanna fetch your gun?'

'But I . . . Where's Mrs Van Winkle?'

'Never heard of her. You got the wrong address.'

'Sure you've heard of her, Mary,' said the man who came out with his gun. 'She was the old lady lived here before us. Husband disappeared. Lived here all alone. Fell down the step and broke her neck – she was old, mind.'

Rip Van Winkle fell back a step or two. These people were not lying. The cow in the yard was not his cow. The axe on the woodpile was not his axe. Bark whimpered at the unfamiliar smells. 'Disappeared, you say? Rip Van Winkle disappeared?'

The woman on the porch scratched her head. 'Sure. Now George calls it back to my mind . . . disappeared 'bout fifty years back. Walked off one day into Watkins Glen, they say, and never came back. Folks said the fairies took him, but then folks would. Fell in the stream and drowned hisself, more like.'

Now you might think that losing your farm, losing your feather bed, losing fifty years – and all in one day – might make a man a little bleak, unsettled and resentful. But no. That was not the way it struck Rip Van Winkle. Rip Van Winkle could see a good side to most things. From the gate of his no-longer home, he walked directly into town with his dog, sat down at the bar of the saloon, and told his story to anyone who would listen.

Within a fortnight, he was the toast of Finger Lake County.

The Raven and the Moon

AN INUIT MYTH

ONCE, WHEN THE night was too dark to bear, the fishing people of the north longed for some relief from the solid black sky and its cold hail of stars. What they did not realize was that a moon had been made for the hours of darkness, just as the Sun had been made for day. But a miserly old man and his miserly young daughter, wanting to keep it for their own, locked it away with their other treasures.

Now Raven, like the magpie, likes shiny things – stones, bones, buttons and the like – and when he heard the two whispering one day about their secret hoard, he set his heart on having something out of that chest for his own collection of pretties.

There was no chance that Loona would ever marry: her father gave away nothing that was his, and Loona would never by choice leave the cottage with its chest full of valuables. So instead of courting her, Raven, with a beat of his black wings, changed himself into two wing-shaped green leaves drooping from the bough of a waterside tree. When Loona came and sat on the bank to fish, the bough brushed her face, and the leaves fluttered in at her mouth. She did not spit them out; they slipped easily down her throat and turned to a baby in her womb.

It was a little startling to find herself pregnant, but as she pointed out to her father, 'Having a baby is like getting something for nothing.'

Her old father agreed. 'And now I need never share our pretties with any son-in-law.'

So they made a crib out of furs, on rockers of whalebone, and when the child was born, laid it in the cradle. They called it Beaky, poor mite, because of its enormous hooked nose.

Beaky started to cry.

'Perhaps it's hungry,' said Loona, and fed it. But still the baby cried.

'Perhaps it's wet,' said her father, and turned over the furs in the cot. But still the baby cried.

'Perhaps it's cutting teeth,' said Loona, and gave it her forefinger to mumble on. 'Ouch! What a bite!' But still the baby cried.

'Perhaps it's sick,' said the old man, and they took turns to walk the baby up and down, up and down, up and down. But still it cried.

'Perhaps it's bored,' said Loona. 'It must have a toy to play with.' So she made it a toy horse and a toy fish and sewed it a ball out of felt. But still the baby cried.

The old miser sank his head in his hands and his fingers in his ears. He needed his sleep. He longed for peace and quiet. But his home was full of bawling, the cries so piercing, so loud, that they seemed to lift the roof and split the plank walls of the hut. They took the baby outside and showed it the lap-lap of the sea and the big skuas circling. Beaky only hid its head under Loona's clothes and howled.

'We could always show it the Moon,' said the old man, his hair quite grey and his forehead puckered with misery. Loona thought for a moment and nodded.

Together they bolted the door, hung rugs over the windows and dragged the chest into the centre of the room. Loona scraped at the dirty floor and unearthed a large key. With it she unlocked the chest. Inside was another chest and inside that was a large square box.

Inside the box was a wicker basket like a lobster pot and inside the basket was a box shaped like a tube.

Inside the tube was a leather bag and inside the leather bag was a sack.

Inside the sack was a bucket, and inside the bucket was a wooden pyramid.

Inside the pyramid was a smaller vellum container studded with stars. (Their shine was reflected in the beady black eyes of the watching baby.)

Inside the star-box was a bundle of orange cloth and, shining through the cloth, a light so bright that all shadows were banished from the room. When Loona unwrapped the cloth, out across the floor rolled a glorious silver ball shining more brightly than any coin, brighter than any flame, brighter even than the stars.

At last, to their immense relief, the baby stopped crying. It clambered out of its crib, crawled across the floor and reached out for the . . .

Loona picked up the Moon and threw it in the air playfully to make Beaky laugh. 'Higher! Higher!' chortled the baby.

The old man threw the shining ball higher still – almost as high as the smoke-hole in the centre of the ceiling. 'Higher! Higher!' cooed the baby and flailed its little arms with joy.

Loona tossed the Moon higher still, and all eyes were on the glittering treasure. So no one saw at what particular moment Raven recovered his true shape, put on black feathers and blacker beak, hunched his wings and scrabbled his claws among the ashes of the hearth.

Suddenly he sprang into the air, seized the Moon in his beak and flew with it once round the room, while Loona and her father chased him with outstretched hands. Then, with a flutter and a short cough amidst the smoke, Raven disappeared through the smoke-hole and into the night sky, carrying the Moon in his gaping beak.

Beneath him, the night shoreline was lit by moonlight for the first time. The wave tips turned to silver, the stones on the beach glimmered, the fish scales scattered along the wharf glittered. Phosphorescent algae glowed in the rockpools.

Raven, greedy to add all these pretties to his collection, let go of the Moon which, instead of falling to earth, remained floating in the sky, out of reach of Loona, her father or anyone else. It floated too high, at last, for even the circling skuas, though some greedy beak must surely slash away at its prettiness every month, for something pares the Moon down to the tiniest sliver. Then, just when it seems to have been carried away entirely to some treasure-trove nest in the sky, there it is again, healing, growing, waxing big and white and beautiful.

Sir Patrick Spens

A SCOTS LEGEND

LEXANDER, KING OF Scotland, sat in Dunfermline Town, drinking blood-red wine. His chair stood at the heart of a firelit room, the room at the heart of a castle. The rain outside could never wet the King's hair. The wind beat in vain against the castle walls. The courtiers loosened the fastenings of their velvet jackets and revelled in the warmth, the food, the dancing.

'Where are the men who will sail me a ship to Norway?' the King said.

'At this time of year, your majesty?'

'Why not? What's a little weather to one of *my* ships? I have betrothed my daughter Margaret to the Prince of Norway. But who shall have the honour of taking her to her marriage?'

An old knight sitting beside the King, half-asleep and remembering summer days, mumbled, 'Well, of course, Sir Patrick Spens is the best sea captain in all Scotland.' So the King wrote a letter commanding Sir Patrick to set sail the next day.

When the letter reached him he was walking on the beach, his grey hair tangled with the salt wind. As he read, he laughed out loud. 'Is this a joke? No one puts to sea at this time of year!'

The King's messenger neither answered nor looked him in the eye. Then Spens knew that the letter was in earnest. Deathly pale, the letter crumpling in his hand, he turned back towards the harbour. The grey sea wall curved like a beckoning arm.

He thrust his head in at the lighted door of the inn and bellowed for his crew. 'Make ready the King's ship! Men to the rigging! Men to the sheets! We sail today for Norway with the King's daughter for cargo!'

His first mate pursued him out into the cold and caught him by the sleeve. 'You don't mean it, Captain! You'll never sail today! Last night the new moon held the old in her crescent: there'll be a storm before noon, or I never read the weather in a sailor's sky!'

Spens narrowed his eyes and looked out to sea, as if he could read more than the weather in the cursive waves. 'I saw it too, old friend, but the King's command is our duty.'

A crowd of rowdy courtiers tripped and trotted down the jetty, holding on to their hats and hinnying excitedly. They thought it would be jolly to accompany the Princess Margaret. 'Oh, look now!' said one, mincing up the gangplank. 'I've wetted my new cork-heeled shoes!' Bright silk handkerchiefs fluttered on the jetty, as ladies waved goodbye to their pretty beaux.

It was only a short voyage. They reached Norway in safety, and delivered the Princess up to strangers and foreigners. Then Sir Patrick Spens and his cargo of courtiers turned back for Scotland.

At that time of year, storms prowl the Firth of Forth like winter wolves, seeking ships to devour. Only a short voyage, but the longest any man ever makes. The wind plucked off the sails like petals from a flower, and broke the mast like a green stalk. Waves rose up as high as the walls of Dunfermline Castle, and fell on the ship like stone. Out of the noise and frenzy of the storm they sailed, down, down into green silence, down, down into black cold, down, down to where the weed beckons and the fishes kiss.

That new moon has waxed and waned many times since the ladies waved goodbye to their beaux. But come moon, go moon, they will never meet again. For the courtiers are at the bottom of the sea, ranged at the feet of Scotland's finest sea captain. Only their cork-heeled shoes and fine-feathered hats float like sea birds on the sea's shining swell.

The Saltcellar

A SCANDINAVIAN MYTH

I N THE DAYS when the sea was sweet (though the people round it were no sweeter than now), the King of Denmark visited the King of Sweden.

'Denmark salutes you!' said King Frodi. 'May you live a thousand years!'

'Thank you,' said King Fiolnir. 'Sweden welcomes King Frodi. May your fame fill the ear of the world as the sea fills a seashell . . . Now, let's eat, and you can tell me why you've come.'

King Frodi and King Fiolnir linked arms and walked in to dinner. All through the meal, Frodi eyed the two girls who brought him his food – big, strapping Swedish girls with plaits as long as bell-ropes and muscles like bell-ringers. 'I hear they pull men like wishbones,' he said wistfully, to King Fiolnir.

'Were you looking for a wife, perhaps?' asked Fiolnir politely.

'Good heavens, no! We have plenty of *pretty* women in Denmark. No, I'm looking for two strong sla . . . workers,' said Frodi mysteriously. 'I have . . . I have some work that needs doing.'

'Then you shall have Fenia and Menia!' declared King Fiolnir. He would be sorry to lose the girls, but hospitality demanded he should give his visitor what he most desired.

Fenia and Menia were women you could moor a boat to with an easy mind. Their knees were as big as capstans and their plaits hung like ships' hawsers past shoulders like harbour moles. They were jolly, willing workers, too. King Frodi accepted them eagerly and took them home – the prize he had sought far and wide.

For at home in Denmark, King Frodi had a mill, and now he had someone to turn it.

The mill had been given him by the King of Giants, two round stones balanced one on the other like twin pillows of rock. But they were so huge that no one in all Denmark had been able to move the grindstones round. What a reward awaited Frodi, now that Fenia and Menia could make the stones turn! For it was a magic mill: from between its bulging lips poured whatever was asked of it.

Frodi asked for gold, and the girls turned the treadwheel, and the mill ground gold dust.

Frodi asked for peace, and the girls turned the treadwheel, and the mill ground peace.

Frodi asked for happiness for all of Denmark. But he never gave a thought to Fenia and Menia, who turned the magic mill. He chained them to the treadwheel, and day and night they worked.

'When may we rest?' asked the millers, toiling round their wheel.

'When the cuckoo stops singing,' said Frodi, feeling the gold dust run through his fingers.

'But the cuckoo sings day and night. When may we sleep?' asked the giant millers, walking their wheel.

'Only while you are singing,' said Frodi, and laughed to see the barrels filling up with peace.

Fenia and Menia could not sleep while they sang, as Frodi well knew, but then Frodi did not know that they could sing at all. He certainly did not know that Fenia and Menia could sing magic songs. 'Sleep while you're singing,' said Frodi unkindly, so the sisters began to sing a song in their own mellifluous language:

> 'Come some army with millions of horses;
> Come some army with myriads of men;
> Come some fleet with battalions of pirates,
> And kill this king who has chained us here!
>
> Come you foes of dirty Denmark;
> Come you foes of Frodi King.
> Come you foes of peace and prosperity,
> And kill this man who has made us slaves!'

That very night, despite the reefs of peace piled round Frodi's palace, pirates came raging up the rocky shore. A sea-king called Mysing and an army of mermen killed Frodi in his treasure-house, and left him head-down in a barrel of peace.

They stole the mill and they stole its millers. They stole the treadwheel and they stole the gold. They carried them all on to their flagship and put out to sea before Denmark even woke.

'Welcome aboard, sweet maidens!' said Mysing, smiling.

'You have set us free!' said Fenia. 'We can breathe again!'

'We can see the sky,' said Menia, 'and feel the starlight running down our hair!' And they danced on deck as the ship crossed the bar.

'Grind, sweet maidens,' said Mysing, smiling.

'For our rescuers? Anything! Name it!' said the girls.

'Grind me out *salt*,' said Mysing, smiling. 'Fine white salt, more precious than gold. For I am a salt merchant and sell rare salt to the kings of the world, to flavour their royal meat.'

'Fine white salt for the sea-king Mysing!' sang Fenia and Menia, skipping round their wheel. 'Fine white salt for the tables of royalty!' and the salt poured down into the holds below.

On and on till midnight Fenia and Menia trotted round the treadwheel, grinding. The moon rose up as white as salt and the Dog Star licked it. Then the ship's brass bell rang midnight.

'Time to rest,' said Fenia and Menia. 'More salt tomorrow, but now we are sleepy.'

'Grind more salt!' said Mysing, and lashed shut the door with anchor chains. 'You'll stop when I say, and not before!'

Fenia looked at Menia. Life had not been fair. Workers in Sweden, slaves in Denmark, and now captives even on the sweet free-running sea. 'Let's grind our salt, then,' they said to each other. 'Enough and more than our dear master Mysing wants.'

They ground out salt till the holds were full.

Then they ground out more, even when Mysing thanked them and asked them to stop.

They ground out salt while the crew was sleeping, and they ground out salt till the sun came up. The sun lit a ship blizzard-white with salt. Mounds rounded the decks, dunes buried the bridge, and the ship wallowed as low as a basking whale.

'Stop! Stop! *Stop!* screamed Mysing for the thousandth time, ladling salt overboard with his two hands. But Fenia and Menia went on working.

Still the salt poured from the magic mill, stifling the mermen in their hammocks. Still Fenia and Menia skipped round their tread-wheel, making more salt than ever Mysing had carried over the sea.

At last, with a groan, the overladen ship dipped its prow beneath the waves. Mysing, who was halfway up the mast, climbing up towards the sky, saw his precious cargo of salt turn transparent under the first green flood. Then his ship fell away from under him, into the deep sweet ocean.

The might of the sea and the strong sea tides are still turning the magic mill. Like a prayer wheel it revolves in the sea's dark cellars making salt. If it had been grinding peace when the ship sank, there might be fewer wars. If it had been grinding gold, then sailors would all be as rich as emperors. But the mill was grinding salt when it sank to the sea's cellars and it has ground out salt now for a thousand years and more.

That is why the seas are salty and all salt merchants poor. None is poorer than Mysing, however, who lies trapped beneath the mill-stones, his bones ground down and his soul salt-corroded away.

As for Fenia and Menia, they escaped from the treadwheel as it rolled along the sea bed, struck out for the surface and swam for home. Their knees were like capstans and their plaits ships' hawsers, and their shoulders as big as harbour moles. So it may well be that they reached dry land, where they pulled more men like wishbones, or sang magic songs, and savoured the salty starlight running down their golden hair.

The Bronze Cauldron

A WELSH LEGEND

THREE PACES FROM the door, three paces from the window, three paces from where Boy Gwion slept on the floor, stood the witch's bronze cauldron on three bronze legs. It was always bubbling, always steaming, filling the room with horrible smells. Boy Gwion had to gather twigs to feed the fire under it. He had to weed the garden, feed the dogs, sweep the floor, bake the bread, and wash the clothes – though the Old White Sow never changed hers. No one dared come near the witch's house, so Boy's life was lonely. But he was not one to complain.

In the next room, Afagddu the witch's son slept in a white bed and never went hungry. But Boy would not have changed places with Afagddu. His face was as ugly as a dish of eels, and the rest of him all clenched up like a fist. He was the reason why the Old White Sow came and went, to and fro, day and night, feeding the great bronze cauldron.

She brought things soft and hard, blue things and red, nameless things and things too horrible to name. Sometimes she took a ladle and poured a drop of the brew down Afagddu's throat. But he only gaped back at her like a cuckoo chick, his two eyes dull as mud. 'Not yet, not yet,' crooned the Old White Sow kissing his scurvy head, 'but one day soon, my darling, I shall give you better than beauty.'

Seven times each day she kicked Boy Gwion. 'Don't you ever go stealing that broth, brat. The day you do is the day you die.'

Boy nodded. He was always hungry, but not so hungry that he wanted to taste the horrible slop in the bronze cauldron.

At all hours of day and night the witch's hooves scuffed the floor as she brought things from the forest and things from the pond, things from the hedgerow and things from the drain; dry things and wet things, cold things and hot. She fed that cauldron till its brew bubbled treacly, close to the brim. 'Stir it and don't stop,' she told Boy, 'But not a taste, not a lick, for the day you do is the day you die.'

Boy shrugged. He had no wish in the world to taste the brew in the cauldron.

One night the Old White Sow was merrier than usual. 'Nearly there, nearly there,' she crooned to Afagddu, as she tucked him into bed. 'Soon now, I know it!' She put on her cloak and took down her basket from the roofbeam. 'Stir, brat! Stir!' she told Boy, and with one more kick, scuffled out into the dark.

Boy stirred with one hand and held his nose with the other, while next door Afagddu snored. The seething bubbles brought nasty, shapeless things to the surface which sank again with a sigh. There were glittering shapes, too, and threads of scarlet. The cauldron spoon was as long as a broom, but Boy went on stirring and stirring all night.

Just before dawn, a rising bubble burst, and three drops spurted on to Boy Gwion's hand.

'Ow!'

He rammed his thumb into his mouth to ease the pain. The three drops left three tastes on his tongue: sweet, salt and sour. Then, into Boy's head burst three stars, and he reeled and staggered and fell.

He saw hill-forts and earthworks, stone circles and bonfires.

He saw the King, the butcher, the beggar and the maid.

He saw machines that could fly, buildings sky-high and mines as deep as hell; saw guns and geysers of oil.

He saw how and why and when and where and who, and all in the space of his brainpan, like magnesium burning.

He saw the past and how, long ago, the witch had stolen him from his cradle. He saw the present and how, that very moment, she was coming up the path. He saw the future and how she would kill him for what he had done. All time was inside him, as well as words in millions – as many as the stars – all waiting to be said.

The Old White Sow pushed open the door with a grunt. She saw at once what had happened. 'Wretch! Rascal! Robber! That was for Afagddu! That was for my boy!' She snatched up the ladle and carried a slopping scoop through to her son, splashing it, hot, into his open mouth. But all the liquor's magic had been in those three drops that burned Boy's thumb. The moment of perfection was past, and Afagddu would have no genius to make up for his ugliness.

Before the witch came back from the bedroom, Boy Gwion fled through the open door. He had glimpsed the mysteries of magic now, and he knew how to change his shape. So he ran his hands through his hair, until his hair turned to ears; he stretched out his body and ran . . . into the shape of a hare.

The Old White Sow came after him, turning herself into a greyhound, the better to catch him.

'Stop and stay, thief,' she barked, 'for if you've seen the future, you know that I shall kill you!' Her lean and bony body gained on the hare, jaws agape and tongue lolling. A river lay in their path. Boy was trapped.

Feeling hot breath on his back, Hare Gwion read magic words off the inside of his eyelids and, speaking them aloud, turned himself into a fish. *Plop*, the squealing hare splashed into the water – a glitter of scales, a flutter of fins – and swam away. The greyhound tumbled in behind.

But as she sank, the Old White Sow turned herself into an otter. A lithe writhe of sleek brown fur sped after the fish, claws ripping the water to foam. The fish flickered through a streaming forest of weed; his dappled back almost invisible over the mottled riverbed. But the otter only came on, with ravenous jaws.

'Stop and stay, villain, for if you've seen the future, you know I shall eat you!'

In his terror, Fish Gwion leapt clear out of the water, and hearing magic words pound in his ears, he spoke them aloud – and turned into a bird. Steep as a lark he soared into the sky. But the Old White Sow only shook the water off her back and turned herself into a hawk. High as the treetops, high as the hilltops, high as an arrow can be shot, flew Bird Gwion. But between him and the sun, casting a cold shadow over him, stooped the hawk-witch, talons spread.

'Stay and die, filcher,' she shrieked, 'for if you have seen the future, you know that I shall swallow you down!'

Down.

Down swooped Bird Gwion, in at the gaping door of a barn, down on to the threshing floor where harvested ears of corn lay waiting to be threshed. Every ear held a hundred grains, and each grain exactly like every other. Feeling his heart thud out magic words, Bird Gwion spoke them aloud and . . . changed himself into a grain of corn: one grain among a million.

But grain cannot run.

Bck-bck-bck.

The witch turned herself into a chicken and came strutting into the barn. She pecked from morning till night. Scratch-peck. Scratch-peck. 'Lie there and die, Grain Gwion, for if you have seen the future, you know I shall . . . *bck-bck-bck.*'

The grain that was Boy Gwion went down the chicken's throat. She stretched up her head and crowed in triumph, then shook off her feathers and went home to where the cauldron stood cold and congealing.

Did you know, did you know, that grains grow in the dark?

Nine months later, the Old White Sow put a hand to her great belly and gave a scream, like a chicken before its neck is wrung.

'*Is there no ridding the world of that thieving Boy?*'

She gave birth to a child so beautiful that his forehead shone like bronze and his small hands plucked music from the witch's lank hair.

His brightness hurt the witch's eyes. She bundled her baby into a sack and slung it over her shoulder. 'Wretch! Thief! Slave! I will not love you! I shall not love you! Let no one say I ever gave you life!' Then she went to the river, where, as an otter, she had chased Fish Gwion, and she flung her baby into the water to die.

Currents caught the sack, eddies spun it, and the undertow dragged it down into dark, drowning depths. It rolled over the stones where the salmon spawn, it washed over the weir where the salmon fishermen fish. And there the sack was found by the King's own fisherman, wound three times round with golden fishline.

They called the baby Taliesin, which means 'bright brow': a child so handsome that the King prized him in the way he prized the work of his goldsmiths. But only when Taliesin opened his mouth did the King realize what riches had come to him in a hessian sack. For Taliesin the poet spoke of the past, present and future, of how, why, when, where, and who. And when he sang songs, to the music of the King's harpist, he had at his beck words in millions, as many as the stars and twice as bright.

The Battle of the Drums
A NATIVE AMERICAN MYTH

THERE WERE MAGICAL marks on his forehead, and magic in the way he grew – from baby to child in the beat of a heart, from child to youth in another. Lone Man had magical powers, so when he wanted a thing he was inclined to take it. He wanted a coat, and Spotted Eagle Hoita had one, a fine white one. Lone Man whistled up the wind and sent it to blow on Hoita, and the white hide coat was whisked from his back and carried away, away and away.

It blew through the arch of a rainbow which touched it with seven colours along with a glisten of dew. When travellers found it, they said, 'This is so beautiful it must belong to Lone Man.'

So Lone Man came by his coat, but in doing so, he made an enemy. For Hoita *knew* the coat was his. And Hoita also knew how to bear a grudge.

Soon afterwards, there came from the north the beat of a drum like the thud of a heart. It woke the animals on the plain, and stirred them to their feet – every buffalo and dog, every quail and coney and mouse. Every day, Lone Man saw them pass by his home – a huge migration of animals, their colours fading to a whiteness, their white forms fading into the northerly distance. Then his stool stirred its three legs and walked away, whitewash white, along with his hogan and hives, his fishing rod and shoes.

Day and night: *thum-thum-thum*. Night and day: *thum-thum-*

thum. Powerless to resist, the animals moved north towards the sound, towards the place called Dog Den. When even the growing things on the plain began to grow pale, Lone Man knew he must act before his people starved. So he turned himself into a little white hare, and loped away north in the footprints of the rest.

When he reached Dog Den, the noise of drumming filled the air from snow to sky, from drift to cloud, filled Lone Man's ears and set his long feet thumping. There was Hoita, leading the animals in a dance, chanting out famine, chanting out strife.

> *'Lone Man shall have his coat;*
> *Lone Man shall have no more;*
> *Lone Man shall have no food or joy*
> *From hill to shining shore.'*

The drum Hoita beat was a huge roll of hide taken from the largest buffalo in the world.

> *'Lone Man shall have no luck;*
> *Lone Man shall have no chance;*
> *Lone Man shall have no powers at all*
> *While Hoita leads the dance.'*

Now Lone Man knew what he must do: find a drum bigger and more magical than Hoita's. He searched the world over, then he searched the world under, and there he found the two Turtles who swim with the Earth on their back, balancing the world on their shells.

'If I were to beat on your shells,' said Lone Man, 'I could raise magic enough to overpower Spotted Eagle Hoita.'

'If you were to beat on our shells, the world might tumble from our backs and sink into the Waters like a stone in a pond,' replied the Turtles. 'But you are quite right. Our shape has magic enough. Look carefully, Lone Man, and copy what you see.'

So Lone Man felled an oak tree and built a frame. He took the hides of a hundred buffaloes, and stretched them over the oak frame. And he made a drum the shape of an Earth Turtle, and almost as big. When he beat it, the sea quaked, the sky vibrated, the hills jumped and hopped like fleas around the plain. It sounded like the heartbeat of the Earth itself.

'What is that sound?' said Hoita, far away at Dog Den in the north. 'Go and see, Coyote.'

So Coyote went to see what was making the noise. But Lone Man was waiting, and put a lead round his neck.

'What *is* that sound?' said Hoita. 'Go and see, Birds.' So the Birds went to see what was making the sound. But Lone Man was waiting with nuts and seed, to feed them.

'WHAT *IS* THAT SOUND?' demanded Hoita. 'Go and see, Buffaloes.' So the Buffaloes went to see what was making the noise, and the magic of the Great Drum scattered them across the Great Plain, scattered them once again within reach of Lone Man's hungry people, where they were needed most.

The Hoita realized that the sound was not the Earth's heartbeat but the beat at the heart of Lone Man's magic, and he let all the animals go, sent them south again, to recover their colours and roam the lands of Lone Man and his kin.

Spotted Eagle Hoita had glimpsed the future, and knew how much the plains people were going to need Lone Man.

> *'Lone Man shall need my coat;*
> *Lone Man shall need his lance.*
> *The dangers ahead are many*
> *For this leader of the dance!'*

Cupid and Psyche

A ROMAN MYTH

How could anyone be more beautiful than the goddess of love? Unthinkable, or so Venus thought. But then thought was not her greatest strength. She was all passion, all instinct, all rash impulse and emotion. There is a cool, deep stillness in a thoughtful woman, which attracts like a deep lake on a hot day. Perhaps that is why mortal Psyche's quiet, pensive beauty was so appealing. Some said she was even more beautiful than Venus, the goddess of love.

'Kill her!' Venus told her son. 'Chain the wretch to a rock and let's see how lovely she is after Typhon has chewed on her!'

Venus's son, Cupid, was accustomed to being sent on errands by his mother. Armed with his bow and quiver of golden arrows, he would lie in ambush, on her behalf, and fire into the heart of man or woman an arrow tipped with the poison of love. But to wound someone with love was one thing: chaining them to a rock to feed a sea monster was different. Cupid went about his task with horror and disgust. Psyche struggled and pleaded with him. 'Who told you to do this? Who hates me this much?' The golden arrows were spilled across the barnacled rock, and Cupid scratched himself in gathering them up. But obedient to his mother, Cupid overpowered the girl and left her there, silently weeping. The sea writhed in blue-green coils around the bare rock.

Typhon smelled the small, sweet, subtle smell of Psyche and started up from the deep-sea trench. Its back and wings were black-feathered like the cormorant, its bulk so great that the ocean churned up its sandy bed, and undersea volcanoes erupted. Jaws agape, Typhon came for its puny meal. Fishy breath blasted the trees on shore, and Psyche, pale as snow, closed her eyes.

Suddenly she felt a new wind, fresher and sweeter. The chains around her turned to flowers, and the rock beneath her feet was suddenly a distant speck on a blue mirror. Zephyrus the Breeze had lifted Psyche and was flying with her through the sky. He carried her to a palace where the sound of the sea whispered everlastingly through whorled walls of shining shell.

Zephyrus himself had no shape. So whose were the steps that echoed each night through the seashell palace? Psyche feared them at first, feared she had been abducted by some monster or collector of pretty women. But when, after several days, she had seen no one, she became easier in her mind, and settled to thinking, which made her happy. So did the flowers which she found every day outside her door.

Then one night, the echoing footsteps came to the side of her bed and out of the darkness a voice said, 'It was I who rescued you from the rock, Psyche. I love you, and I want you for my wife. But you must never see me, never see my face.'

'Are you Zephyrus?' she asked.

'He only brought you here to my palace. Don't ask my name. Don't try to see my face, or we shall be lost to each other.'

Psyche thought for a moment. 'I never cared about anything but the beauty of a person's mind and soul,' she said. 'If in a while I find you are as kind and gentle as you seem, I shall be your wife and never wish for the sun to shine on us both.'

Psyche and her mysterious lover knew nothing but happiness within the seashell palace. For a time, Psyche barely thought about anyone else, anywhere else. But she knew that her parents must think her dead, eaten by the sea monster. So one day she asked to be allowed to visit them, to set their minds at rest. Her lover did not want her to go, feared her going, but he did not try to keep her a prisoner. 'You may go,' he said. 'Only promise me you will pay no attention to your sisters if they try to turn you against me.'

Zephyrus kindly carried Psyche home to her father's house, where the family were overjoyed to see her alive – oh, so much more than alive! By the time she had finished describing her life at the seashell palace, her sisters were sea-green with envy. 'Free to do as you like all day? Showered with presents? He must be really hideous, that lover of yours, or he could have had *anyone!* You should take a look – just one peep – see what an ogre you've won for yourself. Why don't you?' But when they looked up, Psyche had gone, gone with the wind.

Still, Psyche was a thinker, a ponderer and puzzler over riddles. Her fingers told her that her mysterious lover was not furred or scaley, warty, feathered or clawed. His face was smooth between her hands. He felt like a perfect young man. So why must she never see him? Every day her curiosity grew until, at last, she could bear the mystery no longer. So when he was asleep, deep asleep, his breathing slow and steady, she crept to the lamp and lit it, carried the lamp to the bedside and let its gentle light fall on his face. '*You!*'

Oozing from the lamp like great tears, three fat drops of oil fell on to the chest of the sleeping man. His lids lifted; the pupils of his eyes contracted; his mouth opened to reproach her. 'What have you done?' Then he was gone.

Gone, too, were the seashell palace, the bed, the flowers, the lamp. They melted away. Psyche found herself on the dark surface of the cold world, all alone. Her foolishness had returned her to the very rock where she had awaited death.

Once again Typhon scented the small, sweet smell of Psyche, but she was too impatient to wait for death in Typhon's jaws. In her despair, she threw herself into the seething sea.

'Oh no!' said the wave. 'I will not drown you!'

'Live, Psyche!' said the saltwater. 'I will not kill you.'

'Go, Psyche!' said the sea. 'Your death would stain me black with shame. You must find some other way to die!' And an arching wave flung her ashore.

Refused permission to die, Psyche resolved to live. She turned her wet face towards the rainy sky. 'I shall never rest till I've found you!' she shouted, she who had never raised her quiet voice. After that nothing frightened her.

She searched hill and plain, mountain and valley. She took ship and sailed the seas, even beat on the doors of the Underworld to ask if her lover were there. From Pole to Pole and through the core of the Earth she searched.

And the gods watched from their mountaintop.

Psyche visited every temple, laying sacrifices on the altar, praying aloud for help to find her lover. At last she came to the temple of the goddess of love, and never suspecting Venus's hatred for her, went inside.

'No! Not there!' cried the gods out of Heaven, but Psyche did not hear.

'Oh dear goddess, loveliest of the Immortals, protector of all those who truly love. Help me find him! Help me, please!'

Behind her, Venus became gradually visible, like a spider's web in the morning dew. 'There, there. I will, child, I will! Dry your tears! Of course I shall help you find your lover . . . just one thing. *You must be my slave for seven years.*'

Such torments and trials, such cruelties and dangers Venus poured on Psyche's lovely head that the gods on Olympus covered their eyes. For seven years Venus sent her slave on errands to the hearts of volcanoes, to the bottom of the sea. She sent her to winnow sand and to dig quicklime, to gather bird's eggs from cliffs and to sweep marshes dry. Psyche did it all.

And every day the gods liked Venus a little less and admired Psyche a little more.

'You see how she does everything that's asked of her!' said Cupid to Jupiter, King of gods.

'Someone's helping her, that's how,' protested Venus sulkily. 'She could never do it alone.'

'You see how she brings a smile to the very faces of the Dead,' said Cupid to Jupiter.

'Silence, son!' raged Venus. 'It's you I sent to kill her in the first place! Why aren't you down there now, setting dogs on her trail, loosing monsters on to her scent?'

'*Because I love her, Mother,*' said Cupid. All Heaven gasped in astonishment. '*Because it was I who rescued her. And it is I who have helped her survive your spite!*' He showed the three small burns on his chest, where Psyche's oil lamp had spilled. 'That's why I beg you, my Lord Jupiter: *make my love immortal!*'

All eyes turned to Jupiter, King of the gods.

'*NO!*' said Venus.

'*YES!*' boomed the god. 'Thanks to Venus's cruelty, Psyche has earned her place among the Immortals. Marry her, Cupid, and when her mortal part falls away I shall set her in the night sky – a bouquet of stars in the arms of the night!'

That is how Psyche's long search ended. Cupid simply walked down from the foothills of Olympus and took her in his arms.

But what Cupid had forgotten – and Venus, too – was the monster Typhon. Woken and rising still from the seabed, with oily feathered wings of black it broke surface now, its thousand jaws snapping; it found no tasty morsel of mortal chained to the sea rock. So it dragged itself ashore, lumbered out of the sea, and came looking for its old enemies – the gods. Its search was a long one, longer than Psyche's. But at last it found a fitting prey: Venus, goddess of love, and her son Cupid.

They fled him far and fast, but when nothing else could save them, they changed themselves into little fishes and leapt up into the sky. Starry fishes, they swim still through the reefs of nebullae, the dark pools of space. And no fish in the ocean is as happy as Cupid, because Psyche is there too, as gentle and silent as a sea anemone caressing the liquid night.

Doctor Faust

A GERMAN LEGEND

FAUST, SAID HIS friends, was too clever for his own good. Faust, said his enemies, had no respect for God or religion. The truth was, Faust had a thirst for knowledge and would let nothing, friend nor enemy, stand in the way of his learning. So he took for granted nothing his parents told him, nor his teachers, nor even the priests. Instead, he read every book, consulted ancient charts and arts, and dabbled in chemistry.

Soon he could read the language of the stars and twelve other languages besides. Soon he could utter spells, work magic and, when he summoned up the Devil from Hell itself, the Devil came.

He came in the shape of a black dog with blazing red eyes and gaping jaws.

'Too ugly! Leave me!' Faust cried in commanding tones. 'Come back in some other form, or I shall die of looking at you!' And the dog obediently turned and went. In that instant, Faust felt as powerful as God himself, for he could command the Devil and the Devil obeyed.

When the Devil reappeared, he called himself Mephistopheles and had a human shape, though his face was the saddest Faust had ever seen and there was a look in his eyes like a lost child. 'Why do you summon me, Faust? What do you want?'

'Knowledge,' said Faust. 'Knowledge and power! Everything you can give me that plain, ignorant men cannot have!'

'I can give you that,' said Mephistopheles. 'But everything has a price. You won't want to pay mine.'

'Name it!' said Faust, drunk with his own daring.

'Very well. For twenty-four years I serve you – do anything you ask, fulfil your every wish. After that time, I shall have your soul. Is that agreed?'

All his life Faust had been cleverer than anyone he met, able to outwit the sharpest wit. Here was a dog in human shape. Surely he could outwit him too – take the magic but keep his soul – especially after twenty-four years of learning to be cleverer still. 'Agreed,' he said.

From beneath his cloak, the Devil produced a scroll of paper. 'Sign to it.'

'Of course.'

'*In blood.*'

While the blood was still wet, Faust was already asking questions. How many stars? How large the universe? How old the sun? How does a bee fly? Who rules the universe?

'That last I shan't answer,' said the Devil sulkily.

'Then God is greater than you?'

'Do you like pretty women?' asked Mephistopheles, changing the subject.

He fetched for Faust the most beautiful woman in the history of the world. (At least he fetched a likeness of her, which Faust could admire but not touch, an illusion rather than flesh and blood.) He played tricks on Faust's enemies. He did conjuring tricks for Faust's friends. Anything Faust could think to ask for, Mephistopheles did for him. Having seen the most beautiful woman in the world, of course, no other real, live woman could interest Faust. So he took no wife, no one who would care what became of him. But what did that matter? He had everything else.

He had more money than he could spend; houses and clothes, coaches and castles. But as for knowledge, all he found out was that facts bored him and the truth scared him: that good men went to Heaven, whereas bad men went to . . .

'Help me, books! How am I to trick my way out of this deal?' But his books told him nothing. 'Help me, Wagner! How can I save my skin?' But his serving man did not know, and seeing Faust afraid of some impending doom, Wagner fled his master.

The days went by like bees on the wing, each stinging Faust into an awareness of his terrible predicament. Suddenly he was a middle-aged man, fat and slow from eating the Devil's rich food, lonely and bowed down under all the facts he knew. Faust's contract with Mephistopheles was due to expire, and suddenly Mephistopheles was not so harmless or helpful. Beyond his lonely, red-rimmed eyes, Faust could glimpse a bottomless fiery pit bigger than the universe itself, a black-cogged machine whirring like the workings of an everlasting clock. At midnight, Faust must forfeit his soul to the Devil.

That last night, he considered the money, the laughter, the luxuries, the learning . . . and all of it seemed worthless alongside his little soul. He thought of hiding, of arguing, of pleading, but he knew that the Devil was coming to collect what was owed, and would not leave without it.

He barricaded the door, he loaded a gun, he stopped the clock. But time still moved on unstoppable. Ten o'clock, eleven, twelve. As the clock began to strike, Faust fell on his knees, sobbing and mouthing prayers. But the words turned to pitch in his mouth, and the contract in his pocket burned like phosphorus.

'Turn me into water drops and sprinkle me over the ocean,' he prayed, 'but don't let me fall into the Devil's hands! Don't let him take me to Hell!'

The clock in answer struck the twelfth stroke of midnight. Beneath the floorboards there was a roaring fire. Beyond the curls of smoke issuing between the floorboards, Mephistopheles stood – locked door or no locked door – holding the contract unfurled. The blood of Faust's signature was still wet . . .

'No. No! *No! No! NO!*'

Next morning Faust was nowhere to be found. Neighbours told of shrieks and cries, of lightning flashes and blood-red rain. But of Faust there was no trace, no bone, no hair. No books written, no sons or daughters to outlive him, no loyal friend to remember him. Nothing remained of the man who had been Faust; only wild stories of screaming in the night, and a slight smell of brimstone near the broken clock.

Alone

A NATIVE AMERICAN MYTH

A WOMAN LIVED on the shores of the sea. Her name was Copper Woman, though she was made of flesh and bones: flesh and bones and loneliness. One day she was so lonely that she wept, and then, to her shame, was seen weeping by a band of travelling women.

'Don't be ashamed, Copper Woman. Loneliness is not a crime; nor is crying,' said the women. 'There is even magic in a woman's tears. Didn't your crying fetch us here to cheer you?'

It was true. While the visitors stayed, Copper Woman was blissfully happy – talking, laughing, asking questions about the rest of the world, answering questions about her daily life.

'I catch bass here, gather seaweed there, and this is where the best shellfish grow. I made this dress from the silver skin of a seal, this soup from seaweed . . .'

But when the travelling women left, Copper Woman felt more lonely than ever, because now she knew how it felt not to be alone. She stood on the shore and wept, and her tears wetted the sand more than the sea ever had.

Remembering the magic the women had taught her, Copper Woman scooped the wet sand into a little shell and left it on the tide-line. By next day it had grown, not into any recognizable shape, but too large for the shell. So she transferred it to a sea-urchin's shell, then to a crab's. One day it reached out a tiny hand and clasped her finger tight, and would not let go, so that she had to carry it with her everywhere. She brought it shellfish to eat and fish stock, gull-bones to play with as well as bright pebbles and seal's fur.

Copper Woman had given life to Sand Man, and when he was fully grown, his muscles were ropes of sand, strong to help with the fishing, tender to embrace her. Laughing with delight, she worked alongside her mate, chattering and singing, telling him all about herself and the shoreline, asking questions but never waiting for an answer, so glad was she of his company. They slept together in a big bed of sealskins, pillowed on gull feathers. His face was whiskery against hers, like a sea-lion's, and his chest had a soft, silvery fur. Copper Woman thought she would be happy for ever, now that she had a friend.

'I love you,' she said, kissing her handsome Sand Man.

He smiled and turned towards her, his eyes bright with affection. He opened his mouth and she listened eagerly for him to say he loved her too.

But the only sound which emerged was the shrill cry of a seagull. '*Awwwkkhh! Awwwkkhh!*' Sand Man was, after all, the stuff of shells and birdbones and weed; of sand and tears and wishing. Copper Woman cried as she had never cried before, and was lonelier than she had been when she worked alongside the sobbing sea.

The Golden Vanity

AN ENGLISH LEGEND

THE PENNONS AT the masthead were new, the gold paint on the figurehead gleaming, and the sailors were still thinking of home when it happened. Not three weeks out of Portsmouth the *Golden Vanity* was overtaken by a Turkish caravel, light and fast and with guns enough to send the ship and all its crew to the bottom of the sea.

Slow and ponderous, the great English treasure galleon wallowed on the swell, while stone balls and chain-shot smashed away the spars and rigging like twigs falling from a tree. 'We're lost! We're taken!' groaned the Captain, and he cursed his crew, his vessel and the admiral who had sent him on this fatal voyage.

Up jumped the cabin boy, Billy. 'There's something I could do, sir! There's something I could try! What would you say to me sinking the Turk deep down where the whale bones lie?'

'I'd say five thousand pounds and marry my daughter,' said the Captain surlily, 'but since when did cabin boys win battles?'

From his belt Billy pulled a little bradawl, a tool for boring holes in wood. 'What say I swam across and holed the Turks under the waterline – let in the sea to wet their heathen feet?'

The Captain threw aside his spyglass and turned to look at the boy for the first time. 'Reckon you could do it?'

'He can if anyone can!' exclaimed the second mate. 'The lad swims like a fish, he does!'

Cannonfire like the crack of lightning rived the smoky air, and a ball whistled by the Captain's ear. He put out a paw and clasped Billy's little hand in his. 'Then do your best for us, son, and do your worst to them!'

They tied a rope round Billy's waist and lowered him into the sea: he trembled like a fish on a line. But no sooner was he in the water than he untied the rope and struck out strongly, gliding through the wave tops like a very porpoise. 'Tell your daughter I shall buy her a fine house with five thousand pounds!' he called back with a laugh.

The water was cold. Now and then it exploded into spray as a cannon-ball fell short or a piece of rigging crashed down into the sea. But by closing his eyes and imagining – Billy the Beau! Little Billy Gentleman! – he somehow reached the Turkish hull. She had heaved-to to empty her cannon into the *Golden Vanity*, and the hull stood still in the choppy ocean. Holding his breath, he dived – clawed away the pitch and tallow coating, and bored through the wooden hull.

Again and again Billy dived, until his lungs were burning and his body blue with cold. Not until he heard the cries aboard the caravel – 'Awash! Awash! We're holed!' – did he push the bradawl back into his belt and begin the long swim back.

Chilled to the marrow and tired past all enduring, Billy closed his eyes and thought of his mother's face the day he rode to church in a carriage, to marry the Captain's daughter; frock coat of red velvet, with a spyglass and a shiny sword, his brothers would say, 'There goes our little Billy; he saved the day, you know!' When he opened his eyes again, the hull of the *Golden Vanity* loomed huge above him, steep as a cathedral wall.

'Throw down a rope, Captain!' he called, and saltwater slopped into his throat. 'I can't . . . much longer . . . so tired.'

'Raise the topsail and let's put on some speed, men!' said the Captain on his bridge.

The crew stared at him. They ran to the rail. They pointed to Billy, in case the Captain had not heard him. Someone ran for a longer rope.

'Billy did no more than his duty, and now you can do yours,' barked the Captain. 'Man the yard-arms, or I'll blow your heads off for scurvy mutineers!' And he actually primed his hand pistols, then and there. As he did so, he muttered. 'Does he think I have money and daughters to spare on the likes of him?'

'For the love of God, Captain! Keep your money and keep your daughter! But pull me up or I'm dead and done for!' called Billy.

The Captain pursed his thin lips, put his spyglass to his eye and watched the crow's-nest of the Turkish ship sink with a fountaining flurry beneath the cold sea waves. 'Lay on more canvas, men,' he said.

Young Billy pulled the bradawl from his belt. His clammy hand slapped the slow-moving hull. 'I should do to you . . .' His face sank once beneath the surface, his sodden clothes seemed to weigh like lead. 'I should do to you as I did to the Turk . . .' He sank a second time and his fist rapped on the moving hull. '. . . but that I love my friends, your crew!' And so saying, he rolled over in the sea, face-down. The bradawl fell away, away out of his hand, down to where the whale bones lie.

The Founding of London
A VIKING LEGEND

THE FOUR SONS of Ragnar were playing chess when the news came that their father was dead.

'Dead? The mighty Ragnar Lodbrok?' said Ivar.

'Dead? Greatest of the Vikings?' said Bjorn.

'Who killed him?' said Hvitserk.

'How, when he wore his magic shirt?' said Sigurd.

They listened in horror to how Ella, King of Northumberland, had routed the army of Ragnar, captured the noble old warrior and thrown him into a pit of snakes. 'At first the snakes could not pierce the shirt, it's true,' panted the messenger. 'But at last Ella guessed there was magic in it and had it torn from your father's back . . . Then the snakes, oh the snakes . . . !' The messenger broke down and wept at the memory of it.

But Ivar had no time for tears. 'Lift me on to my shield, brothers, and may the gods shut me for ever out of the halls of Valhalla if I do not destroy this Ella of Northumberland!'

'Too late! Too late!' wailed the messenger. 'His army is close on my heels – his and a dozen armies besides! They outnumber us twenty to one! The glory of the Viking eagle is falling, falling!'

'My oath is sworn!' replied Ivar. 'I must fight.'

Ivar, crippled from birth, was lifted on to his shield. Each brother held it high on one hand while with the other he drew his brazen sword. Raised up high, Ivar wielding his archer's bow was a rallying point for the Viking warriors. He loosed arrows like rain in a storm, and every one found its mark.

But Ella's army was huge. Among his allies was King Alfred of high renown, and soon the Norsemen for all their bravery were utterly defeated. Bjorn and Hvitserk and Sigurd set their brother down at the feet of King Ella like a payment of ransom, and the haughty King spat on him.

'Do you admit defeat?'

'We do,' said Ivar.

'Am I the victor?'

'You are,' said Ivar. 'And I swear I will never raise weapon against you, if you will grant me just one boon in your mercy.'

'What is it?' snapped Ella suspiciously.

'As much of this sweet land of England as may be enclosed by the skin of an ox, a little ox.'

Ella beamed magnanimously. 'One ox skin? Take it. That should give you just enough ground to be buried in, ha ha!'

An ox hide was brought, and a sharp knife, too. Ivar began to cut the hide into the thinnest of strips.

'What are you doing?' said Ella uneasily.

'No more than you permitted,' Ivar replied.

Thousands of strips he cut from that one ox hide. On the banks of the River Thames, Bjorn laid down the first. Hvitserk laid another end-on to it. Sigurd placed a third. End-to-end the strips were laid, along and along the green watermeadows . . . over several hills, across a bridge, round the houses clustered by the river. By the time the last strip of skin met with the first, the sons of Ragnar had encircled thirty acres of prime land, and laid claim to the Middle Thames.

King Ella was furious, but what could he do? He had given his word. As he watched the four brothers and their defeated army build a wooden city-stronghold in the middle of his kingdom, he comforted himself that Ivar had given his word too: never to fight him again.

They called the city Lunduna Berg, which became London, in time. There Ivar Lodbrok made his home, at the heart of Ella's empire, though his brothers went back to Denmark. He did not sit idle. He did not chafe at his confinement within these wooden walls. During his childhood, while other boys played, sickly Ivar had studied the magic of the runes. Now he cast the runes all day long, and the

Saxons outside his walls heard the click of these mystical stones which could foretell the future: *click, click, click*.

Every day, Ivar propped himself against the city wall and talked to the Saxons who went past. 'Drink my health tonight, won't you, at the inn?' he would say and throw down a gold coin. 'Please accept this small wedding gift,' he would call as a wedding party danced by, and throw down his jewelled cloak clasp. 'Would you care to dine with me?' he would say to the starving beggars curled up against the palisade. The music of his minstrels carried far beyond the bounds of Lunduna Berg.

Ella meanwhile ruled with cruelty and spite. He taxed the people till they groaned, he worked them till they dropped. He quarrelled with his allies, brawled with his ministers and sacked the generals in his army.

'How goes the world with you?' Ivar called down genially from his city's wooden towers.

'Worse than bad,' came the reply from hungry Saxons driving skinny cattle out to plough ground as stony as Ella's heart.

'That's the trouble with kings,' Ivar would murmur. 'Kings take the credit for victories but never take the blame for the bad times.' Little by little, he and his fellow Londoners befriended the Saxons . . . and having befriended them, stirred them up to rebellion!

'*You* should lead us! *You* should be our king,' the Saxons were soon saying. But Ivar always shook his head.

'I gave my word never to fight Ella. I cannot break it.'

'Listen to him! Such an honourable man!'

Ivar smiled. '*I* gave my word . . . But, of course, my brothers never did . . .' So the unhappy Saxons sent word to Denmark, begging Bjorn and Hvitserk and Sigurd to come back and save them from Ella's tyranny. When the brothers landed, everyone rallied to their eagle flag.

This time there was no King Alfred to fight at Ella's side, no alliance of nations, no army of thousands. Though Ivar kept his word and never raised a bow against him, Ella was utterly defeated. It was the enemy within which beat him – an enemy citadel built at the heart of his own kingdom, yes, but also that cruel snake-pit of a heart within his barbarous breast.

The Monster with
Emerald Teeth

A MAYAN MYTH

EVEN THE GODS make mistakes. First they populated the world
by carving little wooden men and women. But the carvings
were so badly behaved that their very belongings rose up
against them. Their knives stabbed them, their chickens pecked them,
their houses fell on them, their millstones ground them to splinters.

But the giants who replaced the wood-men were no better. Vukub-
Cakix and his two sons, Earth-Mover and Earth-Shaker, were proud,
vain and cruel. Even after the gods had produced their masterpiece –
humankind – the three giants made life a misery for everyone on
earth. They had to be got rid of. But how?

The heavenly twins, Hun-Apu and Xbalanque were sent to rid the
earth of the three giants, and went at once to the nanze tree where
Vukub-Cakix picked fruit each day. Hiding in the branches, they
waited till Vukub had climbed right to the top of the tree before
levelling their blowpipes and taking aim.

'Owowo!' cried the giant, and fell, clutching his face. Though he
crashed to the ground like a meteorite, the fall did not kill him.
Indeed, now he could see strangers in his fruit tree, he came after
them, silver eyes flashing, grinding his emerald teeth. He grabbed
Hun-Apu's arm and pulled it clean off before the heavenly twins were
able to make their getaway.

'I need it back!' said Hun-Apu when they stopped running. 'I can't
go back to Heaven without my arm!'

305

'Don't worry,' said Xbalanque. 'But now our friend the giant has the most fearful toothache. Our darts hit him in the mouth.'

'I'm not feeling too good myself,' said his twin.

But they put on cloaks and masks and went to the house of Vukub-Cakix, where the giantess Chimalmat was just roasting Hun-Apu's arm for dinner.

Terrible groans came from the bedroom, for the giant was in agony. 'I'd just reached the top of the tree,' he told his wife, 'when this terrible toothache started up. If it hadn't been for that, I'd've have brought you home both those thieves to eat.'

The twins knocked at the door.

'We were just passing . . . couldn't help hearing . . . wondered if we could help . . .' they told Chimalmat, '. . . we being dentists.'

She hurried them in to where Vukub lay writhing on his bed, swearing horribly and promising to make the world pay for his misery. Green lights flickered over the ceiling as the firelight reflected off Vukub's emerald teeth.

'Say "aaah",' said Hun-Apu.

'Mmm. Just as I thought. All rotten. Those teeth will have to go,' said Xbalanque, peering into the cavernous mouth.

'But all his power is in his teeth!' whispered Chimalmat in awed tones. 'All his strength! How will he bite off his enemies' heads? How will he grind their bones?'

'We shall give him a new set, of course,' said Xbalanque and began, with pliers, to pull out the emerald teeth one by one. A whole emerald mine never held so many jewels as Vukub-Cakix's mouth.

In place of the emeralds, Hun-Apu and Xbalanque left grains of maize. No more did the green fire flicker on the ceiling, no more did Vukub's silver eyes shine. He faded, faded, faded, like a fire going out. Powerless to lift a finger, he watched the darkness close in on him like a rising flood and carry his soul away.

'What about my arm!' said Hun-Apu when the twins got outside. Xbalanque threw back his cloak and brandished the limb he had rescued from over Chimalmat's fire. 'A little magic,' he said, 'and you'll be as good as new.' And so he was.

Earth-Shaker was a braggart and a show-off. That made him easy to flatter and easier still to find. When the heavenly twins tracked him down, he was busy juggling three small mountains.

'Stupendous!' exclaimed the brothers, bursting into applause. 'So clever! Such strength!'

Earth-Shaker looked down at them, pleased. 'Yeah. There's no mountain I can't move. Name one, any one. I'll show you. Nothing's beyond me.'

Xbalanque pointed to a distant snowcapped peak. 'That one?'

'Easy,' bragged the giant.

'It must make you hungry, all this pushing and juggling,' suggested Hun-Apu. 'Perhaps we could shoot you something to eat?'

Earth-Shaker liked that idea. He was always hungry, always devouring the wildlife tenderly placed by the gods, in the woodlands and hills. As a flock of macaw flew over, the twins put their blowpipes to their lips and brought down a pair of birds. Then smothering them in mud and baking them over a fire, they presented the meal reverently to Earth-Shaker. They did not mention that the darts in their blowpipes were poisoned with curare, that the mud they had used was poisonous, too. By the time Earth-Shaker had eaten his meal, his head was spinning and his silver eyes were dim. He could barely even see the mountain he was supposed to move.

Xbalanque and Hun-Apu led him there, ignoring his whimpers, saying that he was trying to worm out of a challenge. 'He can't do it, you see, brother? He was just bragging,' they said.

So Earth-Shaker, in his insane pride, pushed against the mountain till his sweat ran down it in rivers. He pushed so hard that he left hand prints, a fathom deep. But then his heart burst with the strain of so much poison and so much showing off.

Which left only Earth-Mover, proudest giant of them all.

He was nosy by nature. So the heavenly twins dug a pit which looked like the foundations of an enormous house, and waited. When Earth-Mover came along, he at once climbed down to inspect the pit, thinking what a big house must be planned and how he might just take it for himself.

He saw the huge pile of timber logs stacked beside the hole, but he did not realize, until too late, that Xbalanque and Hun-Apu stood behind the logs with crowbars, levering them forward.

One by ten by hundreds, the huge tree trunks tipped, rolled and fell into the pit on top of Earth-Mover. They fell with the noise of an avalanche, and when the noise stopped, all was silent.

'Come one, come all and build on the ruins of the Giants!' declared

Xbalanque. 'Build a fine home for yourselves over the broken bones of Earth-Mover; you and your families will be safe now from his bullying!'

The young men did just that. Four hundred of them built a log house big enough for all of them to live in, and when it was built, they had a party to celebrate.

But beneath them, Earth-Mover was not dead at all. He had found himself a crevice safe from the falling logs, and there he had bided his time, silver eyes gleaming, grinding his emerald teeth. At midnight he got to his feet, flinging up his head, flinging out his arms, tossing the house and its four hundred occupants into the night sky. It was like the eruption of a volcano.

So high were the young men thrown, so wide their eyes with terror, that Xbalanque looked up and saw the moonlight glimmer in eight hundred eyes. And in that instant, he transformed the boys into stars to keep them from falling to their deaths.

Heartsick and angry, the heavenly twins worked alone to avenge the young men. They undermined two mountains towering over a deep ravine and, when Earth-Mover walked through the ravine, Xbalanque toppled one mountain on top of him and Hun-Apu toppled the other.

Like a blanket, the rocks and earth rucked and folded over the fallen giant. This time he must surely die! But out between the boulders reached a hand, grasping, clawing. Out through the solid earth burst another. And so Xbalanque and Hun-Apu invoked the magic of the heavens, the magic of the gods which had made the giants a thousand years before.

And Earth-Mover was turned to stone, petrified, stopped stock-still and lifeless in the very act of grasping for life.

The Golem

A JEWISH LEGEND

IN THE COURSE of any day, there are dull, repetitive jobs to be done. The more intelligent the man, the more wearisome routine seems to him. So that when the rabbi, Judah Loew ben Bezabel, contemplated the daily round of cleaning, bell-ringing, winding of clocks, checking of candles, mending of vestments, it seemed to him that no man (or even woman) should waste his God-given life doing it. So he built a creature – without mind, without soul, with little shape and no family – to do all the tedious tasks within the Prague synagogue. He called it the Golem, which means 'lifeless lump of earth'. Under its tongue, Judah put a tablet, and the tablet empowered the limbs to move, the shapeless trunk to heave itself about.

It was hideous to look at, but who would see it? The Golem went about his work in the gloomy unlit synagogue when no rabbi or worshipper was present. It pulled the candle stubs from their sconces and fetched new ones, polished the brass and swept the floor, muttered meaningless words from no living language, as it sewed the vestments, washed the windows and scared cats off the front steps.

Perhaps Judah should have written GOLEM on his creature's forehead. But as it was, he wrote the word he loved best: AMETH, which means truth. Once, when old Mordecai the grocer accidentally caught sight of the creature scrubbing amid the shadows, he gave a cry of, 'Oh! Death has come for me!'

Judah sent the Golem away, and laughed, and soothed the old man's fright. 'It's not Death. That's only my Golem.'

'But he has "Death" written on his forehead!'

'No, no. Not METH, but AMETH,' said Judah, and smiled at the mistake. 'The "A" was hidden in the shadows, you see?'

Through his dull, glintless years, the Golem looked out on a world of stone and brass and wood. Sometimes he heard singing and liked that. Sometimes the sun shone through the coloured window-glass and splashed over the Golem like a shower of gems. His last sight each night was of Rabbi Judah's face, large near his own, fingers reaching into the Golem's mouth to remove the tablet. Then darkness closed over him like a coffin lid.

But one day, Judah Loew ben Bezabel forgot to remove the tablet. (He was an intelligent man, and such routine little jobs tended to slip his mind.) The Golem moved on around the empty hall of the synagogue, though all his tasks for the day had been done. He went to check the steps, but there were no cats. The night street stretched away like a dark corridor, so naturally, he began to sweep it.

The broom wore down to a stump. Dawn came up, and the sun shone full in the Golem's face for the first time.

He went mad with joy.

It was the ferocious joy of the Earth as it shakes down trees and houses. It was the destructive joy of a young child who knows no better than to break things. When people saw the Golem on the streets, they screamed, 'A monster! A ghoul!' and he did not like that. He hurled the people through windows, for the joy of seeing the glass shatter. He hurled carts into the river, for the sake of the splash. The tablet under his tongue suffused his body with more strength than ever before, his rudimentary mind with new thoughts. He must taste more of this new, brighter world!

But the light hurt his eyes, the screams hurt his ears, and he could not find his master. People were throwing things at him now, and firing loud guns. The Golem began dimly to feel pain and fright and rage. He tore the walls out of buildings, looking for Judah. He climbed church spires and threw down clocks and gargoyles. Though they tried to kill him, no one could, because he was never truly alive – a lump of clay.

But then God made Man out of a lump of clay, and Judah had made something very like.

When the statues would not speak to him, the Golem pushed them down. The colourful market stalls intrigued him: he snatched down the awnings. The army got in his way, and so he shooed the soldiers away, like the cats from the synagogue steps.

But where was Judah? The cacophony of a city in panic maddened and amazed the Golem, and he ripped off doors and punched down fences, looking for his master, calling for him in a shapeless language nobody understood.

He was hurt. He was lost. By the time Judah Loew ben Bezabel came running, robes flapping, face aghast, the Golem blamed *him* for the dazzled turmoil of his mind. He left tearing up horse-troughs, and turned on Judah with a grotesque snarl. His shapeless hands closed round the rabbi's throat, and they both fell to the ground.

Judah, half-throttled, saw the world shrink to a dim, half-lit confusion. His strength was puny in comparison with the Golem; he knew he could never fight it off. But with his last conscious thought, Judah reached up and struck the Golem's forehead – smudged out the letter 'A' from the world *ameth*: left the word *meth*: *death*.

The Golem's eyelids flew open; the eyes beneath were not dim, but flashing bright. '*Life, not Death!*' he said, quite plainly, then fell forward with the weight of a horse on top of Rabbi Judah.

I ought to mention: the Golem was only tiny, only waist-high to a real man. You may see for yourself. What remains of the Golem stands in a glass case in Prague Museum, a clay figurine as ugly as sin, the Hebrew for 'Death' still scrawled on his forehead.

Mummy's Baby

AN INUIT MYTH

EVERYONE KNOWS THAT babies are a treasure. But most have forgotten that once babies had to be come by in the same way: by digging. All sons and daughters lay underground, like spring bulbs: girls near the surface, boys deeper down. And a woman who wanted a family had only to take a spade and go mining. Consequently, strong, fit, hard-working women had whole armies of children, whereas lazy women might have only one or two.

Then there were the accursed women – luckless wives who, dig as they might, never found the treasure they were seeking. Kakuarshuk was just such a woman. More than sleep, more than food, more than sealskin coats or a fine house, Kakuarshuk wanted a baby. But wherever she sank her spade, however deep she dug and for however long, she turned up nothing but ice and snow, lichen and frozen earth. Sometimes it seemed as if she had dug up all Greenland in her search.

In desperation, she went to visit an *angekkok*, a conjuror, who plucked magic out of the air rather than children out of the earth. 'Please tell me!' cried Kakuarshuk. 'Where must I dig to find a child? I've worn out five spades digging, and all I have to show for it is a basketful of loneliness!'

The *angekkok* scratched in the dirt with a magic stick – a map with glaciers and mountains and villages. 'Dig here,' he said, closing his eyes and driving the stick hard into the ground. 'Here or nowhere.'

The place was a great journey from Kakuarshuk's village, but she took nothing with her – only a spade over her shoulder and a great yearning in her heart. Like a goldminer she struck her claim. Like a prospector after diamonds she broke open the hard crust of the earth. No girl baby lay near the surface. But perhaps a boy lay deeper down, waiting for her, with joy clenched in his tiny fists. So Kakuarshuk dug and went on digging. Deeper than any reasonable woman would have dug, deeper than any woman had *ever* dug, Kakuarshuk shovelled up the soil, until the sky was no more than a grey speck high above her head. Through permafrost and fossil layers, rocky strata and soft loam she dug, until like a black mole, she was lost inside the very earth. When her spade broke, she dug on with the shaft until, exhausted, she lay down and waited to die.

A moment later, a spade sliced past her head, and sunlight streamed into her face. Somebody was tunnelling in the opposite direction!

'Oh, yes! Yes! I have found one!' cried a voice. 'A dear little lady one! Oh! Oh! My very own little mummy!'

A baby, huge as a polar bear, as pink and bare as a crayfish and without a tooth in her head, scooped up Kakuarshuk and hugged her close. Overhead, a brilliant blue sky spilled hot sunshine over a green wonderland of flowers and trees. There was no ice, no snow in this land peopled with giant babies. Crawling, toddling, laughing or crying, there were babies everywhere. Some were digging with little trowels, and some had already found what they were after. Here, on the other side of the world, the babies dug for mummies and, having found them, cradled them in their arms, while the mummies grew younger (and wiser) day by day.

It took some getting used to for Kakuarshuk. She was accustomed to working hard all day, and yet here all she had to do was ride in the crook of her baby's arm and be sung to. The babies did everything for their mummies, fetching them food, washing and dressing them, settling them to sleep under the shade of the flickering trees.

She explained, as she was dandled on her baby's knee, about her long journey through the earth, about the differences between her world and this. She told of her longing for a baby of her own. Her baby looked at her with tear-filled eyes.

'When you are young enough, my darling, I shall show you where to dig for your heart's desire. But you will need all your strength, so close those pretty eyes and go to sleep now. There's my good little mummy.'

Kakuarshuk's child was true to her word. One day she took Kakuarshuk to a place called Troll Mountain and gave her a scarlet trowel. 'Dig here, my pet lamb,' said Baby, 'and never give up, come trouble, come terror, come troll. If you are spared, you may see your world again, though I'm sorry to lose you – sorrier than you will ever know.'

Kakuarshuk began to dig. She dug so deep that soon the brink of the hole was no more than a speck of blue high above her. This time she struck a tunnel, and wandered along it, in utter darkness, hoping to find an exit on her own side of the earth. But the tunnel linked with others – with a maze of tunnels – and every one *dug by a troll!*

They pounced on her out of the darkness, huge grotesque beasts as white as slugs, with snuffling noses and blind, white eyeballs. They slashed at her with their long claws, thrashed at her with dead seals and walruses whose tusks made deep and bloody wounds in Kakuarshuk's side.

She ran, while she was able to run, but as more and more trolls attacked, fell to her knees and crawled, sobbing and calling for help. The trolls kicked and rolled her down endless rocky subterranean passageways, but just when she decided her life was at an end, a soft paw closed around her hand and drew her aside into a daylit shaft.

While the blind trolls blundered by, cursing and groping and kicking, the red fox kept its paw to its lips. Then, when they were gone, it helped her upwards, up the shaft of what seemed like a well.

Kakuarshuk lost consciousness as they neared the light. A terrible, irresistible desire to sleep overwhelmed her, and she was afraid that, as she fell asleep, her hand might slip out of the silky paw of her dear red fox . . .

When she woke, she was asleep on the floor of her own hut. Around her were the smiling, familiar faces of her neighbours, making strange gurgling and cooing noises in the backs of their throats.

'They've all become babies while I was away!' she thought, with a moment's panic. Then she realized that there was something in her arms, looked down and saw a little baby boy blearily waking, too: her neighbours were talking to the baby.

'I hear you found yourself a fine son, Kakuarshuk,' said the *angekkok*, putting his head in at the door. 'I wish you joy of him, and few tears.'

Kakuarshuk thought of the other side of the world, and even in that moment of perfect happiness – *because* of that perfect happiness – she knew exactly what had made her mummy-baby cry at their parting.

Dear Dog

A JAPANESE MYTH

G OD KNOWS, THE old man and his wife had little enough to call their own. There was rarely enough food on their plates, enough fuel for a fire, or enough money to repair the roof when it let in the rain. But they did have a dog and a pretty garden, too, and, in those, Sane and Sode believed themselves rich indeed.

A cherry tree grew in the garden – Sane's pride and joy. When it put on blossom in the spring, no princess in all Japan was more glorious. The milky foam of blossom sat like a blessing over the little garden, and every morning Sane and Sode would stand, hand in hand, gazing in rapture.

'Delightful!' said the old man.

'A wonder!' said the old woman.

'Woof,' said the dog, and wagged his tail.

One day, the dog began to dig near the cherry tree. He scrabbled and burrowed until his paws made a hollow scratching on something buried underground.

The chest was ancient – far older than Sane or Sode or even the house where they lived. It was too heavy for the elderly couple to lift, so they opened it where it stood, and there, laid bare to the spring sunlight, were gold coins, gems and chalices, silver spoons and small vases of exquisite alabaster.

As Sane handed the treasures up to his wife, a long shrill whistle sounded beyond the fence. Their neighbour Bozo poked up his head, grinning mouth agape, eyes bulging like marbles. Nothing showed of his nagging wife but one knobbly finger poking and prodding at Bozo's head and a shrill voice demanding, 'What is it? What they got? What they doing? Don't just stand there whistling! Tell me!'

'Please, please, honoured neighbours,' said Sode, 'you must share in our good fortune. Our house is small and our needs are smaller. Please have some of this gold.'

But Bozo was not satisfied with sharing his neighbours' good fortune: he *envied* it horribly. The thought of that mangy dog unearthing a mint of money made him writhe with envy. 'They don't even know how to spend it!' he complained to his wife. 'Now if it were me, I'd know how to make the most of a stroke of luck like that!'

And while Bozo seethed, his wife nagged like a toothache. 'I told you, *we* need a dog like that. What are you going to do about it. Eh? Eh? You've got to get hold of that dog. You've got to get that dog to dig in our garden!'

So in the end, Bozo went round to his neighbours and asked to borrow their beloved dog. And because Sane and Sode never refused anything it was in their power to give, they lent their dear dog to the next-door neighbours.

Bozo shouldered a spade and hauled the dog roughly down his garden by its lead. Pointing at the ground, he snarled, 'Now find treasure, pooch.'

The dog sat down.

'Find treasure, I said!' raged Bozo, instantly furious. The dog whined and lay down, its paws over its nose. '*Find*, you lazy pile of flea-bitten bones!' shouted Bozo, and shook the spade.

The dog rolled on its back and tucked up its paws, as if asking to be tickled. But then, when Bozo only swore and wagged his spade, the dog finally began to dig. He scrabbled and scraped and burrowed till his paws unearthed the lid of a chest – just as he had done next door. Bozo kicked the dog aside and began to dig with his bare hands, scrabbling frenziedly for the padlock and latch.

But as the weary dog dozed, and Bozo threw handfuls of earth at his wife's feet, the chest flew open and all its treasures were laid bare. Worms and weevils, centipedes and millipedes, ants and snails, bugs and slugs burst out of the chest, swarming up Bozo's trouser legs and into his wife's shoes. In his disgust and disappointment, Bozo brought down his spade – thwack, crack – on the dog's head and killed it where it lay.

'The spade slipped. Sorry. Couldn't be helped,' said Bozo as he handed back an armful of dead dog to the heartbroken owners. They wept bitter tears over their dead friend, and buried him under the cherry tree: the most beautiful spot in the garden.

The year grew older, the tree grew taller. Times grew harder for everyone in Japan. Drought reached its gnarled and twiggy hands through all the fields, blighting the rice crop, leaving fish dead in the dried-up river beds.

But the cherry tree was not stunted by the drought. On the contrary, its branches pushed outwards until they were touching the very roof of Sane's dismal old shack. The boards of the walls opened, the tiles of the roof were pushed out of place and the rain poured in.

'I shall have to cut back those long branches,' he said.

'Oh, please don't!' said Sode. 'It would be like maiming a dear friend to set a saw to our lovely cherry tree!'

But by wintertime the safety of the whole house was at risk. Like a great fist, the cherry tree was pushing off the roof, laying open the rooms below to wind and rain and snow. Regretfully, the old man took his saw and cut off the jutting limb. 'At least we shall have firewood for a week or two,' he said.

'No.' Sode was adamant. 'We shan't burn the wood! I feel sure a little of our dear dog is in that cherry. You can make it into a grinding jar for me. That way at least we shall put it to some use, and I'll think of our dear friend every time I grind my rice.'

'What rice?' asked Sane, with a wry smile. 'If this famine goes on much longer, we shall be laying our own old bones down in the dust beside our dear dog. There's no rice to be had for a hundred miles. Not even for gold.'

It was true. By the time he had carved the cherry wood into a grinding jar, Sode had only a handful of rice left in the house. Their gaunt faces looked tenderly at one another over the grinding jar. 'I'm glad our dear dog did not live to suffer and starve with us,' said Sode, and Sane nodded gravely.

Scrrr scrrr scrrr, the pestle ground the rice in the grinding jar. The jar filled with powdered rice – filled and spilled over, making snow-white mounds on the kitchen table. The soul of the dog had indeed fused with the soul of the cherry tree, and his love for his owners was in the very fabric of the jar, making it as magic as the dog himself had been. Not once, but every time Sode used it, the cherry-wood jar filled with food enough for five, so that Sode and Sane were able to feed the whole street.

'I want it. They owe it to us! Worms and slugs, that's all we got from that wretched mutt of theirs. They could at least lend it to us!' carped the woman next door.

'But they are sharing their food with us, my dear,' said her harassed husband, sucking his chopsticks at the end of a good meal.

'Typical! They just give it away!' she raged. 'If you and I had the only source of food in the whole province, just think! We'd be as powerful as the Emperor himself!' And she did not stop nagging until her husband at last agreed to go next door and steal the magic grinding jar.

A handful of rice was all it took to start the magic, so in went a handful of rice.

And suddenly the room was full of humming, the air black. Flying insects banged clumsily into their faces, crawled into their ears and clothing. Bees and wasps and hornets.

Husband and wife fled – out of the house, across the garden, into the lily pond and out again, through the river and into the woods. But in their desperate rage, they had achieved one last piece of wickedness. When old Sane and Sode poked their heads in at the open door, worried by the noise, wanting to know if they could help, they saw the blackened shape of their magic grinding jar falling to ashes in the fire grate.

Weeping, Sane swept together all the ash into a pan, and went sadly to sprinkle it on the grave of his dead dog. 'If your spirit was in the vessel,' he said aloud, 'it returns to you now, little friend. Be happy.'

The weather was cold. The drought had lasted all summer and autumn; now even the dark snowclouds refused to slake the earth's thirst. And yet surely that was snow on the boughs of the cherry tree? Surely there were snowflakes whirling in the bitter wind? Either snow or . . . *blossom?*

How could there be blossom in winter? How could the flowers bloom and the fruit be taking shape in the orchards? How could the rice plants be spiking green through the bleak bare landscape, turning the whole countryside a cheerful green? The cherry tree in the old couple's garden foamed with so much blossom that the whole town came out to see it. On their way out to the fields to reap a miraculous harvest, on their way to celebrate with friends and neighbours, they stopped and stared open-mouthed at the cherry tree, a fountain of petals splashing the sky with pink and white.

Monkey Do:
The Story of Hanuman

A HINDU MYTH

FOURTEEN THOUSAND GIANTS Prince Rama slew in a single day, and the only one left alive crawled to the feet of Ravana the Demon King, with news of the defeat.

'All my warriors dead?' raged Ravana, tossing his ten heads till they cracked together and thrashing the air with his twenty arms. 'Well, if my fighting men can't kill Rama, at least I can break his heart! I shall rob him of that perfect wife of his!' So, mounted in his magic chariot, scorching the forest with the sparks from its wheels, Ravana snatched Sita – lovely Princess Sita – by her hair and carried her off. The sap in the flowers froze at the sight of it: the birds in the trees choked on their song. Rivers stopped flowing, and the moon flushed sickly green. 'Sita! Sita! What is life without Sita?' cried the whole realm of nature.

Sooner than see Sita in the clutches of the vile Demon King, the King of Vultures hurled his very life under the chariot's wheels. The horses shied and smashed loose, the bladed wheels clashed together like cymbals, and the chariot sagged, buckled and broke apart.

. . . But Ravana simply took to the air, Sita's hair still twined around one of his twenty arms, his ten ghastly mouths laughing aloud. The tree-tops lashed in lament, parakeets shrieking, monkeys jabbering in the topmost branches. Seeing a family of monkeys gazing at her with round, stricken eyes, Sita pulled the golden bangles off her wrist and threw them, calling, 'Tell Rama! Tell Prince Rama!'

321

The monkeys caught the bangles in clever paws and were gone, swinging away under the leaf canopy. Beneath the winged chariot, forest gave way to shimmering sea.

Rama was picking lotus flowers when the Monkey General found him: Hanuman, Chief of Staff to the King of Monkeys and most marvellous of all his breed. 'Stir yourself, my prince! Ravana the Revolting has ravished away your wife! You and I have work to do! My troops and tricks are yours to command, but we must hurry!'

'Where has he taken her?' asked Rama, jumping to his feet.

'No one knows, but my monkey millions are already searching!'

As the monkeys soon discovered, Ravana had taken Sita to the island of Sri Lanka. There, on the highest mountain, he had a palace – a mirage of loveliness built by the gods themselves, but annexed by the ugly and the wicked. Out of the jungles of the world, the monkey millions rallied to Hanuman's battle cry: an army of apes ready to lay down their lives for the lovely Sita. But between them and the Princess stretched the impassable straits of Pamban, swilling with monsters. On the seashore, the frustrated monkey cohorts bared their teeth at the unfriendly sea.

But Hanuman had magic. He wore the very wind in his tail! What is more, he could change shape whenever he chose. There, on the over-crowded beach, he began to grow, until his legs were large as siege engines, flexed like catapults, powerful enough to propel him over surf, over sea, over miles of sea! A veritable mountain of monkey. A great gasp went up from his monkey warriors as Hanuman made that prodigious leap. In a second, he was only a speck in the sky, and a hooting, whooping shout followed him out over the water. But a terrible silence followed.

Out of the ocean depths, bigger than a breaching whale, reared up the head of the Naga-Hag. Green-tressed with slimy seaweed and pocky with barnacles, her mouth gaped, dark, wet and jagged. Powerless to stop himself, Hanuman hurtled inside.

The Naga-Hag meant to chew on Hanuman and swallow him down. But the Monkey General used his magic to grow still larger, wedging his head into the roof of her mouth, his feet into her hollow teeth. And he forced open her jaws as wide as they would go. Then, with a flick of his magic tail, Hanuman was tiny as a flea: he shot out of her ear, leaving her teeth to clash shut on her tongue. '*Ah-hooeurghh!*'

Back on the beach, Prince Rama exhorted the monkeys, 'Build me a bridge! A bridge, my friends! We must reach Sri Lanka!'

They built it not from wood or canes, but from clasped hands, linked tails and braced backs. Balancing with acrobatic skill, monkey on monkey on monkey, they bridged the Pamban.

Meanwhile, Hanuman landed – softly, softly, magic monkey – on Sri Lanka, and entered Ravana's palace. His green eyes blinked at the sheer opulence of the Demon King's lair. Everywhere, the walls were studded with gemstones, the doors inlaid with diamonds. Banners of silk rippled at every flagstaff, and Persian carpets draped every wall, while baskets of saffron stained the air gold with blowing pollen, and joss sticks gave off coils of coloured smoke. But no amount of incense could mask the rank, mouldering stench of Evil. And everywhere, in every alcove and dormitory, at every sentry post and turn of the stairs, squatted hideous rakshasas, whose name means 'destroyers'!

'Give me your love, sublime Sita!' Ravana's bullfrog croak echoed along the cloistered walks. 'Give me your love to feed on!'

Hanuman padded the silk-fringed stairs, poking his nose in at every door, until at last he found the turret where Sita was held prisoner.

As soon as Ravana had gone, Hanuman darted inside. 'Jump on to my back, lady, and I will carry you out of this cesspit!'

'Oh, I can't! I couldn't,' whispered Sita, her lovely cheeks hot with maidenly modesty. 'No man must touch me but Rama my husband!'

'I'm not a man,' Hanuman pointed out. 'I'm a monkey.' But Sita was adamant: even Ravana had held her only by her hair. So there was nothing for Hanuman to do, but wait for the monkey army to cross the Pamban. Nothing to do? Well, while he waited, he could at least kill rakshasas.

Thousands of these vile demons served the Demon King. Some had bulbous bodies and long trailing arms, some elephant trunks or horses' heads. Some were giants with three eyes and five legs; some looked like gorillas but for their blood-red eyes and ginger beards. They infested the palace like rats or cockroaches, and they liked nothing better than a fight. Still, Hanuman took them on single-handedly, and by jumping and weaving, dodging and ducking, narrowly kept out of their claws. Up and down stairs they chased him, along passageways, through cellars and over rooftops. Ex-hausted, overheated, some dropped in their tracks, wheezing and fanning themselves. 'By the time the Prince arrives,' Hanuman taunted, 'not one of you will have breath enough to whistle!'

But at that moment, a lasso fell round the Monkey General's shoulders, tightened round his throat, and dragged him, sprawling and spitting, under the boot of Ravana's hideous son. 'What shall I do with him, Father? What? Shall I eat him, or tear him limb from limb?'

'Monkey meat is tough,' said Ravana, sneering on all his ten faces. 'Set him alight and let's see him burn!'

Oily rags were tied to the monkey's tail. Sita prayed, her hands over her face, but it seemed nothing now could save Hanuman from a hideous death. Smugly the Demon King held a lighted spill to the monkey's tail; there was a smell of burning fur.

Hanuman seemed to shrivel with the heat. He *was* shrivelling! He shrank down just enough to slip free of the rope binding him, and bounded clean out of the window!

From sill to parapet he sprang, from awning to flagstaff, his blazing tail held stiffly out behind. Silk banners and brocade pavilions were kindled by the burning rag. Squirming in through open shutters and with his tail for a spill, he lit bed-hangings and Persian rugs, tapestries and wicker baskets. Soon the whole palace was ablaze, and 'destroyers' of every shape and smell were jumping from the windows, or sliding down knotted sheets to escape the inferno.

That was when Rama arrived, crossing his bridge of monkeys which dismantled itself behind him into an army. A hundred thousand billion monkeys swarmed over the burning ruins of Ravana's palace, pelting rakshasas with white-hot gemstones.

Ravana was unrepentant. He thumped his chest and bellowed for reinforcements. And out of the sea came the Naga-Hag, out from the mountains came the terrible Kumbha-Karna who could swallow a thousand men at one gulp. Soon Prince Rama was forced to retreat, bleeding from a dozen wounds. Though his courage was undimmed, his strength began to fail. He fell to his knees and his monkey legions re-formed to shield him from a sleet of poisoned arrows.

'Fight on, boys!' cried Hanuman. Once more he transformed himself – into a bird, this time – and flew away. Was he turning tail? Had his burns weakened him? Was he afraid? Not Hanuman! Within the hour he returned, from the flowery slopes of the far-off Himalayas, his paws bunchy with herbs. Tenderly he tended to

Rama's wounds, and before Ravana could regroup his shattered army, led his monkey millions into the attack once more.

The gods themselves looked down on that desperate day. Their hearts were stirred by the heroic deeds they saw, and Indra sent down his chariot for Rama to ride in, while Brahma leaned down out of heaven to hand the Prince a single golden arrow.

It was that arrow which finally pierced the heart of Ravana. As it did so, as the fiendish demon crashed to earth, like a gusher of oil, the strangest smell pervaded the battlefield of Sri Lanka. Perfumed flowers of every colour began to rain down out of the clouds, covering the faces of the fallen, lying in drifts upon the ruins of the gutted palace.

Princess Sita stepped into the golden chariot beside her husband, the monkey millions re-formed their living bridge, and Prince Rama drove home over the straits of Pamban, his General dancing on wiry shanks behind him and squealing shrilly for joy.

A Bouquet of Flowers

AN ABORIGINAL MYTH

IT WAS FROM a piece of the sun that Baiame made the world, but his home was among the stars, and it was there that he returned when his work of creation was done.

'Don't cry, little ones,' he told the people and animals as he said goodbye. 'I have to go. Otherwise you would forever run to me with your troubles – like children never learning to grow up. You know I love you and that I'll still be watching over you from my home.' He pointed to the galaxy of the Milky Way stretched like a silver hammock across the night sky.

The animals nodded their heads and wandered off, far and wide. The men and women also understood, but stayed waving long after Baiame the Creator had risen into the sky. Some lay down on soft clumps of flowers to gaze up at the sky and remember their long talks with the Father Spirit. Then they too got up and walked home, thoughtful, wistful, trailing tardy feet through the flowers which carpeted every fold and furrow of the shining new Earth. Wherever Baiame had trodden, flowers had sprung up: every colour of the rainbow and a thousand shades between – scarlet, umber, purple, gold and white. From horizon to horizon they cloaked the rocky ground, cushioned and pillowed it into the sweetest of resting places.

But what were those flowers feeling now? Flowers have no power of reason, no instinct to guide them. They could not comprehend why dear Baiame, who had given them life, should no longer be nearby.

So some migrated. Like birds in winter, they rose in huge flocks, fledged with their own petals, flying, flying towards the object of their love. Into the sky they fluttered, on outwards into space, swagging the sky with coronas of colour. The rest died.

Soon the air was filled with cries of women searching, searching, then realizing that there was not a single flower left living on the whole bare, brown face of the Earth. The air was filled with something else, too – with swarms of frantic bees searching in noisy millions for one speck of pollen, one sip of nectar. There was no golden honey to be had either, and life was much less sweet in those drab days after the flowers died.

In time, of course, the sadness faded. Those who remembered the flowers grew old. Naturally, they told their grandchildren about them and the wonder that had once been, but the grandchildren hardly believed such far-fetched fairy tales. Those children, as they grew older, remembered talk of flowers, but not, of course their colours. Who can remember something they have never seen, or describe it to their grandchildren? So flowers bloomed only in the mouths of story-tellers – a wonder of times long gone. And colour was only in the skins of animals, in insects and the sky, in fishes and the sea. And in the eyes of the story-tellers.

Watching with gentle multicoloured eyes, Baiame felt sad at this one flaw in the Earth's loveliness. So one night, along with the starlight, he rained down dreams on sleeping humanity. Those with listening hearts were stirred by a voice: they seemed to hear it telling them to make a journey. By first light they set off – like sleepwalkers unable to resist the yearning within them. And every man, woman and child who answered the yearning found that their journey brought them to the selfsame spot. From north and south, near and far, hither and yon they came, to the mountain where Baiame had long ago stepped off into space – and to which he had now returned!

There he sat, reaching out his arms like a father inviting his children to sit on his knee. 'Come with me, little ones,' he said. 'I have something to give you.'

Gathering them up into his hands, into his hair, into the crook of his arm and the folds of his robe, he carried them into the sky and on out into space, to where the Milky Way stretched like a silver hammock. He took them over dunes of darkness to valleys invisible from Earth . . . and their cries of amazement set the stars swinging.

For there lay swathes of colour they had never seen before, colours even their women of vision had not dreamed nor their painters imagined.

'These are the "flowers" your story-tellers speak of,' said Baiame. 'Pick them. Pick as many as you can carry, and take them back with you to the Earth. On the day I took a piece of sun and made the world for you, I meant there to be flowers. You have been without them too long. So take them, and when they die, sprinkle their seed on the brown ground, and I will send warmth and rain enough to make them come again.'

In sheaves and armfuls they reaped flowers and carried them down out of the sky. Like conquering heroes they returned to their separate villages, laden with colour, to astound their families and amaze their friends with bouquets of such dazzling glory that it seemed a rainbow had crashed to Earth and scattered its debris over their homes.

And though Baiame's helpers were not able to carry as many flowers as had once bloomed on Earth, they took enough to paint every corner of the world with every colour in the mind of God.

The Curious Honeybird

A BANTU MYTH

L EZA SAT IDLY juggling the magic of the world: three calabashes, perfectly round and red, picked from the Tree of Everything. 'Why three?' asked the curious Honeybird.

'How could I juggle with two?' answered Leza. 'Or eight?'

Leza, Lord and Creator of the Bantu people looked down from his plateau of sky. He did not live so very high above the people he had newly created – just high enough to see what they were doing and watch that they came to no harm. He wished them no harm. Indeed, he wished them all the good in the world – which was why he had decided to pick the three calabashes.

'Take these down to First Man and First Woman, Honeybird,' he said, stringing the three scarlet globes around the bird's neck. 'I need both hands free to climb down. Tell them that they may open these two. Tell them I'm coming, and that I will explain how to use what's inside. Also, I'll tell them the purpose of the third . . . Oh, but Honeybird!'

'Yes, master?'

'Mind you don't go opening those calabashes!'

'Would I?' twittered the Honeybird, and flew off.

Leza began to climb down the immense spider's web which hung from the sky. Though its fabric was almost too fine to see, it was strong enough to bear his weight: so much of him was sunshine.

Meanwhile, the Honeybird wondered about the three calabashes round its neck: whether they contained any magic for birds, whether First Man and First Woman deserved such a gift, and whether they would be grateful. The gourds were very light to carry: had Leza even remembered to fill them?

That was Honeybird's excuse to peck a small hole in the first calabash.

Out spilled seeds and grain, hips and haws, bulbs and corms – all good things to plant in the newly made Earth. Honeybird cocked first one curious eye and then the other over the seed . . . and could see no harm in opening the second calabash.

Out spilled herbs and spices, gold-dust and ore, pollen and resin – all useful things for a life in a new young world. Honeybird turned each marvel over with its delicate claw . . . and saw no harm in opening the third calabash.

Out spilled termites and leeches, sickness and madness, weariness and disease, the roaring of a lion, the sharpness of a thorn; vipers and scorpions, misery, pain. And Death. Slithering away faster than thought, each evil thing wriggled into the cracked ground, into hollow trees, into rock crevices or in under the beds of First Man and First Woman.

'What have you done, you fool!' Leza's voice boomed out behind the Honeybird and ruffled all its feathers with the blast of his breath. 'Could you not have waited a few short moments? My people will never forgive you for this!'

He tried with all his superhuman might to recapture the wild beasts and vile evils let loose, but they were already gone, already lurking in the Earth's dark places.

With infinite care, Leza-the-Infinite explained to First Man and First Woman what to do with the seeds and bulbs and herbs, the metal and the pollen. He told them how to worship him, how to get by amid the troubles Honeybird had brought on them. Then he kissed them and climbed back up the spider's web.

But First Man and First Woman did not want to be left alone. They were so alarmed by the scrabblings under their beds, at the slitherings among their flowers, at the hoots which haunted their sleep, that they picked up their belongings and followed Leza.

'He's safe in the sky; why shouldn't we live there with him?' they reasoned. 'After all, *we* are more special than any of the *other* creatures he made. We'll be safe there!' And they began to scramble up the spider's web.

The web stretched. Its intricate pattern was pulled out of shape by their weight and the weight of all their belongings. At last, with a twang as loud as a hair breaking, the web shredded and tore and fell, tumbling First Man and First Woman back to Earth in a tangle of gossamer.

Leza was appalled at their arrogance, astonished at their presumption. 'Try and climb up to my home?' he cried. 'Is there no end to their ambition?' And he kept himself to himself after that, confined himself to his shelf of sky-blue vapour, and did not come and go between Earth and Sky as he had done before.

The Honeybird, meantime, does what it can to make amends. Whenever it comes across Man or Woman, Son or Daughter, it darts down, uttering its piercing cry of 'Follow, Follow!', leading the way to golden hoards of hidden honey, to crystalline combs of sweetness, in the hope that one day they will forgive the matter of the third calabash.

The Sky-Blue Storybox

A LEGEND FROM GHANA

By NOW, YOU have heard many stories. Forget them. Imagine you have never heard any; that there are no stories to hear. That is what the world was like when Anansi was young – when all the stories were kept in a strongbox, up in Heaven.

Everyone needs stories, not least Anansi the Spider Man. He wanted them for himself and for his family. He wanted the power that stories bring, the respect that comes to the story-teller, the taste of those stories in his mouth. So he wove a web and climbed up it to Heaven, and he said to Sky-God, 'Tell me the price of the Sky-Blue Storybox.'

'Aho,' said Sky-God. 'Many have wanted to buy my Storybox: kings and sorcerers and millionaires. But none could muster the price.'

'What is the price?' asked Anansi.

'All the spots on the leopard, a handful of hornets, a rainbow python and a fairy. Bring me all these and the stories are yours.'

Anansi bowed. 'I'll be back,' he said.

The leopard part was easy.

All he had to do was dig a pit and brew a keg of beer. Then, inviting Leopard home for a drink, he took sips, while Leopard drank deep. By the time Leopard reeled home he was in no fit state to see the pit in his path. In he fell, and with such a thud that his spots all fell off. Then Anansi brought a ladder and, with tender concern, helped Leopard out.

Later, all that remained was to gather up the spots . . . Which left the hornets, the python and the fairy.

At this point, Anansi felt a little uneasy, for he had no idea how to catch a handful of hornets.

'What you need,' said his wife, 'is a gourd, a leaf from a banana tree and a cup of water.'

'I see what you mean!' said Anansi. The gourd he cut a hole in; the leaf he put on his head. The cup of water he threw in the air.

'Hornets! Oh, hornets!' called Anansi. 'What will become of you, now that the rains have come?'

A passing swarm of hornets looked at Anansi. The rains surely had come. Why else would anyone be standing with a dripping banana leaf on his head?

'Shelter in this gourd, friends, and be quick about it!' urged Anansi, 'or the rains will smash your silver wings!'

At once the hornets flew into the gourd, thanking Anansi as they did so. As soon as they were inside, Anansi plugged the hole. There it was. A hand-grenade of hornets . . . Which left only the python and the fairy.

At this point Anansi was in a bit of a quandary, for he had no idea how to catch a rainbow python.

'What you need is a tree trunk and a length of twine,' said his wife.

'I see that, plain as day!' said Anansi. Immediately, he went and cut down a tall palm tree and stripped it bare. Then, with the tree tucked under two or three arms, he walked through the jungle, talking to it as he went. 'He is, I tell you,' said Anansi to the tree, and then, 'I tell you he *is!* I'll prove it to you!' and then, 'Don't argue!'

The rainbow python was puzzled (as anyone would be) to see Anansi talking to a tree. 'Ho there, Anansi! What gives, man?'

'My friend here,' (said Anansi to the python) 'says that he's longer than you, but I say you're longer. Won't you settle the argument, once and for all?'

'Of course, of course,' said the python, flattered, and lay down alongside the palm tree. Round once, round twice, round three times, Anansi bound the twine, until he reached the python's head. 'I believe,' he said, 'that now you're mine for the giving . . . Which leaves only the fairy.'

Now Anansi had not the remotest idea how to catch a fairy. His wife said, 'What you need is a wooden dolly and some sap from the gum tree.'

'Of course,' said Anansi, and then, 'Why's that?'

'To make a gum baby, of course!' said his wife.

'Of course! Of course! said Anansi. 'A gum . . . what was that?'

'And some banana mash for it to hold,' said his patient wife.

At last Anansi saw what she was driving at, and went to make a little wood carving of a child. This he covered in gum, and into one wooden hand he tied a bowl of banana mash. On the face he painted a smile. Then he propped the whole thing against a tree, and hid in the branches.

Before long a fairy came by and, seeing the figure holding out a bowl of banana mash, politely asked if she might have some.

Dolly didn't say 'Yes', didn't say 'No'; it just smiled. So the fairy helped herself. She even said, 'Thank you.'

Dolly didn't say 'Stay', didn't say 'Go'; it just smiled.

'What's your name?' asked the fairy.

Dolly didn't say 'Jess', didn't say 'Mo'; it just smiled.

'Are you deaf?' asked the fairy.

Dolly didn't say 'Guess', didn't say 'So'; it just smiled. At which the fairy started to feel seriously put out, and gave the dolly a push on the shoulder. 'Speak, can't you?'

Dolly didn't speak fast, didn't speak slow; it just smiled. But it didn't let got of the fairy's hand either, seeing as its shoulder was sticky as flypaper.

'Don't just stand there grinning!' snapped the fairy. 'Give me back my hand!' And she slapped the other shoulder. There she stuck, like a wasp in jam. She gave the dolly a kick with both feet, and butted it, too.

Dolly didn't say 'Cease', didn't say 'Ow!'; it just smiled its sticky smile, hard up against the fairy's face.

That was when Anansi climbed down out of the tree, picked up the dolly and the fairy (stuck as fast together as the two sides of a sandwich) and carried her up to Sky-God, along with the rainbow python, the gourd full of hornets and purse full of leopard spots.

Sky-God looked at the great squeaking, buzzing bundles laid down at his feet and his eyes were round as full moons. 'What's this you've brought me, Spider Man Anansi?'

'The price of the Sky-Blue Storybox, master,' said Anansi. 'The gourd is full of hornets, so be careful how you take off the lid.'

'Many have asked to buy the Storybox,' said Sky-God 'but only Spider Man Anansi has managed to pay the price, tricky devil that he is.' So saying, Sky-God laid one finger on each bundle: 'I have touched them; they are mine!' he said, trying to unstick his finger from the gummy fairy. 'The Storybox is yours, Mister Anansi!'

So Anansi climbed down his web out of the sky, the box tucked under four of his arms. And half-way down he cracked it open and began spilling out the stories: riddles and fables, parables and sagas, ballads and myths and legends.

'Wey, Spider Man!' called Sky-God. 'What you doing, man? Ain't you gonna sell them or keep them for a treasure all to yourself?'

'I know what I'm doing,' said Anansi. 'They're mine, so they're mine to let go!'

Pretty soon, Sky-God let go the rainbow python and the leopard too, the angry hornets and the fairy; they were his, so they were his to let go. Naturally, they were livid with Anansi, and went looking for him, to pay him back.

But by then, the people of Earth were so grateful to Anansi for the stories he had spilled that they hid and harboured their hero safe and sound.

It took a while for those stories to spread world-wide, but not so long as you might think, given the size of the world. Wherever a traveller made tracks he carried a wealth of stories, to pay for his supper or a bed for the night. And that's how stories spread far and farther than far.

But answer this riddle. If there were no stories before Spider Man Anansi fetched down his prize, where did I find the story of Anansi and the Sky-Blue Storybox? . . . eh?

A Question of Arithmagic
A LEGEND FROM ICELAND

IF ALL THE villains in the world were stupid, it would not matter whether or not kings were wise. But many of the wickedest people are dangerously clever, and most cunning of all are the trolls.

Fortunately, Olaf Tryggvason was not merely a king, he was a scholar, too. He could read, write and add up; sometimes even do all three at once. The warriors who manned the oars of his ship were strong and fearless, loyal and handsome – men like Thorgeir the Bold – but they held the King in awe and admiration, because he was a scholar and a thinking man.

Sailing one day through the dank Icelandic mists of winter, King Olaf commanded his navigator to steer close by the cliffs. 'If we keep land within sight,' he said, 'we cannot lose our way in this infernal fog.' So carefully, gingerly, the dragon-prowed ship moved along the rocky coastline, close enough inshore to see gannets and cormorants riding on the updraught, close enough to see seals sleeping in the coves, sea pinks growing in the rocky crevices. They sailed so close, they even caught sight of an old man balanced precariously on a narrow shelf of rock half-way up the cliffs. The King hailed him through cupped hands.

'Are you stranded?' he called. 'Do you need help?'

'Not at all,' the old man called back in a voice clear and strong. 'Greetings, King Olaf Tryggvason. Hail and all hail.' Something about the voice made Thorgeir miss his oar-stroke.

'What's your name? Where do you live?' called the King, for it was a wild, inhospitable coast with not a house in sight.

'I live in this cliff, of course: I and all my fighting men.'

King Olaf was intrigued. He knew nothing of any warlord living in this part of his kingdom, nor of any army, although he made it his business to know such things. 'And how many men do you command, sir?'

The old man began to chant:

> 'Twelve ships have I with oaken keels;
> In every boat there ride twelve crew.
> Each rower kills a dozen seals,
> To make our daily meal of stew,
> And cuts each skin in twelve and then
> Each strip is cut in twelve again;
> Each portion cut must serve ten men:
> How many are my followers, then?'

The King laughed and clapped his hands. A riddle! There was nothing he liked better. Calling for paper, he began to work the problem out. 'Twelve ships and each one has twelve . . . that's one hundred and forty-four rowers . . .' The King sucked the feather of his pen and frowned as he struggled with the mathematics.

Thorgeir, meantime, noticed a certain side-slipping motion of the ship. The birds of the cliff seemed bigger than before.

'One hundred and forty-four rowers kill twelve seals each: that's . . . one seven two eight . . .' The King's quill scratched busily.

Thorgeir, meantime, stood up to get a proper look at the old man on the cliff. He seemed to be chanting under his breath. More poetry, perhaps? Or there again, perhaps not.

'One thousand, seven hundred and twenty-eight sealskins, all cut into twelve,' mused the King. 'That's four, carry one – eight – one, carry one . . . By the gods, this man has a bigger army than I do . . . !'

Thorgeir, meantime, felt a faint grating on the ship's hull. It was being pulled steadily inshore, closer and closer to the snarling rocks. As a whirlpool sucks ships into its swilly mouth, the old man's chanting was dragging the King's ship to its destruction. 'Your Majesty . . .' he began.

'Don't interrupt, I'm multiplying,' muttered King Olaf, and went on counting imaginary strips of sealskin.

The old man was clearly visible now, much closer than before. Thorgeir could see how his yellow eyes glinted and his snaggled teeth were bared in an evil grin. The oarsman pulled his oar out of the rowlock, but it was too short for the job. He cut through the sheets of the mainsail and heaved the mast itself out of its socket in the deck. Resting it on the ship's rail, he put his chest against its end and prepared for a jarring shock.

'. . . and if each portion feeds ten men . . .' muttered the King.

'I think, master, that this old man . . .' grunted Thorgeir, struggling with the weight of the mast.

'You'll make me lose my place,' said the King, bending over his sums.

Then the tip of the mast struck the cliff with a force which broke three of Thorgeir's ribs. Still he strained to hold the ship away from the cliff which would rip out its side.

The old man on the cliff, seeing Thorgeir's efforts, scowled at him and chanted faster and louder, a magic chant, a troll chant to wreck the King of Iceland. He cursed Thorgeir, with all the black arts of trolldom.

The magic dragged on the ship as though the very cliff were a magnet and the ship a twopenny plug of iron. Thorgeir felt his breastbone bend, his heart falter within him, but still he held the ship off the cliff.

'So I make that fifty-one thousand, eight-hundred and . . .' said King Olaf Tryggvason. But his answer was never finished. With a noise like a lightning-strike, the mast snapped as, with one final mighty effort, Thorgeir levered the dragon-prowed ship out into deeper water. That great jerking thrust was enough to break the power of the old man's magic. He had to watch his prize escape him, pitching and rolling out of harm's way.

The King lost his footing and fell on his back, ink spilling over the workings of his sum. Looking up, he was in time to see the old man on the cliff change back into his rightful shape – three coils of a hideous nose, and a face like mouldy cheese. 'By the gods, it was a troll!' – he cried. 'D'you see that, Thorgeir? It was a troll trying to lure us on to the rocks!'

Thorgeir said nothing, but lay in the bottom of the boat, content to have saved the King and his comrades from a miserable death on the rocks. 'It is a wonderful thing,' he consoled himself, 'to have a scholar for a king.'

But a bit of common sense doesn't go amiss, either.

The Alchemist

A CHINESE LEGEND

MR CHIA WAS a laundryman. All day he beat the soapy washing clean on a huge block of stone using a long wooden bat: a tedious, wearisome job. But he passed the time thinking about money and what he would do with it if he ever had any.

One day he saw a cart offloading furniture at a house nearby. Chia went at once to call on his new neighbour – his new and *affluent*-looking neighbour – to introduce himself. But the gentleman seemed always to be out. In the end, Chia resorted to hiding in a bush and jumping out as the man put his key in the door. Then he bowed politely and presented a bottle of wine: 'A gift of welcome from your humble neighbour,' he said.

'Charmed, charmed,' said the gentleman. 'Come indoors and let us share this wine! My name is Chên.'

It was a hot day. The wine slipped down deliciously, and the two got on well. There seemed nothing exceptional about Mr Chên except perhaps his good looks and musical speaking voice. When the wine was almost gone, he fetched a large jade jug and poured the last drop into it.

At once the jug filled to the brim with the best wine Chia had ever tasted. 'What a trick!' he gasped. 'Can you do any more?'

Chên smiled benignly and took out a small shiny black stone. He spoke a few words, rubbed the stone against a vase – and at once the vase turned to silver.

Chia gasped. 'Where did you get that stone? What is it? I want one! Where can I get one? Where?'

Mr Chên sighed. 'I was afraid of this. I was told in Heaven that you are a greedy man, Mr Chia.'

'Greedy? Me?'

'That's why I tried to avoid meeting you. You must understand: we Immortals are not permitted to teach alchemy to you mortals. Imagine the chaos it could cause here on Earth.'

'Oh, absolutely. Chaos! I quite understand!' said Chia. 'Have another drink.'

Twenty drinks later, as Chên slithered like a pickled eel out of his armchair and on to the floor, Chia searched his robe, found the lodestone, let himself out and went home.

It was no use, of course. He did not know the magic words, and so, although he rubbed pots, bottles, cups, melons and the dog, his alchemy simply did not work.

It was some hours before Mr Chên woke up. When he realized his lodestone was missing, he assumed he had lost it by sheer careless-ness, and scoured the house, the garden, the street – even went over to the laundry to tell his neighbour of the disaster.

But Chia greeted him with good news as he opened the door: 'Ah! My friend! I found something of yours this morning!'

'My lodestone?'

'Your lodestone, yes! In the street! You must have dropped it.'

Mr Chên was overjoyed. 'How can I ever thank you! I should be in such trouble in Heaven if they found out I'd lost it!'

Chia bowed. 'Don't mention it . . . only I suppose you might see fit to reward me by letting me use the stone. Just once!'

Chên was flustered. 'Impossible! I mustn't! It's forbidden!' But Chia looked so hurt, made Chên feel so ungrateful and mean, that finally he agreed. 'I'll show you – but you must *promise* not to be greedy. Change a few lead coins perhaps, or a pebble. Otherwise the gods are bound to find out what I've done.'

'Something like this, say?' said Chia, holding up a bar of soap.

Chên mopped his brow with relief. 'Clearly the rumours I heard about you in Heaven were quite ill-founded!'

Chia put the tiny morsel of soap on the huge wash-slab where every day he beat the washing clean.

'Now say:

'As Earth is to Heaven, as little is to much,
Lodestone raise the nature of whate'er you touch.'

Chia's fingers, clutching the shiny black stone, hovered for a moment over the sliver of soap as he spoke the magic words . . . Then they dodged aside and quickly rubbed the wash-block. Instantly, half a ton of silver stood gleaming amid the laundry.

'No! *No!* What have you done?' cried Chên. 'My name will be struck from the Book of Angels for this! How could you! What will become of me? No! No!' He rushed out of the laundry tearing his hair and reproaching Chia bitterly for his deceitful trick. But Chia hardly heard. He was busy staring at his reflection in the shining silver slab.

A year went by. One day, an elegant gentleman arrived in town and knocked at the laundry door, asking for Chia. But Mr Chia was out: 'At the hospital, probably,' he was told.

He was on his way there when he met Chia coming the other way. The two recognized each other at once.

'My dear Chia!'

'My dear Chên! How have you been, all this time?'

'Not bad! Of course, at first my name was struck from the Book of Angels, as I said it would be. The gods were furious with me for sharing the secret of alchemy. But after you built the new school and all those houses for the poor, and the hospital, the monastery – those orphanages, and planted all those blossom trees . . . Well, I was summoned to Heaven. "We misjudged you, Mr Chên!" they said. "Through this man, you have done more good on Earth than we have managed in many a year . . ." I must admit, though: for a time *I* misjudged *you*, my dear Chia.'

'What? You didn't really think I'd spend all that silver on myself? With so much poverty all around me? I used to dream, while I beat those clothes, how I'd wash away a thousand miseries if I ever had the money. And you, my friend, you gave me the opportunity.'

So they shared a bottle of wine, and parted. 'Until we meet again in Heaven!' said Mr Chên.

'You really think there's place in Heaven for a poor laundryman like me?' exclaimed Mr Chia delightedly. 'Ah well, yes, I suppose the angels need their clothes washed just like everyone else. Till we meet then, in Heaven's laundry!'

Workshy Rabbit

A WEST AFRICAN LEGEND

THEY SAY THAT rabbits hate hard work, but that's a filthy slur on rabbits. I know of one who put himself to infinite pains, took tremendous trouble, expended endless energy on a project . . . even if it was to get out of working. Of course, it happened long ago – before most animals had ever met, and before they knew how each other looked. Only Rabbit, who scurried about seeing all that was to be seen and getting what was to be got, knew that here lived wildebeest and there a tortoise, here a lion and there a jackal, here an elephant and there a giraffe.

The corn needed planting, so Rabbit went to Elephant and said, 'We animals should help one another. If you'll push down the trees to clear the ground, I will burn them.' Elephant agreed at once, and spent all day barging trees out of the ground with his massive head. It was hard work: he was not the biggest of his breed.

Meanwhile, Rabbit went to Giraffe and said, 'I've done all the hard work rooting out the trees. If you burn off the timber, we can plant as soon as the rains come. We animals should cooperate, don't you agree?' Giraffe agreed. She burned off the fallen timber, amazed that little Rabbit had been able to flatten so many trees single-handedly.

The rains came in like blades of silver slicing through the heat and drenching the ashy earth of the clearing. Rabbit went to Elephant and said, 'If you do the sowing, I'll do the hoeing.' Which Elephant did.

343

Then Rabbit went to Giraffe and said, 'I've done the sowing. It's your turn to do the hoeing.' Which Giraffe did.

The corn grew tall and golden. When it was ripe, Rabbit went to Elephant and said, 'You reap and afterwards I'll gather . . . Oh, but look out for an animal called Giraffe. I hear she's a terrible thief of ripe corn.' Elephant slashed down the corn with scything sweeps of his long tusks, but of Giraffe he saw not a nose nor a neck.

Meanwhile, Rabbit went to Giraffe and said, 'I've reaped the corn. Time for you to gather up the cobs . . . But do look out for that thieving beast called Elephant; he'd steal the corn from his own granny.' Giraffe gathered up the corn cobs into a pile almost as high as her head, but of Elephant she saw not a tail nor a trunk.

Rabbit sat by and watched, just working up an appetite. 'Reckon that Elephant is bound to come sniffing round tomorrow, wanting to steal our corn,' he called out to Giraffe.

'He'll be sorry if he does,' said Giraffe, stamping all four elegant feet in turn.

Before going to bed, Rabbit called on Elephant, too, and said, 'Reckon that Giraffe may come filching our corn one day soon.'

'She'll regret it if she does!' snorted Elephant.

Now the plan was that Rabbit would get up early next day and help himself to as much corn as he wanted before the others arrived. They would simply blame each other for the theft.

But Rabbit overslept: he had quite worn himself out with all that to-ing and fro-ing and mischief-making. When he got to the field, Giraffe was already there. Rabbit thought once and thought again.

'Oh! Look out! Here comes that thieving Elephant to help himself to our corn!' he cried.

'Where? Where?' said Giraffe, baring her teeth and bridling.

'There! There!' said Rabbit, pointing to a mountain.

'Over that mountain?' said Giraffe.

'What mountain?' said Rabbit. 'That IS Elephant!'

At that Giraffe's long legs bowed and her neck sagged and her ears hung down like yellow banana peel. 'God help us! We can't fight a monster like that!' she cried, and promptly fainted clean away.

Rabbit took the opportunity to nibble a breakfast of corn, tossing the chewed husks all around. Before long, around the mountain and down the road came Elephant – not the biggest of his kind – looking all around him for corn thieves. 'Seen any sign of that Giraffe?' he asked Rabbit, and Rabbit nodded furiously.

'Yes! She was here just now! See where she made a start on our corn! She said it was so sweet she'd fetch her mate, and together they would polish off the lot!'

'Cheek! Didn't you chase her away, the impudent whippersnapper?' asked Elephant, outraged.

Rabbit wiffled his nose and trembled his ears and looked as timid as any . . . well, as any rabbit. 'Who me? Tackle a brute like that? Giant Giraffe?'

'Why? Is she very big?' snorted Elephant, contemptuous and swaggering. 'Not too big for *me* to handle, I'll bet!'

Rabbit spread his paws wide, seeming to search for some way of describing the enormity of Giraffe. 'Well, look, that's her guitar lying on the ground,' he said, pointing at the sprawling Giraffe. 'That will give you some idea how big she is.'

At that, Elephant folded his ears on top of his head, picked up his big feet and took off at a run. 'That's her guitar. In that case I'm getting out of here before she uses me for a bongo!'

As soon as Giraffe came round, she too hurried to make her excuses and leave. 'Never really liked corn much anyway,' she said. 'You have it, Rabbit. You eat what you can before that Elephant gets here. Look at the size of him! Big as a hill! Big as a mountain, almost! I'm off!' And away she ran, stretching out her long neck for all the world like the fretboard of the world's largest guitar.

So Rabbit had plenty of time to eat his crop of corn, all the time in the world to laze in the sun and figure out why God made Elephant so big and Giraffe so tall . . . but gave all the brains to rabbits.

Cat v. Rat

A LEGEND FROM THE CONGO

THERE WAS A time, before times changed, when Cat and Rat got along pretty well. They got on like the best of friends, because that's what they were. They lived on an island so far out to sea that the mainland was only a rim of dark along the horizon, and Cat ate the birds out of the trees and Rat ate the roots of the cassava trees.

Still, there was only one kind of bird on the island, and cassava is cassava, call it manioc or tapioca or what you will. Both Cat and Rat craved variety.

'I bet there's all kinds of food out there,' said Rat, pointing with her stringy tail over the sea.

'As many different birds as there are stars,' agreed Cat gloomily, 'but not for us.'

'We could always go there,' said Rat, but Cat's fur stood on end at the thought of all that water.

'I can't swim.'

'You never tried. Anyway, we could make a boat.'

'My dear old furless friend,' gasped Cat, 'what a genius you are!'

Together they dug up a tough old cassava root and, while Cat scraped off the dirt outside, Rat gnawed out a hollow, eating the white pulpy strands as she went. 'When I get to the mainland,' she said, her little belly bulging. 'I never want to see another cassava.'

Now it so happens that cassava juice is a powerful strong drink, and by the time the canoe was finished, the two animals were singing slurred songs, trying to dance and stand on their heads and juggle crabs and so forth. They just leapt aboard and paddled excitedly out to sea.

It was much further than it looked to the mainland.

Paddling was hot, hungry work. When they stopped, the canoe stopped too. It looked as though the journey might take days.

'We forgot to bring any food,' said Rat.

'At least you ate before we set out. All that cassava,' said Cat. 'I'm hungry.'

'Go to sleep. You won't notice then,' said Rat, and they both curled up in the circle of their tails, at either end of the boat, and tried to sleep. Cat was soon dreaming of birds, his paws making little pat-patting movements in his sleep. But Rat could not sleep. A few hours before, she had never wanted to see another cassava root. Now a little cassava sounded very appetizing. 'And if I just scoop out a little more of the canoe, Cat will never know.'

She scooped and nibbled, nibbled and scooped the cassava canoe hollower than before. But not enough for Cat to notice.

Next night, while Cat slept, Rat scooped and nibbled a little more. Scoop, nibble, nibble, scoop. Whoops. One scoop too many.

It spurted a fountain of seawater. The sleeping Cat felt a sudden coldness around the tail area, and woke up to find the boat awash.

'You greedy guts! You peabrain gobbling twiddler! You've chewed through the bottom of the boat! Argghh! I hate water! I ought to eat you here and now, you treacherous little scrabbler!'

'Quite right, quite right!' squealed Rat, paddling furiously while the water came up around her haunches. 'I'll just help you get ashore, and then you really must eat me up from head to tail.'

So Cat paddled, too, though by the time they reached the mainland shore, they were up to their necks in the briny, and their canoe was entirely swamped. 'Just wait till I get my claws on you,' hissed Cat, crawling up the beach. He did not know whether anger or hunger made him keenest to eat Rat.

'Oh, your lovely fur!' cried Rat. 'Don't let it dry with all that salt in it! Poor dear Cat! Don't catch cold! Get dry, do! Groom yourself! I couldn't bear it if you caught pneumonia on my account.'

So Cat sat and licked his salty coat till it was dry and shining, savouring the moment when he would bite off Rat's head.

But when he looked round, all that he found was a small hole dug in the beach. 'Rat? Are you down there?'

'Mmmm,' said Rat. 'I have to admit I am.'

'Then come out at once and let me eat you.'

'We-e-ll. Perhaps not just yet,' said Rat.

'I can wait,' said Cat. 'You have to come out some time.'

'I'll just prepare myself for death, then, and be out directly,' said Rat.

So while Cat sat guard at the entry to the hole, Rat dug deeper and deeper – a longer and longer tunnel which broke surface under the shadow of the trees. Rat slunk off, snickering.

For three days Cat sat and waited for Rat to give herself up, before realizing that he had been duped once again. He swore then a vengeance so terrible that the palm trees shook, and rained down coconuts on his head.

So now the hunt is really on. From town to town, country to country, Cat hunts Rat, determined to kill that perfidious, cheating, no-good, scrabbling rodent. Generations of cats have taught their kittens to hate and hunt the whole ratty breed. And wherever there's a hole with a rattish sort of shape to it, you will find a cat waiting his chance to pounce . . .

The Pied Piper

A GERMAN LEGEND

ONE DAY FRAU Fogel put her hand into the bread bin, and something brushed against it, warm and furry, which sank its teeth into her palm and drew blood.

Next door, Frau Reuzel went to kiss her baby, and found something grey and sleek curled up against the baby's cheek, the cot full of droppings.

At the inn, the innkeeper opened his cellar doors and was met by a flood of fur, a sea of rats, which washed over his feet and streamed away into every corner, squealing.

The little town of Hamelin was infested with rats. Not a house was free of them, not a corner safe to set down a child or a plate of food. Rats moved along the Mayor's white tablecloth, even while the Mayor ate his dinner. Evil, filthy, beady-eyed, with tails like earthworms and teeth like needles, they no longer ran away from the brooms which tried to sweep them out-of-doors, but chewed on the broom bristles and swarmed where they passed.

'Get rid of them! Please!' pleaded the people, banging on the Mayor's door. 'Do something, or what do we pay taxes for?'

'I sent the public rat-catcher, didn't I? With his bucket and pole,' said the Mayor from an upstairs window. 'What more do you want?'

'But the rats ate him!'

'And his bucket!'

'And his pole!'

'*Do something!*'

It was at this moment that a stranger arrived in town. He attracted stares, but no friendly greeting, for he was an odd-looking creature in parti-coloured clothes like a jester – one stocking green, one red, one sleeve blue, one yellow. He wore his hair long, slicked down against his head and shoulders, and a jacket with long tapering tails right down to his dusty boots. He played a pipe, too, and Hamelin was not accustomed to music; the people there had never yet discovered what purpose it served, what profit was to be made from it.

The children liked him, of course, but then children are notoriously bad judges of character. They like a person because he makes them laugh, and ignore a man with ten thousand in the bank. In the town square, the stranger raised his pointed nose in the air and cocked his head, as if those small round ears so high up on his head could hear something out of the ordinary.

'What d'you want?' shouted the town beadle. 'Keep right on going. We have rodents enough round here already.'

'Perhaps I can help you, then . . .' said the stranger.

He said that he could rid the town of rats. For one hundred gold pieces, he would drown them in the river and end the plague.

'Give him the money! Give it!' shouted the crowd gathered outside the Mayor's house. 'Pay the Piper!'

'Anyone can make grand promises,' said the Mayor. 'But can he keep them? First let him do it, and then I'll pay!' From the eaves and sills, crouched on shop signs and along the rim of the ornamental fountain, a million rats looked on with glittering eyes.

'A hundred pieces of gold when I've rid you of rats,' said the stranger. And the Mayor blustered, 'Yes, yes.'

So the Piper put his pipe to his lips and played a tune. It had four beats to the bar, because rats go on four feet. It had a bleak, grey, scampering squeal which set everyone's teeth on edge. But the rats loved it.

The rats were spellbound by it. Captivated. Out of the houses and drains, the gutters and lofts and cellars, out of the cradles and cupboards, the breadbins and rubbish, the water butts and covered carts, a tide of grey vermin swirled down towards the playing of the pipe. Men and women alike screamed at the sheer number – they had never realized! – old men fainted at the stench. But the Piper just went on playing, strolling down towards the bridge, towards the river.

He sank them in the river: he played them to their deaths. Rafts of rats floated down the Weser River, their tails trailing like so many extinguished candle wicks. A strange silence replaced the ceaseless whistle of rodents squealing, the ceaseless scrabble of their claws. There was only the pleasant sound of children playing. Nothing but the rats' droppings and their teethmarks in the cheese remained to prove they had ever been there. And those were soon cleared away.

'What rats!' said the Mayor when the Piper asked for his money. 'I see no rats. I recall no rats.'

'You promised me one hundred gold pieces.'

'Promised? I remember no promise.'

The Piper turned towards the stallholders in the market-place. He was wearing black and white now – pied like the thieving magpie – though no one had seen him change his clothes, or could see where he had carried such baggage. They heard his argument with the Mayor, but they said nothing. After all, the hundred gold pieces would have been paid out of *their* taxes.

'Pay him!' said a child. But then children have no sense of business. They would squander money on anything.

Then the Pied Piper put his pipe to his lips and played another tune. For a man cheated out of money it was a remarkably cheerful tune – a dance, a caper full of laughing trills. And it had *two* beats to the bar.

The children loved it. The children were captivated by it. Enchanted. Throughout Hamelin they left their desks, their toys, their books and games. The older ones picked up their baby brothers and sisters and carried them. They walked and skipped and danced and toddled down towards the bridge and over the river.

Their parents were busy – so much to do now that the rats had gone. They did not realize what was happening. A strange silence replaced the crying of babies, the chant of children playing or reciting their lessons. It was not until the schoolmaster stood at his school gate, screaming himself blue, that the parents noticed their children – all their children – topping a rise on the mountain road, following the Pied Piper. Following, following. Leaving, leaving, leaving them behind.

How those mothers and fathers ran and called and hallooed. Shoes sliding in the dirt, aprons clenched in fists, shouting children's names, shouting promises: 'We'll pay you! A hundred gold pieces! A *thousand* gold pieces! *Come back!*'

The Koppenberg Hill resounded with their shouts, shook with them. It fractured and tore itself apart, opening a rift in the rocks as great as a cathedral door. In at the door went the Pied Piper and behind him the children, without a backward glance. The hill healed itself, closed and knit so completely that no trace remained of the door by the time mothers started clawing at it with their bare hands. *'Don't go! Come back!'*

The human heart does not mend so easily as rock, and that day every heart in Hamelin was broken.

'It's your fault they're gone! You should have paid him!' they shouted, beating on the Mayor's door. 'Where are our children!'

'Children? What children?' said the Mayor in terror. 'You have no children now. Forget them! They're gone. What purpose did they serve, in any case? What are they good for – babies, children? I never understood. Work! Profit! They're the only things that really matter! That's all we have to worry ourselves about now. Work! Profit! And —'

'*Death!*' cried the people of Hamelin as they stormed the Mayor's house like a pack of ravenous rats.

Gull-Girl

A LEGEND FROM SIBERIA

THE DAY WAS so hot that the cats took off their fur, the seals their skins and even Gregor took off his jacket. The fish gaped for air in the tepid lake, and a flock of geese and gulls floated overhead like ash over a bonfire. If it had not been for his mother's nagging, Gregor would never have bothered to go hunting on a day like this.

Idly, he watched the birds sweep in to land on the bank of the lake, watched them strip off their white feather cloaks, watched the goosemaidens and gull-girls inside wade into the water and swim. Quick as a whistle, Gregor ran and snatched up as many cloaks as his arms could carry.

'Oh, no! Thief! Give them back!' came the raucous cries from the lake. 'Don't take our feathers from us, or how shall we fly?' White arms reached out to him; white hands implored him. And Gregor did give back his trophies, cloak by beautiful cloak. All except one. One of the gull-girls was beautiful. Gregor could not bear to let her go.

'You're mine,' he said to the gull-girl.

'I'm promised to the Chief of the Sea Birds!' protested Gull-girl. But Gregor took her promise and broke it, for he was too much in love to care.

Gregor was not a bad man. This one unkindness was the first and last in his life. Gull-girl Chaika had no complaints after she married

353

him, and they came by two pretty children as well as a big feather
bed.

Life was as sweet as a melon. But every melon has pips and, as it
happened, Gregor's mother was about as pleasant as a whole
mouthful of pips.

'Call that a pie?' she would say, when Chaika cooked. 'I've thrown
tastier logs on the fire!'

'Call that clean?' she would say, when Chaika tidied the house.
'I've seen pigs keep their sties cleaner.'

'Call that washed?' she would say, when Chaika did the laundry.
'I've seen scarecrows better dressed than my son since you married
him!' On and on she nagged. 'You, you haven't wits enough to stuff a
cushion! I knew my Gregor was stupid, but I never knew he was
stupid enough to marry a dumb-cluck chicken!'

Chaika bore it until she could bear it no longer. One day, when she
was alone at home with the children, she slit open the feather bed
with a knife, stuck feathers to the arms and shoulders of her son and
daughter, and flew away with them to the Land of Birds. Gregor
heard her shrill gull-squawk of farewell as she swooped overhead,
then away and away.

'Good riddance,' said his mother, but Gregor stamped his boot.

'This is all your doing! So you can just sit down and sew me ten
pairs of boots. When they're made, I'll search the world till I've found
Chaika and the children and brought them home again!'

He was as good as his word. With nine pairs of boots in a sack over
his shoulder, he set off to search the world. High summer turned to
deepest winter, and one by one he wore out the boots in searching.

He had just laced on the ninth pair when he reached the
mountain-top eyrie of a golden eagle. There he bowed down low
in respect and said, 'Mighty King of the Birds, I married a gull-girl,
but she has flown away and left me. Help me to find her and my two
children.'

Golden Eagle was astounded at Gregor's courage. 'Don't you
realize I could tear out your heart with my beak, or carry you into the
air in my claws and drop you from top to bottom of this mountain of
mine?'

'Without Chaika and my little chickabiddy children, I don't much
care if you do,' said Gregor forlornly.

So the eagle took pity on him and sent him down to the seashore – a long journey from a mountain top. 'Go down to the sea and see what you can see,' said Golden Eagle.

Gregor had just laced on his last pair of boots when he reached the seashore and saw an old carpenter building a boat down by the sea.

'Can you tell me the way to Bird Land?' he asked.

'What will you pay for my answer?' replied the carpenter.

'Sir, I've nothing left in the world but one pair of boots.'

'They'll do,' said the giant looking him over, and he ran his plane one last time along the curve of a newly made canoe, struck his chisel against the carvings on its prow. 'This canoe will take you there,' he said, sliding open the wooden bow-cover – a bark lid carved with miraculous beasts and birds, letters and numbers, signs, symbols and mysteries.

Gregor helped him carry the boat down to the water, climbed in and sailed away. He had only to speak his wishes and the magic canoe sped over the water, so he asked it to take him to the Land of Birds, and who should he see when land came in sight, but his own two children playing on the beach.

'Daddy! Daddy!' they cried, flinging their arms round his legs.

'Where's your mother?' asked Gregor.

'Albatross, Chief of the Sea Birds, has claimed her for his own!' said the children. 'Oh, don't cross him, Daddy! He's powerful strong!'

But Gregor spat on his fists and marched right up to Chief Albatross's tent and flattened it with a single blow. When the big white bird came fluttering out, the two of them tussled and wrestled from one day's end to the next until at last Albatross, looking as scruffy as a half-plucked chicken, flapped away into the chilly sky with a dismal mewing.

Gregor kissed his wife and felt altogether pleased with himself. But Albatross had only gone to stir up the people of Bird Land.

All of a sudden, the sky turned dark with bird-wings, the wintry sun eclipsed by flocks of sharp-beaked ravens and crows and rooks. They plucked the feathers from their own wings and threw them at Gregor like black darts. But he shielded his family with the canvas from the tent, and fought back with stones and tent pegs and pieces of driftwood.

The crows and ravens and rooks fell back – only to be replaced by flocks of kites and buzzards and hawks as densely packed as swarms of gnats. All of the eastern sky was black with them, the morning light blotted out.

'We're done for now, my foolish hero,' said Chaika, and a freezing wind gave an ominous moan: *Hoowoo hoowoo!*

'Not if I have my way,' panted Gregor. 'Fetch me a bucket of fresh water and a mop.'

As though he were about to paint the heavens a better blue, Gregor soaked the mop in the water and wagged it at the sky. The water drops fell as sparkling diamonds on to the wings and backs of the flying battalions . . .

. . . and the wind froze that water into flakes of ice!

Weighed down by their little cloaks of ice, the birds fell from the sky like stones. Stalling in flight, their wings failed them. Freezing in flight, they plummeted down and lay about in thousands, winded, on the chilly ground. They were powerless to stop Gregor or his wife or his children climbing aboard the magic canoe, and long before the bird army had shaken the ice off their wings, the canoe sailed over the horizon, homeward bound.

Exhausted, the little family reached the beach where the carpenter still stood planing boat keels. In exchange for the magic canoe, he returned Gregor's last pair of boots . . . hardly enough for the immense journey which lay ahead of them.

'Look out! They've come after us!' cried Chaika, as giant wings over-shadowed them. But it was only the golden eagle Gregor had visited on the mountain top.

'Here, borrow my cloak,' said the eagle, stepping out of his feathers. 'I want it back, mind! Flying was never meant for the human breed.'

Gratefully, Gregor pulled on the feathery pinions of the naked eagle and, tucking his family under his wings, flew as straight as an arrow, home through the sky. What a feeling that was! What a sympathy it gave him for the dipping, diving, soaring, swooping creatures he had watched so many times in the past! Gregor vowed never again to hunt wild birds, or to cage songbirds for the sake of their music.

His mother, meanwhile, having no one to nag, had found herself a husband and left Gregor's little cottage altogether. So Chaika agreed to stay, never more to put on feathers, never again to fly away. And that night, the eagle robe, lying discarded by the cottage door, flew back to its owner who was swimming luxuriously in the waters of a warm spring lake.

Arion and the Dolphins
A GREEK MYTH

KING PERIANDER HAD music in his soul. That is to say there were pleasant, melodious strains and, deep down under that, a dark, reverberating bass. Just below his cultivated surface lay a temper like a shark. He was light and dark, soft and loud, generosity itself and utterly unforgiving. He surrounded himself with artists, poets, musicians; also soldiers, torturers, hangmen.

Most prized of all his friends was Arion the poet, the musician, the genius. Arion could, in playing the cithara, pluck the very heartstrings of his audience. And while he played, he sang – words of his own invention, spare and sonorous and sublime. No one who heard him could hold back either their tears or their smiles. Even the birds fell silent to listen; even the wild animals left off hunting to listen, ears cocked, eyes closed, entranced.

Arion was a quiet man, and would never have put himself forward. But Periander wanted the world to know that his court contained the very best of talents. So when he heard tell of an arts festival in Sicily, he sent Arion – 'No arguments now!' – to compete for its prizes. 'For the honour of Corinth!' he declared, so that Arion could hardly refuse.

He entered everything . . . and won, of course; trophies and laurels, chalices and purses of gold. To his shy embarrassment, he was carried through the streets shoulder-high, while young women threw flowers at him and young men begged to study at his feet. He was chaired down to the harbour and carried aboard ship: a Corinthian ship bound for its home port. 'Now take great care of Arion!' the crowd told the sailors. 'He has won every single prize at the festival. *Every single prize!*'

Now it would be wrong to impugn the honesty of Corinthian sailors, but there was a saying in those days: shake hands with them, but count your fingers afterwards. When they saw the prizes they welcomed Arion aboard. But five miles out to sea, they tipped him out of his hammock and put a dagger to his throat. 'Sorry, harp-plucker, but it's time for you to go swimming!'

Arion was not ashamed to beg for his life. 'Take the prizes; I don't want them! Just let me live!'

'Ah, but then you might say who took them,' said the Corinthian Captain, in a rasping, piratical way, trying on a golden laurel wreath. 'Whereas dead men tell no tales. Heave him over, lads.'

'I'll sing for you! I'll scrub the decks! Anything! Only don't kill me!' His back was against the ship's rail now, their hands under his armpits.

'Sing for the fishes,' said the Captain, and turned his back.

'One last song!' cried Arion. 'Let me offer up a song to the gods. Then maybe they'll pity my soul, if you won't pity my body!'

The Captain was against the idea. But the sailors could see no harm in letting Arion play, before they flung him overboard. So his beloved cithara was laid in his arms once more, and he began to sing – a wild, Corinthian lament fit to break the granite hearts of mountains.

The waves curled with pleasure at the sound. The sails, stretched taut as drumskins, throbbed with ecstasy. Fish, like a million sequins, glinted on the surface of the sea, drinking in the liquid strains of Arion's song. Seagulls perched along the yards, flightless with wonder.

Unfortunately, the sailors' idea of music was a rollicking sea-shanty. They could beat out a jig or obey a ship's whistle, but as for Corinthian laments . . . 'Very nice, I'm sure, if you like that kind of thing,' sneered the Captain. 'Now throw him over.' Their hearts were as hard as the wax in their ears. They dropped Arion into the sea like an anchor, and he sank as though he were made of lead.

Down and down he went through a green silent world where no music sounds but the song of the whale. Though his mouth was open, no music came from it – only a stream of silver bubbles – minims of silence in a green auditorium.

Then something brushed the playing-fingers of his hand – as gently as the strings of a cithara. And a second later, a great grey flank slammed into his ribcage and another drove between his legs. He lost consciousness thinking he was being eaten by sharks.

When he opened his eyes again, the sea was a black dazzle of sunlight and his fingers were trailing through white foam. He was astride a dolphin, his face resting on a grey back as smooth as polished marble. In elegant lunges the dolphin leapt through the water, now swimming, now flying, scarcely even wetting Arion's face. Alongside swam a dozen more, leaping and plunging, chanting their strange, clicking, whistled language.

Ravished by the music coming from the ship, the dolphins had gathered round the hull to listen. Then, as the musician plunged to his supposed death, they had caught him and carried him – like the Sicilian crowds – shoulder-high across the lapis sea.

Venturing as far inshore as they dared, the dolphins dropped Arion in shallow water, then saluted him with crackling whistles before turning back out to sea. From a nearby port, Arion took ship for Corinth and was ashore before the Corinthian ship even crossed the harbour bar, telling his whole story to Periander.

They were startled to see King Periander, mighty tyrant of Corinth, standing watching them disembark. 'I was waiting for a friend,' he told them. 'Arion the poet. I thought he might have come home on your vessel.'

'Who? Ooh no,' said the Captain. 'No passengers this voyage. Arion? Sounds familiar. I recall someone of that name in Sicily. Won all the prizes at the festival. Liked the place so much he decided to stay.'

'Is that right?' said Periander mildly. 'How I'll miss his singing. I shall just have to think of some other form of entertainment.'

Suddenly the harbour was full of soldiers, their hands full of swords, ropes and chains, their mouths full of curses. The sailors offered to sing in return for their lives, to row galleys, to dive for pearls. But Periander was as deaf to their entreaties as if his ears had been full of wax. They had stirred up the blackest mud from the seabed of his soul and, by the time it settled, those Corinthian pirates wished they had never been born.

Arion did not watch. His mind was on dolphins, on the poetry and music of dolphins, on the sun-spangled sea and the sweetness of life, and on washing the sea salt out of his hair.

Thunder and Smith

A CHINESE MYTH

GENERALLY, WHEN people say they don't like thunder, they mean that it scares them. Not Smith. His dislike was personal. He hated Thunder with the same seething, unreasonable loathing that a man feels for a noisy neighbour. And it was mutual. Thunder would come round from time to time and beat on Smith's roof with his axe, while Smith shouted abuse at him up the chimney, and Smith's little daughter and son sat in the corner crying, 'Please don't, Daddy! Please don't! Couldn't you make things up with him and be friends?' Their father took no notice.

One day, Smith made a cage – an iron cage too big to fit through the front door – and a long iron pitchfork. He left the cage outside in the garden, camouflaged by leaves, then he sat himself down in a chair by the front door, fork in hand. He waited, waited and waited for the hot weather to break, watched the rainclouds fill up with dark rain, heard the distant grumbling of Thunder as he dragged his axe about the heavens. And he waited, still and patient, until Thunder's temper finally broke in the heat and he came rampaging over the countryside, splintering trees, knocking down chimneypots, swinging his axe like a hooligan.

Smith was ready for him. He put his thumbs in his ears and wriggled his fingers at Thunder, sticking out his tongue. When the god made a lunge at him, he jumped aside and, catching Thunder off-balance, bundled him into the cage with the fork.

'Aha! Eehee! Yahoo! Yippee!' Hopping round the cage, whooping and yelping with glee, Smith poked and jabbed through the bars. 'Got you now, you old rogue! Tee-hee! Got you, and now I'm going to cook you and eat you, braised with dumplings!'

Thunder rattled at the bars, and chewed on the lock with his yellow zigzag teeth, but because the cage was iron, he could not break free.

Little Nuwa and her brother, cowering in the doorway, hand in hand, stared and trembled. 'Oh, please, Papa! Let him go!' begged Nuwa.

But Smith was busy saddling his horse. 'I'm going to town to buy herbs – cloves and cinnamon and cardamom. I like my meat tender and tasty. You'll be quite safe: he can't get out. Just don't listen to any of his wheedling lies and you'll be fine.' And away he went, down the road, at the gallop.

He was no sooner gone than Thunder trained his steely eyes on the children and began to shout at them, 'Let me out!'

Nuwa covered her ears and told her little brother to go inside and lock the door.

He was no sooner gone than Thunder turned his grey eyes on Nuwa, and burst into tears. 'Please, oh please, oh please, please, please!' he sobbed. 'Let me out or I'll die!'

Nuwa turned to face the wall, so as not to see him, and shook her head.

'Oh please, pretty-pity-please! Have mercy!' begged Thunder. 'How would you like it if a man with a cage trapped *your* father, and cooked him with herbs and spices and ate him for dinner?'

Nuwa bit her lip and put her arms over her head, trying not to listen.

'Well, all right, little one, I understand. Won't you just give me a drop to drink? Is that too much to ask?'

Nuwa thought this was the least she could do for the poor beast in the cage. She ran at once and got a cup of water. Telling Thunder to go right to the other end of the cage, she put it through the bars.

The water was gone in one slurp, and Thunder's eyes turned an interesting blue. Then, to Nuwa's horror, the whole of him began to change – to swell – to grow, bigger and bigger, until he filled the cage like a dog in a cat-basket. He bulged through the bars, bent them, burst them like a whale bursting a string bag. Pieces of metal flew in every direction, some embedding themselves in the house wall, while

Thunder funnelled into the sky in a single dark column of cloud. As he passed the tree-tops, he picked a gourd from the branches and threw it down to Nuwa, calling, 'One kindness deserves another!'

Seeing the commotion in the distance as he rode home, Smith dug in his heels and came back at the gallop. The awful truth was all too plain: his captive gone, his hopes of dinner, too. And over his house hung Retribution: enough rain to flood not only his home, his garden, his country, but the wide world!

So Smith began work. 'I'll deal with you later!' he snarled at his two terrified little children.

The wreck of his cage made the keel, and his iron barn made the walls. He was the best blacksmith for miles around and he worked fast, but long before he finished, the rain had begun to fall. First drizzle, then sprinkling rain, then a downpour, then hail and sleet and snow all mixed together tumbled out of the sky to the noise of a thousand kettledrums, as Thunder wrought his revenge.

But when Smith's iron ship was finished, the last rivet hammered home, no one but he went on board. 'What do I need with two such worthless children?' he shouted down from the quarterdeck. 'Sink or swim, but don't look to me for any help: you brought this on us, and now you can pay!'

The floodwater soon came up to Nuwa's waist. It set the iron ship afloat to grate and bump about. Swiftly, Nuwa picked up a knife and cut a hole in the gourd, and she and her brother climbed inside.

The Flood rolled over the Earth in swirls and eddies, joining lake to lake, river to river. Soon all the houses in the world disappeared from sight – all the trees, all the hills, all the mountains. Still Thunder poured down rain on to the Earth. People riding out the Flood in boats and bath-tubs and basins called out to God to help them, but God was sound asleep, lulled by the hush-shushing of the falling rain. Their puny voices could not rouse Him.

Not until the floodwater reached Heaven itself did He stir.

Bang bang bang. 'Wake up, won't you?' he heard. *Bang clang bang* 'Wake up, you old fool! What does it take to get your attention?' It was foul-tempered Smith, beating on the floor of Heaven from underneath with his iron fork, CLANG BANG CLANG.

Startled and bleary, God looked around him. He saw the Earth and sky full to the brim with floodwater, and the pavings of Heaven starting to lift. 'Waters, be gone!' He commanded.

And the Flood was gone.

It did not drain away, soak in, evaporate in the hot sun. No. It just went. One moment it was there, then, with a clap of God's hands, it was gone. One thousand miles deep and as wide as the world, it just disappeared, leaving a mighty long way down for those who had been floating around on its surface.

The iron ship plummeted down, like a bell falling from a cathedral steeple one thousand miles high. It landed with a single dull CLANG.

But the gourd, of course, fell as any gourd falls from trees: gently, with a spongy PLOP, into a puddle of mud. And Nuwa and her little brother climbed out unharmed.

Thunder saw to that.

'One kindness deserves another,' growled the dark and distant clouds. So Nuwa and her brother planted the seeds from inside the gourd, and from those grew the first plants of the new Earth, and Nuwa and her brother lived all alone beneath their shade, while the world began anew.

A Prickly Situation

A NATIVE AMERICAN MYTH

BEAVER HAD BEEN beavering away all summer. Busy, busy, busy. His dam was built, he had plenty of food for the winter. 'My larder is full,' he said, congratulating himself as he pushed an arrowhead ripple across the pool with his nose. 'Not like hers,' he thought as he saw Porcupine sitting idly on the bank. She was still sitting there later in the day. '*My* larder is full,' Beaver thought gleefully as he pushed another ripple back across the pool, swimming homeward.

His larder was empty.

Beaver caught up with Porcupine on a forest path, pushing a large barrow full of food. 'You stole my food, you bone-idle bunch of no-good knitting needles!'

'Me? Never. I'm a porcupine. Porcupines don't steal,' replied Porcupine.

Beaver took a look into the barrow. The food was familiar. Beaver-type food. So he went to take a large bite out of Porcupine's nose.

At the last moment, Porcupine tucked in her nose and fanned out her spines. It was like biting on a pincushion. Beaver jumped backwards, yelping and whimpering, with a noseful of spines, while Porcupine rattled away, swinging her rump about like a mace.

When the Beaver People saw the state of Beaver's nose, they felt the smart as though it were their own. 'This is war!' they declared. 'That porcupine has eaten her last dinner!'

An army as huge and plush as a bearskin lay siege to Porcupine's house, and when she would not come out, knocked it down and dragged her away. This time they used ropes. There wasn't a thing Porcupine could do to save herself. Over leaves and stones, over beach and out to sea they towed the thief, marooning her on an island seven miles offshore. Not husband, child, friend or neighbour could find hide or spine of her, though they searched and searched.

Dismayed and discomforted, Porcupine listened to the rhythmic splash of her enemies' oars as they rowed away and left her. Then shaking herself, with a noise like spillikins, she looked around the island. No berry bushes, no farm crops, no shops. There was not even so much as a tree to chew the bark off, not a string of seaweed washed up on the beach. 'They mean me to starve!' said Porcupine, choking back a sob. 'Well, I shan't give them the satisfaction! I'll drown myself in the sea! . . . in a minute or two.' Being an idle creature, Porcupine sat down for a rest.

A gentle breeze was blowing across the island, and in it the first bitter seeds of winter. Also a voice. At least, it *sounded* like a voice in Porcupine's ear, saying, *'Call the North Wind, your kin! Call on the North Wind!'*

Porcupine was not of a mystical turn of mind. She had no faith in chants or spells. So she paid no heed – only hunched and slumped her way around and around her barren prison until, in her hunger, she could count her ribs as easily as her spines. Her eyesight was smeary and her ears rang. They rang with that same voice: *'Summon the North Wind, your kin! Summon up the Wind!'*

Porcupine had nothing to lose, and there was no one close by to snigger, so she lifted up her nose and sang the chant:

> *'Come you North Wind, full of winter!*
> *Come you North Wind, full of snow!*
> *Come you steel-grey, glass-sharp splinter*
> *In the sky's eye, North Wind BLOW!'*

Spiny with hail and sleet, rattling and bristling with icicles, the North Wind heard, and came howling down from the Arctic. There were no trees to groan or bend, no beasts but Porcupine to shiver in the icy blast. But the sand swirled in eddies across the beach, and the sea slopped gelatinous against the shore.

Yes, the sea gelled and stood still. Its waves were trapped under a crust of ice as, gradually, the sea froze solid as far as the horizon. Sadly, poor Porcupine was too feeble to move, too weakened by hunger to crawl out on to that magic ice and escape!

Porcupine's relations, searching the shoreline, were amazed at the sight of the sea freezing over. They set off at once across its furrowing, fretful surface, to search all the islands offshore. Last of all, they came to a knoll so small and bare they would never even have spotted it but for the dark spiny shape rolled up in a ball on the sand. Porcupine!

She had to be carried home and fed cabbage broth through a quill straw. The sight of her was so piteous that her family quite forgot the crime which had been her undoing. 'This is war!' they declared. 'That beaver must pay!'

An army as prickly and numberless as the conker cases under a chestnut tree stormed Beaver's lodge. And though his huge dam proved as impenetrable as a castle wall, the porcupines did manage to take one prisoner. Beaver himself was captured and dragged away, over mud, over stones and through the forest.

'You marooned Porcupine and left her to starve! Now we'll maroon you, Rug-tail!' They dragged him over tree-tops and up the trunk of the tree. Like a lynch-mob they swung him from one branch up to the next, until he burst headfirst out of the very crown of the tree. 'Bet you didn't know porcupines could climb trees, did you? Eh? Eh, Bugs-beaver? Now see how you like a taste of your own medicine!' And so saying they left him, marooned him, abandoned him at the top of the tallest tree in the forest.

Around him a sea of trees waved in late autumnal tides of orange and gold. Beaver shook the leaves out of his fur and listened to the rattle of a dozen porcupines shinnying down the tree. Then he hummed a small tune to himself – not a magical chant or a mystical incantation – just a tune.

As he hummed, he began to gnaw. Gnaw, gnaw, gnaw. Beaver liked to keep busy. Busy, busy, busy. By next morning, he had gnawed his way through the entire tree, top to bottom. Then he trotted home to his pool, his dam and his lodge under the dam, to spend a peaceful winter relaxing with his family.

How the Fairies Became

A EUROPEAN LEGEND

BEFORE THERE WAS an earth to walk on or human feet to walk it, God parted Light from Dark. Pushing the darkness downwards, He lived above, in the Realms of Light, beside a glass sea. The darkness settled into a bottomless tarry lake, while the upper light crystallized into spires and domes surrounded by walls of cloud. Flitting about that heavenly citadel, like starlings at dusk, were the angels, doing whatever God asked.

That was the time of perfect happiness, so peaceful that God was free to begin His next creation: Earth. Once begun, it took up all His time – parting sea from land, colouring the animals . . . While He was away, rebellion stirred among the angels. Returning one day from creating the great fishes, God found His cherubim and seraphim brawling in the streets of Paradise. They talked of taking over from God and turning Him out of Heaven. They had even crowned a leader to take His place: an angel calling himself Lucifer, the Carrier of Light. That was the start of the Heavenly Wars, when comets were hurled like slingshot and the skies rained meteors – God's men against Lucifer's.

Some, though, did not take sides. Whether they were cowards, or just wanted to be sure of siding with the winners, these "undecided" angels kept to the hidey-holes of Heaven, biding their time. In their smallness of spirit, they actually shrank, and their wings became transparent.

God won out, of course. Lucifer and all his troops were defeated and toppled out of Heaven. They hurtled down into the tarry pool and the bottomless region of dark. The cloud walls were mended, and everything was the same as before in the marvellous Realms of Light.

Except for the Undecided.

They scurried to sit at God's feet. They sang His praises loudly. But at once He held up a hand to silence them.

'You cannot stay,' He said, and their transparent wings wilted. 'You would not help me when I needed you, and he who is not with me is against me. I shall not throw you into the tarry lake, but you must go and live in this new place I have made – on Earth. Live in the hills and under the ground; live among the tree roots and long grass. From today you shall be called fairies and pixies, brownies and sprites – not angels; not ever angels.'

'Do you hate us so much, then, Master?' said the tallest of the Undecided.

'I neither hate nor love you,' said God, 'because you neither loved nor hated me.'

The Undecided who flew down that day from Paradise to Earth were as plentiful as the dragonflies and thistledown: the people who lived there caught sight of fairies every day. But somehow, there have come to be fewer over the years. Perhaps their magic wore out and they became mortal and died. Or perhaps they shrank to a size human eyes cannot see.

Some people say that God, in His Kindness, forgave them one by one, and let them go home to Heaven, and that there their magic was put to grander use, building the Universe and hanging up the stars. But we shall not find out the truth yet awhile. Not in this life.

The Gods Down Tools
A SUMERIAN MYTH

'**E**NOUGH!**' SAID ENKI, throwing down his spade. 'For a thousand years we've dug out rivers and piled up hills. There has to be more to life than this!'

Around him, the other gods nodded and muttered. Spade after pick dropped to the ground. 'Let Enlil do it himself!'

It was a surly rabble of weary immortals which picketed the home of Enlil, Lord of the Winds. 'What's the matter?' he asked, when he came to the door. 'Why have you stopped working? You still have the River Tigris to dig! We must have that meander by Monday!'

'We're sick of digging,' said the gods. 'You've worn us out, Enlil. We're all agreed: no more digging.'

To their astonishment, Enlil burst into tears. 'I'm sorry! I never realized. I was a fool! I resign as world-planner! I do, I resign!'

The strikers shuffled their feet, embarrassed and a little shame-faced. The Lord of the Winds was a sensitive, passionate soul; they had not meant to hurt his feelings.

We-e coughed awkwardly. 'Suppose – just suppose,' he said, 'that we created some kind of creature to do the work for us?'

And thus humankind was invented – Nintur made them out of earth and blood – to finish digging the river and planting the fields.

They did very well, worked as industriously as the ants, *and* worshipped the gods as well, which gave the gods a warm and happy feeling they had not felt before. Nintur did not need to make

371

thousands: they reproduced themselves. And when they were worn out and could not work any more, they died. Cities grew up, like ant hills, with homes and shops, bath houses and meeting halls. Carts trundled from place to place, and street sellers shouted all day long:

'Buy your fish! Fresh fish today!'

'Lots of lovely lemons!'

'Cage-birds, songbirds, going cheap!'

'WHAT IS THAT DIN?' demanded Enlil one day.

'It's the People,' Enki replied. 'Busy little things, aren't they?'

Enlil groaned and covered his ears. 'The noise! The racket!'

Now Enki had grown rather fond of humankind, and the noise did not much trouble him – except perhaps women who sang off-key and crying babies at night. 'Each separate one doesn't make much noise. It's just that there are so many these days.'

'Then *thin them out*!' hissed Enlil, his nerves frayed from lack of sleep. 'Send Plague to kill them, one in three.'

Regretfully, Enki summoned Plague and told her. But then he hurried ahead to the cities of Sumer, and warned the little workers.

When Plague arrived, everywhere was silent. The cartwheels were muffled with cloth, the babies were all feeding, women passed by their neighbours without a word, and street sellers mimed on the street corners. What is more, delicious offerings were burning on every altar. Plague had not the heart to slaughter one in three, not even one in ten. Not one, in fact.

Enlil did not insist. The cities were silent. He was able to sleep at night and snooze in the afternoon. And he needed workers to build the Zagros Mountains.

For a thousand years, all went as well as it can in the best of all possible worlds. Parents told their children to be quiet, but the children forgot to tell their children. The noise gradually increased. Husbands nagged their wives, children squabbled over toys, women insisted on singing, in and out of key.

'Where can a god go to have some peace and quiet, with this chatter-chatter-chatter?' Enlil complained. 'Let the rivers dry up, let the lakes turn to salt. Perhaps when they are dead of thirst, these human beings will be silent!'

Enki hurried down to the cities of Sumer and warned them: unless they quieten their noise, a fearful drought would kill whole families, neighbourhoods, towns! The priests rushed to the temples of An, the water god, and heaped them with gifts. The men held their fingers to their lips, babies sucked their thumbs, and the din once more fell silent. An had not the heart to take their water, and Enlil had gone back to sleep.

For a thousand years all went as well as it can in the best of all possible worlds. Parents told their children to be quiet, and their children told theirs. But then someone said the story of the drought had never happened. A woman argued with him, and people took sides. Tempers flared, punches were thrown, and the fight that followed made more noise than all the street-traders in Sumer.

Enlil closed his windows. Enlil closed his doors. But still he could hear the din of the cities of Sumer. 'I WILL NOT HAVE THIS NOISE!' he bellowed. 'If they must open their mouths to shout and jabber, let them have no food to put in them, and let them starve and die, but GIVE ME SOME PEACE!'

The famine began instantly; there was no time for Enki to warn anybody. Crops withered, trees cankered, the berries were eaten by birds. The People grew thin as sticks, and had nothing but water to give their children. They called on Enki to save them.

But how to help? Enki paced the banks of the Tigris, stalked the fruitless woods, thinking. Then with a cry of inspiration, he ran to the river and threw in a handful of magic.

Thirty thousand fish tumbled down the river – a coppery shoal of bream and carp overspilling the banks and leaping clear of the waves. There were so many that the People had only to reach out a hand to grasp a fin, a tail, a fishy feast. After that, their mouths were too crammed to talk. Also, fishing is a quiet pursuit, so that Enlil, though angry, let the famine end. 'Next time . . .' he muttered. 'Next time . . .'

For a thousand years, all went as well as it can in the best of all possible worlds. Parents told their children to hush, and their children told their grandchildren. But babies will cry, and neighbours will quarrel. A man must sell his wares. People laugh at jokes, and children cry when they fall over.

Enlil tried to sleep on one ear, then he tried to sleep on the other. But the noise of the cities of Sumer was howling pandemonium in his head.

'AWAY WITH THE LOT OF THEM!' he thundered. 'Let the Earth know silence again. Drown every mortal!'

With the winds in his keeping, he piled up the waves of the sea and thrust rain into the rivers till they burst their banks. He plugged up the tunnels under the earth and gathered the rainclouds like a flock of sheep. This time Enki could see no way to save the People: no possible way . . . unless he were to save just one . . .

'Beware! Beware, Atrahasis!' he whispered to the best of his mortal friends. 'The Lord of the Winds is sending a flood! Build a boat – a big boat – and take your family aboard, along with two of every kind of animal . . .'

Perhaps you have heard the story, or some version of it.

For seven days and seven nights water rolled down the rivers and cascaded out of the sky, drowning all the crying and laughing, shouting and music, traffic and building and singing. The last sounds to trouble Enlil came from swimmers crying for help to the gods, and rooks shrieking in the drowning trees. Then everything was silent.

The gods looked down in horror at the world they had dug and shaped and peopled. They saw their altars and the flowers from their altars float by on the Flood. All this for the sake of peace and quiet?

As the Flood soaked away, Atrahasis' boat ran aground on a mountain top, and he set loose the animals. They ploughed, muddy-legged, through the ruined crops and fallen buildings, the wreckage of the Flood.

'We must offer thanks to the gods that we were saved,' was the first thing Atrahasis said.

When Enlil woke from his peaceful sleep, he looked down at the empty earth and saw . . . Atrahasis.

'Kill him!' he cried, bursting into tears. 'Kill him, or he'll breed! I can see it now! People marrying, people multiplying! Soon it will be as bad as ever! Kill Atrahasis!'

He gave the order, but none of the other gods moved.

'Kill him!' screamed Enlil, making more noise than anyone.

'I'm hungry,' said Enki.

'The fields need tending,' said Nanna. 'Who will do it, if not Atrahasis and the sons and daughters of Atrahasis?'

'There's a lot of *mending* to be done,' said An, pointedly.

'Must we do it all ourselves?' said We-e.

'Must we do everything?' they asked. And one by one, Enki led the gods away, leaving Enlil amid the silence of solitude.

They say Atrahasis was a soft-spoken man, and that he raised his children to speak softly, too. Even with all the gods but one on his side, Atrahasis knew better than to take chances.

Balder and the Mistletoe

A NORSE MYTH

BALDER WOKE SCREAMING from a terrible nightmare, and laid his hand against his chest. 'Weep!' he cried.

His wife, waking beside him, tried to calm him. 'Think, my love! What can possibly harm you? Nothing can pierce your golden skin. Nothing can bruise your soft flesh. And you've no enemies! Everyone loves you as much as I do. Shsh now. There's nothing to be afraid of.' But she could not rid his eyes of terror or the stain of that dreadful dream.

Freya, Queen of the gods, heard her son cry out. It was not for the first time he had dreamed of danger, of dying, and she was worried.

'Who would want to harm our son?' snorted Odin, Balder's father and the King of all gods. 'He's the darling of the world!'

But Freya, like her dream-plagued son, could not rest easy. She decided to exact a promise from every living thing; never to harm her son.

She asked the birds, including the ravenous ravens, the scavenging vultures and the soaring eagles. They all swore never to hurt Balder.

She asked the wild beasts and the tame; the savage lion, the strangling snake and all the venomous hairy spiders. They swore never to hurt Balder.

She asked the flies and the flowers, the fish and the whales, the anemones and the octopuses. and they all swore never to harm a hair of Balder's handsome head.

She asked the thorn bushes and the heather, the smallest herb and the highest oak tree never to harm her beloved son. But she did not see, clinging to the oak like a lantern of luminous green, the gentle mistletoe which grows among the oak leaves, but which is neither leaf nor seed nor berry nor twig of the tree itself.

'All is well, son. You can sleep sound tonight,' she told Prince Balder.

But in the sunny woods, hidden between the tall timber and taller sunbeams, Loki the Trouble-Maker grinned to himself. A piece of mischief had occurred to him, the kind of work for which only he, Loki the Trickster, Loki the Outsider, Loki the Anarchist was framed. He saw how Freya had missed the mistletoe. She had not asked Loki for his promise, either.

Loki bore Balder no hatred, but, for Loki, a peaceful world was as loathsome as dead calm to a sailor. He needed a storm to fill his sails.

'Is it true what they say, Balder?' said Loki. 'That nothing can harm you?'

'Nothing,' said Balder, all his good humour restored. 'Try me! Hit me! Punch me! Go on!' and he offered the flat, steely muscles of his stomach for Loki to punch.

Loki saw misgiving flash through Queen Freya's eyes; she knew how unpredictable Loki could be. But Loki only shrugged his shoulders and shook his head. 'Couldn't possibly. You know me. Wouldn't harm a fly.'

Even so, thanks to Loki's question, all the other gods were soon cheerfully heaving rocks and spears and trees and goats and cats and clouds and all manner of everything at the magnificent figure of Prince Balder – just to test the magic. And nothing so much as grazed his golden skin.

Even Balder's blind brother, Hodir, was easily caught up in the game. Loki had only to slip a loaf, a fir-cone, a pigeon in between Hodir's fingers and he joined in the throwing. After that, Loki had only to slip a stem of mistletoe into Hodir's hand . . . The tender white berries trickled to the ground between Hodir's fingers.

No kiss came with this mistletoe, no loving kindness. It flew, stuck fast, and pierced Balder's chest, sharp and deep as any needle. Balder looked down with an expression of faint surprise on his lovely face. Then he dropped like the oak tree on which the mistletoe had once grown, while the other gods gasped and cried out, and blind Hodir asked, 'What? What's happened? What's wrong?'

Queen Freya held her hair in both hands and screamed a scream which shivered the glass windows of the sky. 'NO!' she cried. 'NO! NO! He shan't die! My son shan't die!'

Hermodir, younger brother of Balder and Hodir, ran to King Odin. 'Lend me your horse, Father! If I ride fast enough, maybe I can stop him – snatch back his soul before it reaches Helheim!'

Odin did not hesitate. He tossed the reins of Sleipnir, his eight-legged horse, into the hands of his youngest son. 'Tell Queen Hel she must wait for my son. Tell her we cannot spare him yet to her Kingdom of the Dead!'

And so, while the gods held their breaths, and the forests of the world quivered with shock, Hermodir spurred on Sleipnir to gallop as the beast had never galloped before.

Faster than thought, Sleipnir's eight hooves covered the miles. For a whole day Hermodir rode, and at every moment he expected to see the soul of Balder flying ahead of him towards the Underworld.

Faster than light, Sleipnir's eight hooves sped down deep valleys and ravines. For nine whole days Hermodir rode until at last he came to a golden bridge spanning a rushing river of ink-black water, and he heard, along the planks of the bridge, the footsteps of his dead brother still echoing. He knew he was entering the Kingdom of Helheim, territory of Queen Hel, Goddess of Death, but his courage never wavered. Into the hall of Hel herself, rode Hermodir, just as she reached to clasp Balder's ghostly hand.

'WAIT!'

Hermodir rode between them. Sleipnir snorted and sweated and steamed, stamping his eight feet.

'Wait, Goddess of Death, and listen! The world cannot bear to part with Balder! Hodir will never forgive himself! The great god Odin's heart will break, and Queen Freya may flood the earth with her tears! Let him go! Let his soul go back to his body! Spare him to his mother and father and brothers and friends! Have pity, Queen Hel!'

Hel stroked the neck of Sleipnir, so that the horse's sweat turned to ice and fell to the ground like gravel. 'If all the creatures of the earth are ready to shed a tear for Balder, and if I may have all those tears to slake my thirst, you may have back your brother. I would not grant as much to any other man. Tell Freya this.'

So for nine days, Hermodir rode back – across the golden bridge, up valleys and ravines, to the sunlit world, and there he returned to the forest clearing where Balder's dead body still lay, a sprig of mistletoe piercing his chest. Hermodir proclaimed the price of Balder's life.

'Then he's free!' cried Freya, laughing through her tears. 'Every creature in Creation is *already* weeping for my boy!'

It was true. It was almost true. It was true of all but one. For when Freya came face-to-face with Loki, she saw no tears in his eyes.

'Weep, Loki!' she commanded. 'You more than anyone should be sorry! You put the mistletoe into Hodir's hand!'

But Loki would not weep. 'I am framed to bring disorder where there is peace, storm where there is calm.'

'Weep, Loki!' raged the Queen.

But Loki would not weep. 'I was framed to trick the simple and teach the innocent not to be so trusting.'

'Weep, Loki, I beg you!' pleaded the Queen, falling to her knees.

But Loki would not weep. 'What's done is done, and I did it. Nor shall I shed one tear of regret. Let Hel hold what she has!' And he laughed in Freya's face, laughed and glared, dry-eyed.

'Launch a great ship,' said Odin, straightening his ancient back. 'A warship. Lay Balder's body on the deck. His soul will not be returning. Thanks to Loki, my son is lost to us everlastingly.'

But as that ship sailed out to sea – as torches were thrown into Balder's funeral barge, and its sails billowed into rags and flags of scarlet fire – Odin took hold of Loki the Trouble-Maker and lashed him in chains, buried him in the earth, and set the poison of a giant serpent to drip, drip, drip everlastingly on to the god's face.

No death came to the rescue of Loki-the-Trickster. No pity came from any creature in the wide world, except his wife, whose tears, falling in his face, diluted the poison. Now, whenever the Mischief-Maker writhes in agony under the drops of poison, the whole Earth shakes and quakes with seismic horror.

Still Loki does not weep – not for Balder, and not for himself. For what he did, he was framed to do. It was in his nature to do it, just as it is in the nature of all living things to die.

About the Stories

All these stories have been passed down from generation to generation by word of mouth and changed a little by each successive storyteller, growing and altering to suit the listener. I have retold them – sometimes from the briefest passing reference in dusty old volumes – to please you, the reader.

In doing so, I have made sometimes small, sometimes large changes, but have tried to preserve an inkling of the pleasure each story gave to its original audience.

G McC.

The Golden Wish

In Greek mythology, King Midas of Phrygia represented the height of foolishness. The story of his greedy wish is just one of the follies attributed to him.

Shooting the Sun

This Chinese myth of the Fun Sang tree and the divine family in its branches dates back to the sixth century BC. For his actions here, the archer Yi is banished to earth and mortality, but becomes a hero figure in later myths.

George and the Dragon

When the early Church recorded the life of a young martyr, George of Lydda (possibly d. 313 AD), they embellished it with local legend. But the dragon-slaying story predates Christianity; Theseus, in Greek myth, slew a sea monster and rescued a princess on virtually the same spot.

SKINNING OUT
The idea of God entrusting animal messengers with crucial information recurs throughout Africa. In Ethiopia, it is the holawaka bird which takes the blame for human mortality.

ROBIN HOOD AND THE GOLDEN ARROW
Tales concerning the outlaw Robin Hood have set his adventures variously in Nottingham and in Yorkshire, in the 1190s and the 1320s. But all depict him as a champion of the oppressed, who robbed the rich to help the poor.

BRAVE QUEST
This story is adapted from a Sioux myth explaining the origins of the famous Sun Dance – a ritual of cleansing and endurance offered up by a warrior in thanksgiving – not to the Sun, but to Wakan Tanka, the Great Creator.

SAVING TIME
Maui is the trickster hero of Oceanic mythology: a rebel who broke every taboo. He is also said to have created the archipelagos by hauling up each island from beneath the ocean with his fishing line.

THE LAKE THAT FLEW AWAY
Many Estonian myths concern lakes and rivers, for water has a holy, magical quality. God is seen as having filled certain water courses from his own golden bowl, pouring water out on to a riverbed prepared by all the beasts of creation.

ADMIRABLE HARE
We traditionally describe the moon's pitted surfaces as looking like a man with a dog. Many other cultures, including India and Mongolia, make out the shape of a hare. This Sri Lankan myth explains how the hare came to be there.

ALL ROADS LEAD TO WALES
The *Mabinogion* is a collection of eleven ancient Celtic stories. This one can be thought of as an expression of wonder, by post-Roman Britons, at the legacy of straight metalled roads left behind by the Roman occupation.

RAINBOW SNAKE

The Rainbow Snake's writhings through the Australian landscape are held to account for very specific landmarks, rivers and mountain ranges – a common function of myth.

JUNO'S ROMAN GEESE

Geese were sacred to the Roman goddess Juno, for they were said to share her attributes of love, guardianship and good housekeeping. Camillus (and perhaps the temple geese) is said to have saved Rome from Gaulish invaders in 365 BC.

JOHN BARLEYCORN

Wherever barley is grown, the agricultural cycle of sowing, growing, ripening, reaping, threshing and brewing has been celebrated in song. The subject of the song? John Barleycorn himself, indestructible spirit of the crop.

THE SINGER ABOVE THE RIVER

On the banks of the River Rhine, just south of Koblenz in Germany, a rocky bluff disturbs the flow of the river, creating dangerous currents and dismal rumours of evil magic . . .

HOW MUSIC WAS FETCHED OUT OF HEAVEN

A sixteenth-century Nahua poem written in Nahuatt, language of the Aztecs, revealed this myth dating from a thousand years earlier. Quetzalcoatl, the feathered serpent, appears in Mesoamerican myth in all manner of guises, from the wind to the planet Venus.

WHOSE FOOTPRINTS?

Eshu turns right into wrong, wrong into right. So runs the Yoruba song. The Fon people of Benin call him Legba, that mischievous assistant of God, who causes chaos and strife wherever he goes.

THE DEATH OF EL CID

By 1080, most of Spain was occupied by Moorish Africans. Rodrigo Díaz de Vivar entered Moorish Spain and made conquest after conquest. In doing so, he achieved fabulous wealth, glory and a place in Spanish history, his life and character hugely romanticized into an heroic ideal.

THE MAN WHO ALMOST LIVED FOREVER

The stories discovered in the Sumerian library of Nippur are probably the oldest in the world, already ancient when written down during the Third Dynasty of Ur (about 2000 BC). The true end of Adapa's story is missing, and can only be guessed at.

STEALING HEAVEN'S THUNDER

Thor, with his mighty hammer, Mjollnir, was the best loved of the Norse gods in Norway and Iceland and the last to be ousted by Christianity, probably as late as 1100 AD. In this story, unusually, Loki's mischief is committed in a good cause.

ANANSI AND THE MIND OF GOD

Anansi is a descendant of the many trickster heroes in African mythology. Travelling over in the slave-ships, spider-man Anansi took up residence in the plantations of the West Indies, resourceful, witty, and with a strong instinct for self-preservation.

HOW MEN AND WOMEN FINALLY AGREED

The Kikuyu people of Kenya believe that God had three sons. From the other two sprang the Masai and Kamba peoples. But God's favourite was Kikuyu, which is why God took him to the top of holy Mount Kenya and showed him all creation.

FIRST SNOW

Coyote is the foremost mythical character in western deserts of America. Without his meddling interference, life would be much easier and pleasanter – and yet he is credited with the introduction of fire, agriculture and snow.

RAGGED EMPEROR

Magic plays a great part in Chinese legend, and though Yu Shin's story is a moral tale of virtue rewarded, it is also just as much of a fairy story as *Snow White*. In longer versions, Yu Shin's guardian fairy repeatedly saves his life in fantastical ways, as his father tries to kill him.

THE BOY WHO LIVED FOR A MILLION YEARS

This gypsy horror story is from Romania, from where the 'travelling people' take their origins and their more correct title of 'Romanies'. It captures something of the restlessness of the roaming soul, though it is a cautionary Christian tale.

SEA CHASE
The *Kalevala* is Finland's epic myth cycle and this story only one episode from the huge enthralling saga. Lapland is an ethnic region straddling the northlands of Finland, Sweden and Russia.

DRAGONS TO DINE
In the land now covered by Syria and Turkey, two thousand years before Christ, the Hittite peoples worshipped the weather god Taru. When Roman invaders took over the country, they also adopted and adapted the myth of Taru and Illuyankas, the chaos-dragon.

GUITAR SOLO
This myth is told on the banks of the upper Niger River by the Songhay people. Though their lives are complicated by countless tricky, malicious spirits, this story shows that evil magic can be overcome by very ordinary individuals.

SADKO AND THE TSAR OF THE SEA
The *byliny*, epic poems of old Russia, tell of a race of demi-gods, ancient champions, *bogatyri*. Massively strong, amazingly brave, capable of magic, they were nevertheless Christian heroes. One, transformed into stone, is still to be seen in Kiev Cathedral which he supposedly built.

THE ARMCHAIR TRAVELLER
Ganesa is the Hindu god most honoured by poets and writers. His likeness – pot-bellied, four-armed, elephant-headed dwarf demon – is found in many houses in India, and offerings of fruit and vegetables are made to him.

UPHILL STRUGGLE
In Greek mythology, Sisyphys is the grandfather of Bellerophon, another thorn in the side of the gods. For Bellerophon, even more ambitious than his grandfather, tried to reach the halls of Olympus, flying upwards on his winged horse.

BOBBI BOBBI!
Most Australian myths are set during the Alchera or 'Dreamtime'. This story, told by aboriginal Australians in the north, is one of them.

THE GINGERBREAD BABY
Many familiar stories begin with a woman unhappy because she cannot have children. In Arab Palestine, it is a particularly common theme, and childlessness is portrayed as the one fault no husband can forgive. Originally, this old lady made seven helpful trips abroad while waiting for her bread to rise.

THE PRICE OF FIRE
Every culture has a myth to explain how fire fell into mortal hands. Mostly the fire is stolen from God at great peril, and someone has to suffer for it, as in this tribal myth from Gabon in West Africa.

THE HUNTING OF DEATH
In some parts of Rwanda, death is blamed on the man who disliked his mother-in-law so much he would not let her come back to life. But this is an alternative explanation.

YOUNG BUDDHA
Two and a half thousand years ago, in the city of Kapilavastu, a prince was born to the King of Shakyas. According to legend, until the age of twenty-nine he lived a life of blissful luxury, then gave it all up to seek perfect wisdom and a solution to suffering and death. It took him six years of trial and error. After his enlightenment he taught the 'Middle Way' which is at the foundation of Buddhist thinking, not just in India but all over the world.

THE WOMAN WHO LEFT NO FOOTPRINTS
The Inuit tribes of Alaska set this story in the village of Na-ki-a-ki-a-mute during the month of Naz-re-rak-sek, or October. This is surely an indication of the myth's significance: a celebration of the coming of the winter freeze, when rivers mystically turn to solid ice.

SUN'S SON
Tonga, loveliest of the Polynesian islands, gave rise to this story of

pride. Properly speaking, the boy's choice is between Melaia and Monuia, abstract magical words not easily translated.

Biggest
Japanese merchants measure soft goods, such as material, with one yardstick, and solid goods, such as metal, with another. The soft 'whale yard' is five centimetres longer than the other – surely the origin of this legend . . . unless the legend is the origin of the difference. Castastrophic storms have destroyed much of Kamakura, including the temple, but the huge Buddha still stands.

'I Love You, Prime Minister!'
The epic French *Chansons de geste* or 'songs of deeds' written by troubadours in the eleventh and twelfth centuries, mostly concerned the Emperor Charlemagne, his champions and enemies. Robert Southey, the English poet, translated the one from which this story is taken.

And the Rains Came Tumbling Down
This myth from Papua New Guinea claims to recount the origin of traditional building techniques used universally in this wild, wet territory.

Four Worlds and a Broken Stone
The Black Mesa stands at Four Corners, Arizona and is crucial to the religion of the ancient indigenous Hopi tribe. The word 'Hopi' itself means 'Peace'. The Hopi currently consider that the time of the Great Purification has begun, which will result in the destruction of the Fourth World and establishment of the Fifth.

The Needlework Teacher and the Secret Baby
The Langobardic cycle of legends are just as complex as the more famous tales of King Arthur. Set down in the fifteenth-century Book of Heroes, these stories – of Constantine and the Amelings, of Ice Queens, bear-witches and more – date back six centuries earlier than that. All trace is lost of whatever true-life events and people gave rise to them, but they originated in a region known then as Pannonia (now Hungary and its surrounding territories). The action roams, though, as far afield as Sweden and Greece, Heligoland,

Constantinople and Germany, depicting a war-torn Europe rich in chivalry.

CULLOCH AND THE BIG PIG
The oldest Culloch legend is actually older than King Arthur. It gave rise to (or arose out of) various piggy place-names and landmarks in Wales and Cornwall. The name Culloch itself means 'pig-boy'. Long ago, haircutting once had ritual significance, too. Culloch, for instance, promised his mother on her deathbed that only King Arthur would cut his hair for the first time

THE CALL OF THE SEA
Generally, the mythical mermaid is brought ashore as an unwilling wife and ultimately returns to the sea. This legend from the Island of Jersey in the English Channel is different. It also involves historical events

THE CRYSTAL POOL
The people of Melanesia, like so many other places, widely recall a Great Flood turned back by a serpent during the dawn of time. This particular story, however, from the Bainang peoples of New Britain, accounts for the origins of the oceans.

The creation myths of the Maori people of New Zealand are epic and complex. Tane, both the god of forests and of light, is often found in conflict with his scheming brother. This battle is the third and last war to involve the seventy immortal offspring of Rangi and Papa (Earth and Sky). The original story in fact accounts for many very specific rituals of worship among priests and worshippers.

LAMIA
Legends of lamias are amazingly widespread. From Greece to China people have believed in snake-women deadly to their human mates, unmasked only by goodness or wisdom. John Keats wrote a poem about one. This legend, though, comes from Kashmir.

ISIS AND OSIRIS
Even after the wondrous Old, Middle and New Kingdoms had declined, and the Romans subjugated Egypt, Isis and Osiris were still being worshipped far and wide. Her tears swelling the Nile was the

mythological explanation of a yearly event, when the river, swollen by rains upriver, overspilled its banks. Though dangerous and unpredictable, it spread the banks with fertile black silt: a greater blessing to Egypt than all its gold and silver.

THE FLYING DUTCHMAN
For at least two centuries, sailors have been telling tales of a ghost ship regularly sighted off the coast of the Cape of Good Hope. Given the distances sailors travel, and their liking for a good yarn, the story quickly circled the world on the trade winds. It was Sir Walter Scott's theory that the legend originated in a plague-ship forbidden permission to dock anywhere, its crew forced to live out their short, doomed lives at sea. It took more detailed shape in the nineteenth century, in a short story written by Auguste Jal and entitled *The Flying Dutchman*. In the opera of the same name, Wagner allows the Captain finally to find the salvation of true love.

PROUD MAN
The Algonquin tribe who inhabit the northern forests of the United States have a richly complex culture. They tell a great, widely renowned poetic cycle of stories about Gluskap (or Glooskap), their creator god, and his brother Malsum the Wolf, the evil antithesis of Gluskap's goodness. When Malsum has been defeated, the world perfected, and Gluskap's many adventures are complete, he sails towards sunrise in his canoe, watched by the animals who love him, perhaps to return one day.

THE SILVER-MINERS
Bolivians enjoy an almost personal relationship with the landscape that surrounds them. I am indebted to M. Rigoberto Paredes and his book *Mitos, Supersticiones y Supervivencias Populares de Bolivia* for the contents of this story.

THE MEN IN THE MOON
The Chaga people of Kenya display, in this story, a unique concept of the Moon being attached to the Earth by a causeway.

DREAM JOURNEY
The dangers, frustrations and responsibilities of leadership are a large aspect of this Maori story about an exceptionally enlightened chief.

ROLAND AND THE HORN OLIVANT
In 778 AD, Basque warriors annihilated the rearguard of Charlemagne's retreating army. As the story was retold, Saracens were substituted for the Basques. The epic poem, *Chanson de Roland*, recounting Roland's heroic last stand, was written in the early twelfth century.

A QUESTION OF LIFE AND DEATH
During the fourth century BC, The Boeotian city of Thebes was briefly the leading power-base within the Greek Empire. Sophocles wrote a play about Oedipus, a legendary king of Thebes – a sorry tale from start to finish, but for his defeat of the Sphinx.

THE HARP OF DAGDA
The Dagda, or Daghdha, was the Irish 'good god' or 'great father'. 'The Mighty One of Great Knowledge'. He could kill and restore life with his giant club, and had control over harvests and the weather. His worship was prevalent around 200 BC.

A NEST AND A WEB
In 622 AD, Muhammad moved from Mecca to Medina, on a journey now called the Hejira or migration. It marks year one of the Muslim calendar. This is a story told about that journey.

ASH
This is a shortened retelling of the life and feats of strength of Duktuthl, or 'Dirty Skin', told by the Tlingit tribe inhabiting the north-west coast of North America and Canada.

THE TOWER OF BABEL
The plain where the tower was said to have been built is the Tigris-Euphrates basin where Mesopotamian civilizations erected ziggurat temples as gateways to Heaven. It was originally told, not as a warning against pride and ambition, but simply to explain the origin of languages.

SAINT CHRISTOPHER

'Thou hast borne all the world upon thee, and its sins likewise,' says the child to Christopher in an antique English telling of the traditional European tale. Dr Brewer in *Myth and Legend* writes, 'This is an allegory: Christopher means Christbearer; the child was Christ, and the river was the river of death.'

GOD MOVES AWAY

Togo is one of the smallest countries in Africa, sandwiched between Ghana and Benin, in the west. Its chief crop is maize, so it is no surprise that the pounding of maize with pestle and mortar features in its myths.

WILHELM TELL

It has never been possible to track down a real-life figure on whom Wilhelm Tell might be based. He seems to be a fifteenth-century invention, exactly mirroring the Norse *Saga of Thidrek* in which Egil the Archer shoots an apple off his son's head.

A HEART OF STONE

The Greek myth of Pygmalion, as told in the Latin poet Ovid's *Metamorphoses,* was the basis for George Bernard Shaw's modern comedy, *Pygmalion*, and thus for the musical *My Fair Lady*. Aphrodite was the Greek goddess of love: Ovid used the name of Venus, her Roman equivalent.

BABUSHKA

'Babuskha' simply means 'grandmother' in Russian, and is used of any old peasant lady. She is the Russian equivalent of Saint Nicholas, her poignant story explaining the tradition of giving presents to children at Christmas.

THE PIG GOES COURTING

Kamapua'a's name means 'hog child', and his hilarious mythology largely explains features of Hawaiian geology and natural phenomena. He is impulsive and unpredictable – a good friend to have around, but something of a liability, too.

CAN KRISHNA DIE?
Though Krishna's name means 'the black one', he is usually depicted as having a blue face of ineffable beauty. He features in the ancient Hindu text the *Bhagavad-Gita* as an avatar (or incarnation) of the god Vishnu.

THE LIGHTHOUSE ON THE LAKE
The hurricanes which frequently rage across Japan's Lake Biwa in August are called Hira hurricanes, because they blow from the Hira mountain range. The myth of the lighthouse-keeper is an attempt to explain this seasonal cataclysm.

KING ARTHUR GIVES BACK HIS SWORD
The ninth-century *Historia Britonum* mentions a warlord called Arthur leading the Saxons in twelve battles culminating in a triumphant victory in about 500 BC. The Arthurian tradition has little to do with him, however, and grew up during the Age of Chivalry, feeding off Celtic legend and Christian allegory.

A BLOODTHIRSTY TALE
Hathor, benign and gentle goddess of Egyptian mythology, was also the fearful Sekhmet – Powerful One. On her feast day, the preparation of strong drink was entrusted to girls instead of men, and toasts drunk to the goddess. She thus became goddess of wine.

RIP VAN WINKLE
American writer Washington Irving gave him a name in his *The Sketch Book of Geoffrey Crayon, Gent*. But Rip Van Winkle existed long before that, in legend and rumour, among the Catskill Mountains.

THE RAVEN AND THE MOON
There are many variants of this story. Its original function was to explain why the moon waxes and wanes. Raven is the Inuit animal of creation, responsible for making the world and unearthing the sun from the ground.

SIR PATRICK SPENS
In 1266 AD Norway renounced claims on the Hebrides in return for a

marriage between Prince Eric of Norway and Princess Margaret of Scotland. In 1281 the Princess embarked for Norway and her wedding. On the return trip, a terrible storm sank the ship which had carried her.

THE SALTCELLAR
The many variants of this worldwide myth have littered the sea bed with mills and cellars, all churning out salt. This version is Scandinavian. Though it may seem odd for the pirates to rate salt a precious cargo, it was once a vital and priceless food preservative.

THE BRONZE CAULDRON
In sixth-century Wales there lived a gifted poet named Taliesin. But even if he were the dim and distant origin of this legendary figure, the stories told about 'bright brow' contain truly ancient and recurring elements of myth: shape-changing, prophecy, the 'thumb of knowledge' (as it is in Ireland). Legendary Taliesin even sailed with King Arthur to Other-world to recover British treasures stolen by the forces of evil.

THE BATTLE OF THE DRUMS
The Mandan tribe of native North Americans live on the plains, dependent on the buffalo herds for food and shelter. Lone Man is their 'founding father' and protector, this story the origin of their ritual chants, dance and drumming.

CUPID AND PSYCHE
Here is a remarkable ancestor of a fairy tale now popular the world over. *East o' the Sun, West o' the Moon* is easily recognizable in this Roman myth. It may have been first set down in writing by Apuleius, in the second century AD, in his book *The Golden Ass*. Since Psyche means 'soul' and Cupid represents physical love, the story is also about the two elements at work in true love.

DOCTOR FAUST
Georgius Sabellious lived in sixteenth-century Germany: a doctor, fortune-teller, astrologer and magician. He roused the anger of the Church, but had several rich and influential clients. After his death, the rumours about him were wild and inventive. 'Faustus Junior' (as he called himself) became the subject of fairground puppet shows.

ALONE
The Native Americans of the North-West Pacific coast tell this story of a time before the region was populated. It is extraordinary not only for its wistful melancholy, but also for the picture of a primeval world devoid of men, heroic or otherwise.

THE GOLDEN VANITY
This story is usually sung as a ballad. There are many versions, the oldest of which names the treacherous Captain as Sir Walter Raleigh, no less, and the ship as his vessel *Sweet Trinity*.

THE FOUNDING OF LONDON
The founding of London is one small incident in the thirteenth-century saga of Ragnar Lodbrok (or Ragnar Leather-Trousers). In it England figures simply as one overseas colony among all the others which the Danesmen conquered.

THE MONSTER WITH EMERALD TEETH
Most knowledge of the Mayan culture of Central America comes from the *Popul Vub* (Collection of Written Leaves). Lost in the seventeenth century, it turned up after two hundred years in Guatemala, and contains stories collated by the Mayans themselves before they, like the giants, disappeared from the earth.

THE GOLEM
The 'historical' Golem of Prague in Czechoslovakia probably gave rise to a latter, better-known fiction – *Frankenstein*. Its brief life was the subject of a novel by Gustav Meyrink in 1916, written three hundred years after the supposedly true events.

MUMMY'S BABY
This story is told by the Eskimos of West Greenland. Though only a guess, it seems fairly plain that Kakuarshuk's subterranean journey is a mystical depiction of labour and childbirth itself.

DEAR DOG
The Japanese tell countless variations of this story, the good kami of an animal or person passing into other living things, bringing help to the deserving, punishment to the wicked. Plants in particular are seen

as selflessly devoted to those who treat them tenderly, and it is a heinous crime indeed to cut down a beautiful tree.

MONKEY DO: THE STORY OF HANUMAN

Hanuman, son of the Hindu wind god, is a divine being. For helping Rama, he is rewarded with eternal youth. The exploits of the two are set down in the seven-volume *Ramayana,* one of the great epic works of Sanskrit literature, composed by the poet Valmiki in 500 BC. Even to read the *Ramayana* is an act so holy as to absolve the reader of sin. When Hanuman's fame spread to China, he became hugely popular there, too, and the subject of new adventures.

A BOUQUET OF FLOWERS

The aboriginal peoples of Australia tell various stories of Baiame, the 'Father Spirit', who lived on Earth as a man for a short time so as to rest after completing Tya (the world). He promised to return to visit them, now and then, in human form.

THE CURIOUS HONEYBIRD

This Bantu version of Pandora's Box also incorporates the belief of one section of Bantu – the Kaonde – surrounding Leza's withdrawal from his creation. This apparent aloofness of the creator, taking offence after a period of initial tenderness, recurs time and time again throughout Africa.

THE SKY-BLUE STORYBOX

The Ashanti tribe of Ghana were once rich and powerful masters of the 'Gold Coast'. The first outsiders to hear their tales of Anansi the Spider Man and Nyame the Sky God were Portuguese merchant-sailors. But they cared more for the local currency – gold dust – and the strong slaves to be had, than for the wealth of vivid stories.

A QUESTION OF ARITHMAGIC

Olaf Tryggvason ruled Norway from 995 to 1000 AD. A series of stories recount his various confrontations with heathen gods and malevolent trolls, all of which give the impression that the Old Magic is more potent than the new (Christianity), though the King does always win *in the end.*

THE ALCHEMIST
Two thousand years ago, alchemy – the magical chemistry of transmuting valueless substances into precious ones – intensely interested the Taoist priests of China. Whereas alchemists in Europe were usually seen as in league with the Devil, the Chinese ones were virtuous Immortals revisiting Earth.

WORKSHY RABBIT
The Hausa tribes of West Africa tell this particular fable of small outsmarting big. Wherever Rascal Rabbit pops up (as far apart as North America, Japan and Asia), his trickery and cunning are always admirable rather than reprehensible. Rabbit rarely meets with retribution.

CAT V. RAT
This story would have been told in scores of Congolese villages by the 'Alo Man' or story-teller, who travelled about spreading his repertoire of entertaining fables.

THE PIED PIPER
The German Pied Piper dates from 1298, when Hamelin's children were reputedly lured away by a magician and never seen again. The legend has been used to explain where isolated Germanic-speaking groups came from – the lost children of Hamelin re-emerging elsewhere from underground. Another theory is that the story masks the real-life tragedy of the Children's Crusade when whole populations of children did willingly leave their homes, incited by the Pope to fight a holy war. They never returned.

GULL-GIRL
This Chukchi myth from the bleak landscapes of Siberia is very like the European mermaid myths in which a fisherman takes a 'sulkie's' tailskin and hides it so that she cannot return to the sea. Torn between husband and natural instincts, the mermaid inevitably finds the tail and swims away, mourning the children she is forced to leave behind on dry land.

Arion and the Dolphins
Arion really was a poet at the court of the tyrant Periander – probably around 625 BC, though the legend of his rescue is pure poetic licence. In an older Greek myth, Dionysius, god of agriculture, is captured by pirates who leap overboard in terror when they realize who he is. He transforms them into the world's first dolphins.

Thunder and Smith
Almost every culture has its own Flood myth – a cataclysm in prehistory when the world was cleansed by water and begun afresh. This Chinese Flood is brought about by the pride of a mortal who foolishly believes he can tame the elements. For once God escapes responsibility for the destruction: Thunder is blamed instead.

A Prickly Situation
In the original Haida myth, both Beaver and Porcupine are spirit animals (though Porcupine's spines are no less substantial for that). The Haida are a Native North American people living both on the British Columbian mainland and the offshore Queen Charlotte Islands. And North American porcupines *can* climb trees!

How the Fairies Became
An apocryphal story dating from the time when the Christian Church was trying to absorb beliefs into Christianity. Thus a belief in fairies was no longer incompatible with being a good Christian.

The Gods Down Tools
Creator gods are not generally pictured as manual labourers, but the Sumerian gods of Babylonia are credited with creating mankind to take their place after the gods downed pick and shovel themselves, and went on strike.

Balder and the Mistletoe
Among the Scandinavian gods of Asgard, Balder was god of light. In another version, Hodir is his rival in love and kills him in a fight – but one idea remains constant: Balder's death begins the Twilight of the Gods, the destruction of the halls of Asgard – Ragnarok, the Day of Doom.